The Pocket Companion to

OPERA

John Allison

Mitchell Beazley

CONTENTS

Edited and designed by Mitchell Beazley,
an imprint of Reed Consumer Books Limited
Michelin House, 81 Fulham Road, London SW3 6RB
and Auckland, Melbourne, Singapore and Toronto

© 1994 Reed International Books Limited

Editor Katherine Martin-Doyle
Designer John Grain
Commissioning Editor Sarah Polden
Art Editor Ashley Western
Art Director Jacqui Small
Production Controller Michelle Thomas

The publishers will be grateful for any information which will assist
them in keeping future editions up to date. Although all reasonable
care has been taken in the preparation of this book, the publishers cannot accept any liability for any consequences arising from the use
thereof, or the information contained herein.

A CIP catalogue record for this book is available from the British Library

ISBN 1-85732-253-3

Set in Caslon 540 and Gill Sans
Produced by Mandarin Offset International Limited
Printed in Malaysia

INTRODUCTION

Despite recent attempts to persuade us otherwise, opera is more than a series of 'highlights' sung by superstars in parks in bad weather. Besides some of the best tunes, opera has some of the most gripping stories, and it obviously helps those attending a fully-staged performance to understand the intricacies of the plot. Opera comes alive as an all-embracing theatrical experience for those hearing it in a familiar language, but for many English-speakers, a great part of the repertory remains less accessible, unless they are hearing it sung in English translations. In the last ten years the opera world has been swept by the fashion for 'surtitles'—translations projected above the proscenium arch—but these hinder as much as they help, distracting attention away from the drama on stage and even from the singing itself. There is no substitute for knowing the plot, and the purpose of this book is to simplify the 'homework' required. Many operas are complicated, and synopses can be dense: this book aims to provide a helpful outline that will lead to deeper understanding and enjoyment.

The emphasis is on information which will help the reader follow performances better—a full list of characters and a concise synopsis are provided for each work—and there is also a short 'programme note' placing each opera in context. Despite its concise format, this guide covers representative works from every period and major school of operatic composition, from Monteverdi's *L'Orfeo* (1607) to Schnittke's *Life with an Idiot* (1992). Most of the works featured are performed with reasonable frequency in opera houses today, but also included are some neglected operas which seem to be coming back into fashion.

Operas are generally to be found under their original titles, with translations given where appropriate, though familiar English titles are given and cross-referenced to guide the reader. Exceptions are operas in Slavonic languages, given their familiar English titles: for example, *Prodaná nevěsta* is listed only as *The Bartered Bride*, and *Zolotoy petushok* as *The Golden Cockerel*.

I gratefully acknowledge the friendly criticism of Max Loppert, the advice of Rodney Milnes, the patience of my editors at Reed Books, Katie Martin-Doyle and Sarah Polden, and the support of my wife, Nicole.

John Allison

THE FEATURED COMPOSERS AND WORKS

Béla Bartók (1881-1945)
Duke Bluebeard's Castle

Ludwig van Beethoven
(1770-1827)
Fidelio

Vincenzo Bellini (1801-1835)
Norma
I Puritani

Alban Berg (1885-1935)
Wozzeck
Lulu

Hector Berlioz (1803-1869)
Béatrice et Bénédict
Les Troyens

Harrison Birtwistle (b.1934)
Punch and Judy

Georges Bizet (1838-1875)
Les Pêcheurs de perles
Carmen

Alexander Borodin (1833-1887)
Prince Igor

Benjamin Britten (1913-1976)
Peter Grimes
Albert Herring
Billy Budd
The Turn of the Screw
A Midsummer Night's Dream
Death in Venice

Alfredo Catalani (1841-1893)
La Wally

Domenico Cimarosa (1749-1801)
Il matrimonio segreto

Claude Debussy (1862-1918)
Pelléas et Mélisande

Gaetano Donizetti (1797-1848)
Anna Bolena
L'elisir d'amore
Lucia di Lammermoor
Maria Stuarda
Roberto Devereux
Don Pasquale

Antonin Dvořák (1841-1904)
Rusalka

George Gershwin (1889-1937)
Porgy and Bess

Philip Glass (b.1937)
Akhnaten

Mikhail Glinka (1804-1857)
A Life for the Tsar
Ruslan and Ludmila

Christoph von Gluck (1714-1787)
Orfeo ed Euridice
Alceste
Iphigénie en Tauride

Charles Gounod (1818-1893)
Faust
Roméo et Juliette

George Frideric Handel
(1685-1759)
Agrippina
Giulio Cesare
Alcina
Ariodante
Serse

Hans Werner Henze (b.1926)
Elegy for Young Lovers
The Bassarids

Engelbert Humperdinck
(1854-1921)
Hänsel und Gretel

Leoš Janáček (1854-1928)
Jenůfa
Katya Kabanova
The Excursions of Mr Brouček
The Cunning Little Vixen
The Makropoulos Case
From the House of the Dead

Ruggero Leoncavallo (1857-1919)
Pagliacci

Pietro Mascagni (1863-1945)
Cavalleria rusticana

Jules Massenet (1842-1912)
Manon
Werther
Thaïs
Cendrillon
Don Quichotte

Olivier Messiaen (1908-1992)
Saint François d'Assise

Giacomo Meyerbeer (1791-1864)
Les Huguenots

Claudio Monteverdi (1567-1643)
L'Orfeo
Il ritorno d'Ulisse in patria
L'incoronazione di Poppea

Wolfgang Amadeus Mozart
(1756-1791)
Idomeneo, re di Creta
Die Entführung aus dem Serail
Le nozze di Figaro
Don Giovanni
Così fan tutte
La clemenza di Tito
Die Zauberflöte

Modest Mussorgsky (1839-1881)
Boris Godunov
Khovanshchina

Jaques Offenbach (1819-1880)
Orphée aux Enfers
Les Contes d'Hoffmann

Francis Poulenc (1899-1963)
Les Mamelles de Tirésias
Les Dialogues de Carmélites

Sergey Prokofiev (1891-1953)
The Gambler
The Love for Three Oranges
The Fiery Angel
War and Peace

Giacomo Puccini (1858-1924)
Manon Lescaut
La Bohème
Tosca
Madama Butterfly
La fanciulla del West
Gianni Schicchi
Suor Angelica
Il tabarro
Turandot

Henry Purcell (1659-1695)
Dido and Aeneas

Maurice Ravel (1875-1937)
L'Heure espagnole
L'Enfant et les sortilèges

Nikolay Rimsky-Korsakov
(1844-1908)
Christmas Eve
Sadko
The Golden Cockerel

Gioachino Rossini (1792-1868)
L'italiana in Algeri
Il barbiere di Siviglia
La Cenerentola
La gazza ladra
Semiramide
Le Comte Ory
Guillaume Tell

Camille Saint-Saëns (1835-1921)
Samson et Dalila

Aulis Sallinen (b.1935)
Kullervo

Alfred Schnittke (b.1934)
Life with an Idiot

Arnold Schoenberg (1874-1851)
Moses und Aron

Dmitry Shostakovich
(1906-1975)
The Nose
Lady Macbeth of Mtsensk

Bedřich Smetana (1824-1884)
The Bartered Bride

Karlheinz Stockhausen (b.1928)
Licht

Johann Strauss (1825-1899)
Die Fledermaus

Richard Strauss (1864-1949)
Salome
Elektra
Der Rosenkavalier
Ariadne auf Naxos
Capriccio

Igor Stravinsky (1882-1971)
Oedipus Rex
The Rake's Progress

Pyotr Ilyich Tchaikovsky
(1840-1893)
Eugene Onegin
Mazeppa
The Queen of Spades
Iolanta

Michael Tippett (b.1905)
The Midsummer Marriage
King Priam
The Knot Garden

Giuseppe Verdi (1813-1901)
Nabucco
Attila
Rigoletto
La traviata
Il trovatore
Les Vêpres siciliennes
Un ballo in maschera
La forza del destino
Macbeth
Aida
Simon Boccanegra
Don Carlos
Otello
Falstaff

Richard Wagner (1813-1883)
Der fliegende Holländer
Tannhäuser
Lohengrin
Tristan und Isolde
Die Meistersinger von Nürnberg
Das Rheingold
Die Walküre
Siegfried
Götterdämmerung
Parsifal

Carl Maria von Weber
(1786-1826)
Der Freischütz

Kurt Weill (1900-1950)
Aufstieg und Fall der Stadt
Mahagonny
Street Scene

THE ABDUCTION FROM THE SERAGLIO
see **Die Entführung aus dem Serail**

AGRIPPINA
George Frideric Handel (1685-1759)

THREE ACTS. LIBRETTO BY VINCENZO GRIMANI. PREMIERE IN VENICE, 26 DECEMBER 1709.

Agrippina, Handel's earliest operatic masterpiece, was the high point of the composer's four-year sojourn in Italy. A satire based on characters and events from around AD 50, the opera was first given during the Venice Carnival at the end of 1709.

CHARACTERS
Agrippina, wife of Claudio (SOPRANO); *Nerone* (Nero), Agrippina's son (SOPRANO); *Poppea* (Poppaea), a gentlewoman (SOPRANO); *Ottone* (Otho), Roman general (ALTO); *Narciso* (Narcissus), aide to Agrippina (ALTO); *Giunone* (Juno), goddess (ALTO); *Claudio* (Claudius), Roman Emperor (BASS); *Pallante* (Pallas), aide to Agrippina (BASS); *Lesbo*, servant of Claudio (BASS)

ACT I
When the Empress Agrippina learns that her husband, Claudius, away in England, is dead, she resolves to establish Nero, her son by a previous husband, as Emperor of Rome. She enlists the help of Pallas and Narcissus, but their plans are thwarted by Claudius's rescue and return. Moreover, Claudius has rewarded his deliverer, the general Otho, by naming him Caesar. Agrippina plots to turn Claudius against Otho: she deceives Otho's mistress Poppaea (also pursued by both Claudius and Nero) into thinking that Otho is willing to surrender Poppaea to Claudius in return for the throne, and suggests that to keep Otho, Poppaea will have to set Claudius against him. This Poppaea succeeds in doing, and Otho is denounced.

ACT II
Pallas and Narcissus curry favour with Otho in the hope of political reward. They are astonished when Claudius castigates Otho. Agrippina, taking advantage of the situation, persuades Claudius to favour Nero instead, and urges Narcissus and Pallas to murder Otho. Otho has meanwhile convinced Poppaea of his love, and she realizes that she has been tricked by Agrippina.

ACT III
Poppaea now receives her three admirers in quick succession, and deludes Claudius into thinking his rival is Nero. Agrippina realizes that her schemes have failed, but manages to convince Claudius that she has been acting in his interests all along. He tries to resolve the situation by giving the throne to Otho, and Poppaea to Nero. But Nero's political aspirations are not satisfied until Otho renounces the succession in order to gain Poppaea's hand. Claudius accepts the arrangement and calls on the goddess Juno to bless the union of Poppaea and Otho.

AIDA
Giuseppe Verdi (1813-1901)

Four acts. Libretto by Antonio Ghislanzoni, after a scenario by Auguste Mariette. Premiere in Cairo, 24 December 1871.

Aida, arguably Verdi's most popular opera, was premiered in Egypt, but not, as is often supposed, at the opening of the Suez Canal, nor at the inauguration of the Cairo Opera House. The opera, whose story is based in Egyptian antiquity, reached the new theatre only at the end of its second season. Though *Aida* came late in Verdi's operatic output, its structure is conservative, almost a throwback to the grand operas of the earlier 19th century—epitomized in the famous Triumphal Scene.

CHARACTERS

Aida, Amneris's Ethiopian slave (SOPRANO); *High Priestess* (SOPRANO); *Amneris*, the King's daughter (MEZZO-SOPRANO); *Radamès*, Captain of the Guards (TENOR); *Messenger* (TENOR); *Amonasro*, King of Ethiopia, father of Aida (BARITONE); *The King of Egypt* (BASS); *Ramfis*, High Priest (BASS)
With *priests, priestesses, ministers, captains, soldiers, slaves, prisoners*

ACT I

SCENE 1 *The King's palace in Memphis*
Egypt is threatened by Ethiopian armies. Ramfis, High Priest of Egypt, has consulted the goddess Isis to learn who will lead the Egyptian forces. Radamès hopes that he has been chosen: victory will help him to win the hand of Aida, Ethiopian slave to Amneris, the King's daughter (herself in love with Radamès). The King arrives to appoint Radamès commander, leaving Aida torn between her love for Radamès—enemy of her country—and her duty to her father, the Ethiopian king Amonasro.

SCENE 2 *Inside the Temple of Vulcan, Memphis*
In a solemn ceremony led by Ramfis, Radamès is invested with the consecrated sword.

ACT II

SCENE 1 *A room in Amneris's apartment in the palace*
The Egyptian army has defeated the Ethiopians, and Amneris, helped by her slave-girls, is preparing for the victory celebrations. Suspicious of Aida, Amneris tricks her slave into confessing her love for Radamès and declares her rivalry.

SCENE 2 *One of the gates to Thebes*
A huge crowd has assembled to welcome back Radamès and the triumphant army. Aida recognizes her father among the prisoners of war, but does not disclose his rank. Although the Egyptian King believes that Amonasro has died in battle, Aida's father is kept as a hostage when the other Ethiopians are freed. The King offers Radamès his daughter Amneris in marriage—thus promising succession to the Egyptian throne.

ACT III
The banks of the Nile

Amneris arrives by boat at the Temple of Isis, to pray on the eve of her marriage. Aida comes to meet Radamès, but is startled to find her father, who, aware of her love for the Egyptian captain, begs her to find out Egyptian military secrets (the Ethiopians have renewed their campaign). Radamès promises to flee Egypt with Aida to escape Amneris, but reveals the route guarded by the Egyptian army. Amonasro appears from hiding to admit his identity, and Radamès realizes that he has betrayed his country. Amneris discovers his treachery, and as Aida and her father escape, Radamès gives himself up to Ramfis.

ACT IV
SCENE 1 *A hall in the King's palace*

Amneris—who discloses that Amonasro has been killed—urges Radamès to save himself by renouncing Aida. He refuses, and is sentenced to death by Ramfis's priests, despite Amneris's pleas for pardon. She rushes out, denouncing the verdict of the priests.

SCENE 2 *The temple of Vulcan*

Radamès is entombed alive in the crypt of the temple, and discovers Aida hiding there. They die in each others' arms, as Amneris prays above on the tomb.

AKHNATEN
Philip Glass (b. 1937)

THREE ACTS. LIBRETTO BY SHALOM GOLDMAN, ROBERT ISRAEL, RICHARD RIDDELL AND THE COMPOSER. PREMIERE IN STUTTGART, 24 MARCH 1984.

Akhnaten is the third of Glass's full-length operas, and completed a trilogy of what the composer described as 'portrait' works, each depicting a 'thinker' in world history. The first was *Einstein on the Beach* (1976), followed four years later by *Satyagraha*, which dealt with Gandhi; Akhnaten, a 14th-century-BC Egyptian pharaoh, was a religious reformer. Together the operas also cover the three major issues of science, politics, and religion. *Akhnaten* is perhaps the Glass opera to have achieved widest success, despite the fact that his minimalist style—endless repetitions of simple musical cells—has many detractors. Few would deny, though, that Glass has brought a new audience to contemporary opera.

Akhnaten was the name taken by Amenhotep IV, who introduced worship of the sun, abandoned the Egyptian capital of Thebes, and built his own splended new city, Akhetaten.

CHARACTERS
Queen Tye, Akhnaten's mother (SOPRANO); *Nefertiti*, Akhnaten's wife (ALTO); *Akhnaten*, King of Egypt (COUNTER-TENOR); *High Priest of Amon* (TENOR); *Horemhab*, General and future Pharaoh (BARITONE); *Aye*, Nefertiti's father and Akhnaten's advisor (BASS); *Tourist Guide* (ACTOR; VOICE-OVER)
With Akhnaten's six *daughters* and *Funeral part* (eight men's voices)

ACT I
Thebes, 1370 BC

The priests of Amon, god of Thebes, prepare for and conduct King Amenhotep III's funeral. His son is crowned as King Amenhotep IV (Akhnaten), and sets about his religious reforms, but the High Priest of Amon is offended by the abolition of old rites. He departs, and Akhnaten, his wife Nefertiti and mother Queen Tye dance sacrilegiously through the Temple of Amon.

ACT II
The Temple of Amon

The priests of Amon conduct their rituals, but it is not long before they are deposed and their temple destroyed. Queen Tye teaches her son a poem in praise of Aten (the sun), which he in turn imparts to Nefertiti. Monotheism is thus established, polygamy is revoked, and the new order is celebrated in the building of a new city and temple at Akhetaten.

ACT III
Akhetaten, 1358 BC

Akhnaten is depicted living contentedly with his family. However, preoccupation with his new life leads to isolation from his subjects, and he ignores the warnings of Aye and Horemhab that his people are restless and plotting against him. Frustrated, Aye departs, taking with him Nefertiti and her oldest daughter. The High Priest of Amon returns, now allied with both Aye and Horemhab, and Akhnaten is overthrown. His city is destroyed and Amon reinstated. In a shift to the present day, tourists wander around the ruins of Akhetaten, over which phantoms of its founder and his family linger.

ALBERT HERRING
Benjamin Britten (1913-1976)

THREE ACTS. LIBRETTO BY ERIC CROZIER, AFTER GUY DE MAUPASSANT'S SHORT STORY *LE ROSIER DE MADAME HUSSON*. PREMIERE AT GLYNDEBOURNE, 20 JUNE 1947.

Albert Herring, Britten's fourth opera, was his first comedy, yet in common with all the composer's darker works one senses therein his identification with the vulnerable, alienated hero. Set in Loxford, a small market-town in Britten's native East Suffolk, the opera tells of how Albert, repressed by his mother and ridiculed by his peers, is turned into an outsider.

CHARACTERS
Lady Billows, an elderly autocrat (SOPRANO); *Miss Wordsworth*, head teacher (SOPRANO); *Nancy*, from the bakery (MEZZO-SOPRANO); *Mrs Herring*, Albert's mother (MEZZO-SOPRANO); *Florence Pike*, Lady Billow's housekeeper (CONTRALTO); *Albert Herring*, from the greengrocer's (TENOR); *Mr Upfold*, the mayor (TENOR); *Sid*, a butcher's assistant (BARITONE); *Mr Gedge*, the vicar (BARITONE); *Superintendent Budd* (BASS)
With *Emmie* and *Cis* (SOPRANOS); and *Harry* (TREBLE); village *children*

ACT I

SCENE 1 *The breakfast room of Lady Billows's house*
The Loxford town worthies assemble at Lady Billows's house to elect the May Queen. Lady Billows has offered a £25 prize as encouragement, but none of the town's young women meet her stringent standards of virtue. After much indecision, the police superintendent offers a solution, that they choose a May King instead. Albert Herring, who leads a sheltered life serving in his mother's greengrocer's shop, is selected.

SCENE 2 *Mrs Herring's shop*
Sid, from the butchery, appears in the shop and begins to tease Albert about what he is missing out on in life—chiefly poaching and dating. Sid's girlfriend Nancy soon joins him, and their flirting embarrasses Albert, who, left alone, starts to yearn for independence. He is interrupted by the arrival of the festival committee, who bring their news: Albert rejects the idea, but is over-ruled by his mother, eager for the prize.

ACT II

SCENE 1 *A marquee in the vicarage garden*
During preparations for the crowning ceremony, Sid laces Albert's glass of lemonade with rum. The presentation commences and speeches flow; Albert is only able to stammer a few words in reply before downing his drink. He starts to hiccup.

SCENE 2 *Mrs Herring's shop, the same evening*
Albert returns jauntily to the shop. He overhears Sid and Nancy, outside, sympathizing over his plight, and eventually resolves to break free. Mrs Herring returns to find her son gone in search of adventure.

ACT III

Mrs Herring's shop, the following afternoon
Rumours abound as to Albert's whereabouts. Mrs Herring believes he is dead, and everyone is saddened when his May King wreath, crushed and muddied, is brought in. At the climax of their threnody, Albert pops in—not to a welcome but to general recrimination. Defiantly, he shocks everyone (except Sid and Nancy) with an account of his experiences and thanks them for providing the wherewithal. The townsfolk depart, disgusted. Sid and Nancy join with Albert in celebrating his newly-won liberty.

ALCESTE
Christoph Willibald von Gluck (1714-1787)

THREE ACTS. ITALIAN VERSION: LIBRETTO BY CALZABIGI AFTER EURIPIDES. PREMIERE IN VIENNA, 26 DECEMBER 1767. FRENCH VERSION: LIBRETTO BY ROULLET AFTER CALZABIGI AND EURIPIDES. PREMIERE IN PARIS, 23 APRIL 1776.

Gluck has gone down in history as the reformer of 18th-century opera: he sought simplicity of both action and music in place of the convoluted plots and florid music of *opera seria*. *Alceste* was the second of his 'reform' operas, and the preface to the original (Italian) version is one of the most significant documents in operatic history. The opera was heavily revised for Paris nine years after its Vienna premiere, and it is this substantially different version which has usually been performed since.

CHARACTERS (French version)

Alceste (Alcestis), Queen of Thessaly (SOPRANO); *Admète* (Admetus), Alcestis's husband (TENOR); *Evandre* (Evander), leader of the Pherae people (TENOR); *Apollon* (Apollo) (BARITONE); *High Priest of Apollo* (BASS); *Hercule* (Hercules) (BASS); *Thanatos*, an infernal deity (BASS); *Herald* (BASS); *Oracle* (BASS); *Alcestis's and Admetus's two children* (SILENT) With *officers* of the palace, Alceste's *attendants*, *citizens* of Pherae, *deities*, *priests* and *priestesses* of in the temple of Apollo

ACT I

Square in the city of Pherae, with Admetus's palace on one side and the entrance to the temple of Apollo at the back
People crowd the square, lamenting the illness of King Admetus, which, the Herald informs them, will prove fatal. Alcestis enters mournfully, and exhorts the people to follow her to the temple of Apollo to plead with the gods for mercy. A change of scene reveals the solemn ceremony, where the High Priest urges the crowd to hear the Oracle's judgement. It is cruel: Admetus will die unless another is sacrificed in his place. The people, frightened, flee, and Alceste resolves to die for her husband. Alone and torn by love for her children, she prepares to meet her fate.

ACT II

A hall in Admetus's palace
The King's miraculous recovery is being celebrated. Evander tells him of the Oracle's pronouncement, but does not disclose the name of the victim. Admetus is overjoyed to be reunited with his wife, but Alcestis is unable to hide her distress. Eventually she confesses that she is to die, and Admetus rages against the gods—but to no avail. The people grieve with her.

ACT III

A courtyard in the palace/Entrance of the underworld
The deaths of Alcestis and Admetus—who has followed his wife—are being mourned. Hercules arrives to visit Admetus. Evander reveals the tragic events to him, and Hercules pledges to bring them back from the underworld. The scene changes to the entrance of the underworld, where the (invisible) gods are calling Alcestis. She is joined by Admetus, who wishes to die with her, but Thanatos reminds her that only one of them can die. They vow to die for each other, but are interrupted by the arrival of Hercules, who fights the infernal deities and returns Alcestis to Admetus. Apollo appears and restores calm: Hercules is rewarded with a place among the gods, and Alcestis and Admetus reinstated on earth. The opera ends back at Admetus's palace, amid scenes of rejoicing.

ALCINA
George Frideric Handel (1685-1759)

THREE ACTS. LIBRETTO ADAPTED FROM THE ANONYMOUS
L'ISOLA DI ALCINA BASED ON CANTOS VII AND VIII OF ARIOSTO'S
ORLANDO FURIOSO. PREMIERE IN LONDON, 16 APRIL 1735.

Handel's operas can be conveniently divided into three broad
categories—the heroic, the anti-heroic, and the magical. *Alcina*
belongs to the last of these, and is full of the supernatural
effects which were a feature of Baroque theatre. Like
Handel's other operas, *Alcina* suffered two centuries of
neglect, but Joan Sutherland's assumption of the title role in
the late 1950s did much to re-establish it in the repertory.

CHARACTERS

Alcina, a sorceress (SOPRANO); *Morgana*, Alcina's sister (SOPRANO);
Ruggiero, a knight (MEZZO-SOPRANO); *Oberto*, a young nobleman
(TREBLE); *Bradamante*, betrothed to Ruggiero (CONTRALTO); *Oronte*,
Alcina's general (TENOR); *Melisso*, Bradamante's governor (BASS)

ACT I

The sorceress Alcina rules her magic island, on which she lives
with her sister, Morgana, and general, Oronte (who is in love
with Morgana). There Alcina lures suitors, only to transform
them into natural objects, sometimes even wild animals. Her
latest victim is the knight Ruggiero, as yet untransformed but
so besotted with the enchantress that he has forgotten his
betrothed, Bradamante. The opera begins as she lands on the
island in search of him. Bradamante has come disguised as her
brother Ricciardo, and together with her governor Melisso, is
guided to Alcina's palace by Morgana (herself soon smitten
with 'Ricciardo'). There they encounter the young Oberto, on
a mission to recover his father. Ruggiero thinks that he is
addressing Ricciardo, and tells 'him' that he is infatuated with
Alcina; soon he becomes concerned that Alcina has fallen in
love with 'Ricciardo', and urges Alcina to transform his 'rival'.
Morgana, who has transferred her affections from Oronte to
'Ricciardo', warns her new lover of Alcina's plan and urges
'him' to flee the island.

ACT II

Melisso visits Ruggiero, appearing to be the latter's old tutor
Atlante. With the help of a magic ring, the spell over Ruggiero
is removed, and the knight's thoughts return fondly to
Bradamante. She arrives, but has trouble however in convincing him of her identity: for a moment he believes that Alcina is
tricking him again. Eventually persuaded, he escapes from the
sorceress by asking her for permission to go hunting. (Meanwhile,
Oberto renews his attempts to discover his father, and Alcina
promises, insincerely, to assist him.) Oronte announces that
Ruggiero has escaped, taking with him Alcina's sword in which
her supernatural powers are invested. Oronte mocks Morgana
over the loss of 'Ricciardo'. Alcina retreats to a subterranean
cave where she attempts, in vain, to summon up her spirits.

13

ACT III

Oronte forgives Morgano for her disloyalty. Alcina makes a final, unsuccessful attempt to win Ruggiero, but he steadfastly declares his love for Bradamante. Once more, Oberto begs Alcina for the release of his father. This provokes her into giving him a spear with which to kill a lion, but at the last moment he recognizes the beast as his transformed father. Finally, Ruggiero destroys the urn containing Alcina's spells, and the sorceress, together with Morgana, vanishes. At once, Alcina's victims are restored to human form (among them Oberto's father), and all celebrate.

ANNA BOLENA
Gaetano Donizetti (1797-1848)

TWO ACTS. LIBRETTO BY FELICE ROMANI. PREMIERE IN MILAN, 26 DECEMBER 1830.

Donizetti was a prolific composer in many genres. His operatic output numbers approximately 70 works, of which *Anna Bolena*, the 30th, was his first international success. It remained enormously popular for most of the 19th century, but suffered neglect thereafter until its triumphant revival at La Scala in 1957, with Maria Callas in the title role; the magnificent final scene offered her rich histrionic possibilities.

CHARACTERS

Anna Bolena (Anne Boleyn), Henry's Queen (SOPRANO); *Giovanna Seymour* (Jane Seymour), Anne's lady-in-waiting (MEZZO-SOPRANO); *Smeton*, the Queen's page (CONTRALTO); *Percy* (TENOR); *Hervey*, court official (TENOR); *Enrico* (Henry VIII); King of England (BASS); *Rochefort*, Anne's brother (BASS)

ACT I

The opera opens in Windsor Castle, where courtiers discuss the King's neglect of his Queen and the increasing attention he has been paying to her lady-in-waiting, Jane Seymour. Jane is troubled by her own disloyalty, but soon won over by the King's advances. Henry plans to trap Anne by arranging for the return of her former lover, Percy, from exile; Anne's brother Rochefort is astounded to see Percy, and becomes concerned at Percy's indiscretion when the latter admits that his love for her has not waned. Outside the Queen's apartments, her page Smeton sings of his own love for her, contemplating her miniature portrait. He hides as Rochefort appears, who persuades Anne to receive Percy: The former lovers meet, but Anne, distressed, steadfastly refuses to give in to his feelings. In desperation, Percy draws his sword, preparing to kill himself. Anne faints, Smeton comes out of hiding, and despite Rochefort's warnings, Henry arrives to find what he takes to be a conspiracy against him. He denounces them all and orders them to be taken off to cells.

ACT II

Jane visits the incarcerated Queen, urging her to plead guilty in order to receive the King's clemency. She eventually admits that the King has chosen her as his new Queen, and Anne forgives her. During Anne's trial, Smeton, attempting to save her, claims to be her lover, but his ploy fails and Anne and her accomplices are all sentenced to the scaffold. In the Tower of London, Hervey brings word of the King's pardon to Rochefort and Percy, but both refuse to accept it while the innocent Anne remains under sentence. In the final scene Anne, unhinged, reminisces, thinking that she sees Percy. She loses her reason, but the sound of bells and cannon announcing the wedding of Henry and Jane jolt her out of her hallucination into a final, fierce protestation against her plight.

ARIADNE AUF NAXOS (Ariadne on Naxos)
Richard Strauss (1864-1949)

PROLOGUE AND ONE ACT. LIBRETTO BY HUGO VON HOFMANN-STHAL. PREMIERE IN STUTTGART, 25 OCTOBER 1912; REVISED VERSION GIVEN IN VIENNA, 4 OCTOBER 1916.

Ariadne auf Naxos was originally designed as a one-act opera to be given after a condensed, German version of Molière's *Le bourgeois gentilhomme* (for which he also composed incidental music), but the cost to theatres of providing both actors and singers for an evening made revivals impractical. Strauss's solution was to drop the play and write a Prologue on the same subject instead, in which the Opera is commissioned and prepared—hence the 'opera-within-an-opera' scheme.

CHARACTERS
IN THE PROLOGUE
The Composer (MEZZO-SOPRANO); *The Dancing Master* (TENOR); *An Officer* (TENOR); *The Music Master* (BARITONE); *The Wigmaker* (BASS); *A Footman* (BASS); *The Major-Domo* (SPOKEN)

IN THE PROLOGUE AND OPERA
The Prima Donna (later *Ariadne*) (SOPRANO); *Zerbinetta* (SOPRANO); *The Tenor* (later *Bacchus*) (TENOR); *Scaramuccio* (TENOR); *Brighella* (TENOR); *Harlequin* (BARITONE) and *Truffaldino* (BASS) commedia dell'arte players

IN THE OPERA
Ariadne (SOPRANO); *Naiad* (SOPRANO); *Echo*, a nymph (SOPRANO); *Dryad* (CONTRALTO); *Bacchus*, a nymph (TENOR)

PROLOGUE
A stage in the house of a rich Viennese
Preparations are being made for the performance of a new opera commissioned as entertainment for the wealthy man's guests. The Music Master is outraged when the Major-Domo declares that it will be followed by an unrefined *commedia dell'arte* entertainment, and that both presentations have to be finished in time for a fireworks display. The situation is aggravated when he returns to announce that, instead, the two shows will run

simultaneously, sections of each alternating. Meanwhile, both companies prepare themselves, and the Composer tries to rehearse, presenting his arias to the Tenor and Prima Donna. Zerbinetta, leader of the Comedians, soothes the Composer in the hope of extracting details of the opera to use to her advantage, but she soon becomes fascinated by the mythological story of Ariadne, who is abandoned on Naxos by Theseus and who longs for death. The Composer is soon taken with Zerbinetta's charms, and offers a hymn to the sacred art of music.

OPERA

The entrance to Ariadne's cave

The host and his guests watch as the curtain rises to reveal Ariadne lying at the entrance to her cave on Naxos. The three Nymphs, Naiad, Dryad, and Echo, sing sympathetically of her plight, and the four Comedians, watching from a distance, are moved by Ariadne's dream-like recollections. Yearning for death, she takes little notice of Harlequin's serenade; the Comedians appear, but she remains unmoved by their boisterous entertainment. Zerbinetta dispenses with them, thinking she can convert Ariadne to her coquettish philosophy by recounting her own amorous exploits. Unwilling to hear, Ariadne retreats into her cave, and Zerbinetta's scene becomes a monologue (a virtuoso showpiece, one of the most demanding in the repertory). Soon she is pursued by all of her Comedians; she teases them in turn, but only Harlequin succeeds in gaining her favour, to the exasperation of the others. The Nymphs herald the arrival of the virile young Bacchus, whom Ariadne mistakes as the long-awaited messenger of death. They are united in a rapturous duet (Zerbinetta appears momentarily to express satisfaction with the outcome) before ascending heavenwards together.

ARIODANTE

George Frideric Handel (1685-1759)

THREE ACTS. LIBRETTO BY ANTONIO SALVI, AFTER ARIOSTO'S *ORLANDO FURIOSO*. PREMIERE IN LONDON, 8 JANUARY 1735.

The most famous treatment of the Ariodante story is Shakespeare's *Much Ado About Nothing*, and commentators have noted that Handel's *Ariodante* is the closest approach to Shakespearian romance in the composer's output. Certainly, it stands out amongst Handel's operas for its subject—a realistic, human drama, different from the heroic, magical plots which he customarily set. These factors, combined with the fact that *Ariodante* contains some of the composer's greatest music, help to make the opera one of Handel's most appealing.

CHARACTERS

Ginevra, the King's daughter, betrothed to Ariodante (SOPRANO); *Dalinda*, Ginevra's lady-in-waiting (SOPRANO); *Ariodante*, a prince (MEZZO-SOPRANO); *Polinesso*, Duke of Albany (CONTRALTO); *Lurcanio*, Ariodante's brother (TENOR); *Odoardo*, a courtier (TENOR); *King of Scotland* (BASS)

ACT I

At the King of Scotland's palace in Edinburgh, his only child, Ginevra, and her lady-in-waiting, Dalinda, discuss Ginevra's love for Ariodante. Polinesso, ambitious for the throne, arrives to pay court to Ginevra, but she rebuffs him. Schemingly, he decides to use Dalinda's devotion to him to avenge Ariodante. Ariodante and Ginevra meet in the palace gardens, and soon the King joins them to bless their forthcoming marriage and pronounce Ariodante his heir. Polinesso, hypocritically, pledges himself to Dalinda, persuading her to come to their assignation that evening dressed as Ginevra, and to allow him to enter the royal apartments. Meanwhile, Ariodante's brother Lurcanio woos Dalinda, but he is rejected. The act ends with pastoral celebrations of the imminent marriage.

ACT II

Ariodante and Polinesso meet in the moonlight outside Ginevra's apartments. Polinesso, pretending to be unaware of the engagement, claims that he enjoys the princess's favours. Ariodante, horrified, believes him when he sees the disguised Dalinda admitting his rival into Ginevra's suite. Overcome with grief, he is prevented from committing suicide by his brother Lurcanio, but swears revenge. Polinesso revels in his success. The King, unaware of these events, summons his council to inform them of Ariodante's succession, but is interrupted by the news which Odoardo brings of Ariodante's drowning. Ginevra collapses in shock. Lurcanio arrives and pins the blame for his brother's death on Ginevra's behaviour. The King denounces his daughter, and she loses her reason.

ACT III

However, Ariodante has survived. He saves Dalinda from assassins sent by Polinesso, and she reveals how he was deceived. Ginevra has been sentenced to die, and Polinesso arrives to defend her from Lurcanio. She refuses his offer, but the King insists. Lurcanio inflicts mortal wounds on Polinesso; no sooner is he carried off than a second, unknown knight appears to protect Ginevra. He is soon revealed to be Ariodante, and when Polinesso's and Dalinda's confessions reach the King, he pardons his daughter. The court celebrates the reunion of Ginevra and Ariodante, and the King renews his blessing on them.

ATTILA
Giuseppe Verdi (1813-1901)

PROLOGUE AND THREE ACTS. LIBRETTO BY TEMISTOCLE SOLERA AFTER ZACHARIAS WERNER'S *ATTILA, KÖNIG DER HUN-NEN.* PREMIERE IN VENICE, 17 MARCH 1846

Attila is one of Verdi's Risorgimento operas, a reference to the Italian nationalist movement which the composer supported. The name 'Verdi' became code for 'Vittorio Emanuele, re di'Italia'—hence the Risorgimento slogan 'Viva Verdi'. *Attila*'s subject matter, dealing with the Hun invasion of Italy, ensured that the opera was one of Verdi's most popular works in the 1850s, and the Roman general Ezio's line to Attila, 'Avrai tu l'universo, resti l'Italia a me' ('You may have the whole world, leave Italy to me'), helped to heighten anti-Austrian feeling. As with all of Verdi's early operas, the music lacks refinement (swaggering oompah accompaniments are prominent), but well conducted it can sound thrilling.

CHARACTERS

Odabella, daughter of the Lord of Aquileia (SOPRANO); *Foresto*, a knight of Aquileia (TENOR); *Uldino*, Attila's slave (TENOR); *Ezio*, a Roman general (BARITONE); *Attila*, King of the Huns (BASS); *Leone* (Pope Leo) (BASS)

PROLOGUE

SCENE 1 *The city of Aquileia, 452 AD*
Attila's army celebrates its victory in the piazza of the fallen city. Soon the warrior himself arrives, and soldiers sing his praises. In defiance of orders, his slave Uldino has saved a small group of enemy women, and their leader, Odabella, steps forward to proclaim their indomitable resolve. Attila is so impressed by this display of bravery that he offers her any favour she chooses: Odabella requests his sword, and resolves to seek revenge with it. Ezio, an envoy from the Roman Emperor, enters. In private, he proposes a bargain: Attila can have the world if he leaves Italy to Ezio. The Hun, outraged, rejects the proposal and announces his march on Rome.

SCENE 2 *A mudflat in the Adriatic lagoons*
As a storm subsides, dawn reveals a group of refugees from the sacked city of Aquileia. Their leader, Foresto, laments the fate of his beloved Odabella, held prisoner by Attila. He urges his people to build a new city on the lagoon, equal in splendour to the one they have fled (a reference to Venice, city of the opera's premiere).

ACT I

SCENE 1 *A wood near Attila's camp*
Odabella mourns her father's death in the fighting. Foresto enters, disguised as a Hun, and having seen Odabella with Attila, accuses her of betrayal. She, however, reveals her plot against their enemy, and Foresto forgives her.

SCENE 2 *Attila's tent*
In a nightmare, Attila sees himself barred in the name of God at the gates of Rome. No sooner has he told Uldino of his vision, than a procession of hymn-singing women and children appear, led by Leone, the old man of Attila's nightmare. The Hun is terrified when Pope Leo utters the very words of his dream.

ACT II

SCENE 1 *Ezio's camp outside Rome*
Ezio, reading a dispatch from the Roman Emperor informing him of a truce, reflects on Rome's weak leadership. A group of Attila's men invite Ezio to a banquet, and as they leave, the

disguised Foresto remains behind to tell him of his plot against Attila. Ezio eagerly supports him.

SCENE 2 *Attila's camp*

Festivities are already underway when the Roman guests arrive. A sudden gust of wind extinguishes the torches, and the Huns superstitiously take this to be a bad omen. Undeterred, Attila proposes a toast, but Odabella prevents him from drinking the wine which Foresto has poisoned (she relishes personal vengeance). In return for his deliverance, Attila grants Odabella's plea to spare Foresto, but insists that he will marry her the following day. Foresto flees swearing revenge, and hostilities between the two sides are resumed.

ACT III

Outside Attila's camp

Foresto, tormented, waits for news of Odabella's wedding. Ezio urges Foresto to battle, but they are interrupted by the arrival of Odabella who is distracted by the ghost of her father who Attila killed. She tries to convince Foresto of her love, but they are interrupted by Attila, in search Odabella. Attila confronts them and Ezio, but when the noise of battle reaches them, Odabella stabs the Hun. She and Foresto are reunited.

AUFSTIEG UND FALL DER STADT MAHAGONNY
(The Rise and Fall of the City of Mahagonny)
Kurt Weill (1900–1950)

THREE ACTS. LIBRETTO BY BERTOLT BRECHT. PREMIERE IN LEIPZIG, 9 MARCH 1930.

Weill wrote for the musical theatre on both sides of the Atlantic, in his native Germany and—forced to flee from the Nazis—in America. Though he adapted his musical style to each location, all the works have in common his biting wit and deep humanity. *Mahagonny*, which belongs to the German period, is an anti-capitalist satire set in an imaginary American city given over to hedonism.

CHARACTERS

Jenny Hill (SOPRANO); *Leokadja Begbick* (CONTRALTO); *Jim Mahoney* (TENOR); *Fatty* (TENOR); *Jack O'Brien* (TENOR); *Toby Higgins* (TENOR); *Trinity Moses* (BARITONE); *Bill* (BARITONE); *Joe* (BASS)
With six *prostitutes* and the *men* of Mahogony

ACT I

The widow Begbick, Fatty, and Trinity are on the run after breaking out of prison. Their car breaks down in a desolate place, and unable to move on, they establish the 'paradise city' Mahagonny. Soon it acts as a magnet to malcontents from far and wide: the tart Jenny arrives together with six other women, followed by the four lumberjacks Jim, Jack, Bill and Joe. Jim and Jenny develop a relationship based both on money and affection. All devote their lives to drinking, sex, and gambling. Abiding by the rules drawn up by the city's founders, life goes so smoothly that the inhabitants get bored and begin to protest at its purposelessness. Their existence is threatened by news of an approaching hurricane. In terror, Jim discovers a new code of behaviour: 'Do what you like. Everything is permitted.'

ACT II

Word comes that the storm has missed Mahagonny. The people rejoice, and take it as approval for their new way of life. Once again it is given over to eating and drinking, sex and sport. Jim runs out of money, but none of his friends are willing to help. Having committed the capitalist crime of being unable to meet his debts, he is tied up and led away.

ACT III

Jim is to be tried by Mahagonny's 'court', consisting of Begbick (judge), Fatty (defence), Trinity Moses (prosecution). In the preceding case, Toby Higgins offers a substantial bribe and is acquitted of murder, but Jim is unable to produce a sweetener. Even Jenny refuses to help, and accused of several offences, Jim is sentenced to death. His execution sparks off a riot, and as Mahagonny burns, the crowd chants 'Can't help ourselves or you or anybody!'.

UN BALLO IN MASCHERA (A Masked Ball)
Giuseppe Verdi (1813-1901)

THREE ACTS. LIBRETTO BY ANTONIO SOMMA AFTER EUGENE SCRIBE'S LIBRETTO FOR AUBER'S *GUSTAVE III*. PREMIERE IN ROME, 17 FEBRUARY 1859.

Verdi's original scenario for his opera was based on the assassination of the Swedish King Gustavus III, who was shot during a masked ball in Stockholm in 1792. However, after the attempted assassination of Napoleon III by an Italian revolutionary in 1858, the censors objected to the subject and after delays the opera was salvaged by moving the action back a century and to Boston, where the ruler became an English governor. Several modern productions of *Un ballo in maschera* have restored the Swedish setting successfully.

CHARACTERS

Amelia, Renato's wife (SOPRANO); *Oscar*, a page (SOPRANO); *Ulrica*, a fortune-teller (CONTRALTO); *Riccardo*, Count of Warwick, Governor of Boston (TENOR); *Renato*, Riccardo's secretary (BARITONE); *Silvano*, a sailor (BASS); *Samuel* and *Tom*, enemies of the Governer (BASS) With a *Judge*, Amelia's *servant, officials, populace*

When the Swedish setting is restored, the names are as follows: *Amelia* - Amelia, *Oscar* - Oscar, *Ulrica* - Mam'zelle Arvidson, *Riccardo* - Gustavus III, King of Sweden, *Renato* - Anckarstroem, the King's secretary, *Silvano* - Christian, *Samuel* - Count Ribbing, *Tom* - Count Horn

ACT I

SCENE 1 *Reception room in the Governor's residence*

A crowd of loyal subjects (but also containing a group of conspirators, led by Samuel and Tom) awaits the arrival of the Governor, Riccardo, for his morning audience. He enters with his page Oscar, who shows him the guest list for the masked ball being planned. He is distracted when he sees the name of Amelia, wife of his loyal secretary Renato, on the list, for he is secretly in love with her. Renato himself enters and attempts to warn Riccardo of a plot against him, but the Governor obstinately refuses to believe it. The next caller is the Judge, who tries to persuade Riccardo to sign an order banning the fortune-teller Ulrica, but Oscar intercedes on her behalf. Riccardo resolves to visit her in disguise to test her clairvoyant powers, and invites the assembled company to join him there.

SCENE 2 *Ulrica's hut*

Riccardo arrives disguised as a fisherman, and before long he is astonished to see Amelia appear too. She has come to ask for a cure for her infidelity, and Ulrica prescribes a magic herb which can only be gathered at midnight from beneath the gallows outside the city. She promises to do so, and Riccardo makes plans to follow her. When the disguised Riccardo's turn comes, Ulrica foretells that he will soon be assassinated, moreover by the first person to shake his hand. Suddenly Renato appears, and, unaware of the prophecy, rushes up to the Governor. The sight of the loyal Renato makes everyone sceptical of the grim prediction, and the crowd celebrates, relieved.

ACT II

A deserted field outside the city

Amelia, frightened, comes in search of the magic herb. She is surprised when Riccardo arrives. At first she resists when he declares his love for her, but she soon admits her feelings. Footsteps are heard: it is Renato, coming to protect the Governor, and the agitated Amelia draws a veil over her face. Renato warns Riccardo of the lurking conspirators and persuades him to return to town; Riccardo agrees only when Renato promises to escort the unknown, veiled woman back to safety. But the latter two are intercepted by Samuel and Tom, who demand to see whom the Governor had been meeting. They mock Renato when his wife is exposed, and he, in a rage, agrees to meet with the plotters the following day.

ACT III

SCENE 1 *Renato's house*

Renato plans to kill his unfaithful wife, but grants her request to bid their son farewell. Reflecting on the circumstances, he decides that it is Riccardo who has betrayed him and that he will spare Amelia. Samuel and Tom are astonished when he joins forces with them. He orders Amelia to draw lots to establish who will kill the Governor, and the deed falls to him. He recognizes his opportunity when Oscar arrives with an invitation to the Governor's masked ball.

SCENE 2 *The Governor's study*
Riccardo resolves to send Renato and Amelia back to England. Although troubled by premonitions of death, he ignores the warning of Oscar that he risks assassination at the ball.

SCENE 3 *A brilliantly-decorated ballroom*
Oscar reveals to Renato how the Governor is disguised. Amelia, too, has established who Riccardo is, but is unable to persuade him to flee. Renato shoots the Governor, and in the ensuing confusion Oscar unmasks the killer. As he dies, the Governor convinces Renato of Amelia's innocence and pardons him for the assassination.

THE BARBER OF SEVILLE
see **Il barbiere di Siviglia**

IL BARBIERE DI SIVIGLIA (The Barber of Seville)
Gioachino Rossini (1792-1868)

TWO ACTS. LIBRETTO BY CESARE STERBINI AFTER BEAU-MARCHAIS. PREMIERE IN ROME, 20 FEBRUARY 1816.

Beaumarchais's play *Le barbier de Séville*, first part of his Figaro trilogy (the second part was set by Mozart as *Le nozze di Figaro*), had attracted several composers before Rossini came to it. Indeed, one setting (by Paisiello) was so popular that Rossini's opera was considered unable to take the same name, and was first called *Almaviva*; only two months after Paisiello's death was Rossini able to call his work by its now familiar title. In spite of its famously chaotic premiere, Rossini's opera has gone on to become one of the best loved operas ever written.

CHARACTERS
Rosina, ward of Bartolo (MEZZO-SOPRANO); *Berta*, Bartolo's house-keeper (MEZZO-SOPRANO); *Count Almaviva* (TENOR); *Figaro*, a barber (BARITONE); *Dr Bartolo* (BARITONE); *Don Basilio*, music teacher (BASS); *Fiorello*, Almaviva's servant (BASS); *Ambrogio*, Bartolo's servant (BASS)
With *Notary*, *Officer*, *musicians* and *soldiers*

ACT I
SCENE 1 *A square in Seville, at dawn*
Count Almaviva is in love with Rosina, the rich ward of old Dr Bartolo. Assisted by Fiorello and a band of musicians, he serenades her, but she fails to appear. Almaviva despatches the players, but remains in the square where, before long, the crafty barber Figaro appears. Figaro's job has given him entrée all over the city, and he is familiar with Rosina's circumstances. He tells Almaviva of the strict regime she lives under, that Bartolo jealously guards her beauty and money since the old man wants to marry her himself. Rosina, who has noticed her secret admirer, contrives to drop him a note from her balcony, asking his name. The Count replies that he is Lindoro, a poor student. Before Rosina has a chance to respond, Bartolo closes the shutters; he is

already trying to arrange his wedding. In return for a rich reward, Figaro helps Almaviva hatch a plan: he must enter Bartolo's house disguised as a drunken soldier and request lodgings.

SCENE 2 *A room in Dr Bartolo's house*
Rosina has just written a letter to 'Lindoro' when Figaro enters, but they are unable to talk, because Bartolo and her music teacher, Basilio, appear. Basilio tells the old doctor that Almaviva has arrived in Seville, but Bartolo is too preoccupied with his wedding arrangements to be interested in Basilio's slanderous scheme to force the Count out of town. Figaro, who has over-heard their conversation, goes to report it to Rosina. She, equally, is too preoccupied with 'Lindoro' to worry, and gives her letter to Figaro to deliver to her admirer. As soon as he departs, Bartolo confronts her with evidence that she has written a letter to her lover. Almaviva arrives and demands lodgings. Bartolo questions him, but amid the chaos Almaviva manages to identify himself to Rosina. Challenged by a guard, the Count reveals his true identity and is allowed to go free, much to Bartolo's chagrin.

ACT II
A room in Dr Bartolo's house
Almaviva now enters disguised as a music teacher, 'Don Alonso', claiming to have come in place of Basilio. He ingrati-ates himself with Bartolo by 'exposing' the Count's designs on Rosina, and the 'lesson' goes ahead. Figaro arrives to shave the old doctor, and succeeds in getting the balcony key required for Rosina's escape. He is followed by the real music teacher, Basilio, easily bribed to leave. But Bartolo has overheard the lovers' plans to elope, and in confusion the two plotters are chased away. He convinces Rosina that she has been deceived and that she would be better off marrying him after all, and wastes no time in sending for the Notary. During a storm, Almaviva and Figaro steal back using the balcony key, and although Rosina at first rejects him angrily, the Count reveals his true identity and wins her back. Figaro saves the situation by instructing the Notary to marry Rosina and the Count. Bartolo arrives back too late, in time only to receive Rosina's dowry as compensation. He accepts his fate.

THE BARTERED BRIDE
Bedřich Smetana (1824-1884)

THREE ACTS. LIBRETTO BY KAREL SABINA. PREMIERE IN PRAGUE, 30 MAY 1866.

Smetana, the 'father of Czech opera', was a leader of the mid-19th century Czech musical revival, and almost single-handedly estab-lished a national operatic style. Of his eight operas, *The Bartered Bride* remains the best known, admired for its lively dance music.

CHARACTERS
Mařenka, daughter of Krušina and Ludmila (SOPRANO); *Esmerelda*, circus artist (SOPRANO); *Ludmila*, Krušina's wife (MEZZO-SOPRANO);

Háta, Mícha's wife (MEZZO-SOPRANO); *Jeník*, Mícha's son by his first marriage (TENOR); *Vašek*, son of Mícha and Háta (TENOR); *Ring Master* (TENOR); *Krušina*, a peasant farmer (BARITONE); *Kečal*, marriage broker (BASS); *Mícha*, a landlord (BASS); *Indian*, circus artist (BASS)
With *villagers, circus troupe*

ACT I

The village green beside a tavern

The Bohemian spring is being celebrated by the villagers and all are in high spirits except for the lovers Mařenka and Jeník. They are downcast at the news that her parents plan to marry her off to a wealthy man she has never met. The couple depart and Mařenka's parents appear with the village marriage broker, Kečal, who sings the praises of Vašek, son the rich Tobias Mícha. Krušina, Mařenka's father, believes that Mícha has two sons, but Kečal counters this, saying that the one by an earlier marriage has been missing for years, presumed dead. Mařenka joins the trio, declaring that she is already engaged and objects to the plan. Their confrontation is interrupted by a lively polka danced by the villagers.

ACT II

Inside the tavern

Merriment in the tavern gives way to the entrance of Vašek, who turns out to be a stuttering simpleton. Mařenka recognizes him as the man she is supposed to marry and, taking advantage of the fact that he does not yet know her, attempts to discourage him by describing herself in the bleakest terms. The marriage broker Kečal, as persistent as ever, makes another attempt to get Jeník out of the way, offering him a substantial sum if he will renounce Mařenka : this Jeník does, but in favour of Mícha's elder son only. Kečal is satisfied, thinking the other son to be dead, but Jeník knows that the elder son is none other than he himself. The broker calls on the villagers to witness the document, and all are satisfied until it is revealed that Jeník has renounced Mařenka for money. They are shocked by his apparently callous treatment of her.

ACT III

The village green beside a tavern

Vašek, puzzled by events, is distracted by the arrival of a circus troupe in the village. He is enchanted by the beautiful dancer Esmerelda. She, in turn, flirts with him, and when it is announced that the man who plays the performing bear is too drunk to appear, she teaches Vašek to dance. In spite of his parents' pleas, Vašek refuses to go to meet Mařenka , of whom he has heard bad reports. The jilted Mařenka enters, and spurred on by Jeník's cheerfulness, agrees to marry Vašek after all. The villagers assemble to witness the marriage of Mařenka and 'the son of Tobias Mícha'. Suddenly Mícha and his wife Háta recognize Jeník as their long-lost son. Mařenka understands Jeník's scheme and the two are reunited. The outwitted Kečal storms off as the village celebrates.

THE BASSARIDS
Hans Werner Henze (b. 1926)

ONE ACT (FOUR MOVEMENTS AND AN INTERMEZZO). LIBRETTO
BY W.H. AUDEN AND CHESTER KALLMAN AFTER EURIPIDES'S
THE BACCHAE. PREMIERE IN SALZBURG, 6 AUGUST 1966.

One of the most significant post-1945 German composers, Henze has written extensively for the operatic stage. *The Bassarids*, his sixth full length opera, was his second collaboration with Auden and Kallman. Henze's setting of the Greek tragedy remains perhaps his greatest success to date. Its layout, in four 'movements', suggests symphonic structure.

CHARACTERS
Agave, Cadmus's daughter and mother of Pentheus (MEZZO-SOPRANO); *Autonoe*, Agave's sister (SOPRANO); *Beroe*, old slave (MEZZO-SOPRANO); *Dionysus* (also sings *Voice* and *Stranger*) (TENOR); *Tiresias*, an old, blind prophet (TENOR); *Pentheus*, King of Thebes (BARITONE); *Captain of the Royal Guard* (BARITONE); *Cadmus*, Pentheus's grandfather, founder of Thebes (BASS); *Young woman*, slave in Agave's household (SILENT); *Child*, her daughter (SILENT)
With *Bassarids*, *citizens* of Thebes, *guards* and *servants*

FIRST MOVEMENT
After the abdication of Cadmus, founder of Thebes, a crowd in the royal palace acclaim their new king, Cadmus's grandson Pentheus. They are interrupted by an off-stage Voice, who announces that the god Dionysus has arrived in Boeotia. Almost immediately the Theban people become his followers, the Bassarids. Although Pentheus issues dire warnings against the cult, even the prophet Tiresias, as well as Agave and Autonoe, are lured to Mount Cytheron by the sensuous new religion.

SECOND MOVEMENT
The headstrong Pentheus ignores Cadmus's advice and commands the Captain of the Guard to arrest Dionysus and the Bassarids. Most of the prisoners are taken off to be tortured, but Pentheus interrogates his family members and Tiresias himself. They provide no explanation for their behaviour: his mother Agave, still in a trance, can only sing of the delights of Cytheron. Pentheus orders the torture of a stranger (whom Beroe recognizes as being none other than Dionysus).

THIRD MOVEMENT
An earthquake hits Thebes as the stranger is tortured and the prisoners escape back to Cytheron. In the Intermezzo (a parody of 18th-century French musical style), Dionysus reveals to Pentheus the latter's dream-like sexual fantasies in a play on the Judgement of Calliope. Dionysus persuades Pentheus to join the Bassarids on the mountain, where a mob, led by Agave who does not recognize her son, kills him.

FOURTH MOVEMENT
The ecstatic Agave returns to Thebes parading the head of her

son; still hallucinating, she maintains that she has killed a lion. When she finally comes to her senses, horrified, Cadmus pins the blame for the murder on Dionysus. The god arrives and banishes the royal family from Thebes. He orders the palace to be burnt, first raising his mother Semele from her grave there. Dionysus and Semele (now called Thyone) become joint objects of the Bassarids' worship.

BÉATRICE ET BÉNÉDICT
Hector Berlioz (1803-1869)

TWO ACTS. LIBRETTO BY THE COMPOSER AFTER SHAKE-SPEARE'S *MUCH ADO ABOUT NOTHING*. PREMIERE AT BADEN-BADEN, 9 AUGUST 1862.

Béatrice et Bénédict was Berlioz's final opera. After his epic *Les Troyens*, he turned to Shakespearian comedy to provide some-thing light-hearted for the opening of a new theatre in Baden-Baden. Though he condensed Shakespeare's text, Berlioz fol-lows the play closely for much of the opera; only the non-Shakespearian character Somarone was the composer's invention. The Sicilian setting gave Berlioz the opportunity to include street dances and to score for tambourines and guitars.

CHARACTERS

Héro, Léonato's daughter (SOPRANO); *Béatrice*, Léonato's niece (MEZZO-SOPRANO); *Ursula*, Héro's attendant (MEZZO-SOPRANO); *Bénédict*, an officer (TENOR); *Claudio*, an officer (BARITONE); *Somarone*, music master (BASS); *Don Pedro*, a general (BASS); *Léonato*, governor of Messina (SPOKEN)

ACT I
The governor's garden

The town of Messina is celebrating Don Pedro's defeat of the besieging Moor army. Among the officers returning will be Claudio, betrothed to Héro. She sings excitedly of his home-coming; in contrast, Béatrice is not looking forward to seeing Bénédict, with whom she frequently squabbles. No sooner have the soldiers arrived when Béatrice and Bénédict begin to pro-voke each other. When the wedding of Héro and Claudio is announced for that evening, the conversation of Don Pedro, Claudio, and Bénédict turns to marriage. The latter insists that he intends to hang on to his bachelorhood, and as a challenge the other two resolve to deceive Béatrice and Bénédict into admitting tenderness for each other. Somarone appears to rehearse his musicians for that evening's celebrations. Bénédict, eavesdropping on an arranged conversation, learns that Béatrice is in love with him and softens his attitude towards marriage (and she overhears corresponding talk in the house). Héro and Ursula close the act with a nocturne in the moonlit garden.

ACT II
A hall in the governor's palace

The wedding guests are making merry and Somarone offers a

drinking song. Béatrice discloses that she is now in love with Bénédict, and is joined by Héro and Ursula in extolling the virtues of love. The two reluctant lovers admit their mutual feelings, while nevertheless continuing to taunt each other. A double wedding is celebrated, as Hero and Claudio, and Beatrice and Bénédict are united.

BILLY BUDD
Benjamin Britten (1913-1976)

TWO ACTS. LIBRETTO BY E.M. FORSTER AND ERIC CROZIER AFTER HERMAN MELVILLE'S STORY. PREMIERE IN LONDON, 1 DECEMBER 1951.

Melville's novel drew inspiration from a true event in the US Navy in the mid-19th century, but it (like Britten's opera) is set on board a Royal Navy ship during the French Wars in 1797. The ship can easily be taken as a metaphor for other institutions, but whatever interpretation is chosen, Britten illuminates the plot with music of great psychological power; though only male voices are used, he avoids monotony with scoring of equal brilliance.

CHARACTERS

Captain Vere, in command of the HMS Indomitable (TENOR); *Billy Budd*, able seaman (BARITONE); *Claggart*, master-at-arms (BASS); *Red Whiskers*, an impressed man (TENOR); *Novice* (TENOR); *Squeak*, a ship's corporal (TENOR); *Maintop* (TENOR); *Mr Redburn*, First Lieutenant (BARITONE); *Mr Flint*, Sailing Master (BARITONE); *Donald*, a sailor (BARITONE); *Bosun* (BARITONE); *First and Second Mates* (BARITONES); *Novice's Friend* (BARITONE); *Arthur Jones*, an impressed man (BARITONE); *Lieutenant Ratcliffe* (BASS); *Dansker*, an old seaman (BASS)
With *cabin boy, midshipmen, seamen, officers, petty officers, marines, drummers*

PROLOGUE
Vere in old age
The old Captain Vere, long in retirement, is haunted by his actions way back in 1797.

ACT I
SCENE 1 *The deck of the HMS 'Indomitable', 1797*
Sailors are at work on the deck. When a Novice annoys the Bosun he is taken off for a flogging. A guard-boat returns from a passing merchant vessel with three men impressed into service: Red Whiskers, Arthur Jones, and Billy Budd. Only Billy pleases the Master-at-Arms, Claggart, when he questions them, for in spite of a stutter, he displays the qualities of a strong sailor. But the officers worry that Billy's farewell to his old ship, called the 'Rights o' Man', has political significance, and fearing dissent from the other sailors, Claggart instructs Squeak to spy on Billy, even to provoke him. The Novice returns from his flogging, and Billy's expression of sympathy annoys Claggart. Donald and Dansker warn Billy about the sinister Claggart, and advise him to throw his loyalty behind

Captain Vere. When Vere addresses them, Billy leads a chorus of praise, swearing to die for him if necessary.

SCENE 2 *Captain Vere's cabin, a week later*
Vere, reading alone in his cabin at night, is joined by two officers, Mr Redburn and Mr Flint. Their conversation turns to a recent naval mutiny, and the officers suggest Billy as potential bad influence on the men of the 'Indomitable'. Vere is not convinced, especially when the men below decks are heard singing a spirited shanty. Enemy land is sighted.

SCENE 3 *Below decks, that evening*
Billy finds Squeak tampering with his kit-bag. They fight, and before Squeak can reveal that he was only obeying Claggart's orders, Claggart has him detained. But Claggart, obsessed with Billy's good looks, sadistically intends to destroy him. He presses the Novice into trying to bribe Billy to lead a mutiny; the Novice wakes Billy but the latter can only stammer agitatedly. Dansker calms Billy down, and attempts to warn Billy about Claggart's motives. But Billy naively believes that Claggart favours him, and looks forward to promotion.

ACT II

SCENE 1 *On deck, some days later*
Claggart is warning Vere about the danger of a mutiny when they are interrupted as a French ship is sighted. The crew leaps into action and a shot is fired, but the enemy slips away. Claggart tries again to blacken Billy's name, and though Vere does not believe him, he summons both men to his cabin.

SCENE 2 *Captain Vere's cabin*
Billy arrives anticipating promotion. When Claggart makes his accusation, the stammering Billy is left speechless and hits out instead. Claggart collapses, dead. Vere knows that the innocent Billy has brought catastrophe on himself. He is forced to convene a court, but in a moment of weakness gives no evidence against Claggart. Billy is sentenced to die the following morning.

SCENE 3 *A bay of the gundeck, shortly before dawn*
Dansker brings the condemned Billy food and drink. He tells Billy that the sailors will try to stop his execution, but Billy has accepted his fate.

SCENE 4 *On deck, at dawn*
The ship's crew assembles to witness the execution. Billy stoically reaffirms his loyalty to Vere (a cry taken up by the whole company), but his execution sparks off a revolt, soon crushed. Only Vere remains on deck.

EPILOGUE
Vere in old age
Vere recalls Billy's burial at sea, acknowledging that he failed both Billy and himself. But, he says, Billy saved him.

LA BOHÈME
Giacomo Puccini (1858-1924)

FOUR ACTS. LIBRETTO BY GIUSEPPE GIACOSO AND LUIGI ILLICA AFTER HENRI MURGER'S NOVEL *SCENES DE LA VIE DE BOHÉME*. PREMIERE IN TURIN, 1 FEBRUARY 1896.

La Bohème, Puccini's second mature work, combines music of a special, tender glow, with carefully crafted construction—in many ways, a model opera. Debussy, not normally an admirer of Puccini's music, admitted that he knew of no one who had described the Paris of that time better.

CHARACTERS

Mimì, a seamstress (SOPRANO); *Musetta*, a grisette (SOPRANO); *Rodolfo*, a poet (TENOR); *Parpignol*, a toy vendor (TENOR); *Marcello*, a painter (BARITONE); *Schaunard*, a musician (BARITONE); *Colline*, a philosopher (BASS); *Benoit*, a landlord (BASS); *Alcindoro*, a state councillor (BASS); *Customs official* (BASS)

With *students*, *working girls*, *citizens*, *shopkeepers*, *vendors*, *soldiers*, *waiters* and *children*

ACT I

Christmas Eve: a garret overlooking snow-covered Parisian rooftops
In a freezing cold attic both Rodolfo, a poet, and a painter Marcello abandon work because there is no fuel for the stove. Rodolfo attempts to save the situation by burning his latest manuscript, but it produces little warmth. They are joined by the philosopher Colline, and then by the fourth bohemian, the musician Schaunard. He arrives with food, but his companions are too hungry to listen to the bizarre story of how he earned the money for it. They are about to consume it when he suggests that, since it is Christmas Eve, they eat out and store up what he has brought for harder times. Before they can leave, their landlord Benoit comes to demand unpaid rent. They ply him with drink so that he forgets the purpose of his visit, and when he is indiscreet about his womanizing they bundle him out, pretending to be shocked. Only Rodolfo remains behind, to work on an article he hopes to sell, but he is soon distracted by a timid knock on the door. It is his neighbour Mimì, in search of a light for her candle. Weak with illness, she collapses and drops her key. When she is recovered, they search for the key and their hands meet. Soon Rodolfo is telling her about his life, and she responds with an account of her own simple existence. Rodolfo's friends impatiently shout up for him, and the two go together to join the others at the Café Momus.

ACT II

At the Café Momus, later the same evening
Amidst the revellers, the bohemians buy Christmas gifts. Parpignol entertains the children. Once inside the café, Rodolfo introduces Mimì to his friends. They are interrupted by the arrival of Marcello's ex-lover, Musetta, who has brought Alcindoro, a wealthy, ageing admirer, with her. Alcindoro's presence makes Marcello jealous, and Musetta achieves her

goal of winning the painter back. The reunited couple, together with the other bohemians, slip off to join the celebrations, leaving Alcindoro to pay the bill.

ACT III
The Barrière d'Enfer

Rodolfo and Mimì have parted. At dawn on one cold February day, Mimì comes to the entrance to the Latin Quarter, seeking Marcello in the hope that he may be able to help reconcile her with Rodolfo. She pours out her heart—about Rodolfo's jealousy—and then hides as he appears. He confesses to Marcello that she is dying of consumption, and that they must part because he is unable to provide a better place than the freezing garret for her. Mimì emerges: her first reaction is to leave him for good, but soon they resolve to stay together until the spring. Marcello, who has heard Musetta's laughter from the tavern, quarrels noisily with her.

ACT IV
The garret, some weeks later

Both couples have split up. Rodolfo and Marcello are trying to work, but end up reminiscing about the girls. Spirits are raised when Colline and Schaunard appear with a meagre supper for the four. Suddenly Musetta bursts in, bringing with her the dying Mimì, who requested to see Rodolfo. Musetta gives her earrings to Marcello to sell to pay for a doctor, and Colline pawns his coat to help too. The friends go out to seek assistance, and Mimì and Rodolfo recall their first meeting. The others return, and soon realize that Mimì has died peacefully. Rodolfo, the last to comprehend it, falls on her body.

BORIS GODUNOV
Modest Mussorgsky (1839-1881)

PROLOGUE AND FOUR ACTS. LIBRETTO BY THE COMPOSER AFTER ALEXANDER PUSHKIN'S *BORIS GODUNOV* AND HISTORICAL WORKS BY NIKOLAY KARAMZIN. PREMIERE IN ST PETERSBURG, 16 FEBRUARY 1874.

Mussorgsky's epic is perhaps the greatest Russian opera. But of all operas, its genesis is also one of the most complicated, and performers today are faced with the choice of several different editions. The opera as premiered in 1874 was already a revision, for the composer's original, seven-scene conception had been rejected by the theatre authorities in St Petersburg. (The first version has now been successfully staged, but the expanded prologue and four acts described below remains more popular.) After Mussorgsky's death the opera was revised twice by Rimsky-Korsakov: his view of the piece glossed over the dark, crude realism of Mussorgsky, but his second revision helped to establish the opera in the international repertory, and is still favoured by some today. Other editions exist, notably a re-orchestration by Shostakovich, all testifying to the power of the piece and the musical and dramatic attractions of the title role.

CHARACTERS

Xenia, Boris's daughter (SOPRANO); *Marina Mniszek*, a Polish princess (SOPRANO); *Hostess* (MEZZO-SOPRANO); *Fyodor*, Boris's son (MEZZO-SOPRANO); *Xenia's Nurse* (CONTRALTO); *Grigory*, The Pretender Dmitry (TENOR); *Prince Shuisky* (TENOR); *Simpleton* (TENOR); *Andrey Shchelkalov*, secretary to the Council of Boyars (BARITONE); *Boris Godunov* (BASS); *Pimen*, monk and chronicler (BASS); *Varlaam* (BASS) and *Missail* (TENOR), vagabonds; *Rangoni*, a Jesuit in disguise (BASS); *Nikitich*, a police officer (BASS)

With *Boyars, Jesuits, guards, soldiers*, Polish *nobility, maidens* of Sandomierz, *pilgrims, people* of Moscow, *urchins* and *vagabonds*

The opera recalls turbulent events in Russian history at the beginning of the 17th century. In 1591, the nine-year-old Dmitry, son of Ivan the Terrible, in line for the throne, was murdered (assassinated, the opera asserts, by Boris Godunov, though modern historians dispute that fact). His half-brother Fyodor was too weak to rule, and so left government to his brother-in-law Boris Godunov. On Fyodor's death in 1598, Boris was elected Tsar.

PROLOGUE (1598)

SCENE 1 *Courtyard of the Novodevichy Monastery, Moscow*
The police officer Nikitich chides the assembled crowd for its apathy, saying that Boris is reluctant to accept the throne and they must beg him to do so. Too confused by events to respond, they are urged again, this time by Shchelkalov, who fears that without Boris, the country will slide into anarchy. Pilgrims enter the monastery.

SCENE 2 *Square in the Moscow Kremlin*
Boris has been crowned. Shuisky comes from the Cathedral to call upon the crowd to acclaim him. This they do, but the solemn Boris silences them and prays for guidance. Inviting them to a feast, he departs amid scenes of rejoicing.

ACT I (1603)

SCENE 1 *Pimen's cell in the Chudov Monastery*
Five years after Boris's coronation, Russia is in turmoil. In spite of his efforts to rule justly, famine has brought discontent. The old monk Pimen attributes Russia's problems to Boris's crime of murdering the boy Dmitry, and records what he saw (previously a soldier, he witnessed the deed) in the chronicle he is finishing. Pimen hopes to hand his work over to his young apprentice Grigory. When Grigory wakes from a nightmare, Pimen comforts him. Pimen reminisces, and tells Grigory that the murdered Tsarevich Dmitry would now have been Grigory's age. Grigory resolves to avenge Boris.

SCENE 2 *An inn on the Lithuanian border*
The Hostess's singing is interrupted by the arrival of three men, the vagabonds Varlaam and Missail, and Grigory, now posing as the Pretender Dmitry and on the run for fear of detection. He is heading west to Russia's hostile neighbours, hoping to enlist help. Fortified by wine, Varlaam gives a lively account of his

past exploits, and berates Grigory for his downcast mood. Grigory is obtaining directions to the border from the Hostess, when guards in search of him arrive. He tries to persuade the guards (illiterate and unable to make out the warrant) that Varlaam is the fugitive Pretender, but Varlaam himself uses his rusty reading skills to expose Grigory, who escapes just in time.

ACT II (1603)
The Tsar's apartments in the Kremlin
Boris's son and daughter are with their Nurse. Fyodor is studying a map of Russia, but Xenia is weeping for her dead fiancé. The Nurse tries to distract them with games and songs, but Xenia is still upset when her father enters. Boris comforts her, and then left with Fyodor, admires the map uneasily. He is haunted by political troubles and the vision of a dying child. Shuisky's arrival is announced by a boyar, who confides to Boris that Shuisky is in league with conspirators. When Shuisky enters, he is accused of treason. Nevertheless, Shuisky reports on the rise of a Pretender in Poland, who has gained the support of the King as well as the Pope. At the mention of the name Dmitry, Boris panics. He questions Shuisky as to whether the young Dmitry really died and, overcome with guilt, begins to hallucinate.

ACT III (1604)
SCENE 1 *Marina's room in Sandomierz Castle*
Girls are entertaining Marina with their songs. They flatter her, but she shows little interest and sends them away: her mind is on Dmitry (Grigory), through whose love she hopes to reach the throne in Moscow. She is interrupted by the Jesuit Rangoni, who urges her to use the power that will be hers to convert the Russians from Orthodoxy to Roman Catholicism. He silences her objections.

SCENE 1 *The gardens of Sandomierz Castle*
While Dmitry is waiting for Marina at a moonlit fountain, the scheming Rangoni steals up. Hoping to win powerful connections for himself, he attempts to fan Dmitry's passion for Marina. They hide as noblemen, emerging from the court, talk of the campaign against Moscow. When Dmitry meets Marina, he is insulted to find that she is interested only in the throne. But finally he wins her over and they embrace.

ACT IV (1605)
SCENE 1 *Granovitaya Palace in the Kremlin*
The Council of Boyars meet to debate measures against the Pretender. Shuisky arrives late and proceeds to tell them of the Tsar's tormented state. Moments later Boris himself appears, still evidently disturbed. He tries to address the council, but is interrupted by the entry of Pimen. The latter's tale of a blind shepherd whose sight was restored by praying at the boy Dmitry's grave, fills Boris with fear. In desperation he calls for his son and bids him farewell, telling him to rule wisely and to protect his sister Xenia. Boris collapses and dies.

SCENE 2 *A clearing in the forest near Kromy*
Dmitry's supporters are advancing on Moscow. They seize and bait a supporter of Boris, the boyar Khrushchov. Varlaam and Missail rail against Boris and urge the crowd to lynch two Jesuits. Dmitry appears to his enthusiastic followers, and pardons the boyar and the Jesuits on condition of their support. He leads his supporters off towards Moscow, leaving only a dissident Simpleton behind, who laments the fate of Russia.

CAPRICCIO
Richard Strauss (1864-1949)

ONE ACT. LIBRETTO BY THE COMPOSER AND CLEMENS KRAUSS. PREMIERE IN MUNICH, 28 OCTOBER 1942

Capriccio, the last of Strauss's 15 operas, makes a fitting end to the composer's operatic output. It is, in essence, a self-illustrating discussion on the relationship between music and words in opera, a subject of concern to many practitioners of the form. Indeed, initial inspiration came from the libretto of *Prima la musica e poi le parole*, set by Mozart's rival, Salieri. Strauss's opera takes place around 1775, at the time of quarrels prompted by Gluck's operatic reforms. It works at several levels—each protagonist's view of the subject is paralleled in his relationship to the Countess—but most importantly it is an opera of glorious, glowing music.

CHARACTERS

Countess Madeleine (SOPRANO); *Clairon*, Madeleine's actress (CONTRALTO); *Flamand*, a composer (TENOR); *Two Italian Singers* (SOPRANO and TENOR); *Mounsieur Taupe*, a prompter (TENOR); *The Count*, her brother (BARITONE); *Olivier*, a poet (BARITONE); *La Roche*, a theatre director (BASS); *The Major-Domo* (BASS)
With eight *servants*, a *ballerina*, and three onstage *musicians*

A château near Paris
The young, recently widowed Countess Madeleine and her brother, the Count, are listening to a string sextet written by the composer Flamand in preparation for her birthday celebrations. Her reactions are closely watched by the composer, but also by the poet Olivier, since the two are rival suitors for her. Flamand and Olivier are both eager to know whether she is moved more by words or by music, and they discuss their relative merits with the theatre director La Roche (who, favouring lively entertainment, had been lulled to sleep during the music). Olivier has contributed a play in honour of the Countess's birthday, and La Roche prepares to direct it: the Count is to take part, opposite the actress Clairon with whom he is in love (she also happens to have been Olivier's former mistress). Clairon and the Count read from the play, reaching a passionate sonnet which is really Olivier's declaration of love for the Countess. As soon as they go off to the theatre to rehearse, Olivier reads his sonnet to the Countess; not to be outdone, Flamand sets it to music, and sings it. The two men argue over whose work it really is. When Olivier is summoned away to the rehearsal by La Roche, Flamand takes

the opportunity to declare his love to the Countess. She promises to answer him at eleven o'clock the next morning, and clears the air by ordering chocolate for all those in the salon. (At this point an interval is sometimes inserted into the opera.)

The Count joins his sister and they discuss their affairs of the heart. She still cannot decide between the composer and the poet, and speculates that perhaps a collaborative opera will result. As people assemble, La Roche lays on entertainment, first by a ballerina and then by two Italian singers. The dancing and singing give rise to more debate about the importance of words and music, but their reflections are interrupted by La Roche's announcement of a grand spectacle for the Countess's birthday. The serious, allegorical subject 'The Birth of Pallas Athene' is met first with laughter and then with quarrelling. When all have calmed down, La Roche launches into a defence of his art. The Countess requests a collaboration between Flamand and Olivier: subjects are discussed, and eventually they settle for 'the events of today' with the ending to be decided on by the Countess. The company departs and servants who enter to tidy up gossip about what they have overheard. The Major-Domo gives them the evening off; he then encounters the prompter, Monsieur Taupe, who has just woken up after a long sleep in his prompt box. All is quiet when the Countess enters. The Major-Domo brings her a message from Olivier: he will come to her the following morning at eleven to find out how the opera should end. She remembers that she is due to answer Flamand's declaration at that time. She muses over the opera, asking herself whether she is more moved by music or words. But she never decides (or does she?: she goes out humming Flamand's melody to the sonnet) because before long she is summoned by the Major-Domo to supper.

CARMEN
Georges Bizet (1838-1875)

FOUR ACTS. LIBRETTO BY HENRI MEILHAC AND LUDOVIC HALÉVY AFTER PROSPER MÉRIMÉE'S NOVEL. PREMIERE IN PARIS, 3 MARCH 1875.

Carmen's status as one of the best loved and most frequently performed operas in the repertory today makes it easy to forget that its premiere was a failure. Indeed, Bizet enjoyed little operatic success during his lifetime, and his death three months after *Carmen*'s premiere prevented him from basking in the popularity which it soon achieved. It was the opera's low-life characters that upset the Parisian audiences of 1875; few noted its well-proportioned structure or deft orchestration.

CHARACTERS

Carmen, a gypsy (MEZZO-SOPRANO); *Micaëla*, a country girl (SOPRANO); *Frasquita*, a gypsy girl (SOPRANO); *Mercédès*, a gypsy girl (SOPRANO); *Don José*, a corporal (TENOR); *Le Dancaïre*, a smuggler (TENOR); *Le Remendado* a smuggler (TENOR); *Escamillo*, a matador (BARITONE); *Moralès*, a corporal (BARITONE); *Zuniga*, a lieutenant (BASS); *Lillas Pastia*, an innkeeper (SPOKEN)

With *soldiers, cigarette factory girls, gypsies, smugglers, vendors, people* of Seville

ACT I
A square in Seville outside a cigarette factory
Soldiers are watching over the square when Micaëla comes looking for Don José. He is due to appear with the changing of the guard, but she is too shy to wait for him. When José arrives his captain, Zuniga, tells him about the visitor, and José explains that she is a young orphan brought up by his mother. At noon the girls come out of the cigarette factory for their break. One of them, Carmen, turns her attentions on José, throwing a flower at him. He picks it up as soon as she has left, but hides it when Micaëla reappears. She brings a letter from his mother (urging him to marry Micaëla). José resolves to return home as soon as possible, but his thoughts are interrupted by a sudden commotion from the factory. A quarrel has broken out and Zuniga sends José in to investigate. He finds the culprit, Carmen, and arrests her. As he guards her in prison she begins to flirt with him, persuading him to let her escape.

ACT II
Lillas Pastia's inn
There is singing and dancing at the inn as Carmen, Frasquita, and Mercédès entertain the officers. They include Zuniga, who tells Carmen that José, imprisoned for allowing her to escape, is to be released. The toreador Escamillo passes through, showing an interest in Carmen, but she refuses him. After the inn closes Le Dancaïre and Le Remendado try to persuade the girls to join them on a smuggling expedition. Carmen refuses since she is waiting for Don José. When he appears she dances for him, but he is soon distracted by the sound of trumpets recalling him to barracks. She mocks him as he decides to leave, but before he can leave Zuniga comes to order him back. A fight breaks out and José, now forced to desert the army, joins Carmen and the gypsies fleeing to the mountains.

ACT III
In the mountains
Things are going badly in the smugglers' cave. Carmen's and José's relationship is breaking down, and she learns from cards of her impending death. Micaëla arrives in search of José, but hides when Escamillo approaches. He has come for Carmen, and fights José. Escamillo's life is saved by the intervention of Carmen, and he invites her to his next bull fight. Defiantly, José vows that he and Carmen will stay together, even if it means death. Micaëla emerges from hiding to bring news to José of his dying mother.

ACT IV
Outside the bullring in Seville
Festivities are underway and the crowd cheers Escamillo when he arrives for the fight. Carmen's friends warn her of José's presence, but she goes to confront him. When she hears the sound of Escamillo's victory, Carmen attempts to enter the

ring to celebrate with him. José blocks her way and stabs her, giving himself up as Escamillo and the spectators emerge.

CAVALLERIA RUSTICANA (Rustic Chivalry)
Pietro Mascagni (1863-1945)

ONE ACT. LIBRETTO BY GIOVANNI TARGIONI-TOZZETTI AND GUIDO MENASCI AFTER GIOVANNI VERGA'S PLAY BASED ON HIS STORY. PREMIERE IN ROME, 17 MAY 1890.

Though *Cavalleria rusticana* and *Pagliacci* have been almost inseparable for a century, *Cavalleria* predates its partner by two years. It was a success from the start: Mascagni was a provincial music teacher with just one operetta to his name when he submitted *Cavalleria* in a competition for one-act operas and emerged as the winner. *Cavalleria* was the first verismo opera, a term (meaning 'realism') applied to a genre of opera which developed in Italy in the last decade of the 19th century. Operas which dealt with everyday events and the 'low-life' (though verismo meant more than just this: it exploited local colour, too) were immensely popular in a country just emerging from rigorous censorship. The movement had started in the straight theatre, and Giovanni Verga, on whose play telling of peasant life in Sicily Mascagni based his opera, was one of its leading writers.

CHARACTERS

Santuzza, a peasant girl (SOPRANO); *Lola*, Alfio's wife (MEZZO-SOPRANO); *Mamma Lucia*, Turiddu's mother (CONTRALTO); *Turiddu*, a young peasant soldier (TENOR); *Alfio*, a horseman (BARITONE)

A Sicilian village on Easter Sunday, 1880
Turiddu is heard serenading Lola, the young wife of Alfio who is away on business. The villagers, excited by the arrival of spring, are preparing to celebrate Easter when Santuzza appears at Lucia's tavern, anxious for news of Turiddu, Lucia's son and Santuzza's former lover. Alfio enters, singing of his occupation and of his wife's beauty; he mentions in passing that has seen Turiddu near his house that morning. Lucia and Santuzza join the Easter procession, but Santuzza, excommunicated from the church for her affair, remains outside with Lucia when the worshipers enter church. She pours her heart out to Lucia, telling of Turiddu's betrayal of her. He had been engaged to Lola before going off on military service, she says, but in his absence Lola had married Alfio; on his return Turiddu transferred his affections to Santuzza, but continued to visit Lola whenever Alfio was away on business. Santuzza has lost both her honour and her lover, and asks Lucia to pray for her in church.

Turiddu appears in the square and is scolded by Santuzza for his adultery. Lola passes on her way to church, baiting them, and Turiddu turns to follow her. Santuzza begs him to stay with her, but when he rejects her she curses him. Suddenly Alfio comes in search of his wife, and the jealous Santuzza reveals the truth to him. As he leaves in a rage, she realizes what a storm she has unleashed. An orchestral Intermezzo follows, full of foreboding.

As the church empties onto the square, Turiddu invites the villagers for a drink. When he proposes a toast to Lola, Alfio refuses to join him, challenging him to a duel instead. Fearing the worst, Turiddu goes to beg his mother's blessing, asking her to protect Santuzza. He rushes off to face Alfio, and before long women in the crowd cry that Turiddu has been killed.

CENDRILLON (Cinderella)
Jules Massenet (1842-1912)
FOUR ACTS. LIBRETTO BY HENRI CAIN AFTER PERRAULT'S FAIRY TALE. PREMIERE IN PARIS, 24 MAY 1899.

Cendrillon, one of Massenet's most appealing operas, has been unjustly neglected. More fantastical than Rossini's setting of the Cinderella story (*La Cenerentola*), Massenet's opera uses fairy-tale trappings to probe deep into human nature, and contains some of the finest music the composer ever wrote.

CHARACTERS
Cendrillon (SOPRANO); *La Fée* (Fairy Godmother) (COLORATURA SOPRANO); *Le Prince Charmant* (Prince Charming) (SOPRANO); *Noémie*, Cendrillon's step-sister (SOPRANO); *Dorothée*, Cendrillon's step-sister (MEZZO-SOPRANO); *Madame de la Haltière*, Cendrillon's stepmother (MEZZO-SOPRANO); *Le Doyen de la Faculté* (TENOR); *Le Roi* (The King) (BARITONE); *Le Surintendant des plaisirs* (BARITONE); *Pandolfe*, Cendrillon's father (BASS); *Le Premier Ministre* (BASS)
With *spirits, servants, courtiers, doctors, ministers*

ACT I
Madame de la Haltière's house
As Madame de la Haltière and her daughters, Noémi and Dorothée, prepare for the ball, her long-suffering husband Pandolfe regrets remarrying and bemoans his fate and that of his daughter Cendrillon. He is off to the ball too, sad to be leaving her behind. When all have left, Cendrillon falls asleep. Soon the Fairy Godmother appears and gives her a gown and glass slippers for the ball, but orders her to leave by midnight.

ACT II
The royal palace
The ball in is progress. Prince Charming is miserable: he has been commanded by his father to marry, but cannot love any of the princesses brought to him. When a stranger (Cendrillon in disguise) appears, it is love at first sight. At midnight she has to tear herself away, losing a slipper in her haste.

ACT III
SCENE 1 *Madame de la Haltière's house*
Back home, Cendrillon reflects on the events at the ball. Soon the three other women begin to bicker at Pandolfe, who resolves to return to his country estate with his daughter. Cendrillon, however, is anxious not to impose her heartache on her father, and decides to leave home.

SCENE 2 *The fairy domain*

The fairies have arranged for Cendrillon and Prince Charming to appear, but the Fairy Godmother's spell ensures that they cannot see each other. The lovers are separated by a hedge, and when they hear one another they implore the Fairy Godmother to lift the spell. At last, reunited, they lapse into a blissful sleep.

ACT IV

SCENE 1 *A terrace*

Pandolfe nurses his sickly daughter, who has been hallucinating about the ball, her encounter in the fairy domain, and the missing slipper. Her sceptical father is overjoyed at her recovery. Madame de la Haltière arrives to bring news of the Prince's search for the princess who can match the missing slipper, and Cendrillon realizes that it is she who is being sought.

SCENE 2 *The palace*

Everyone celebrates as Cendrillon claims the slipper.

LA CENERENTOLA (Cinderella)

Gioachino Rossini (1792-1868)

TWO ACTS. LIBRETTO BY JACOPO FERRETTI, AFTER PERRAULT'S *CENDRILLON* AND ETIENNE'S LIBRETTO FOR ISOUARD'S *CENDRILLON*. PREMIERE IN ROME, 25 JANUARY 1817.

The Cinderella story has been the subject of several operas; apart from Rossini's most notably Massenet's *Cendrillon*. Rossini wrote his version—famously, in just over three weeks—the year after *Il barbiere di Siviglia*. Cenerentola mixes the light comedy of his previous masterpiece with elements of sentiment and pathos, as befits the rags-to-riches story.

CHARACTERS

Cenerentola (Angelina), Don Magnifico's step-daughter (MEZZO-SOPRANO or CONTRALTO); *Clorinda*, Magnifico's daughter (SOPRANO); *Tisbe*, Magnifico's daughter (MEZZO-SOPRANO); *Don Ramiro*, Prince of Salerno (TENOR); *Don Magnifico*, Baron of Monte Fiascone (BARI-TONE); *Dandini*, Ramiro's valet (BASS); *Alidoro*, a philosopher (BASS) With *ladies* and *gentlemen* of the Prince's court

ACT I

SCENE 1 *A room in Don Magnifico's rundown castle*

Magnifico's daughters, the Ugly Sisters Clorinda and Tisbe, argue while their downtrodden stepsister, Cenerentola, is busy with the housework. (As she works she sings a lament about a king who, looking for a wife, prefers as his bride a woman of goodness rather than beauty.) Prince Ramiro's tutor Alidoro enters disguised as a beggar: he has come to assess the suitability of Magnifico's daughters as candidates for his master's hand. Disgusted by his appearance, Clorinda and Tisbe mock him, and only Cenerentola takes pity on the stranger. Prince Ramiro's impending arrival is announced. His courtiers appear first, to invite Magnifico's daughters to the Prince's ball, at which he plans to choose the most beautiful girl there as his bride. Clorinda and Tisbe, excited by the prospect, bully Cenerentola into helping them prepare for the ball, but their noise disturbs Magnifico's sleep. He emerges, and relates the dream he has just had, which he interprets as foretelling royal connections for the family. Ramiro finally enters, but disguised as his valet Dandini. Alidoro has assured him that there is a worthy bride in Magnifico's household, and Ramiro has come to see for himself. He and Cenerentola fall in love at first sight. Dandini now enters disguised as his master, and they overhear Cenerentola begging Magnifico to allow her to go to the ball too. but he refuses, and when confronted by Ramiro, Dandini (each of them still posing as the other) and Alidoro, Magnifico tells them that his third daughter is dead and Cenerentola is only a servant. Cenerentola tries to deny this, but Magnifico threatens her violently; the others come to her defence. When all except Cenerentola have departed for the ball, Alidoro returns to help Cenerentola get there too.

SCENE 2 *Don Ramiro's castle*
Dandini (disguised as the Prince) is so impressed with Magnifico's drinking prowess that he appoints him cellar-master. As the guests proceed to dine, Ramiro confides to Dandini that he is mystified by Alidoro's confidence in one of Magnifico's daughters. Clorinda and Tisbe appear in search of their 'Prince', but he tries to palm them off onto his servant (in reality Ramiro). They are interrupted by the entry of a beautifully attired lady. Although Magnifico and his daughters note her resemblance to Cenerentola, they do not realize the truth.

ACT II
SCENE 1 *A room in Don Ramiro's castle*
Magnifico has misgivings about the success his daughters are having, each of whom thinks she has wooed the Prince (in reality Dandini, for he is still disguised). Dandini is now in love with Cenerentola, but she spurns him in favour of his 'valet' (the real Ramiro). When Ramiro proposes to her, she gives him a bracelet, one of a pair, saying that he must find her by the matching piece. When Magnifico challenges Dandini, requiring to know which daughter he will be marrying after all, Dandini reveals the hoax. Magnifico is outraged to realize that he has been paying homage to a valet.

SCENE 2 *A room in Don Magnifico's castle*
Clorinda and Tisbe are jealous of Cenerentola, who resembles the beautiful stranger at the ball. A storm blows up, causing the Prince's carriage to overturn outside the castle. He and Dandini take refuge inside, where Ramiro recognizes Cenerentola and claims her. She is scorned by her family and Ramiro rebukes them. Alidoro gives thanks for the success of his scheme.

SCENE 3 *The throne room in Don Ramiro's castle*
Cenerentola can scarcely believe her fortune. She pardons Magnifico and her step-sisters, and all rejoice in her happiness.

CHRISTMAS EVE
Nikolay Rimsky-Korsakov (1884-1908)

FOUR ACTS. LIBRETTO BY THE COMPOSER AFTER GOGOL'S STORY. PREMIERE IN ST PETERSBURG, 10 DECEMBER 1895.

Gogol's collection of folk tales *Evenings on a Farm near Dikanka* has served as a rich source of inspiration for composers. When Rimsky-Korsakov wrote *Christmas Eve* in 1894-5, he had already based one successful opera on another of Gogol's tales, *May Night* (1878-9), and perhaps his only reason for not having used *Christmas Eve* earlier was that Tchaikovsky had done so in *Cherevichki*. Significantly, *Christmas Eve* was the first opera Rimsky wrote after the death of the Tchaikovsky in 1893, an event which seems to have 'freed' Rimsky and encouraged him to write prolifically for the stage thereafter.

CHARACTERS
Oxana, Chub's daughter (SOPRANO); *Solokha*, a witch (MEZZO-SOPRANO); *Woman with a Purple Nose* (MEZZO-SOPRANO); *Woman with an Ordinary Nose* (SOPRANO); *The Tsaritsa* (MEZZO-SOPRANO); *Vakula*, the blacksmith, and Solokha's son (TENOR); *Devil* (TENOR); *The Priest* (TENOR); *The Mayor* (BARITONE); *Panas*, Chub's friend (BASS-BARITONE); *Patsyuk*, a medicine man (BASS-BARITONE); *Chub*, an elderly Cossack (BASS)
With *Major-Domo, Brooch Fairy, Ballet Mistress, Girls, Boys, Cossack and Woman, Witches, Wizards, Spirits of Darkness and Light, Venus Star, Morning Star* and other *Stars, Courtiers, Lackeys*

ACT I
On Christmas Eve in the Ukranian village of Dikanka, the widow Solokha (a part-time witch) is joined by the Devil. They flirt, and she agrees to help him in his plan to steal the moon and whip up a blizzard. The Devil has hatched his scheme to prevent the blacksmith Vakula, who has insulted him, from paying court to Oxana; the Devil reasons that the weather will keep Oxana's father, Chub, at home, and thus Vakula away from their house. In spite of the raging storm, however, Chub and his friend Panas set out to visit the Priest for a drink. The beautiful but capricious Oxana is left alone and before long she is joined by Vakula. But when the storm proves too much for Chub he returns home, and Vakula, mistaking him for a rival, uses force to eject him. Oxana rebuffs Vakula, saying that she will marry him only if he is able to bring her a pair of the Tsaritsa's slippers from St Petersburg.

ACT II
At her cottage, Solokha and the Devil are celebrating the success of their moon-stealing expedition. The Devil makes advances to Solokha, but they are interrupted by a knock at the door. It is the Mayor, and the Devil hides in a sack. Solokha is popular with the village men, and the Mayor is soon disturbed by the Priest, and he in turn by Chub. Each is hiding in a sack by the time Solokha's son Vakula returns home. When the villagers assemble outside Solokha's cottage to sing carols, Vakula

is too downcast to join them. He sets off to fulfil Oxana's demand, unaware that the sack on his back contains the Devil.

ACT III

Vakula, desperate to fulfil Oxana's request, consults the mysterious medicine man Patsyuk. He expects Patsyuk to tell him that only the Devil can help, but is astonished when Patsyuk reveals that in fact he has the Devil on his back. When the Devil jumps out of his sack, Vakula forces him to fly them to the Tsaritsa's court in St Petersburg. Vakula manages to enter the palace and is dazzled by the festivities. His wish is granted.

ACT IV

On Christmas morning the village square is filled with people celebrating. Vakula appears, and is reunited with Oxana. When he shows her the slippers, she is hardly interested: his expedition was in vain, because Oxana admits that she loves him anyway.

LA CLEMENZA DI TITO (The Clemency of Titus)
Wolfgang Amadeus Mozart (1756-1891)

TWO ACTS. LIBRETTO ADAPTED BY CATERINO MAZZOLA FROM PIETRO METASTASIO. PREMIERE IN PRAGUE, 6 SEPTEMBER 1791.

La clemenza di Tito was commissioned to mark the coronation of Leopold II as King of Bohemia in 1791, the year of Mozart's death. It was composed at the same time as *Die Zauberflöte* (The Magic Flute), but the two operas are utterly different: the latter is a light *Singspiel* (in the German vernacular), and *Tito* is an old-style Italian *opera seria*. As Mozart had proved in his earlier *Idomeneo*, he was capable of breathing new life into an unfashionable form, and *Tito* was to enjoy immense success in the years after its premiere (it was the first of Mozart's operas to reach England, in 1806). A century-and-a-half of neglect followed, and it is only comparatively recently that the opera's great richness has begun to be appreciated again.

CHARACTERS

Vitellia, daughter of the deposed Emperor Vittelius (SOPRANO); *Servilia*, sister of Sextus (SOPRANO); *Sesto* (Sextus), friend of Titus, in love with Vitellia (SOPRANO); *Annio* (Annius), friend of Sextus, in love with Servilia (SOPRANO); *Tito* (Titus), Roman Emperor (TENOR); *Publio* (Publius), captain of the praetorian guard (BASS) With *senators, ambassadors, guards, people of Rome*

ACT I

Vitellia, jealous that Emperor Titus intends to marry the Judaean princess Berenice rather than herself, has plotted to assassinate him. She persuades her new lover Sextus to join the conspiracy, but when the latter's friend Annius arrives with the news that Titus has sent Berenice away, she puts off the plan in the hope that she will become Empress after all. Annius wishes to marry Sextus's sister Servilia, and begs his friend to obtain the Emperor's permission for the marriage. Meanwhile, the

Romans celebrate Titus's victories, and Publius announces that a temple will be built in the Emperor's honour; Titus, however, prefers the funds to go to the survivors of the eruption of Vesuvius. Before Sextus can raise the matter of Annius's proposed marriage to Servilia, Titus announces that he is planning to marry her himself. Annius and Servilia reaffirm their love, but he nobly resolves not to deny her the opportunity to become Empress; Titus, on learning this, unselfishly stands down in Annius's favour and decides that he will marry Vitellia after all. She, however, hears only of Titus's plans to marry Servilia, and puts her assassination plan into action, sending Sextus off to set fire to the Capitol. Soon Annius and Publius appear with news that she is to be Titus's wife, but it is too late for her to stop Sextus. In the confusion at the Capitol, Sextus—horrified by his task but spurred on by the thought of Vitellia—stabs someone he believes to be Titus, but the Emperor escapes.

ACT II

Annius tells Sextus that the Emperor has survived after all, and advises his friend to beg Titus's forgiveness; in contrast, Vitellia, anxious that her role in the plot will be revealed, urges Sextus to escape while he can. Publio arrests Sextus, who is sentenced to death. Titus refuses to believe that his friend has conspired against him, and he summons the prisoner. Sextus reveals nothing of Vitellia's collusion and is led out, but the merciful Titus destroys the death warrant. Urged by Sextus's friends to intercede, Vitellia goes to plead with Titus on her behalf. She is filled with remorse for her part in the plot, and confesses all to Titus, who pardons both parties. The Romans praise his clemency.

LE COMTE ORY (Count Ory)
Gioachino Rossini (1792-1868)

Two acts. Libretto by Eugene Scribe and Charles-Gaspard Delestre-Poirson after their own play, based on a popular ballad. Premiere in Paris, 20 August 1828.

The witty *Le Comte Ory* sparkles so naturally that one would never guess that much of its music was originally composed for another opera. But Rossini had conceived *Il viaggio a Reims* (written for the coronation of Charles X in Paris, 1825) as a *pièce d'occasion*, and realizing that it would not survive as a repertory work he pressed its music into service again. *Il viaggio* had been Rossini's first opera for Paris but was nevertheless in Italian; his next two operas were French adaptations of earlier Italian works, so *Le Comte Ory* was the first composed to an original French text. It is also his second last opera; the following year, after composing *Guillaume Tell*, Rossini retired from operatic work, though he went on to write in other genres.

CHARACTERS

Adèle, Countess of Formoutiers (SOPRANO); *Alice*, a peasant girl (SOPRANO); *Ragonde*, companion to Countess Adèle (MEZZO-SOPRANO); *Isolier*, Ory's page (MEZZO-SOPRANO); *Comte Ory*, a young, libidinous

nobleman (TENOR); *A young Nobleman*, Ory's friend (TENOR); *The Tutor* (BARITONE); *Raimbaud*, Ory's henchman (BARITONE)
With *Ory's men, ladies, Crusaders, peasants*

ACT I

The Count of Formoutiers and his men are away on crusade, leaving his sister Adèle and the other ladies of the castle without protection. Count Ory, eager to woo Adèle, pretends to be a hermit and loiters outside the castle. With the help of his loyal friend Raimbaud, word gets out that the hermit can advise on matters of the heart. Ragonde reveals on behalf of Adèle that the lonely woman seeks the hermit's wisdom, but before he enters the castle Ory encounters his page, Isolier. Isolier himself has fallen in love with Adèle, and tells his master of his plan to gain access to the castle disguised as a pilgrim. Ory gives his consent, but once inside, the 'hermit' warns Adèle both against Isolier and Comte Ory, with whom she admits she is in love. Ory's tutor exposes him, and even though the return of the crusaders is imminent, Ory realizes that he has time to try another ploy.

ACT II

Adèle and the ladies celebrate their escape from Ory. A storm blows up and 'pilgrims' outside the castle—none other than Ory and his friends dressed as nuns—who claim to be fleeing from the dangerous Ory, are given refuge. The 'Mother Superior' (Ory) thanks Adele for her generosity. Raimbaud locates the wine cellar, and the 'nuns' indulge in revelry, reverting to their plaintive chant the moment Adèle appears. Isolier discloses the ploy to Adèle. Together they plan to ensnare Ory: in her darkened bedroom, Adèle hides near Isolier, and Ory, responding to Adèle's own voice, propositions the page instead. The scene is interrupted by the homecoming of the crusaders, leaving Ory just enough time to escape.

LES CONTES D'HOFFMANN
(The Tales of Hoffmann)
Jacques Offenbach (1819-1880)

FIVE ACTS. LIBRETTO BY JULES BARBIER, AFTER A PLAY BY BARBIER AND MICHEL CARRÉ, BASED ON STORIES BY E.T.A. HOFFMANN. PREMIERE IN PARIS, 10 FEBRUARY 1881.

Offenbach, whose music exemplified the spirit of Second Empire Paris, established his name through a string of frivolous *opéras bouffes*. With *Les contes d'Hoffmann* he made a bid for recognition as a serious composer, but died during rehearsals, leaving the work unfinished (hence the many different versions of the piece). *Hoffmann* is now recognized as Offenbach's masterpiece, since it combines his characteristically lyrical music with a rich, fascinating subject. Offenbach took as his source a play in the which the poet E.T.A. Hoffmann is depicted in his own stories. Hoffmann's decline is traced through a series of loves—from the mechanical doll Olympia to the courtesan Giulietta.

CHARACTERS

Olympia, a doll (SOPRANO); *Antonia*, Crespel's daughter (SOPRANO); *Giulietta*, a courtesan (SOPRANO); *Stella*, a prima donna (SOPRANO); *Nicklausse*, Hoffmann's friend (MEZZO-SOPRANO); *A Ghost*, Antonia's mother (MEZZO-SOPRANO); *Hoffmann*, a poet (TENOR); *Spalanzani*, a physician (TENOR); *Andrès*, Stella's servant (TENOR); *Frantz*, Crespel's servant (TENOR); *Cochenille*, Spalanzani's servant (TENOR); *Pittichin-accio*, Giulietta's servant (TENOR); *Nathanaël* and *Wolframm*, students (TENORS); *Lindorf*, a councillor (BARITONE); *Coppélius*, a scientist (BARITONE); *Dr Miracle* (BARITONE); *Dapertutto*, a sorcerer (BARITONE); *Luther*, an innkeeper (BARITONE); *Hermann*, and *Wilhelm*, students (BARITONES); *Crespel*, a violin maker (BASS or BARITONE); *Peter Schlemil*, Giulietta's lover (BASS or BARITONE); *The Muse* (SPOKEN)
With *students, waiters, party-goers, Venetians, servants*

ACT I Prologue
Luther's tavern, adjoining the opera house in Nuremberg
The scene for an evening of drinking is set when the poet Hoffmann's Muse laments his love for the prima donna Stella, wishing that he would devote all his energies to creative work instead; the Muse then takes on the identity of Hoffmann's friend Nicklausse. Lindorf, an influential town councillor and rival for Stella's hand, intercepts a letter from her to Hoffmann arranging an assignation. A noisy crowd enters with Hoffmann, and persuades him to sing his song about the dwarf Kleinzach. He is startled to see Lindorf, who, he relates to his friends, has thwarted previous love affairs. He begins to tell them about his three great loves.

ACT II Olympia
Spalanzani's laboratory
Hoffmann loves Olympia, who he thinks is Spalanzani's daughter, but who turns out to be Spalanzani's mechanical invention. Coppélius, her co-maker, arrives to demand his share in the profits which Spalanzani hopes the invention will bring, but to get rid of him before guests arrive Spalanzani tricks Coppélius of his money. At the party Hoffmann is danced off his feet by the phenomenal Olympia, and he sings of his love for her. But Coppélius reappears, angry at having been tricked out of his cut, and smashes the doll to pieces. Hoffmann realizes he has been fooled, and the guests mock him.

ACT III Antonia
Crespel's house in Munich
The musician Crespel has hidden his daughter Antonia away from her lover Hoffmann, who he believes in some way to be responsible for Antonia's serious illness. Hoffmann, together with Nicklausse, succeed in finding her, and the lovers are re-united. They sing together, but she tells him that she is forbidden to sing (singing is somehow connected to her sickness, as it was to her mother's early death); when Crespel returns, Hoffmann hides and soon overhears the evil Dr Miracle who has gained entry. Crespel holds the Doctor accountable for his wife's death, and drives him out. When

Antonia is alone, Dr Miracle returns and, taking his violin out, encouraging her to sing. Their duet becomes a trio when the Doctor raises the spirit of Antonia's mother, but before long the girl collapses. Crespel and Hoffmann find her dying.

ACT IV Giulietta
A palace on the Grand Canal in Venice

Hoffmann, at a party, hears a barcarolle as Nicklausse and the courtesan Giulietta arrive in a gondola. More interested in wine than women, Hoffmann sings a drinking song, but he is soon attracted to Giulietta. The sinister Dapertutto promises Giulietta a diamond if she will capture Hoffmann's soul (in the form of his reflection). Hoffmann is unable to resist Giulietta's advances, and she easily obtains the reflection. However, her lover Schlemil enters and a duel ensues, which Hoffmann wins. He takes the key to Giuletta's room from the dead Schlemil, but finds her departing in the arms of her servant Pittichinaccio. Once again he is mocked.

ACT V
Luther's tavern

Back in Nuremberg, Hoffmann is concluding his tale. As the opera house closes for the night, the prima donna Stella, fresh from her stage success, enters the tavern. Hoffmann, seeing in her his three lost loves, disdains her, and she leaves with Lindorf. Nicklausse is transformed back into Hoffmann's Muse, and comforts the now drunk poet with the thought that his work will have been enriched by his sad experiences.

THE CORONATION OF POPPAEA
see L'Incoronazione di Poppea

COSÌ FAN TUTTE (Thus do all women)
Wolfgang Amadeus Mozart (1756-1891)

Two acts. Libretto by Lorenzo Da Ponte. Premiere in Vienna, 26 January 1790.

Così fan tutte was the third of the operas Mozart wrote to a Da Ponte libretto, but unlike the other two, *Le nozze di Figaro* and *Don Giovanni*, it has not always enjoyed success. For almost 150 years it was regarded as immoral, and though that view no longer persists, audiences are still disturbed by its dark side. It leaves ambiguity as to what the characters have indeed learned in 'the school for lovers' of the subtitle, and enough disquiet to make the traditional happy-ever-after ending seem false.

CHARACTERS
Fiordiligi (SOPRANO); *Dorabella*, her sister (SOPRANO or MEZZO-SOPRANO); *Despina*, their maid (SOPRANO); *Ferrando*, an officer, Dorabella's lover (TENOR); *Guglielmo*, an officer, Fiordiligi's lover (BASS); *Don Alfonso*, an old philosopher (BASS)
With *soldiers, sailors, servants, wedding guests*

ACT I

SCENE 1 *A coffee-house*
The officers Ferrando and Guglielmo brag about the constancy of the sisters Dorabella and Fiordiligi, to whom they are engaged. But the cynical Don Alfonso is determined to prove that like all women, he says, given a chance they will be unfaithful. They enter into a bet.

SCENE 2 *A garden by the sea*
The sisters are extolling the virtues of their lovers when Alfonso—putting into action the first part of his plan—arrives to break news to them of the officers' departure for war. The men arrive to say their farewells, and Dorabella and Fiordiligi are overcome with emotion.

SCENE 3 *A room in the sisters' house*
Despina is preparing drinking chocolate for the ladies, who soon enter, still in despair. The down-to-earth maid offers them little sympathy: she believes the opposite of Alfonso—that men cannot be trusted to remain faithful—and advises them to find new lovers. The sisters protest indignantly. Alfonso comes to enlist Despina's help: without revealing the details, he tells her that he will be bringing two new admirers to visit, but when the two 'Albanian' strangers arrive (Ferrando and Guglielmo in disguise), even Despina fails to recognize them. Following Alfonso's orders, each man attempts to woo each other's lover, but, they are relieved to discover, in vain.

SCENE 4 *The garden*
Alfonso redoubles his attack on the sisters when the men, 'downcast' at their rejection, pretend to take poison. Alfonso and Despina go in search of a doctor, who soon appears (Despina in disguise). 'He' cures them by magnetizing out the 'poison', and though the sisters are relieved, they steadfastly refuse the men a kiss.

ACT II

SCENE 1 *A room in the sisters' house*
By now the women are receptive to a spot of flirtation, and need little prompting from Despina. Dorabella worries only that the visitors might set tongues wagging (but Despina is happy to let it be known that they are her admirers) and has already got her eyes on the dark-haired suitor (Guglielmo in disguise). Fiordiligi is content to pass a little time with the fair-haired one.

SCENE 2 *In the garden*
The shy couples are encouraged to join hands by Alfonso and Despina. The disguised Guglielmo conquers Dorabella's emotions easily, but although Fiordiligi is unfaltering in the face of Ferrando's wooing, once left alone she admits to herself that her resolve is softening. Guglielmo smugly receives news of Fiordiligi's constancy, but Ferrando is furious to hear of the ease with which Guglielmo overcame Dorabella.

SCENE 3 *A room in the sisters' house*
The sisters discuss the situation, and Fiordiligi, racked by her conscience, decides to escape the snare by joining her betrothed on the front. But before she can depart, Ferrando appears and she finally submits. Alfonso, whose wager is won, struggles to quieten the angry Guglielmo. To prove his point Alfonso wants the rearranged couples to go through a wedding ceremony, and he sends Despina off to find a notary.

SCENE 4 *A room prepared for a wedding*
Despina supervises the wedding preparations, and soon enters disguised as a notary. The sisters are signing their marriage contracts when they are interrupted by the sounds of their officers returning from war. The 'Albanians' flee in 'dismay', only to return half changed, still in their costumes but no longer disguised. They confront their astonished fiancées, who beg forgiveness. Alfonso confesses his plot, and the original lovers, now a little wiser, are reunited with each other.

THE CUNNING LITTLE VIXEN
Leoš Janáček (1854-1928)

THREE ACTS. LIBRETTO BY THE COMPOSER AFTER RUDOLF TĚSNOHLIDEK'S STORIES. PREMIERE IN BRNO, 6 NOVEMBER 1924.

Janáček composed *The Cunning Little Vixen* in his 70th year, and though there was operatic life left in him—he completed two more important scores—the *Vixen* has a valedictory feel about it. Its theme of death and renewal is illuminated by the natural, seasonal cycle which forms a background. Janáček's initial inspiration came from an unlikely source—a series of newspaper cartoons depicting the adventures of a vixen—but he responded with some of his most personal, glowing music.

CHARACTERS
Bystrouška, 'Little Sharp Ears', the Vixen (SOPRANO); *The Fox* (SOPRANO); *The Cock* (SOPRANO); *Chocholka*, the hen (SOPRANO); *Woodpecker* (SOPRANO); *Lapák*, the dog (MEZZO-SOPRANO); *The Owl* (CONTRALTO); *The Mosquito* (TENOR); *The Badger* (BASS); *The Innkeeper's Wife* (SOPRANO); *The Forester's Wife* (CONTRALTO); *Pásek*, the innkeeper (TENOR); *The Schoolmaster* (TENOR); *The Forester* (BARITONE); *The Parson* (BASS); *Harašta*, the poacher (BASS)
With *birds, flies, cricket, grasshopper, hens, squirrels, hedgehog, fox cubs*

ACT I
Summer; afternoon in the forest
The animals, playing in the forest, are disturbed by the Forester, who stops on his way home to have a sleep. Before long they are at play again. When the Frog, being pursued by the Vixen, lands on the Forester, the man captures the Vixen and takes her home.

Autumn; the farmyard
The Vixen is being kept as a pet. But she still has to endure the

advances of the Dog and the teasing of the Forester's children. She falls asleep when night comes, and dreams of her spirit being freed. Next morning she baits the hens, urging them to fight for their rights. Disgusted by their apathy, she pretends to kill herself. When the Cock comes to investigate, she catches him and then proceeds to kill off all the hens too. Afraid of being punished by the Forester's family, she escapes into the forest.

ACT II

The forest; late afternoon
The Vixen taunts the Badger until he leaves his home. She moves in.

Winter; the inn
The Forester, Schoolmaster, and Priest are playing cards. Each is teased about his foible: the lonely Schoolmaster about his hopeless love for Terynka, a young gypsy girl; the Priest about his sexual guilt; and the Forester for having let the Vixen escape.

Winter; the forest in the moonlight
As the Schoolmaster and Priest stumble home along different pathways, each catches sight of the Vixen: the first man mistakes her for Terynka, the second for a young girl he was wrongly accused of seducing in his youth. Both are startled when the Forester fires his gun after the Vixen.

Summer; the forest in the moonlight
The Vixen meets a Fox. Their love-making scandalizes the gossiping Owl and Jay, but soon their wedding is celebrated by all the forest creatures.

ACT III

Winter; the forest at midday
Harašta is passing through the woods when the Forester confronts him, suspecting that he has been poaching. But Harašta is only on his way to visit Terynka—who he tells the Forester he is soon to marry—and when he leaves the Forester lays a trap for the Vixen. She appears with the Fox and their large family of cubs, and they scoff at the rudimentary snare. When Harašta returns, the Vixen diverts him so that her cubs can raid his bag. Angrily, he shoots her.

The inn
The Schoolmaster is upset to hear news of Terynka's marriage. Both he and the Forester are sad that their old friend the Priest has moved away, and the Forester, now feeling his age, sets off through the forest on his way home.

Summer; afternoon in the forest
The Forester, lulled by the beauty of the warm forest, thinks back to his youth, even his wedding day, and soon falls asleep. He is surrounded by animals—descendents of the ones that irritated him at the beginning of the opera—and finds himself at peace with them.

DEATH IN VENICE
Benjamin Britten (1913-1976)

TWO ACTS. LIBRETTO BY MYFANWY PIPER, BASED ON THOMAS MANN'S NOVELLA *DER TOD IN VENEDIG*. PREMIERE AT SNAPE, SUFFOLK, 16 JUNE 1973.

Death in Venice was the last of Britten's dozen operas. Like nearly all the others its theme is that of the outsider—in this instance, the elderly writer Aschenbach who becomes increasingly alienated from society as his obsession with a young boy (to whom he never speaks) grows. It is an elusive work—like the original story, concerned with the inner thoughts of one man—offering one of Britten's most taxing roles and an unearthly, atmospheric score summing up the composer's late style.

CHARACTERS

Gustav von Aschenbach, a novelist (TENOR); *The Voice of Apollo* (COUNTER-TENOR); *The Traveller* (BARITONE); *The Elderly Fop* (BARITONE); *The Old Gondolier* (BARITONE); *The Hotel Manager* (BARITONE); *The Hotel Barber* (BARITONE); *The Leader of the Players* (BARITONE); *The Voice of Dionysus* (BARITONE); *The Polish Mother* (DANCER); *Tadzio*, her son (DANCER); *Jaschiu*, his friend (DANCER) With *youths*, *girls*, hotel *guests*, *waiters*, *gondoliers*, *vendors*, *beggars*, *people* of Venice, *choir* of St Mark's, *followers* of Dionysus, *strolling players*, *beach attendants*

ACT I
SCENE 1 *Munich*
Aschenbach, a famous writer, is frustrated by his failing inspiration. On a walk he meets a Traveller, whose tales of distant places inspire him to head south in search of rejuvenation.

SCENE 2 *On the boat to Venice*
On board, Aschenbach encounters high-spirited youths and an Elderly Fop, and begins to wonder if Venice will provide what he needs.

SCENE 3 *The journey to the Lido*
Aschenbach, now content to be in Venice, is rowed to the Lido by the Old Gondolier. He disappears before Aschenbach can pay him, and the writer begins to see the black gondola as a vision of death.

SCENE 4 *The hotel*
The Hotel Manager proudly shows Aschenbach to his room. Aschenbach watches as the guests assemble for dinner, and when the Polish family enters he is immediately struck by the beauty of the boy, Tadzio.

SCENE 5 *On the beach*
Aschenbach, ill at ease, watches the children playing on the beach and buys fruit from a strawberry-seller. When the Polish family appear, he once again admires Tadzio.

SCENE 6 *The foiled departure*
Stifling weather and large crowds make Venice unbearable, and Aschenbach resolves to catch the train back to Germany. But when he learns that his luggage has been sent to the wrong destination he decides to stay. A sense of relief at his foiled departure comes over him when he sees Tadzio playing on the beach.

SCENE 7 *The Games of Apollo*
In the boys' choreographed, Olympian-style sports, Tadzio wins each game. He passes Aschenbach and smiles at him. The old man cannot bring himself to speak to the boy, but admits to himself the love that he feels.

ACT II

SCENE 8 *The Hotel Barber's shop*
From the Barber, Aschenbach hears rumours of a disease forcing people to leave Venice.

SCENE 9 *The pursuit*
Aschenbach follows the Polish family into Venice, where he reads notices giving precautions against infection, and a newspaper report denying that the sickness is cholera.

SCENE 10 *The Strolling Players*
Aschenbach attends an entertainment at the hotel. He quizzes the troupe's leader about the possible epidemic, but his questions are evaded.

SCENE 11 *The travel bureau*
The travel clerk, inundated with people trying to leave the city, admits to Aschenbach that an epidemic is spreading and advises him to leave.

SCENE 12 *The Lady of the Pearls*
Aschenbach resolves to warn Tadzio's mother, the Lady of the Pearls, but again he is unable to speak.

SCENE 13 *The dream*
Asleep, Aschenbach hears an argument between Apollo and Dionysus, representing his own dilemma.

SCENE 14 *The empty beach*
Aschenbach observes Tadzio and a few friends playing on the now deserted beach.

SCENE 15 *The Hotel Barber's shop*
Tadzio's youth has made Aschenbach aware of his own age, and he goes to have his hair tinted.

SCENE 16 *The last visit to Venice*
Aschenbach, feeling young again, trails the Polish family through Venice. He buys strawberries, but finds them over-ripe. Quoting Socrates, he confronts his own turmoil.

SCENE 17 *The departure*
Guests are leaving the hotel. When Aschenbach realizes that the Polish family are to depart, he goes down to the beach for a last glimpse of Tadzio. Aschenbach succeeds in calling out to him, but when the boy responds to him, the old man collapses dead in his chair.

DIALOGUES DE CARMELITES
(Dialogues of the Carmelites)
Francis Poulenc (1899-1963)

THREE ACTS. LIBRETTO BY THE COMPOSER AFTER GEORGES BERNANOS'S PLAY, ITSELF DERIVED FROM GERTRUDE VON LE FORTE'S *DIE LETZTE AM SCAFOTT*. PREMIERE IN MILAN, 26 JANUARY 1957.

Poulenc's opera about a convent of nuns who go to the guillotine proclaiming their faith is an exploration of terror, both within individuals and imposed by the state. Based on historical events—the martyrdom of the Carmelite sisters of Compiègne in 1789—it is compelling theatre. Poulenc's score, which makes use of Renaissance religious music, is subtle and accessible, a far cry from the cynical musings of the enfant terrible 30 years earlier. As he put it, 'It seems that my Carmelites can only sing tonal music. You must forgive them.'

CHARACTERS
Blanche de la Force, the Marquis's daughter (SOPRANO); *Sister Constance of St Denis*, a young novice (SOPRANO); *Madame Lidoine*, the new Prioress (SOPRANO); *Mother Marie of the Incarnation*, assistant Prioress (MEZZO-SOPRANO); *Sister Mathilde* (MEZZO-SOPRANO); *Madame de Croissy*, the Prioress (CONTRALTO); *Mother Jean of the Child Jesus* (CONTRALTO); *Chevalier de la Force*, the Marquis's son (TENOR); *Father Confessor of the Convent* (TENOR); *Marquis de la Force* (BARITONE); *Thierry*, a footman (BARITONE); *M. Javelinot*, a physician (BARITONE)
With *nuns, municipal officials, police, guards, prisoners, townspeople*

ACT I
SCENE 1 *The library of the Marquis de la Force*
The Chevalier de la Force is concerned for the safety of his sister Blanche when he hears rumours of a mob on the rampage. It is late, and she is still out in the carriage. He tells his father, who fearfully recalls how his wife had died giving birth to Blanche after her carriage had been mobbed. Blanche arrives home, and though edgy, maintains her composure enough to announce her intention to enter a Carmelite convent.

SCENE 2 *The parlour of the Carmelite convent, Compiègne*
The aged Prioress interviews Blanche. She is convinced of the young girl's devotion, and Blanche is admitted to the convent.

SCENE 3 *Inside the convent*
Blanche meets Sister Constance, a lively country girl. The two

are completely different. Constance finds it easy to discuss death, and shocks Blanche with her premonition that they will both die young, together.

SCENE 4 *The Prioress's cell*
The old Prioress lies in great pain on her deathbed. Mother Marie, caring for her, tries to restrain the Prioress from blasphemy, but in agony the Prioress curses God. The Prioress feels a special responsibility for Blanche, and entrusts her to Mother Marie. Blanche comes to receive the old woman's blessing and leaves, only to reappear moments before her death.

ACT II
SCENE 1 *The chapel*
After the Prioress's funeral, Blanche stays to watch over the body. Overcome with fear, she runs off, but is met by Mother Marie who calms her. As Blanche and Constance take in flowers, the latter reflects on the Prioress's death.

SCENE 2 *The chapter house*
The new Prioress, Madame Lidoine (not Mother Marie as had been expected), preaches to the nuns.

SCENE 3 *The parlour*
The Chevalier, about to go abroad, has come to see his sister. He fears that she, as both a noblewoman and a nun, is in great danger, but Blanche, stoically, resolves to stay.

SCENE 4 *The sacristy*
The Father Confessor, about to go into hiding, leads the nuns in prayer. The Prioress has just warned the nuns against martyrdom, when commissars arrive to deliver an expulsion order. Blanche tries to carry a statue of the infant Jesus with her, but terrified by the noise of the mob, she drops it and it shatters.

ACT III
SCENE 1 *The ruined chapel*
In their desecrated convent, the nuns are addressed by Mother Marie. In the absence of the Prioress, she suggests that they take a vow of martyrdom, but when they vote there is one dissenter, Blanche. Constance, trying to cover up for her friend, says that the vote was her own, and that she has retracted it. But as Blanche goes up to take her vow, she runs off and escapes from the convent. The Prioress returns and is forced to accept that the vow, made before God, must stand.

SCENE 2 *The Marquis's library*
Blanche arrives at the house her father, who has been executed. She lives in fear, disguised as a servant, but is unwilling to return to the nuns even when Mother Marie tries to persuade her. Soon Blanche hears of the sisters' arrest.

SCENE 3 *The prison*
The Prioress is exhorting her nuns to remain courageous when

the Gaoler enters to announce their sentence of death. In an interlude, Mother Marie (who is still free) hears of their fate and resolves to join them, even though the Father Confessor tries to persuade her that it may not be God's will.

SCENE 4 *Place de la Révolution*
Singing the 'Salve Regina', the nuns file towards the guillotine. Blanche watches with the crowd, but finally steps forward and joins the nuns in death.

DIDO AND AENEAS
Henry Purcell (1659-1695)

THREE ACTS. LIBRETTO BY NAHUM TATE AFTER HIS PLAY *BRUTUS OF ALBA* AND VIRGIL'S *AENEID*. PREMIERE IN LONDON, 1689.

Although Purcell wrote a considerable amount of music for the theatre, *Dido and Aeneas* came early in his career and remained his only real opera. Indeed, it is one of the earliest surviving English operas, also remarkable for its brevity and simplicity. Though the opera moves swiftly to its tragic conclusion it never lacks depth, because the composer concentrates powerfully on the central personal drama.

CHARACTERS

Dido, Queen of Carthage (SOPRANO); *Belinda*, her lady-in-waiting (SOPRANO); *Sorceress* (MEZZO-SOPRANO); *Spirit* (CONTRALTO); *Sailor* (SOPRANO or TENOR); *Aeneas*, a Trojan prince (BARITONE)
With *courtiers*, *witches*, *sailors*, and *cupids*

ACT I
The palace
Dido, the widowed Queen of Carthage, has received the Trojan prince Aeneas at her court after his escape from the ruined Troy. He is on his way to Italy, destined to found Rome, but having been blown off course to Carthage he lingers, enjoying hospitality there. The downcast Queen is hesitant to admit her love for Aeneas, but urged on by her lady-in-waiting, Belinda, she gives in. The court delights in an impending royal marriage.

ACT II
SCENE 1 *The cave*
The Sorceress and her witches, plotting against Dido, plan to trick Aeneas into leaving the Queen.

SCENE 2 *The grove*
Dido and Aeneas celebrate their love with an entertainment by Belinda and another courtier. A thunderstorm, conjured up by the Sorceress, sends everyone rushing for shelter, but Aeneas is waylaid by a Spirit (posing as Mercury) who commands him to leave, reminding him of his responsibilities in Italy. In anguish, he wonders how best to appease Dido.

ACT III

SCENE 1 *The ships*

Aeneas's men are preparing to sail from Carthage, and the witches arrive to exult in the success of their plot.

SCENE 2 *The palace*

Dido and Aeneas bid a bitter farewell. Dido realizes that her death is now inevitable, and having sung her great lament, she dies. She is mourned by a chorus of cupids.

DON CARLOS
Giuseppe Verdi (1813-1901)

FIVE ACTS. LIBRETTO BY JOSEPH MÉRY AND CAMILE DU LOCLE, BASED ON SCHILLER'S DRAMATIC POEM *DON CARLOS, INFANT VON SPANIEN*. PREMIERE IN PARIS, 11 MARCH 1867.

Don Carlos (the third opera Verdi based on Schiller, after *I masnadieri* and *Luisa Miller*) contains some of the composer's most stirring music. In Schiller's dramatic poem, Verdi found rich opportunities for characterization and political events that stirred him, with conflicts between church and state, liberalism and despotism. The large-scale dramatic plan required one of his longest scores, and from the beginning its stage history was fraught with complications: Verdi wrote his five-act original for Paris, whose audiences expected lengthy spectacles, but subsequently he revised and shortened it several times, omitting the first act for the Italian premiere of 1884. Thus there is no 'definitive' edition, but thanks to recent scholarship, much of Verdi's music—even some cut before the Paris premiere—has been restored. Today, even when the opera is given in a shortened form, the first act is almost always performed, an arrangement which makes the best dramatic sense.

CHARACTERS

Elisabeth de Valois, later Philip's queen (SOPRANO); *Thibault*, Elisabeth's page (SOPRANO); *A Voice from Heaven*, (SOPRANO); *Princess Eboli*, Elisabeth's lady-in waiting (MEZZO-SOPRANO); *Don Carlos*, Philip's son, heir to the Spanish throne (TENOR); *Count Lerma*, (TENOR); *A Royal Herald* (TENOR); *Rodrigue*, Marquis of Posa (BARITONE); *Philip II*, King of Spain (BASS); *The Grand Inquisitor* (BASS); *A Monk*, (BASS)

With Flemish *deputies, Inquisitors, lords* and *ladies* of the French and Spanish courts, *woodcutters, populace, pages, guards* of Henry II and Philip II, *monks, officers* of the Inquisition, *soldiers*

ACT I

The forest at Fontainebleau

Elisabeth, daughter of the French King Henry II, has been attending a hunt with her page Thibault. Lost in the forest, she meets her betrothed, Don Carlos, the Infante of Spain but disguised as a Spanish envoy, who has come to catch a glimpse of his future bride. They discuss the politically significant marriage before Carlos reveals his identity. Elisabeth is overjoyed, but their happiness is short-lived: Thibault returns with the Spanish ambassador to announce that as part of the peace treaty between France and Spain, King Henry has offered her hand not to Carlos, but to his widowed father, King Philip of Spain. She assents in the knowledge that the peace and welfare of her own people depend on the marriage. The crowd rejoices, but both Elisabeth and Carlos are shattered.

ACT II

SCENE 1 *The cloister at the monastery of San Yuste*

Carlos seeks refuge in a monastery, which houses the tomb of his grandfather, Charles V. He is startled to meet a monk, whose voice he thinks he recognizes as that of his grandfather. Carlos's friend Rodrigue, the Marquis of Posa, appears, and tries to persuade the Infante to forget his passion for the woman who is now his step-mother. To take his mind off events, Rodrigue enlists Carlos's help on his crusade to free Protestant Flanders from oppression by Catholic Spain.

SCENE 2 *A pleasant spot outside the monastery gates*

Elisabeth's ladies-in-waiting anticipate her return, and to pass the time Princess Eboli entertains them with a Moorish song. When Elisabeth enters, Rodrigue arranges a meeting between her and Carlos. When the two are finally alone together, Elisabeth agrees to help Carlos in his attempt to become Governor of Flanders, but rejects his pleas of love, reminding Carlos of his duty to his father. Carlos leaves, and when Philip enters to find the Queen unattended, he angrily dismisses the Countess d'Aremberg, who had been responsible for attending her. Philip and Rodrigue meet, and the latter candidly begs the King to liberalize his rule in Flanders. Philip, impressed by Rodrigue's honesty, opens his heart to the very man who challenges the politics of Spain: he asks him to keep an eye on Elisabeth and Carlos, and also warns him to be wary of the Inquisition.

ACT III

SCENE 1 *The Queen's Gardens in Madrid*

Carlos has received a letter inviting him to an assignation, from Elisabeth, he believes. A veiled Eboli (author of the letter) appears, and the two embrace. Carlos is horrified to discover her true identity, and out of jealousy of his love for the Queen, Eboli threatens to bring about his downfall. Rodrigue enters, and tries to dissuade Eboli from seeking vengeance. But she departs determinedly, and Rodrigue asks Carlos to let him have any incriminating documents for safekeeping.

SCENE 2 *A square in front of Valladolid Cathedral*

A crowd gathers for an auto-da-fé, the execution of heretics at the stake. Processions have arrived, including those of Elisabeth and Philip, when Carlos boldly intervenes to demand the governorship of Flanders and rights for the people there. When Philip rejects him, Carlos rashly draws his sword, but he is disarmed by Rodrigue. As the auto-da-fé proceeds, a voice from heaven is heard welcoming the heretics.

ACT IV

SCENE 1 *The King's study in Madrid*

Philip, alone, laments the loss of his wife's love. The Grand Inquisitor, brought in to advise on the King's rebellious son, suggests that in fact Rodrigue is a greater threat. Suddenly Elisabeth rushes in, distraught at the theft of her jewel casket. She sees it on the King's table: when he forces it open and a portrait of Carlos falls out, he accuses her of adultery. She faints. Eboli and Rodrigue are called in; once the men have departed, Eboli confesses to the Queen that she stole it out of jealousy, and that she is the King's mistress. Elisabeth curses her, giving her the choice of either exile or a convent.

SCENE 2 *Carlos's prison*

Rodrigue, who has allowed himself to be implicated so that Carlos may go free, visits his friend to tell him of his impending release. As they talk, henchmen of the Inquisition creep in and shoot Rodrigue, who, as he dies, tells Carlos to meet Elisabeth the following day at San Yuste. Philip arrives to free his son, but their conversation is interrupted by a crowd demanding the Infante's release. In the confusion, Eboli helps Carlos to escape, and the crowd is restrained only on the intervention of the Grand Inquisitor.

ACT V

The cloister at the monastery of San Yuste

Elisabeth waits for Carlos. She bids him farewell, encouraging him on his Flanders mission. Philip arrives with the Grand Inquisitor, intending to hand his son over to the Inquisition. Suddenly, as he is about to be arrested, Carlos sees the tomb of his grandfather, Charles V, open: the monk he encountered in Act 2, now dressed in the robes of the Emperor, appears and drags Carlos to the safety of the monastery, away from his father and the Inquisition.

DON GIOVANNI
Wolfgang Amadeus Mozart (1756-1791)

TWO ACTS. LIBRETTO BY LORENZO DA PONTE. PREMIERE IN PRAGUE, 29 OCTOBER 1787.

Countless settings had been made of the popular Don Juan story before Da Ponte used it as the base for the second of his three librettos for Mozart. The legend was first made into a play by the Spanish poet-monk Tirso De Molina in 1630, and during the 18th century it became widely known: Gluck set it as a ballet, and several Italian composers turned it into operas. One, by Giuseppe Gazzaniga, was also written in the year Mozart's version was premiered. Mozart stressed the comic side by calling his *Don Giovanni* a *dramma giocoso*, but the full title (*I dissoluto punito, ossia Il Don Giovanni*) points to the serious moral of the 'dissolute man punished'. Both sides are captured in music which transcends its late-Classical period.

CHARACTERS

Donna Anna, the Commendatore's daughter (SOPRANO); *Donna Elvira*, a lady from Burgos (SOPRANO); *Zerlina*, a peasant girl (SOPRANO); *Don Ottavio*, Donna Anna's betrothed (TENOR); *Don Giovanni*, a young, licentious nobleman (BARITONE); *Leporello*, Don Giovanni's servant (BARITONE or BASS); *Masetto*, a peasant, betrothed to Zerlina (BASS); *Commendatore* (BASS)

ACT I

SCENE 1 *Courtyard of the Commendatore's house*
Leporello is waiting impatiently for his master, Don Giovanni, who has made his way into the Commendatore's house to seduce Donna Anna. Suddenly Don Giovanni emerges, with Donna Anna in angry pursuit; the commotion raises her father, the Commendatore, who challenges Don Giovanni and is killed in the ensuing fight. Giovanni and his servant escape. Anna and her betrothed, Don Ottavio, enter and find the body, and in distress she makes him swear to avenge her father's death.

SCENE 2 *A street at dawn*
Giovanni and Leporello encounter Donna Elvira, one of the former's previous mistresses. When she recognizes him, he slips away, leaving Leporello to deal with her reproaches. He recounts his master's sexual exploits, which so far number 2064. In anger, Elvira leaves swearing vengeance.

SCENE 3 *The countryside near Don Giovanni's house*
As Zerlina and Masetto celebrate their wedding, Giovanni appears and turns his attentions on the bride. He has Leporello divert Masetto's attention, and is about to seduce Zerlina when Elvira arrives and warns her about Giovanni. She takes Zerlina to safety, and returns to find Anna and Ottavio on the scene. Elvira then reveals Giovanni's identity, and in spite of his protestations, Anna recognizes him as her father's killer. Ottavio is not convinced, but realizes that his peace of mind rests on Anna's and so vows to find the truth. Leporello prepares a party.

SCENE 4 *Afternoon in Don Giovanni's garden*
Zerlina reassures Masetto of her love, but his suspicions are raised again when she acts nervously on Giovanni's entrance. To allay suspicion, Giovanni invites the couple into his party, but also admits three masked guests, Elvira, Anna, and Ottavio.

SCENE 5 *A ballroom in Don Giovanni's house*
Giovanni flirts with Zerlina, and after dancing with her slips her out of the ballroom. Soon her screams alert the company, and though Giovanni tries to blame Leporello, the maskers reveal themselves and confront the culprit. Don Giovanni is denounced, but he manages to escape.

ACT II

SCENE 1 *A street at night*
Leporello quarrels with Giovanni, threatening to leave his service because of his behaviour, but Giovanni bribes him to stay

on. Don Giovanni's next intended conquest is Elvira's maid, and to assist him in distracting Elvira, he forces Leporello to swap clothes. Pretending to be Giovanni making amorous advances to Elvira, Leporello lures her away so as to leave the real Giovanni free to pursue his prey. But 'Leporello' is interrupted by Masetto and friends, who, believing him to be the real Leporello, announce their plan to track down Giovanni. 'Leporello' plays along, but soon seizes the opportunity to beat up Masetto. Zerlina comforts him.

SCENE 2 *A courtyard of Donna Anna's house*
Trying to escape from Elvira, Leporello is confronted by Anna and Ottavio, Zerlina and Masetto. They think that they have cornered Giovanni at last, but Leporello reveals that he is in disguise. He escapes, and Ottavio repeats his intention to seek justice. Left alone, Elvira confesses that her feelings for Giovanni are torn between vengeance and love.

SCENE 3 *A graveyard at night*
Giovanni and Leporello have escaped to the graveyard. As they compare exploits, they are interrupted by the threatening voice of the Commendatore's statue. Giovanni makes the terrified Leporello invite the statue to dinner, and it accepts.

SCENE 4 *A room in Donna Anna's house*
Ottavio hopes to marry Anna soon, but she is too distressed to accept his offer yet.

SCENE 5 *A room in Don Giovanni's house*
Musicians play and Leporello serves Giovanni his supper. Elvira arrives, hoping to persuade Giovanni to repent. As she leaves, she shrieks in terror; Leporello goes to investigate and returns petrified, announcing to his master that the statue has arrived for dinner. Refusing food or drink, it commands him repent. Giovanni refuses and is dragged down to hell.

EPILOGUE
Elvira, Anna and Ottavio, Zerlina and Masetto arrive with police, and Leporello is only able to stammer an explanation. Normal life is resumed, and the six join in drawing the moral: evil-doers ultimately receive their just desserts.

DON PASQUALE
Gaetano Donizetti (1797-1848)

THREE ACTS. LIBRETTO BY GIOVANNI RUFFINI AND THE COMPOSER AFTER ANGELO ANELLI'S LIBRETTO FOR PAVESI'S *SER MARCANTONIO*. PREMIERE IN PARIS, 3 JANUARY 1843.

Don Pasquale is Donizetti's comic masterpiece. It stands as one of the finest 19th-century Italian comic operas, not only for its fresh melodiousness, but also for its characterization, which is warmly human rather than stereotyped. In every aspect it shows the composer's sure theatrical touch: it was the product of his experience, written late in his career when he already had more than 60 operas behind him.

CHARACTERS

Norina, a young widow, Ernesto's beloved (SOPRANO); *Ernesto*, Pasquale's nephew (TENOR); *Dr Malatesta*, Pasquale's physician (BARITONE); *Don Pasquale*, an elderly bachelor (BASS); *A Notary*, Malatesta's cousin Carlino (BASS)
With *servants*

ACT I

SCENE 1 *A room in Don Pasquale's house*
Old Don Pasquale has resolved to marry. He plans to father an heir and so disinherit his nephew Ernesto, with whom he is angry because of the latter's love for the merry young widow Norina. Pasquale's physician, Malatesta, assures him of his virility. But Malatesta is also a friend of Ernesto's and Norina's, and so plots to help them. He tells Pasquale that he should marry his sister, 'Sofronia', and plans to disguise Norina as the bride. Pasquale informs Ernesto of his impending marriage and kicks him out of the house.

SCENE 2 *A room in Norina's house*
Norina reads an old romantic story, which she finds quaint and silly. Malatesta arrives to recruit her in his plan against Pasquale, and coaches her in her role as the bride he has described: a beautiful young girl fresh from the convent.

ACT II

A living-room in Pasquale's house
Ernesto laments his fate and sadly prepares to leave for exile. The exiled Pasquale enters, and Malatesta brings 'Sofronia' to meet the old man: she disguises her amusement at the situation by feigning terror of him. Malatesta has also laid on a Notary (his cousin Carlino), who draws up a mock wedding contract. As the 'ceremony' is taking place Ernesto arrives and is forced to witness the contract; he is dismayed at Norina's apparent unfaithfulness, but Malatesta takes him aside and discloses the plot, which is about to unfold further. As soon as the contract is sealed, Norina begins to make Pasquale's life impossible: she demands a long list of extravagances, which drive the old man into a rage.

ACT III

SCENE 1 *A living-room in Pasquale's house*
'Sofronia' is living lavishly, and Pasquale's house is now full of servants handling her orders for jewels and dresses. As she prepares to leave for the theatre, Pasquale confronts her and she slaps him. He now realizes the folly of his ways, and she secretly feels sorry for his predicament. But as she departs, she drops a note that reveals her plan to meet Ernesto in the garden that night, and Pasquale calls for Malatesta's advice. The servants gossip about the strange goings-on. Pasquale tells his physician that he longs to be rid of 'Sofronia', and they plan to catch the lovers.

SCENE 2 *Don Pasquale's garden*

Norina and Ernesto, aware that they are being watched, meet in the garden. Pasquale and Malatesta confront 'Sofronia', and tell her that the following day Ernesto's bride Norina will run the house. 'Sofronia' protests that she would rather leave than live under the same roof, and so Pasquale immediately consents to the marriage of Ernesto and Norina. Malatesta then reveals 'Sofronia' to be none other than Norina herself, and although Pasquale is angry at being fooled, he is relieved to be free of trouble. He joins in the celebrations, and takes the point of the moral, that an old man who marries is asking for trouble.

DON QUICHOTTE
Jules Massenet (1842-1912)

FIVE ACTS. LIBRETTO BY HENRI CAIN, AFTER JACQUES LE LORRAIN'S PLAY *LE CHEVALIER DE LA LONGUE FIGURE*, ITSELF BASED ON MIGUEL CERVANTES'S *DON QUIXOTE*. PREMIERE IN MONTE-CARLO, 19 FEBRUARY 1910.

Cervantes's tale *Don Quixote* is the source of more than fifty operas. Most notably, it provided Massenet, who composed prolifically for the French operatic stage for almost half a century, with his last great success: the cast of the Monte-Carlo premiere included the great Russian bass Shalyapin, for whom Massenet wrote the title role. The colourful score is by turns boisterous and tender, and the characters so affectionately drawn that it is hard not to detect an autobiographical element in the portrait of an elderly man susceptible to female charm.

CHARACTERS

La Belle Dulcineé (MEZZO-SOPRANO); *Pedro* (SOPRANO); *Garcias*, Dulcinée's admirer (SOPRANO); *Rodriguez*, Dulcinée's admirer (TENOR); *Juan*, Dulcinée's admirer (TENOR); *Chef des Bandits* (BARITONE); *Sancho Panza* (BASS-BARITONE); *Don Quichotte* (BASS)

ACT I
A square outside Dulcinée's house

At a fiesta the tart Dulcinée receives the attentions of her four admirers. Soon the eccentric knight-errant Don Quichotte and his servant Sancho Panza enter, to be welcomed by most of the crowd but taunted by the admirers. Don Quichotte begins to serenade Dulcinée, but he is challenged to a duel by one of the jealous admirers, Juan. Dulcinée sends Juan away. Amused by Don Quichotte's flattery, she asks him to prove his devotion by recovering her necklace, stolen by the Bandit Chief.

ACT II
The countryside at dawn

Out on their expedition, Don Quichotte works on a new serenade and Sancho, disgruntled to be out searching for the Bandit Chief simply because of Don Quichotte's infatuation, complains about women. When the mists lift to reveal windmills, Don Quichotte mistakes them for giants and attacks them.

ACT III
In the mountains at sunset
Don Quichotte and his servant are following the bandits' trail. While they rest the bandits attack Don Quichotte; Sancho runs off. The bandits prepare to kill Don Quichotte, but are soon moved by the sight of him praying. Impressed by his apparent piety, they give him the necklace and beg for his blessing.

ACT IV
Dulcinée's garden
At her party, Dulcinée sings of her longing for the excitement of love. Don Quichotte and Sancho arrive triumphantly with the necklace, and the appreciative kiss the old knight receives from Dulcinée leads him to believe that marriage may be in the offing. But she rejects him, explaining that she believes in free love; though Don Quichotte is downcast, he is grateful for her honesty. Dulcinée leaves, and it is left to Sancho to shield his master from the taunts of the crowd.

ACT V
A mountain pass, at night
Don Quichotte, realizing that his life is at its end, is comforted by Sancho. As Don Quichotte dies, he imagines a planet in the starlit sky to be Dulcinée beckoning him.

DUKE BLUEBEARD'S CASTLE
Béla Bartók (1881-1945)

ONE ACT. LIBRETTO BY BÉLA BALÁZS AFTER A FAIRY-TALE BY CHARLES PERRAULT. PREMIERE IN BUDAPEST, 24 MAY 1918.

Duke Bluebeard's Castle is Bartók's only opera, and although it came early in his career it is both one of his major works and one of the most significant operas of the 20th century. All three of Bartók's stage works—the other two are ballets, *The Wooden Prince* and *The Miraculous Mandarin*—deal with the relationship between man and woman, and the opera sets the Bluebeard legend as a Symbolist allegory which can be understood on several levels, most basically as a parable of mankind's impenetrable solitude. Bartók provided music of graphic descriptive power to balance the static, internalized drama.

CHARACTERS
Judith, Bluebeard's wife (SOPRANO or MEZZO-SOPRANO); *Duke Bluebeard* (BARITONE); *Prologue* (SPOKEN); Bluebeard's three former *wives*

A hall in Bluebeard's castle
Before the curtain rises, the Prologue (spoken, sometimes omitted) establishes that the drama is taking place in the inner mind of each spectator. Bluebeard and his new bride Judith enter, and though she is struck by the gloominess of her new home, she resolves to bring light to it. Judith sees seven doors, and requests that they be unlocked. Reluctantly, Bluebeard gives her the key to the First Door, and it opens, blood-red light

pouring out, to reveal a Torture Chamber; its walls drip with blood, but Judith is not daunted. The Second Door reveals bronze-coloured light and Bluebeard's Armoury; Judith notices blood again, this time on the weapons. Bluebeard feels unburdened of his secrets, and gives her three more keys. The Third Door (golden light) and Fourth Door (blue-green light) give way to the Treasury and Garden, and in each case Judith sees blood again. He urges her on to the Fifth Door, which opens in a blaze of bright white light: it is Bluebeard's Kingdom. Now Judith is obsessed with discovering Bluebeard's secrets and the significance of the blood she has seen through every door. But Bluebeard is reluctant to let her through the two remaining doors. As the light fades and the gloom of the opening returns, Judith ignores his warnings and opens the Sixth Door, revealing the still, dark Lake of Tears. Bluebeard at first insists that the Seventh Door must remain shut, but Judith, morbidly fascinated, persuades him otherwise. As she questions him about his former wives, it dawns on her the blood and tears signify that he has murdered them. He gives her the final key, and three beautiful women step out. He explains that they represent the dawn, noon, and evening of his life. Judith, he says, is the most beautiful of them all, and she represents the night: after her is eternal darkness. She goes to take her place with the other wives behind the Seventh Door, and as it shuts blackness envelops the lonely Bluebeard.

ELEGY FOR YOUNG LOVERS
Hans Werner Henze (b. 1926)

THREE ACTS. LIBRETTO BY W.H. AUDEN AND CHESTER KALLMAN. PREMIERE IN SCHWETZINGEN, 20 MAY 1961.

The theme of an artist's relationship to society—common in 20th-century opera—rears its head again in Henze's fourth full-length opera: here it concerns the creation of a poem (the title of which gives us the title of the opera). Set in an Alpine retreat, the music sparkles with a clarity evocative of the landscape. The opera is structured in a sequence of 34 compact scenes divided into three acts.

CHARACTERS
Elizabeth Zimmer (SOPRANO); *Hilda Mack*, a widow (SOPRANO); *Carolina Gräfin von Kirchstetten*, Mittenhofer's secretary (CONTRALTO); *Toni Reischmann*, the physician's son (TENOR); *Gregor Mittenhofer*, a poet (BARITONE); *Dr Wilhelm Reischmann*, a physician (BASS); *Josef Mauer*, an Alpine guide (SPOKEN)
With *servants* at the Schwarze Adle (Black Eagle) inn

ACT I
Every year the poet Gregor Mittenhofer goes to an inn in the Austrian Alps to find inspiration for his poetry in the hallucinations of the widow Hilda Mack, who has lived there since her husband was killed climbing the Hammerhorn during their honeymoon forty years earlier. This year Mittenhofer's

entourage includes his patroness and secretary Carolina von Kirchstetten, his mistress Elizabeth Zimmer, and his physician Dr Reischmann. Before long Reischmann's son Toni joins them. They are interrupted when Josef Mauer, an Alpine guide, announces that he has discovered a frozen corpse which is likely to be Frau Mack's husband. Elizabeth is selected to break the news to Frau Mack, which she does tactfully. But Frau Mack's feelings erupt. The emotional turmoil increases when Toni realizes that he is falling in love with Elizabeth.

ACT II

When Carolina discovers that Toni and Elizabeth are lovers she alerts Mittenhofer. At first he tries to intervene in the affair, but soon he submits. Mittenhofer now has new protagonists and plans a new poem 'The Young Lovers'; but, he says, to complete it he needs an edelweiss from the slopes of the Hammerhorn, and asks the lovers to pick one. Once they leave, his suppressed anger comes out, and he wishes them dead.

ACT III

Frau Mack is now well enough to depart, but before she does so she bids farewell to the lovers as they ascend the mountain. Soon the sky darkens and a blizzard sweeps up, leaving Elizabeth and Toni exhausted. In a loving embrace, they reconcile themselves to death. The scene shifts: in Vienna a fashionable audience is assembled to hear Mittenhofer read his poem 'Elegy for Young Lovers', in which the voices of Frau Mack, Carolina, Elizabeth and Toni are heard.

ELEKTRA
Richard Strauss (1864-1949)

ONE ACT. LIBRETTO BY HUGO VON HOFMANSTHAL AFTER SOPHOCLES. PREMIERE IN DRESDEN, 25 JANUARY 1909.

With *Elektra*, Strauss began his long collaboration with the librettist Hugo von Hoffmansthal, which was to last until the writer's death. Hoffmansthal had adapted Sophocles's tragedy *Electra* as a play in 1903, and Strauss's encounter with it inspired him to write the opera. The drama of family vengeance drew from him his most brutal, atonal music: that he never wrote anything as 'advanced' again probably had less to do with a stylistic retreat than with the realization that with *Elektra*, and the earlier *Salome*, he had exhausted the possibilities of portraying obsessive heroines.

CHARACTERS

Elektra, daughter of Agamemnon and Klytemnestra (SOPRANO); *Chrysothemis*, Elektra's sister (SOPRANO); *Klytemnestra*, widow of Agamemnon (MEZZO-SOPRANO); *Aegisth*, Klytemnestra's paramour (TENOR); *Orest*, Agamemnon's son (BARITONE)
With Klytemnestra's *Confidante*, Klytemnestra's *Trainbearer*, *Overseer*, *Maidservants*, *Young Servant*, *Old Servant*, Orestes's *Tutor*

The courtyard of the palace at Mycenae

The wild Elektra is kept a virtual prisoner by her mother Klytemnestra and stepfather Aegisth. She is so unruly that many of the servants dislike her. When the curtain goes up they are discussing her; only one is devoted, and she is taken off and beaten for her loyalty.

Elektra enters, alone, and recalls the murder of her father, Agamemnon, by her mother and stepfather, vowing that together with her brother, Orest, she will avenge his death. Her younger sister Chrysothemis appears with news of further trouble for Elektra, and although she sympathizes with Elektra she is reluctant to join in the planned revenge; she is distracted by her longings for love.

Klytemnestra is racked by nightmares and summons Elektra for advice. She hopes that the sacrifice of a victim will placate the gods and so stop her torture, but when Elektra implies that the victim will be none other than Klytemnestra herself, she is horrorstruck. Her Confidante runs up and whispers new of Orest's death, and Klytemnestra's terror turns to glee.

When Chrysothemis brings Elektra news of their brother's death, Elektra tries again to enlist her younger sister's help in killing Klytemnestra. Unwilling, Chrysothemis rushes out, and Elektra resolves to do the deed herself. Elektra begins to dig in the courtyard for the axe which killed her father, but she is interrupted by the arrival of a stranger bearing news of Orest's death to Klytemnestra. When Elektra reveals her identity, the man confesses that Orest is not dead. Servants enter and kiss his hand: everyone has recognized him save his own sister.

Her anger gives way to tenderness as she realizes that the stranger is indeed Orest. Immediately he promises to avenge Agamemnon's death. Elektra rejoices, but Orest's Tutor reminds them that they must be quiet for the plot to succeed.

Out in the courtyard Elektra waits to hear the scream which will confirm that Orest has murdered their mother in the palace. Aegisth is puzzled by the commotion and Elektra, more amenable than ever, ushers him into the palace. He too is killed, and the ecstatic Elektra dances triumphantly. She collapses, dead, at the height of her frenzy, and Chrysothemis rushes to the door of the palace calling in vain for Orest.

L'ELISIR D'AMORE (The Elixir of Love)
Gaetano Donizetti (1797-1848)

TWO ACTS. LIBRETTO BY FELICE ROMANI AFTER EUGENE SCRIBE'S TEXT FOR AUBER'S *LE PHILTRE*. PREMIERE IN MILAN, 12 MAY 1832.

Though the Donizetti revival of recent decades has brought new interest in the composer's tragic operas, his best comedies, notably *L'elisir d'amore* and *Don Pasquale*, have always remained popular. *L'elisir* has never been out of the repertory, and with good reason: it is one of Donizetti's most consistent, sparkling scores, and the characterization runs deeper than in many comic operas of the period.

CHARACTERS

Adina, a wealthy landowner (SOPRANO); *Giannetta*, a peasant girl (SOPRANO); *Nemorino*, a peasant in love with Adina (TENOR); *Belcore*, a sergeant (BARITONE); *Dr Dulcamara*, a travelling quack (BASS)

ACT I

SCENE 1 *Outside Adina's farmhouse*

Adina is beautiful, young, and rich. She is loved by both the peasant Nemorino and the sergeant Belcore. Much to the shy Nemorino's despair, Adina seems to be more taken with his rival, so he decides to consult the quack Dulcamara.

SCENE 2 *The village square*

Dulcamara arrives, peddling his medicines. Nemorino uses his last coin to buy a potion which he believes will have effect within 24 hours, but which is nothing more than a fast-acting bottle of cheap Bordeaux. Adina is so disgusted by Nemorino's sudden show of confidence that she resolves to marry Belcore after all.

ACT II

SCENE 1 *Inside Adina's farmhouse*

The wedding guests are celebrating, but Adina insists on waiting for Nemorino to come and witness the contract. When he arrives he buys another elixir from Dulcamara, but he is without money to pay for it. Belcore, on the look-out for recruits, suggests that he enlists in the army to get the cash.

SCENE 2 *A courtyard*

Giannetta and her friends have heard that Nemorino's rich uncle has died, and Nemorino supposes that the attention they suddenly pay to him is due to the effect of the love potion. Adina, too, realizes that she loves Nemorino after all, and after Dulcamara tells her of Nemorino's hopeless love for her, she buys back his enlistment papers from Belcore. Nemorino, still in despair, plans to seek death in battle and so rejects the papers she offers him, but this prompts her finally to confess her love. Belcore graciously gives way to Nemorino, who swears that the potion has worked, and the surprised Dulcamara triumphantly proclaims the potency of his elixir.

L'ENFANT ET LES SORTILÉGES
(The Child and the Spells)
Maurice Ravel (1875-1937)

TWO SCENES. LIBRETTO BY SIDONIE-GABRIELLE COLETTE. PREMIERE IN MONTE-CARLO, 21 MARCH 1925.

Ravel—composer of only two operas, of which this is the second—was a lover of the cinema, a medium which might have been better suited to Colette's quirky libretto than to opera. Indeed, the Ravel-Colette collaboration on *L'enfant et les sortilèges* began as a ballet, but evolved into an opera. Staging it is notoriously difficult, with everyday objects taking on life, and animals singing; the mezzo-soprano taking the part of the child is required to impersonate a six- or seven-year-old. But the score is full of enchanting numbers, not least among them the love-duet in miaows for two cats.

CHARACTERS

The Child (MEZZO-SOPRANO); *His Mother* (CONTRALTO); *The Louis XV Chair* (SOPRANO); *The Fire/The Princess/The Nightingale* (SOPRANO); *The Bat* (SOPRANO); *The Owl* (SOPRANO); *A Shepherdess* (SOPRANO); *The Chinese Cup* (MEZZO-SOPRANO); *The Female Cat* (MEZZO-SOPRANO); *The Dragonfly* (MEZZO-SOPRANO); *The Squirrel* (MEZZO-SOPRANO); *A Shepherd* (CONTRALTO); *The Teapot* (TENOR); *The Little Old Man* (Arithmetic)/*The Frog* (TENOR); *The Grandfather Clock* (BARITONE); *The Tomcat* (BARITONE); *The Armchair* (BASS); *A Tree* (BASS) With *Settle, Sofa, Ottoman, Wicker Chair, Numbers, Frogs, Animals, Trees, Shepherds, Shepherdesses*

SCENE 1 *A room in the house*

The lazy Child, neglecting his homework, is scolded by his Mother. He goes into a rage, attacking every object in sight, setting upon the Cat, smashing the Teapot, and swinging on the pendulum of the Grandfather Clock until it breaks. But he is to be taught the consequences of his violence, as one by one the objects and animals speak out and torment him in return: the Armchair backs away as he is about to sit in it, and Numbers leap out of his torn arithmetic book to tease him with problems. Two cats miaow a love-duet before leaping out into the garden, where the Child follows them.

SCENE 2 *The garden*

The animals whose families the Child has harmed, and even the Trees whose bark he has cut, complain about him. They dance, after which the Squirrel reproaches the Child; he tries in vain to call for his Mother, and sensing his fear the animals torment him more. But when the Child bandages the Squirrel's wounded paw, the animals' animosity vanishes—the 'spell' is broken. They want to help him in return, and learn to call 'Maman!' on his behalf. Finally, the Mother answers his call, and the Child regains touch with the real world.

DIE ENTFÜHRUNG AUS DEM SERAIL
(The Abduction from the Seraglio)
Wolfgang Amadeus Mozart (1756-1791)

THREE ACTS. LIBRETTO BY GOTTLIEB STEPHANIE THE YOUNGER AFTER CHRISTOPH FRIEDRICH BRETZNER. PREMIERE IN VIENNA, 16 JULY 1782.

Hoping to counter the Italian and French domination of the Viennese operatic stage, in 1778 Emperor Franz Joseph founded a National-Singspiel company in his capital. The *Singspiel* form—musical comedy with spoken dialogue instead of recitative, performed in the German vernacular—was already popular in Germany, but it had little success with the musically more sophisticated Viennese. Mozart's *Entführung* was an isolated triumph there: its music is far richer than that of other works commissioned for the theatre, and it played on the then current vogue for Turkish settings—hence the orchestral effects of shrieking piccolo and jingling cymbals.

CHARACTERS

Konstanze, a Spanish lady, betrothed to Belmonte (SOPRANO); *Blonde*, Konstanze's English maid (SOPRANO); *Belmonte*, a Spanish nobleman (TENOR); *Pedrillo*, Belmonte's servant (TENOR); *Osmin*, overseer of the Pasha's house (BASS); *Selim*, the Pasha (SPOKEN)

ACT I

A plaza outside the Pasha's palace, near the sea

The Spanish nobleman Belmonte has arrived in Turkey at the Pasha Selim's palace, where, he has discovered, his betrothed Konstanze is being held. (She had been abducted by pirates, along with her maid Blonde and Pedrillo, the latter's lover, and all three sold as slaves to the Pasha Selim.) Osmin, the Pasha's aggressive overseer, rebuffs Belmonte's enquiries, but Belmonte still succeeds in finding Pedrillo, his former servant and now the Pasha's head-gardener. Pedrillo assures Belmonte that Konstanze is well and has remained faithful to him, in spite of the Pasha's attentions. The two men plot to abduct the women from the harem: Belmonte will gain access to the palace by posing as an architect. Their plotting is interrupted by the arrival on shore of the Pasha and Konstanze, greeted by a chorus of janissaries (Turkish soldiers). The Pasha renews his attempts to woo Konstanze, but she reveals that there is another claim on her heart. When she leaves, Pedrillo takes the opportunity to introduce the 'architect' Belmonte to the Pasha, who invites him to stay at the palace. Osmin remains suspicious and tries to bar them from entering the palace, but Belmonte and Pedrillo force their way past him.

ACT II

The palace garden

Blonde has been promised by the Pasha to Osmin, but she is unmoved and succeeds in outwitting him. Konstanze remains disconsolate, and when the Pasha threatens to torture her into submission, she replies defiantly. Pedrillo informs Blonde that they are to be rescued that evening, and with the help of wine sets about rendering Osmin harmless. Belmonte and Konstanze are reunited, and both couples meet to finalize their escape plans. Konstanze and Blonde reassure their men that in spite of the pressures of life in the Pasha's harem, they have remained faithful.

ACT III

SCENE 1 *The plaza*

Under the harem window Pedrillo sings a serenade as a signal to the women. Both are brought down ladders and the four are about to escape when Osmin is roused and apprehends them.

SCENE 2 *Inside the palace*

They are brought before the Pasha, who recognizes Belmonte

as the son of his sworn enemy, and threatens to take revenge. Belmonte and Konstanze reconcile themselves to death, but unexpectedly the Pasha decides to match Belmonte's father's cruelty with clemency and the four are freed. Osmin is enraged, but the others rejoice and join in praising the Pasha.

EUGENE ONEGIN
Pyotr Ilich Tchaikovsky (1840-1893)

THREE ACTS. LIBRETTO BY THE COMPOSER AND KONSTANTIN SHILOVSKY AFTER ALEXANDER PUSHKIN'S VERSE NOVEL. PREMIERE IN MOSCOW, 29 MARCH 1879.

Eugene Onegin is Tchaikovsky's best-loved opera, and its source—Pushkin's verse novel of the same name—is the most beloved work of Russian literature. It also carried autobiographical significance for the composer: at the centre of the story is an impassioned letter written by Tatyana to Onegin, and it was while composing the opera that Tchaikovsky received a letter in similar circumstances and was drawn into a disastrous marriage. Not surprisingly, the characterization of Tatyana is the greatest in all Tchaikovsky's operas. But the entire subject was ideally suited to his temperament, and he responded with what is perhaps the most deeply Russian work in his output.

CHARACTERS

Tatyana, elder daughter of Madame Larina (SOPRANO); *Madame Larina*, a widowed landowner (MEZZO-SOPRANO); *Filipyevna*, an old nurse (MEZZO-SOPRANO); *Olga*, Tatyana's younger sister (CONTRALTO); *Lensky*, a poet, betrothed to Olga (TENOR); *Monsieur Triquet*, a French tutor (TENOR); *Eugene Onegin*, Lensky's neighbour and friend (BARITONE); *Prince Gremin*, a retired army general (BASS); *Zaretsky*, a retired army officer (BASS); *An Army Captain* (BASS) With *peasants* and ball *guests*

ACT I
SCENE 1 *The garden of Madame Larina's estate*
On a late summer evening Madame Larina and the old nurse Filipyevna are making jam. Prompted by the song her daughters are singing inside the house, Larina recalls her youth and loveless marriage. Peasants return from harvesting in the fields and the girls come out to watch their dancing. The sisters, opposite in character, react in different ways: Olga wants to join in the celebrations, while Tatyana is lost in daydreams. Visitors are announced: Lensky, a young poet betrothed to Olga, has brought with him his new friend Onegin, a St Petersburg dandy who has just inherited the neighbouring country estate. The couples stroll in the garden: Lensky reaffirms his love for Olga, and Tatyana supposes Onegin to be the hero of her dreams. When they return, Filipyevna notices the impression the cold, sophisticated man has made on Tatyana.

SCENE 2 *Tatyana's bedroom*
Distracted and unready for sleep, Tatyana asks Filipyevna

about the old days. She confesses her love for Onegin. Left alone, she pours out her feelings in a letter to him, and is still awake when Filipyevna returns at dawn. She persuades the bewildered nurse to arrange delivery of the letter to Onegin.

SCENE 3 *The garden*

As the women pick fruit, Tatyana arrives agitated at the prospect of seeing Onegin. His reaction to the letter is cold and correct: though touched by her declaration he considers himself unsuited to marriage. He also urges her to greater self-control: other men could have responded unscrupulously.

ACT II

SCENE 1 *A brightly lit room in Madame Larina's house*

At a ball in honour of Tatyana's nameday, Onegin is annoyed to hear gossip linking his name to hers. He peevishly decides to take revenge on Lensky for bringing him to the party, and provokes him by dancing with Olga. Lensky's jealousy is aroused, but the proceedings are interrupted by a set of couplets the French tutor Triquet sings in Tatyana's honour. When the dancing resumes and Onegin once again pays attention to Olga, the two men begin to quarrel. Rashly, Lensky challenges his rival to a duel. Onegin realizes that his joke has gone too far, but there is nothing he can do to calm Lensky, and the ball ends in uproar.

SCENE 2 *Outside the mill, at dawn*

Lensky awaits Onegin and contemplates his love for Olga. When Onegin arrives, Zaretsky, Lensky's second, reminds the antagonists of the rules of duelling. Both realize that reconciliation is possible, but their stubbornness prevents it. Lensky is shot dead, and Onegin is horrified at what he has done.

ACT III

SCENE 1 *The ballroom of a noble house in St Petersburg*

Several years have passed during which Onegin, on distant travels, has tried to erase memories. No sooner has he returned than he finds himself drawn back into society. At a ball attended by Prince Gremin, Onegin is struck by the young Princess Gremina, and recognizes her as Tatyana. Gremin, a retired general, relates to his guests how his new marriage has transformed his life, and introduces Onegin to Tatyana. She is disturbed by their encounter, pleads fatigue, and leaves. Suddenly Onegin realizes that it is he who is consumed with love for her.

SCENE 2 *A room in Prince Gremin's house*

Tatyana, reading a letter from Onegin, is agitated by his reappearance. When he rushes in and declares his love, she reminds him of his earlier coldheartedness, and wonders if his new interest has anything to do with her improved social position. But Onegin's passion and evident self-reproach for his past conduct quell her doubts. She admits that she loves him, but resolves to remain true to her husband and insists that Onegin leaves. Onegin begs her to elope with him, but she rushes out, bidding him farewell for ever. Onegin is left alone, distraught, to curse his fate.

THE EXCURSIONS OF MR BROUČEK
Leoš Janáček (1854-1928)

TWO PARTS (FOUR ACTS). LIBRETTO (PART I) BY THE COMPOSER WITH FRANTIŠEK GELLNER, VIKTOR DYK, F.S. PROCHAZKA AND OTHERS AFTER SVATOPLUK ČECH'S NOVEL *THE TRUE EXCURSION OF MR BROUČEK TO THE MOON*; (PART II) BY F.S. PROCHAZKA AFTER SVATOPLUK ČECH'S NOVEL *THE EXCURSION OF MR BROUČEK TO THE FIFTEENTH CENTURY*. PREMIERE IN PRAGUE, 23 APRIL 1920.

The Excursions of Mr Brouček, Janáček's only comic opera, is based on a pair of novels by Svatopluk Čech, the first concerning an imaginary trip to the moon, the second an excursion back to the 15th century. The satire derives from the simple Mr Brouček's confrontation with two worlds beyond his comprehension. Part II is set during the Hussite wars, and was calculated to appeal to the feelings of nationalism which surged during the creation of a Czech state after the First World War.

CHARACTERS

PRAGUE 1888	THE MOON	PRAGUE 1420
Malínka	*Etherea*	*Kunka* (SOPRANO)
Waiter	*Prodigy*	*Student* (SOPRANO)
Mr Brouček (TENOR)		
Mazal	*Blankytný*	*Petrík* (TENOR)
		Apparition of the Poet (TENOR or BARITONE)
Sacristan	*Lunobor*	*Domsík* (BASS-BARITONE)
Würfl	*Čaroskvoucí*	*Alderman*

With *artists, dancers,* Etherea's *companions,* moon *artists, armed men,* *Hussite people,* Prague and Taborite *soldiers, priests, boys* and *girls*

PART I The Excursion of Mr Brouček to the Moon

ACT I
The Vikárka street, Prague, on a moonlit night
The lovers Málinka (daughter of the Sacristan) and Mazal are interrupted in the middle of a argument by Brouček, staggering home. Málinka threatens to marry Brouček to avenge the infidelities of Mazal, one of Brouček's tenants. More disturbances follow and, looking up to the moon, Brouček dreams of a calmer life there. Mysteriously, he is transported to the moon.

A moonscape
On the moon Brouček meets the lunar poet Blankytný (who bears a striking resemblance to the earthly Mazal) and his betrothed, Etherea (resembling Málinka). Almost immediately Etherea falls in love with Brouček, and in spite of the protests of Blankytn´y and his father Lunobor (the Sacristan on earth), the two elope.

ACT II
The Temple of All Arts
By now Brouček has found that the moon is a giant artistic colony. He and Etherea, pursued by Blankytný and Lunobor,

arrive in the temple of lunar arts and are welcomed by its patron Čaroskvoucí. Brouček is inducted into lunar customs, and at a banquet of flower scents discovers that his hosts survive by sniffing nectar. Brouček, alarmed by what he finds, unwittingly contravenes etiquette and is soon ostracized by the sensitive artists. He succeeds in escaping back to earth and is found, by Würfl, quite drunk in a beer barrel. At dawn Mazal and Málinka return home, reconciled.

PART II The Excursion of Mr Brouček to the Fifteenth Century

ACT I

The jewel-chamber of Wenceslas IV
Voices are heard from the inn: Brouček is arguing with his fellow drinkers about underground passages built in medieval times, which he believes exist under Prague. Making for home, Brouček loses his way, and falls down a hole into a jewel-chamber. He is confronted by the apparition of the author, Svatopluk Čech, who recalls the better days and the great victory of 1420, in which the Czechs successfully defended their Hussite faith.

The Prague Old Town Square
The town is unfamiliar to Brouček, for he is now in 15th-century Prague. He meets the Alderman who finds his 19th-century speech unintelligible and arrests him for being a spy. Brouček realizes that Prague is on the eve of a major battle and that he is in danger, and is only rescued by the intervention of Domšík (the Sacristan), who takes him to the safety of his house.

ACT II

A room in Domšík's house
Brouček is given hospitality in Domšík's house, and introduced to his daughter Kunka (Málinka) and friends. The company discuss the religious affairs of the day. Preparations for the coming battle are made, and Brouček is fitted out in medieval battle-dress. When the men go to battle, he seizes the first opportunity to escape, but is noticed and condemned a traitor.

The Old Town Square
Victory is being celebrated, although Domšík has died in battle. Brouček is sentenced to die in a beer barrel. The scene dissolves: back home, Brouček wakes up in a barrel, and begins to regale Würfl with his adventures.

FALSTAFF
Giuseppe Verdi (1813-1901)

THREE ACTS. LIBRETTO BY ARRIGO BOITO AFTER SHAKE-SPEARE'S *THE MERRY WIVES OF WINDSOR* AND *KING HENRY IV*. PREMIERE IN MILAN, 9 FEBRUARY 1893.

Falstaff, the last of Verdi's 28 operas, was only his second comic opera. Many people thought him too serious to compose a successful comedy (his first comic opera, *Un giorno di regno*, written half a century before *Falstaff*, had not been a success), but Verdi proved them wrong: *Falstaff* is often held to be his greatest work. Yet it is not his most popular. The quicksilver score is full of melodies, but they come and go teasingly and there are no conventional set-pieces. It is with a witty fugue 'Totto nel mondo è burla' ('All in the world's for laughter') that Verdi ended his operatic career in jest.

CHARACTERS

Alice Ford (SOPRANO); *Nannetta*, her daughter (SOPRANO); *Mistress Quickly* (MEZZO-SOPRANO); *Meg Page* (MEZZO-SOPRANO); *Fenton*, a young man (TENOR); *Dr Caius* (TENOR); *Bardolfo* (Bardolph), follower of Falstaff (TENOR); *Sir John Falstaff* (BARITONE); *Ford*, Alice's husband (BARITONE); *Pistola* (Pistol), follower of Falstaff (BASS)

With *Host* of the Garter Inn, Falstaff's *page*, Ford's *pageboy*, *burghers* and *commoners*, *servants*, masquerade of *elves*, *fairies*, *witches*

ACT I

PART 1 *Inside the Garter Inn*
Falstaff, putting the finishing touches to two letters, is disturbed by Dr Caius, who angrily berates him for having allowed his two henchmen, Bardolph and Pistol, to rob him. On dismissing Dr Caius, Falstaff reveals the purpose of the letters to his friends: they are declarations of love, to be sent to two wives of Windsor, Alice Ford and Meg Page. When Bardolph and Pistol refuse to deliver the letters, Falstaff hands them over to a page, and then rails against the men, lecturing them on the subject of honour.

PART 2 *The garden outside Ford's house*
Alice Ford and Meg Page compare the two identical letters they have received and resolve to punish Falstaff. Bardolph and Pistol arrive to warn Ford of Falstaff's designs on his wife. Ford is troubled both by this news and by the fact that his daughter Nannetta loves the young Fenton, of whom he disapproves; he favours Dr Caius as a prospective son-in-law. Ford makes up his mind to probe his wife's relationship with Falstaff by visiting the latter in disguise. The two women, meanwhile, have dispatched Mistress Quickly to the inn to invite Falstaff to an assignation with Alice Ford.

ACT II

PART 1 *The Garter Inn*
Mistress Quickly enters to tell Falstaff of the success of his letters: both wives love him. She invites him to visit Alice Ford that day while her husband is out. Falstaff is musing on his appeal to women when Ford arrives, announcing himself as 'Master Brook'. He pretends to be madly in love with Alice Ford, and when he asks Falstaff for advice on winning her, the old knight takes him into his confidence and tells him about his planned tryst. Falstaff exits to dress up for the meeting,

leaving Ford to erupt in a fit of jealousy. Falstaff reappears, and the two men leave for the Ford house together.

PART 2 *A room in Ford's house*
The women are preparing for Falstaff's visit. Soon he arrives, declaring his love. They are interrupted by the entrance of Meg Page, who—according to plan—paints a frightening picture of Ford's arrival in fury. Soon, however, her lie turns out to be true, when he enters with Bardolph, Pistol and Dr Caius and begins to search the house. Suspicious of the laundry basket, he turns it out, but finds no trace of the old knight. As soon as he begins to search other rooms, the women hide Falstaff in the basket. Ford snatches a screen away, only to discover Nannetta and Falstaff kissing behind it. Before Ford can return, the women empty the basket out of the window into the Thames, much to Falstaff's humiliation.

ACT III
PART 1 *Outside the Garter Inn*
A soaked Falstaff huddles in blanket over a jug of steaming wine. Mistress Quickly arrives with another letter from Alice Ford, this time inviting him to meet her at midnight deep in Windsor Park, dressed as the 'Black Hunter' and wearing a pair of antlers. While everybody plots to humiliate the old knight once and for all, Mistress Quickly overhears Ford promising Dr Caius his daughter's hand in marriage, and decides to help Nannetta escape that fate.

PART 2 *Windsor Forest*
Fenton, musing over his love for Nannetta, is soon joined by the other schemers. Falstaff appears at midnight, but before long his wooing is interrupted by the entrance of 'spirits'. While they tease Falstaff, Nannetta and Fenton slip away, and at the height of the torment Bardolph is unmasked. Other identities are revealed in turn, and Falstaff realizes that he has been fooled. But Ford is also a target of the women: his plan to marry Dr Caius and Nannetta goes astray when one of the couples he has blessed turns out to be Bardolph and Dr Caius; the other is Nannetta and Fenton, and Ford is resigned to the situation. Falstaff, now forgiven by everyone, leads the crowd in laughing at the folly of human ways.

LA FANCIULLA DEL WEST
(The Girl of the Golden West)
Giacomo Puccini (1858-1924)

THREE ACTS. LIBRETTO BY GUELFO CIVININI AND CARLO ZANGARINI AFTER DAVID BELASCO'S PLAY *THE GIRL OF THE GOLDEN WEST*. PREMIERE IN NEW YORK, 10 DECEMBER 1910.

La fanciulla del West, Puccini's seventh opera, was the first work to receive its world premiere at the Metropolitan Opera in New York. Appropriately, it is set in California during the gold rush, and the masculine ambience—unique among Puccini's operas—

is captured in the music: striking harmonies and vigorous rhythms help to evoke the Wild West. Perhaps the incongruity of an opera set in a mining camp and the fact that there is only one big set piece in the work have militated against it achieving the popularity of some of Puccini's other operas, but it is undoubtedly one of the composer's most innovative scores.

CHARACTERS

Minnie (SOPRANO); *Wowkle*, her servant (MEZZO-SOPRANO); *Dick Johnson* ('Ramerrez'), a bandit (TENOR); *Nick*, a bartender (TENOR); *Trin*, a miner (TENOR); *Harry*, a miner (TENOR); *Joe*, a miner (TENOR); *Pony Express Rider* (TENOR); *Jack Rance*, sheriff (BARITONE); *Sonora* (BARITONE); *Sid*, a miner (BARITONE); *Bello*, a miner (BARITONE); *Happy*, a miner (BARITONE); *Jake Wallace*, a minstrel (BARITONE); *Ashby*, a transport agent (BASS); *Larkens*, a miner (BASS); *Billy Jackrabbit*, a Red Indian (BASS); *José Castro*, one of Ramerrez's band (BASS)
With *men* of the camp

ACT I

The Polka saloon, at sunset
As evening falls, miners assemble in the bar to drink, gamble, and sing nostalgically of home. One of them, Larkens, is no longer able to bear his homesickness, and his comrades take a collection to enable him to leave. A fight breaks out over cards, but soon Ashby, an agent for the Wells Fargo Trading Company which is out to arrest the bandit Ramerrez, enters with news of the robber's whereabouts. Another quarrel follows, this time between Rance and Sonora over who will win Minnie's hand; she interrupts them and begins her daily Bible reading. The pony express arrives with further news of Ramerrez. Rance renews his attempts to woo Minnie. A stranger who calls himself Dick Johnson (in reality, the bandit of whom they have been talking) arrives: Minnie recognizes him from a past meeting, and their talk provokes Rance's jealousy. Castro, a member of the bandit gang, is captured; he promises to lead Rance to the gang's hide-out, but uses the opportunity to whisper to Johnson that, at the sound of a whistle, the gang will attack the saloon and steal some gold the miners have left for safe-keeping with Minnie. When the whistle is heard, though, Johnson ignores it: he is deep in conversation with Minnie. She invites him to visit her in her log-cabin.

ACT II

Minnie's cabin, later that evening
With Billy Jackrabbit and his squaw Wowkle in the house, Minnie gets ready for Johnson's visit. Johnson and Minnie discuss life in the camp, before finally declaring their love for each other. A raging blizzard prevents Johnson from leaving, so when Rance and other men arrive on the bandit's trail, he is forced to hide. Minnie is devastated to learn from them the truth of Johnson's identity, and in spite of the bandit's pleading, she sends him away. But as Johnson steps outside he is shot by Rance; Minnie takes pity on him and helps him to hide in the loft. Rance re-enters in search of the fugitive, whose hiding place

is revealed when blood drips through the ceiling. Desperate to save Johnson, Minnie challenges Rance to a game of cards: if he wins, both she and Johnson will be his, but if he loses, Johnson will go free. She wins by cheating, and Rance is forced to go.

ACT III
A forest clearing

Rance and friends are sitting round a fire discussing Minnie's love for Johnson when they hear the noise of the bandit's capture. As arrangements to hang him are made Johnson pleads with his captors to keep his death a secret from Minnie. But she arrives to find him already on the gallows and her appeals for clemency are ignored until she brandishes a pistol. The miners relent and Johnson is freed. The couple set off in search of a new life.

FAUST
Charles Gounod (1818-1893)

FIVE ACTS. LIBRETTO BY JULES BARBIER AND MICHEL CARRÉ AFTER CARRÉ'S *FAUST ET MARGUERITE* AND GOETHE'S *FAUST*. PREMIERE IN PARIS, 19 MARCH 1859.

The two most popular French operas of the latter part of the 19th century, *Faust* and *Carmen*, both originated as *opéra comiques* with spoken dialogue, and both were later re-worked with sung recitatives. *Carmen* has now had its dialogue restored, but *Faust* is still usually given as the quasi-grand opera reworked by Gounod for the Paris Opéra in 1869, and it sometimes includes the Walpurgisnacht ballet added in Act V on that occasion. With changing fashions, *Faust* is no longer the most-performed opera it once was, but its memorable tunes (such as Marguerite's 'Anges purs' and 'Jewel Song', and the 'Soldiers' Chorus') ensure that it maintains a hold on the repertory.

CHARACTERS

Marguerite (SOPRANO); *Siébel* , student of Faust (SOPRANO); *Marthe*, Marguerite's guardian (SOPRANO); *Faust*, a philosopher (TENOR); *Valentin*, a soldier, Marguerite's brother (BARITONE); *Wagner*, friend of Valentin (BARITONE); *Méphistophélès* (BASS)

ACT I
Faust's study

The disillusioned old Faust has resolved to poison himself but is distracted by the bustle of young people outside. Longing for youth, he curses God and calls on the devil, who appears in the form of Méphistophélès. Encouraged by a vision of the beautiful Marguerite, Faust agrees to a pact: on earth Méphistophélès will serve him; in the underworld the roles will be reversed. Faust is transformed into a gallant young man.

ACT II
The village square

Valentin, Marguerite's brother, arrives at a fair and begs her lover Siébel to protect her while he is away at war. He also bids his friend Wagner farewell. Méphistophélès appears, and sings a cynical song before telling the fortunes of the young people: Wagner will be killed in battle, Siébel will cause any flowers he picks to wither, and Valentin will die at the hands of somebody he knows. Rejecting the wine offered to him, Méphistophélès magically conjures up a better vintage and proposes a toast to Marguerite, which angers Valentin. Realising who the stranger is, the students cross themselves and try to drive the devil out. Soon he reappears with Faust, who catches sight of Marguerite.

ACT III
Marguerite's garden

Siébel collects flowers for Marguerite. As foretold, they wither but are restored by holy water. Faust sings of his love for Marguerite, but it is Méphistophélès's scheme that works: he proposes leaving a jewel-casket outside Marguerite's door and she is enraptured by its contents. Méphistophélès distracts her friend Marthe so that Faust and Marguerite can be alone. They declare their love for each other, and though she is at first overcome with shame, under the influence of Méphistophélès she is soon filled with desire.

ACT IV
SCENE 1 *Marguerite's room*

Seduced and abandoned, Marguerite has give birth to Faust's child. Siébel tries to comfort her, but she still longs for Faust's return.

SCENE 2 *A public square*

Soldiers return, and Valentin goes into the house. Outside, Méphistophélès serenades Marguerite on behalf of Faust: enraged, Valentin rushes out to defend Marguerite's honour, but is fatally wounded in a duel with Faust. Marguerite hears her dying brother curse her.

SCENE 3 *A cathedral*

The distraught Marguerite goes to pray, but is mocked by Méphistophélès. She collapses in terror.

ACT V
SCENE 1 *The Harz Mountains*

Faust and Méphistophélès watch the witches celebrating Walpurgisnacht.

SCENE 2 *A cavern peopled with courtesans of antiquity*

Faust is distracted by Méphistophélès's offer of all the famous courtesans of history, but when he sees a vision of Marguerite he demands to be taken back to her.

SCENE 3 *A prison*

Marguerite, having killed her child and been imprisoned for infanticide, is awaiting execution. Faust obtains the keys to her cell and, though they recall past bliss, he is unable to persuade her to flee with him. Instead, she prays for forgiveness: her soul ascends to heaven, while Méphistophélès claims his price from Faust and drags him away.

FIDELIO
Ludwig van Beethoven (1770-1827)

TWO ACTS. LIBRETTO BY JOSEPH SONNLEITHNER AND GEORG FRIEDRICH TREITSCHKE AFTER JEAN NICOLAS BOUILLY'S LIBRETTO *LÉONORE OU L'AMOUR CONJUGAL*. PREMIERE IN VIENNA, 20 NOVEMBER 1805, AND IN ITS FINAL VERSION IN VIENNA, 23 MAY 1814.

Beethoven wrote a considerable amount of music for the stage, but *Fidelio* remained his only complete opera. It took ten years and three versions to reach its final form, because although Beethoven was moving with relative confidence in his orchestral work during this period (with the composition of such works as the 'Eroica' Symphony and the Violin Concerto), he was less at home in the operatic medium. Moreover, he was often overcome by the power of the politically sensitive subject. But he matched the high moral tone of the libretto with music of great nobility, as powerful as anything he wrote. Famously, there are four overtures connected with the opera: the one now played is identified as 'Fidelio'. Of the other three 'Leonore' overtures, the third is still sometimes inserted before the final scene, although this late-19th century practice is now discredited.

CHARACTERS

Leonore, Florestan's wife, and assistant to Rocco under the name of Fidelio (SOPRANO); *Marzelline*, Rocco's daughter (SOPRANO); *Florestan*, a prisoner (TENOR); *Jacquino*, Rocco's assistant, *Don Pizarro*, governor of a state prison (BASS-BARITONE); *Rocco*, a gaoler (BASS); *Don Fernando*, a minister and Spanish nobleman (BASS) With *soldiers, prisoners, townspeople*

ACT I
SCENE 1 *The prison courtyard*
The porter Jacquino attempts to court Marzelline, daughter of the gaoler Rocco. She in turn has fallen in love with the new helper, Fidelio, and when Jacquino is called away, she dreams of married life with Fidelio. Fidelio enters with provisions, and earns Rocco's confidence for his trustworthiness; the jealous Jacquino finds the situation unbearable. But Fidelio is really the disguised Leonore, whose husband Florestan is a political prisoner languishing in an unknown dungeon: she tests Rocco's trust by begging him to take her on his rounds of the gaol. Though Don Pizarro, the cruel governor, has forbidden others to enter the lowest levels, Rocco promises to request permission.

SCENE 2 *The courtyard*
Pizarro arrives with his soldiers. He learns from despatches that the benign minister Don Fernando is on his way to the prison to investigate rumours of maltreatment. He resolves to have

Florestan murdered, and posts a soldier to watch for Fernando's approach. When Rocco refuses to carry out the killing, Pizarro orders him to dig a grave in Florestan's cell. Fidelio is appalled to overhear this. She begs Rocco to allow the prisoners into the fresh air of the courtyard—but Florestan is not among them. Don Pizarro is furious to discover the prisoners out and sends them back, renewing his order to dig the grave.

ACT II
Scene 1 *A deep dungeon*
Florestan, weighed down by his chains, laments his fate. He sees a vision of Leonore, but then falls unconscious. Rocco and Leonore enter on their gruesome mission. Although Leonore is unable to see the prisoner's features, she resolves to help him whoever he is. As they finish digging the grave, Florestan wakes and implores Rocco to send a letter to his wife. Leonore is overcome, but recovers her composure to offer him a piece of bread. Don Pizarro enters to carry out the murder. But Leonore has hidden in the shadows, and as Pizarro is about to stab Florestan, she intervenes, keeping the tyrant at bay with a pistol. At that moment Don Fernando arrives at the prison, and Pizzaro goes out to meet him. Left alone, the ecstatic couple are reunited.

Scene 2 *The parade grounds of the prison*
Don Fernando addresses the people, telling them he has come to release them from oppression. Florestan appears, and the minister is amazed to find his friend, whom he had assumed dead. The story of Leonore's heroism is related to Fernando, and once Don Pizarro has been arrested, Fernando invites her to remove Florestan's chains herself. Florestan and the released prisoners hail Leonore as the noblest of women.

THE FIERY ANGEL
Sergey Prokofiev (1891-1953)

FIVE ACTS. LIBRETTO THE COMPOSER AFTER VALERY BRYUSSOV'S NOVEL. PREMIERE IN VENICE, 1955.

Though *The Fiery Angel* has had a sketchy performance history—it was premiered posthumously, and subsequent productions have been rare—it is one of Prokofiev's most important stage works. He composed the opera in the 1920s during his self-imposed Western exile, but decided against taking it with him when he returned to Russia in 1937: although the ostensible setting is Reformation Germany, its subject matter of demonic possession and religio-sexual hysteria would have been unacceptable in Stalin's Russia. Even before his return Prokofiev had experienced difficulties in getting the opera staged, and, loathe to see a fine score go to waste, had transferred some sections into his Third Symphony.

CHARACTERS
Renata (SOPRANO); *Mother Superior* (MEZZO-SOPRANO); *Fortune-Teller* (MEZZO-SOPRANO); *Hostess* of the Inn (CONTRALTO); *Mephistopheles*

(TENOR); *Jacob Glock* (TENOR); *Agrippa von Nettesheim*, a philosopher (TENOR); *Doctor* (TENOR); *Ruprecht*, a knight (BARITONE); *Mathias* (BARITONE); *Porter* at the Inn (BARITONE); *Inkeeper* at Cologne (BARITONE); *Faust* (BARITONE); *Inquisitor* (BASS); *Count Heinrich* (MUTE) With two young *Nuns*, three *Neighbours*

ACT I

The attic of an inn

Ruprecht, a wandering knight recently returned from the Americas, is shown to a dirty attic room of an inn by the Hostess. His sleep is disturbed by noises in the next room. He investigates, and finds the young woman Renata, who believes that she is possessed by demons. She relates her story: since childhood she been haunted by an angel, Madiel, who protected her until her craving for physical union drove him away, promising to come back as a man. Later she lived with a Count Heinrich, believing him to be Madiel reincarnated. But he had disappeared after a year, and since then she has been wandering, looking for him. The sound of their conversation rouses the Hostess and Porter, who accuse Renata of being a whore. But Ruprecht has fallen in love with her, and agrees to follow her to Cologne in search of Madiel. In spite of the intervention of a Fortune-Teller, Ruprecht carries Renata off.

ACT II

SCENE 1 *A room full of books, in Cologne*

Ruprecht and Renata have resorted to magic to assist them in their search. The bookseller Jacob Glock supplies them with forbidden books, but when Renata begins to cast spells she hears only the familiar knockings that have been tormenting her. Glock suggests that they consult the renowned sorcerer, Agrippa von Nettesheim.

SCENE 2 *Agrippa's studio*

Ruprecht has gone, alone, to seek Agrippa's advice. But the sorcerer refuses to assist in minor dabbling. The intervention of skeletons prove that Agrippa is indeed a practitioner of the most sinister arts.

ACT III

SCENE 1 *The street outside Count Heinrich's house*

Renata has located Heinrich's house, but he dismisses her. Spurned, she appeals to Ruprecht to kill Heinrich, but when Heinrich appears surrounded by light, she imagines that he is her Fiery Angel and begs Ruprecht not to attack him. But it is too late: they duel.

SCENE 2 *On the banks of the Rhine*

Ruprecht lies wounded. Full of regret, Renata declares her love for him.

ACT IV

A square outside a tavern in Cologne

Renata has nursed Ruprecht back to health, but refuses his

pleas for marriage. She resolves to enter a convent, but before running off stabs herself and accuses Ruprecht of being an agent of the devil. Mention of the devil summons up Faust and Mephistopheles, who come to the tavern to eat and drink. When the food does not arrive, Mephistopheles eats the serving boy, and proves his magic powers by disgorging him into a rubbish bin. Faust and Mephistopheles invite the dejected Ruprecht to join them on a tour of Cologne the next day.

ACT V

A convent

Renata has entered the convent and perverted the other nuns with her hallucinations. The Mother Superior resolves to bring in an Inquisitor, but his attempts at exorcism fail. Ruprecht, Mephistopheles and Faust appear unnoticed, and watch as Renata and the others pray to Satan and attack the Inquisitor. He is saved, and condemns Renata to be burnt at the stake.

DIE FLEDERMAUS (The Bat)

Johann Strauss II (1825-1899)

THREE ACTS. LIBRETTO BY CARL HAFFNER AND RICHARD GENÉE, AFTER HENRI MEILHAC AND LUDOVIC HALÉVY'S *LE RÉVEILLON* . PREMIERE IN VIENNA, 5 APRIL 1874.

Die Fledermaus is not only the work most central to the operetta repertory, it is the only work of its genre to have an undisputed place in the great opera houses of the world. It is also the only operetta by the great waltz king of Vienna to be set in that city—even though the original play was French, and by the same writers who supplied Strauss's French counterpart, Offenbach, with his best librettos. Strauss matches the high spirits of the story with a score of sparkle and wit, nostalgia but not sentimentality, underpinned with delicious waltzes.

CHARACTERS

Rosalinde, Eisenstein's wife (SOPRANO); *Adele*, her maid (SOPRANO); *Ida*, Adele's sister (SOPRANO); *Prince Orlovsky* (MEZZO-SOPRANO); *Gabriel von Eisenstein* (TENOR); *Alfred*, Rosalinde's lover, a singer (TENOR); *Dr Blind*, a lawyer (TENOR); *Frank*, a prison governor (BARITONE); *Dr Falke*, a notary (BARITONE); *Frosch*, a gaoler (SPOKEN)
With *guests* and *servants*

ACT I

A room in Eisenstein's house

Eisenstein's wife Rosalinde is being wooed by her lover Alfred, who promises to return that evening. The coast will be clear, because Eisenstein is due to begin a prison sentence for a petty offence. Rosalinde refuses her maid, Adele, the night off, although Adele admits to the audience that she intends to get to the ball at Prince Orlovsky's. Dr Falke arrives, ostensibly to take Eisenstein off to prison, but he has another plan: three years earlier, Eisenstein had made Falke walk home from a party the morning after, still disguised as a bat in fancy-dress, and Falke is plotting his revenge. He persuades Eisenstein to delay starting his prison sentence until the next morning, and takes him to Orlovsky's ball. Alfred arrives back, and has just begun dinner with Rosalinde when the prison governor Frank enters to collect Eisenstein to start his sentence. Assuming Alfred to be Rosalinde's husband, he takes him off to prison. Rosalinde and Alfred are both eager to protect her reputation, so they comply.

ACT II
Prince Orlovsky's villa

The ball is in full swing. Falke explains his charade, 'The bat's revenge', to the prince, and when Eisenstein enters he falls into the trap. First he flirts with the disguised Adele, watched by his wife who has come as an Hungarian countess. Soon he turns his attentions on the countess—unaware that she is his own wife—and shows off his repeater watch, which she succeeds in pocketing. The party continues: Rosalinde proves her Hungarian credentials by singing a fiery csárdás, and Eisenstein regales the guests with the story of how he humiliated Falke by making him walk home dressed as a bat. As more drink flows, spirits are raised, but at dawn Eisenstein hurries off to prison, in fulfilment of his promise.

ACT III
The prison governor's office

The gaoler Frosch is trying to stop Alfred singing in his cell. Adele and Ida come looking for the 'Chevalier Chagrin' (in reality Frank) who they had met the previous evening: Adele hopes that he will be able to launch her career as an actress. Eisenstein arrives to give himself up, and is amazed to find himself being impersonated by Alfred. His suspicions aroused, he swaps clothes with his lawyer, Dr Blind, in order to interrogate both Alfred and Rosalinde, who has come to obtain Alfred's release. Both confess that they were together the previous evening, but when the furious Eisenstein reveals his identity, Rosalinde counters by producing the tell-tale watch. The other revellers arrive at the prison to hear Falke disclose his plot. All are reconciled, and agree that champagne was at fault.

DER FLIEGENDE HOLLÄNDER
(The Flying Dutchman)
Richard Wagner (1813-1883)

THREE ACTS. LIBRETTO BY THE COMPOSER. PREMIERE IN DRESDEN, 2 JANUARY 1843.

It is in *Der fliegende Holländer*, Wagner's fourth complete opera, that the composer's authentic voice is heard for the first time. Its theme of redemption through love, already a preoccupation of Wagner, was one which he was to develop further. The story of a sea captain condemned to sail the seas forever for his rash defiance of the devil had been gestating during the period that Wagner lived in Riga, but it was a rough sea voyage from there to London that provided the impetus: stormy music and shanty rhythms give the score its character.

CHARACTERS

Senta, Daland's daughter (SOPRANO); *Mary*, her nurse (CONTALTO); *Erik*, a huntsman (TENOR); Daland's *Steersman* (TENOR); *The Dutchman* (BASS-BARITONE); *Daland*, a Norwegian sailor (BASS)
With Norwegian *sailors*, the Dutchman's *crew*, young *women*

ACT I

A rocky shore
A violent storm blows Daland, a Norwegian sea captain, off course, where he encounters a ghostly ship. It is that of the Flying Dutchman who, having sworn an oath to travel round a stormy Cape of Good Hope, has been condemned by the devil to sail the seas eternally—unless, in coming on land once in every seven years, he should find a women whose faithful love redeems him. Daland is so taken by the treasures that the stranger offers that he fails to notice anything peculiar about him, and offers him hospitality.

ACT II

A room in Daland's house
Significantly, a portrait of the legendary Flying Dutchman has always hung in Daland's house, and his daughter, Senta, is fascinated by it. As she, her nurse Mary, and other women sit spinning, she admits her love for the man in the painting. The woman tease her for her belief that she can bring him salvation. Senta's admirer, the huntsman Erik, is concerned by her state of mind, and reminds her of their youthful attachment. But when Daland brings the Dutchman in, Senta is enraptured: she recognizes her destiny and the Dutchman wonders if Senta is to be his redeeming angel.

ACT III

A bay, with rocky shore
The Norwegian sailors are celebrating. They taunt the silent crew of the Dutchman's ship, and when the latter come to ghostly life the Norwegians flee in panic. Erik pleads with Senta not to desert him. When the Dutchman overhears this he becomes convinced that Senta is fickle and loses all hope of her being his redeemer. He rushes aboard his ship and reveals his identity to the horrified villagers. As he sails, Senta casts herself into the sea, thus breaking the spell. The spectral ship vanishes, and the Dutchman, redeemed at last, is seen ascending heavenwards with Senta.

THE FLYING DUTCHMAN
see **Der fliegende Holländer**

THE FORCE OF DESTINY
see **La forza del destino**

LA FORZA DEL DESTINO (The Force of Destiny)
Giuseppe Verdi (1813-1901)

FOUR ACTS. LIBRETTO BY FRANCESCO MARIA PIAVE AFTER THE PLAY *DON ALVARO, O LA FUERZA DEL SINO* BY ANGEL DE SAAVEDRA, DUKE OF RIVAS, AND A SCENE FROM *WALLENSTEINS LAGER* BY FRIEDRICH VON SCHILLER. PREMIERE IN ST PETERSBURG, 10 NOVEMBER 1862.

La forza del destino—which comes between *Un ballo in maschera* (1859) and *Don Carlos* (1867) in the Verdi canon—is the only one of the composer's 28 operas with an abstract idea for a title: it reflects the way in which the 'force of destiny' pursues the opera's protagonists. The characters' many conflicting, doomed allegiances make it a complex work, which in inadequate performances can seem sprawling. *La forza del destino*'s dramatic richness is matched in its music, the darkness of which perhaps reflects that it was commissioned for performance in Russia. The version generally heard today is a revision, made for Milan in 1869, which ends more optimistically, without Alvaro's suicide, and includes the famous, full-scale overture.

CHARACTERS

Donna Leonora (SOPRANO); *Preziosilla*, a gypsy (MEZZO-SOPRANO); *Curra*, Leonora's maid (MEZZO-SOPRANO); *Don Alvaro*, a Peruvian nobleman (TENOR); *Trabuco*, a muleteer (TENOR); *Don Carlo di Vargas*, Leonora's brother (BARITONE); *The Marquis of Calatrava*, Leonore's father (BASS); *Fra Melitone*, a Franciscan monk (BASS) With *Surgeon, muleteers, peasants, soldiers, friars*

ACT I
In Seville: the Marquis of Calatrava's house
Leonora is planning to elope with Don Alvaro, despite the disapproval of her father, the Marquis of Calatrava. When their plan is discovered, Don Alvaro gives himself up to the old man, but as he surrenders his pistol it goes off accidentally, fatally wounding the Marquis, who curses his daughter as he dies.

ACT II
SCENE 1 *The village of Hornachuelos and vicinity*
Leonora's brother Don Carlo has come (disguised as a student) to the crowded inn at Hornachuelos on his mission to find Leonora and her lover and to avenge her father's death. Leonora (dressed as a young man) arrives with Trabuco, a muleteer, in search of Don Alvaro. She hears her brother's threats—and claim that Alvaro has escaped back to South America—and prays with a band of passing pilgrims for deliverance while the gypsy Preziosilla urges the men to join the war in Italy.

SCENE 2 *A monastery outside Hornachuelos*
Leonora reaches the monastery of Our Lady of the Angels, frightened and in despair. She begs for sanctuary in the monastery: the reluctant Fra Melitone calls the Father Superior, Padre Guardiano, who allows her to remain as a hermit in a grotto, cut off from the rest of the monastery.

ACT III

SCENE 1 *In Italy: a wood near Velletri, at night*
Under an assumed name Don Alvaro has joined the army and is fighting with the Spaniards against the Germans in Italy. Believing Leonora to be dead, he is lonely and has little wish to live. Don Carlo is also in the army under a hidden identity, and when Don Alvaro saves him from a fight without realizing who he is, the two men become loyal friends. The battle with the Germans resumes: Alvaro is injured and entrusts his papers to the safekeeping of Carlo, whose growing suspicions of his friend's identity are confirmed when he finds a portrait of Leonora among the belongings. When the surgeon sends news that Don Alvaro will live, Don Carlo gloats in the knowledge that can avenge his father's death.

SCENE 2 *A military encampment near Velletri*
Don Carlo confronts Alvaro and in spite of the latter's insistence that the Marquis's death was accidental, forces him into a duel, but not before revealing that Leonora is still alive. The two men fight, but are separated by soldiers, and Alvaro resolves to take refuge in a monastery. Life in the camp goes on, with a sermon from Melitone and a rousing military chorus led by Preziosilla.

ACT IV

SCENE 1 *The monastery near Hornachuelos*
The poor are queuing for soup from the monks. Melitone is dispensing it grudgingly, and the crowd compare him unfavourably with Padre Raffaello—Don Alvaro's new guise. Don Carlo arrives and challenges Alvaro: although Alvaro refuses to fight on the grounds that he is now in holy orders, Carlo succeeds in provoking him and they rush off to duel.

SCENE 2 *A gorge amid inaccessible rocks*
After years of seclusion in her grotto, Leonora is still not at peace with herself. She hears the fighting, in which Alvaro mortally wounds Carlo, and when Alvaro goes to summon the 'hermit' to perform the last rites on the dying man, he and Leonora recognize each other. She hurries to her brother; even in death Carlo looks for revenge and stabs her. Don Alvaro curses fate, but is urged by Padre Guardiano to seek forgiveness. As Leonora dies, he senses redemption.

DER FREISCHÜTZ (The Freeshooter)
Carl Maria von Weber (1786-1826)

THREE ACTS. LIBRETTO BY JOHANN FRIEDRICH KIND AFTER JOHANN AUGUST APEL'S AND FRIEDRICH LAUN'S *GESPENSTER-BUCH*. PREMIERE IN BERLIN, 18 JUNE 1821.

Der Freischütz, Weber's seventh opera, was the first to bring him success, and remained the most popular German opera until the middle of the 19th century. In this work Weber combined four vital elements—the fantastic, the realistic, the comic and the national—for the first time, thus laying the foundation for

German Romantic opera. Weber's music captures both the folk-like and supernatural sides to the story; with its dark atmosphere, the Wolf's Glen scene is a magnificent example of the latter.

CHARACTERS

Agathe, Cuno's daughter (SOPRANO); *Aennchen*, her cousin (MEZZO-SOPRANO); *Max*, an assistant forester (TENOR); *Kilian*, a wealthy peasant (BARITONE); *Ottakar*, a prince (BARITONE); *Cuno*, head forester (BASS); *Caspar*, an assistant forester (BASS); *Hermit* (BASS); *Samiel*, the 'Black Huntsman' (SPOKEN)

ACT I

In front of an inn in the Bohemian forest

In a shooting contest, Kilian defeats Max. Normally a good shot, Max is provoked by the taunts of the villagers, and a brawl between the two men is prevented only by the arrival of the head forester, Cuno. Cuno reminds Max that gaining Agathe's hand and the position of new head forester depend on winning a shooting competition the following day. Left alone, the gloomy Max is soon joined by another forester, Caspar. The latter has made a pact with Samiel (the Devil, known as the 'Black Huntsman') which gave him seven magic bullets in exchange for his soul after a set period of time, soon to expire; only by finding Samiel a substitue soul will he win a reprieve, and he fixes his hopes on Max. Caspar tells Max that the secret to winning the competition is a 'magic' bullet (he proves his point by lending Max his gun, which miraculously hits a distant target). Max, haunted by the fear of losing Agathe, agrees to join Caspar at the Wolf's Glen at midnight, to cast more magic bullets. Caspar rejoices that he has found Samiel a substitute victim.

ACT II

SCENE 1 *Cuno's house*

Aennchen is re-hanging the portrait of Cuno's ancestor that had fallen (at the very moment Max fired the magic bullet), slightly injuring Agathe. Aennchen tries to comfort her cousin, but Agathe is preoccupied by thoughts of an evil omen about which a Hermit warned her. Her anxiety disappears when Max enters, but returns when he says he is off to the Wolf's Glen to retrieve a deer he shot there. The girls beg him not to leave, but Max resolves to go.

SCENE 2 *The Wolf's Glen*

As midnight approaches, Caspar enters the glen and calls on Samiel, who accepts Max as victim in Caspar's place. Max appears and, in spite of frightening visions of his dead mother and Agathe, joins Caspar in casting seven bullets. As they progress, the apparitions become wilder. When Samiel enters, Caspar and Max fall unconscious, and the apparitions vanish.

ACT III

SCENE 1 *The forest*

Max and Caspar are out hunting. When Max has fired three perfect shots, he asks Caspar for more of the magic bullets.

But Caspar discharges his so as to leave just one—the seventh bullet, cast as Samiel entered.

SCENE 2 *Agathe's room*
Agathe is preparing for her wedding to Max, in spite of strong premonitions. She tells Aennchen of her dream, in which she appeared as a white dove at which Max shot. Aennchen tries to comfort her, but the mood darkens when instead of a garland, a funeral wreath is delivered. The sisters fashion a new garland from the white roses the Hermit gave Agathe.

SCENE 3 *A romantic landscape*
Hunters are celebrating. Prince Ottokar sets up the shooting contest, and selects a white dove as the target. Agathe enters and begs him not to shoot, since she knows the dove represents her. When Max's shot goes off it is Caspar who is hit. Agathe collapses but soon recovers, and the dying Caspar curses those around him. Prince Ottokar questions Max and is about to banish him when the Hermit intervenes: the prince is persuaded to give Max a year's probation, after which he can become head forester and marry Agathe. All join in praising God's mercy.

FROM THE HOUSE OF THE DEAD
Leoš Janáček (1854–1928)

THREE ACTS. LIBRETTO BY THE COMPOSER AFTER FYODOR DOSTOYEVSKY'S NOVEL, *MEMOIRS FROM THE HOUSE OF THE DEAD*. PREMIERE IN BRNO, 12 APRIL 1930.

Janáček derived considerable inspiration from Russian literature, so it was appropriate that he should turn to Dostoyevsky for his last opera. As befits the subject, the score is stark, with emphasis on percussion (including jangling chains). The cast (with the exception of one small part) is entirely male, in contrast to Janáček's previous three operas—*Katya Kabanova*, *The Cunning Little Vixen*, and *The Makropoulos Case*—all of which feature female portraits. Also, unlike its predecessors, *From the House of the Dead* has no dominant character, although Goryanchikov might be said to be a protagonist, in as much as his arrival and departure frame the opera. There is no plot, rather a series of incidents; the only action is that remembered and related in the three big monologues.

CHARACTERS
Alyeya, a young Tatar (MEZZO-SOPRANO); *Prostitute* (MEZZO-SOPRANO); *Filka Morosov*, a prisoner under the name of Luka Kuzmich (TENOR); *Skuratov* (TENOR); *Big Convict* (TENOR); *Very Old Convict* (TENOR); *Drunken Convict* (TENOR); *Young Convict* (TENOR); *Kedril* (TENOR); *Shapkin* (TENOR); *Cherevin* (TENOR); *Guard* (TENOR); *Chekunov* (BARITONE); *Small Convict* (BARITONE); *Commandant* (BARITONE); *Cook* (BARITONE); *Priest* (BARITONE); *Convict*, playing Don Juan and Brahmin (BARITONE); *Shishkov* (BARITONE); *Alexander Petrovich Goryanshikov*, political prisoner (BASS); *Smith* (BASS)
With *prisoners*, prison *guards*, *guests*

ACT I

The yard in a Siberian prison; a winter morning

Prisoners begin their morning routine, and soon a fight breaks out. The new political prisoner Goryanshikov is bought before the Command-ant and sent off for flogging. The prisoners are taunting an eagle, but the Commandant intervenes. Some prisoners move off, but Skuratov remains behind, and argues with Luka. Both reminisce: Skuratov is homesick for Moscow, and Luka recounts his previous spell in prison, and how he was punished. Goryanshikov returns badly beaten.

ACT II

The bank of the Irtysh river; summer evening, a year later

Convicts are at work on the river banks, where Goryanshikov befriends the Tartar boy Alyeya, asks about his mother and sister, and tries to comfort the distressed youth by offering to teach him to read and write. Since it is a holiday, the evening is given over to entertainment. Skuratov describes the background to his crime, how he shot the rich man his girlfriend Luisa was made to marry. The prisoners perform two plays for the local townspeople, while another disappears with a prostitute. Goryanshikov and Alyeya drink tea, but another prisoner, jealous of this 'luxury', assaults the Tartar boy.

ACT III

SCENE 1 *The prison hospital; towards evening*

Alyeya, while delirious, talks to Goryanshikov, thus irritating the dying Luka. Shapkin tells the story of his interrogation. As darkness falls, only the moans of the Old Prisoner are heard until Shishkov embarks on his story of the girl he married, Akulka: though she was wrongly accused before their wedding of having lost her honour to a certain Filka Morozov, when it transpired later that she did in fact love Filka, Shishkov murdered her. At his point in his story, Luka dies. Shishkov realizes that the dead man was Filka masquerading under a different name, and curses the corpse as it is dragged out. Goryanshikov is summoned by the guards, much to Alyeya's distress.

SCENE 2 *The prison yard*

The drunken Commandant addresses Goryanshikov, apologizes that he was flogged, and gives orders for him to be freed. Alyeya comes to say goodbye. As Goryanshikov departs, the prisoners release the eagle in a symbolic gesture. They have glimpsed freedom, but the prison routine reasserts itself.

THE GAMBLER
Sergey Prokofiev (1891-1953)

FOUR ACTS. LIBRETTO BY THE COMPOSER AFTER FYODOR DOSTOYEVSKY'S NOVEL *THE GAMBLER*. PREMIERE IN BRUSSELS, 29 APRIL 1929.

Though Prokofiev was a man of the theatre, his operas enjoyed little success during his lifetime. *The Gambler*, his sixth opera (four were juvenilia), was the first to be staged, and had to wait twelve years for its premiere. It was completed for performance in St Petersburg in 1917, but owing to internal problems at the Maryinsky Theatre—and the Revolution—the project was abandoned. It finally reached the stage in Brussels in 1929 (sung in French), and then did not surface again until after Prokofiev's death. *The Gambler* was the first significant opera to be based on Dostoyevsky, whose novella was ideally suited to Prokofiev's sense of irony and fantasy. The score reflects the way in which the composer was trying to break free from operatic convention, and lacks set pieces and even developed themes. Rather, short motifs and declamatory vocal writing match the comic, obsessive nature of the story.

CHARACTERS

Pauline, the General's step-daughter (SOPRANO); *Babulenka*, the General's aunt (MEZZO-SOPRANO); *Blanche*, a demi-mondaine (CONTRALTO); *Alexey*, tutor to the General's children (TENOR); *The Marquis* (TENOR); *Prince Nilsky* (TENOR); *Mr Astley*, a wealthy Englishman (BARITONE); *Potapich*, Babulenka's steward (BARITONE); *The General*, a retired army officer (BASS); *Baron Würmerhelm* (BASS); *Baroness Würmerhelm* (MUTE)
With *gamblers, waiter, page-boy, hotel guests, servants, porters*

ACT I
The garden of the Grand Hotel

The opera is set in Roulettenburg, an imaginary German spa town, where the General awaits news from Russia that his aunt (referred to as Babulenka—literally 'Grandmother') has died, leaving him a fortune. He needs the money to repay the rich French Marquis, and to marry Blanche. The Marquis's grip over the family is considerable: he has seduced the General's step-daughter Pauline, who in turn is the object of the tutor Alexey's attentions.

Alexey has lost all the money Pauline gave him to gamble with. Watched by Blanche, the Marquis, and Mr Astley, the General opens a telegram from Moscow, only to discover that his aunt is in good health. All attempt to dissuade Alexey from further gambling, but he reveals his contempt for his wealthy social superiors. Pauline has grown tired of Alexey's persistence, and in revenge encourages him to insult the Baroness Würmerhelm.

ACT II
The casino

Alexey's rudeness has caused an uproar. The General tries to dismiss the tutor but, fearing a scandal, allows him to stay. Matters get complicated when Alexey learns not only of Blanche's past—she had been banished from the casino at the request of Baroness Würmerhelm, who saw Blanche propositioning her husband—but that the money-lending Marquis is interested in Pauline because of the wealth that her stepfather is due to inherit. Soon, Babulenka confounds them all by arriving at the casino—in good health.

ACT III

A room in the Grand Hotel

Outside the gaming room where Babulenka is wiping out her fortune, the General bemoans his fate. When Prince Nilsky announces the aunt's total losses, Blanche abandons the General. Babulenka returns to Russia penniless.

ACT IV

SCENE 1 *Alexey's attic room*

Pauline comes to Alexey with the news that the Marquis has left her and further insulted her by paying her off (with money from her step-father's debts). Alexey is enraged, and rushes off to the casino, where he hopes to win the money for her.

SCENE 2 *The casino*

Alexey astounds the gamblers by breaking the bank twice.

SCENE 3 *Alexey's room*

Alexey returns to Pauline with the money, but she refuses it. She is angry at being 'bought off' for a second time and, seeing that he is now obsessed with gambling, rejects him. Alexey's thoughts return to the roulette wheel: he is slave to a new love.

LA GAZZA LADRA (The Thieving Magpie)

Gioachino Rossini (1792-1868)

TWO ACTS. LIBRETTO BY GIOVANNI GHERARDINI, AFTER *LA PIE VOLEUESE* BY J.-M.-T. BAUDOUIN D'AUBIGNY AND LOUIS-CHARLES CAIGNIEZ. PREMIERE IN MILAN, 31 MAY 1817.

La gazza ladra is a classic example of *semiseria* (literally 'half-serious') opera, which developed in late 1700s and was recognized as such early in the 19th century. A hybrid of comedy and potential tragedy, the genre typically had a pastoral setting, and its heroine was usually a village maiden whose innocence, at first doubted, was vindicated. Indeed, the plot for *La gazza ladra* derives from real-life events in which a French peasant girl was executed for thefts later discovered to have been the work of a magpie—though in the opera the heroine's innocence is proved at the last minute. For Rossini, who perhaps felt he had exhausted pure comedy in *L'italiana in Algeri* (1813) and *Il barbiere di Siviglia* (1816), *La gazza ladra* (1817) provided him with a subject of great potential: the music moves from lightheartedness to deep pathos (there is a disturbingly scored march to the scaffold), only to return to high spirits at the end.

CHARACTERS

Ninetta, Fabrizio's servant (SOPRANO); *Lucia*, Fabrizio's wife (MEZZO-SOPRANO); *Pippo*, a young peasant (CONTRALTO); *Giannetto*, a soldier, Fabrizio's son (TENOR); *Isacco*, a pedlar (TENOR); *Antonio*, the gaoler (TENOR); *Fernando Villabella*, a soldier, Ninetta's father, *Fabrizio Vingradito*, a rich farmer (BASS); *Gottardo*, the village mayor (BASS); *Giorgio*, the town clerk (BASS); *Ernesto*, a soldier, friend of Fernando With *usher, armed men, villagers, servants, a magpie*

ACT I

Ninetta is in love with Giannetto, her employer's son, soon to return from the wars. His father Fabrizio, a farmer, is happy that they intend to marry but his mother Lucia voices her doubts; she claims that their servant girl is unreliable, and disapproves of the match. Giannetto arrives home and is fêted by all the folk on the farm. Ninetta is in the farmhouse when a vagrant appears whom she recognizes as her father Fernando. He has deserted the army in order to visit his daughter, and gives her a silver fork and spoon to sell to raise cash. Ninetta tries to hide him, but is interrupted by the lecherous, sinister mayor, Gottardo. The town clerk brings news of a deserter, and the mayor, unable to read the description for lack of his glasses, asks Ninetta to help. She changes the description to keep suspicion from centring on her father. While Gottardo is considering the evidence, a magpie steals a silver spoon belonging to Lucia. When Lucia discovers that it is missing, the pedlar Isacco's evidence that he bought one from Ninetta with the initials F.V.—those of both Fabrizio and Fernando—is used against the girl, who is arrested. Gottardo gloats that the girl who repulsed his advances is in trouble.

ACT II

In prison, Ninetta receives three visitors. Thanks to the lenient gaoler, Antonio, Giannetto is allowed in to visit his betrothed, who protests her innocence. The mayor offers her freedom in exchange for favours, but is rejected again. Pippo also visits her, and she asks him to hide some money for her father. Fernando risks all by enquiring at the farmhouse after his daughter. Although Lucia retracts her accusation against Ninetta, the trial goes ahead and she is found guilty; Fernando tries to intervene, but is spotted by the mayor and arrested. In a grim possession to the scaffold, Ninetta pauses in front of the church to pray for her father. He is pardoned, and in another turn of events, Pippo and Antonio discover the stolen cutlery in the magpie's churchtower nest. They are just in time, and Ninetta is reprieved. Everyone rejoices, except the mayor.

GIANNI SCHICCHI
Giacomo Puccini (1858-1924)

ONE ACT. LIBRETTO BY GIOVACCHINO FORZANO, AFTER A PASSAGE FROM CANTO 30 OF DANTE'S *INFERNO*. PREMIERE IN NEW YORK, 14 DECEMBER 1914.

Gianni Schicchi is the third and most popular work in Puccini's triptych, *Il trittico* (see also *Il tabarro* and *Suor Angelica*). Although several of Puccini's earlier works reveal his feeling for comedy, *Gianni Schicchi* is his only comic opera; the humour is often morbid, but the work paints a lively picture of medieval Florence. One aria, Lauretta's 'O mio babbino caro', has gained immortality out of its operatic context.

CHARACTERS

Lauretta, Gianni's daughter (SOPRANO); *Nella*, Buoso Donati's widow

(SOPRANO); *La Ciesca*, Marco's wife (MEZZO-SOPRANO); *Zita*, Buoso's cousin (CONTRALTO); *Gherardino*, Buoso's and Nella's son (ALTO); *Rinuccio*, Zita's nephew (TENOR); *Gherardo*, Buoso's nephew (TENOR); *Gianni Schicchi* (BARITONE); *Marco*, Simone's son (BARITONE); *Ser Amantio di Nicolao*, a notary (BARITONE); *Betto di Signa*, Buoso's brother-in-law (BASS); *Simone*, Buoso's cousin (BASS); *Maestro Spinelloccio*, a doctor (BASS); *Pinellino*, a cobbler (BASS); *Guccio*, a painter (BASS)

A bedroom in the house of Buoso Donati

Soon after Buoso Donati has died, his relatives gather and attempt to out-do each other in their expressions of grief. But they have really come to discover what the wealthy man left in his will, and a rumour that he has endowed everything to a nearby monastery puts an end to all mourning as a search for the document is carried out. Rinuccio, a young man in love with Gianni Schicchi's daughter Lauretta, finds it, but refuses to open it until his Aunt Zita consents to his marriage. Zita agrees; with the prospect of wealth uppermost in her mind, she hardly cares who her nephew marries. All gather round to read the will, and their worst fears are confirmed: they have been passed over. Rinuccio suggests that Gianni Schicchi could help solve the problem, but the others dismiss Schicchi as a country bumpkin. When Schicchi arrives, they treat him with such contempt that he refuses to assist; only his daughter's pleading—Lauretta's marriage to Rinuccio is threatened by the quarrel over her lack of dowry—changes his mind.

Since nobody outside the family circle knows of Buoso's death, Schicchi's plan is to disguise himself as Buoso and dictate a new will. But he has only given instructions for the body to be removed when the Doctor arrives. Hiding behind the bed-curtains, Schicchi imitates the dead man's voice, assuring the Doctor of his miraculous improvement. Next, he sends for the Notary, and the excited relatives make bids for Buoso's most prized possessions: his house, his mule, and the mills at Signa. Rinuccio escorts the Notary in, and Schicchi begins by leaving an insignificant amount to the monks and making other small bequests to the relatives. The family's anxiety turns to impotent rage as he reaches the big items, which he promises to his 'dear, devoted, and much-loved friend, Gianni Schicchi'. When the Notary departs, however, they turn on him and plunder the house. Schicchi chases them out, and—seeing Lauretta and Rinuccio happily in love, she guaranteed a dowry—steps forward to beg the audience's indulgence for what has been accomplished with Buoso's wealth.

GIULIO CESARE (Julius Caesar)
George Frideric Handel (1685-1759)

THREE ACTS. LIBRETTO BY NICOLA HAYM AFTER G. F. BUSSANI'S LIBRETTO *GIULIO CESARE IN EGITTO*. PREMIERE IN LONDON, 20 FEBRUARY 1724.

Giulio Cesare, perhaps the best-known and most frequently performed of Handel's operas, is also one of his longest and richest scores. Its success during Handel's lifetime meant that he revised it several times, leaving no definitive score. Various reconstructions have been made by scholars since it was revived for the first time in almost two centuries, at Göttingen in 1922. Early in its revival the opera's male roles (originally sung by castratos) were transposed down and given to baritones and basses, a procedure which damages Handel's vocal textures. Performers are beginning to appreciate the importance of preserving the original pitches: these roles are now increasingly assigned to women and counter-tenors. Handel's characterization is vivid: the action is based on Julius Caesar's visit to Egypt in 48-47 BC, and though the characters are largely historical, most of the detail is fictional.

CHARACTERS

ROMANS

Sesto (Sextus), son of Pompey and Cornelia (SOPRANO); *Cornelia*, widow of Pompey (CONTRALTO); *Giulio Cesare* (Julius Caesar) (CONTRALTO/COUNTER-TENOR); *Curio* (Curius), tribune (BASS)

EGYPTIANS

Cleopatra, Queen of Egypt (SOPRANO); *Tolomeo* (Ptolemy), King of Egypt, Cleopatra's brother (CONTRALTO/COUNTER-TENOR); *Nireno* (Nirenus), confidant of Tolomeo and Cleopatra (CONTRALTO/COUNTER-TENOR); *Achilla* (Achillas), general, Tolomeo's advisor (BASS)

ACT I

Caesar has pursued Pompey, whom he has just defeated at Pharsalia in Greece, to Egypt. He is welcomed by the Egyptians, and implored by Pompey's wife and son, Cornelia and Sextus, to show mercy. Caesar agrees to a settlement, but is interrupted by the entry of Achilla bearing gifts from Ptolemy; they include the head of Pompey. The devastated Cornelia tries to take her own life, and soon finds herself having to rebuff the advances of Curius; Sextus swears vengeance.

Cleopatra, at her court, plans to become sole ruler of Egypt by forming an alliance with Caesar against her brother Ptolemy. Achilla tells Ptolemy of Caesar's disgust at Pompey's murder, and offers to kill Caesar so long as his reward can be Cornelia's hand. Ptolemy agrees.

Cleopatra enters Caesar's camp disguised as 'Lydia', and Caesar is soon captivated by her beauty. Together with her confidant, Nirenus, she watches as Cornelia pays her final respects to her dead husband. Once again, Sextus swears vengeance, and 'Lydia'plays on their emotions to enlist their help against Ptolemy.

Caesar visits Ptolemy at his palace. Cornelia and Sextus arrive and challenge Ptolemy to a fight, but are arrested: she is sent to the king's harem, and he imprisoned. Achillas offers Cornelia freedom in return for marriage, but is rejected. Mother and son lament their fate.

ACT II

Cleopatra has laid out the scene for Caesar's seduction. He is entranced by what he sees, and by the promise of the attentions of 'Lydia', who will in turn introduce him to Cleopatra.

In the garden of the harem, Cornelia again rejects Achillas's advances, but this time she also receives unwelcome attention from Ptolemy. She makes another attempt at suicide, but Sextus intervenes. When Nirenus advises Sextus on his planned revenge, she urges her son on.

In her apartments, Cleopatra (still disguised as 'Lydia') flirts with Caesar, but they are interrupted by Curius, who warns of an impending attempt on Caesar's life. Cleopatra is forced to reveal her identity, and goes off to quieten the crowd, but she fails and urges Caesar to escape. He, however, is determined to confront the conspirators.

In his harem, Ptolemy shows special attention to Cornelia, thus provoking Sextus, who comes close to killing him but is thwarted by Achillas. The latter brings news of Caesar's apparent death—it is believed that he drowned in the harbour while escaping—and also that Cleopatra is mustering troops against Ptolemy. Achillas's reminder to the king that his efforts should be rewarded by the hand of Cornelia is rejected, and he goes off threatening revenge. In despair at his lack of success, Sextus tries to kill himself, but Cornelia urges him not to give up.

ACT III

Near Alexandria, Achillas resolves to defect to Cleopatra's side. Ptolemy wins the battle, and Cleopatra is sent to prison. Caesar reappears at the harbour-side, having avoided drowning. There he sees the wounded Achillas hand to Sextus the seal which gives command of his troops. Caesar takes over, and sets off to rescue Cleopatra and Cornelia.

Having gained entry to the palace, Caesar is reunited with Cleopatra. Ptolemy makes a final attempt to win Cornelia, but Sextus appears and kills him. Caesar and Cleopatra arrive at the harbour in triumph, and are soon joined by Cornelia and Sextus, who brings news of Ptolemy's death. Cleopatra will rule Egypt under Rome's protection, and all join in celebrating a new era of peace.

THE GOLDEN COCKEREL
Nikolay Rimsky-Korsakov (1844-1908)

THREE ACTS. LIBRETTO BY VLADIMIR IVANOVICH BELSKY AFTER PUSHKIN'S POEM. PREMIERE IN MOSCOW, 7 OCTOBER 1909.

The Golden Cockerel, last of Rimsky's 15 operas, is the only one to have enjoyed much success outside Russia. It is untypical of his work—indeed, it is not his best—but it owes its success in the West to Diaghilev's famous staging in Paris in 1914. The music, highly chromatic (but blended with simpler, folk-inspired material), epitomises Rimsky's way with colourful Oriental subjects. Although the plot seems shallow, its lampooning of autocracy was clearly intended as an attack on the Russian authorities. The opera was written in the wake of political disturbances in 1905 (Rimsky was sacked from the St Petersburg Conservatory for favouring reform), and fell foul of the censors: it was not performed until after the composer's death.

CHARACTERS

The Queen of Shemakha (SOPRANO); *The Golden Cockerel* (SOPRANO); *Amelfa*, royal housekeeper (CONTRALTO); *Astrologer* (HIGH TENOR); *Prince Guidon*, Dodon's son (TENOR); *Prince Afron*, Dodon's son (BARITONE); *Tsar Dodon* (BASS); *Commander Polkan* (BASS)
With *boyars, guards, soldiers, slave girls, crowd*

PROLOGUE

The Astrologer appears to inform the audience that he is about to recall an ancient story.

ACT I

Tsar Dodon's court

Old Tsar Dodon faces an impending attack. He gathers his sons and councillors to seek advice, but General Polkan chooses to ignore the pointless suggestions which Guidon and Afron make. The uncertainty is resolved by the arrival of the Astrologer, who brings a magic Golden Cockerel to Dodon: the bird can warn of danger and also tell Dodon when it is safe to sleep. Put at ease, Dodon is able to sleep—he dreams of a beautiful maiden—between the alarms sounded by the Cockerel. When the time comes, Dodon leads his army into battle.

ACT II

A mountain gorge

Dodon's ill-prepared army has been routed, and in the confusion the brothers Guidon and Afron have killed each other. At dawn a magnificent tent is spotted, which Dodon and Polkan assume to be that of the opposing general. They bombard it, but a beautiful maiden emerges. She is the Queen of Shemakha, who plans to conquer Dodon with her beauty rather than by force. Polkan is sent away, and she sets about seducing the Tsar, whose antics become increasingly ludicrous. They set off for his capital.

ACT III

The capital

Dodon and his bride arrive back amid scenes of rejoicing. But proceedings are interrupted by the appearance of the Astrologer, who demands as a reward for his services the beautiful Queen. Dodon strikes the Astrologer and kills him; immediately, the sky darkens. When Dodon tries to embrace the Queen, she repulses him. Suddenly, the Cockerel gives a loud crow and pecks Dodon to death. When the sky clears, both the Cockerel and the Queen are gone. The people, terrified by this turn of events, lament their dead Tsar.

EPILOGUE

The Astrologer appears again to the audience, reassuring it not to be alarmed: it was only a fairytale, he says, in which he and the Queen were the sole mortals.

GÖTTERDÄMMERUNG
see **Der Ring des Nibelungen**

GUILLAUME TELL (William Tell)
Gioacchino Rossini (1792-1868)

FOUR ACTS. LIBRETTO BY VICTOR JOSEPH ETIENNE DE JOUY,
HIPPOLYTE-LOUIS-FLORENT BIS, AND ARMAND MARRAST
AFTER FRIEDRICH VON SCHILLER'S PLAY *WILHELM TELL*.
PREMIERE IN PARIS, 3 AUGUST 1829.

Guillaume Tell was Rossini's last opera. After five years in Paris,
where the Italian had spent much of his energy revising and
adapting earlier operas for his new public, he sought to offer
Parisian audiences a new work to satisfy their taste for
grandiose spectacle, and in so doing composed the first great
grand opéra. Though *Tell* is still imbued with Italianate lyricism, it shows how Rossini had absorbed experiences of the
Paris Opéra and a developed a feeling for French settings. It
could have initiated a new phase in his career; instead, it represents a creative summing-up, and reflects how over only two
decades Rossini grew from copying 18th-century buffo conventions to establishing the foundations for 19th-century
composers to build on. *Tell* is conceived on a large scale, with
ballets and processions; the chorus is central to the work, since
the drama concerns the Swiss people in rebellion.

CHARACTERS
Hedwige, Tell's wife (SOPRANO); *Jemmy*, Tell's son (SOPRANO);
Mathilde, Gesler's sister (SOPRANO); *Arnold*, Mathilde's suitor, con-
spirator with Tell (TENOR); *Rodolphe*, commander of Gesler's archers
(TENOR); *Ruodi*, a fisherman (TENOR); *Guillaume Tell* (BARITONE);
Melcthal, Arnold's father (BASS); *Gesler*, governor of the cantons of
Schwyz and Uri (BASS); *Walter Furst*, conspirator with Tell (BASS);
Leuthold, a shepherd (BASS)
With *peasants, knights, pages, hunters, soldiers*

ACT I
The shore of Lake Lucerne in Switzerland
On a beautiful spring morning, festivities are about to culminate
in a triple wedding. Only Tell is gloomy, as he contemplates
the repressive rule of the Austrians under the tyrant Gesler.
The venerable Melcthal symbolizes Swiss resistance, and is
thus asked to officiate at the wedding ceremony. But
Melcthal's son, Arnold, has fallen in love with Gesler's sister,
Mathilde; Arnold is troubled by his divided allegiances, but
agrees to help Tell fight Austrian rule. The festivities (including
an archery competition, which Tell's son, Jemmy, wins) continue until they are interrupted by the sounds of Gesler's hunt.
Leuthold appears on the run from the Austrians: he has killed
an Austrian soldier who tried to rape his daughter, and begs for a
ferryman to row him across the lake. With a storm brewing, only
Tell is willing to take him to safety. In retaliation, the Austrians
threaten to sack the village, and Melcthal is taken prisoner.

ACT II
The Rütli Heights, overlooking Lake Lucerne
As work on the hillside finishes for the day, Arnold and Mathilde meet and reaffirm their love. Arnold is convinced that he will have to fight with the Austrians, but news—brought by Tell and Walter—of his father's death at the hands of Gesler persuades him to join the Swiss cause. The three men swear an oath to overthrow Austria, and are joined by representatives of the surrounding cantons in planning a strategy.

ACT III
Scene 1 *A chapel in the gardens of the Altdorf Palace*
Mathilde and Arnold meet but, as her brother has killed his father, he renounces her, and they bid each other farewell.

Scene 2 *The square at Altdorf*
Gesler has imposed festivities to mark the 100th anniversary of Swiss rule. As a symbol of his power, he has commanded that all should bow to his hat, but Tell, who arrives with Jemmy, refuses. When he is recognized as the one who saved Leuthold, both father and son are arrested. The sadistic Gesler announces that he will only release them if Tell manages to shoot an apple from Jemmy's head. Jemmy remains calm, and Tell succeeds; but he lets slip that his second arrow was intended for Gesler, and the two are re-arrested. Mathilde intervenes and persuades her brother to let her care for Jemmy, but Tell is sent to the dungeons of Küssnacht castle.

ACT IV
Scene 1 *Melcthal's house*
Arnold returns to his home. When he is shown where his father and Tell had hidden weapons, he realizes that it is now up to him to lead the rebellion.

Scene 2 *The shore of Lake Lucerne*
Mathilde brings Jemmy to Tell's wife, Hedwige. As an experienced boatsman, Tell has been forced to pilot Gesler across the stormy lake, and when he sees the signal—given by Jemmy—that the uprising has begun, he abandons the boat and makes for the shore. When Gesler lands, Tell kills him. Arnold's men free Altdorf, and as the storm subsides, all join in celebrating their liberation.

HÄNSEL UND GRETEL (Hansel and Gretel)
Engelbert Humperdinck (1854-1921)
Three acts. Libretto by Adelheid Wette after the Brothers Grimm. Premiere in Weimar, 23 December 1893.

Humperdinck's first opera—the only one of his six to have remained in the repertory—was a brother-and-sister affair from the start: it was the composer's sister who initiated it, by requesting incidental music for a play for her children, and when Humperdinck conceived the idea of a full-scale opera, she remained his librettist. *Hänsel und Gretel* is most frequently revived as a seasonal show, but the sinister undertones of the fairy-tale and the Wagnerian musical techniques (Humperdinck was a disciple of Wagner, and assisted him at Bayreuth) make it as suitable for adults as it is for children. Richard Strauss, who conducted the premiere, declared it 'masterpiece of the highest quality'; what sets it apart from other Wagner-influenced works is the freshness and charm of Humperdinck's music.

CHARACTERS

Gretel (SOPRANO); *Gertrud*, mother of Hänsel and Gretel (SOPRANO); *Sandman* (SOPRANO); *Dew Fairy* (SOPRANO); *Hänsel* (MEZZO-SOPRANO); *Witch* (MEZZO-SOPRANO); *Peter*, a broom-maker, father of Hänsel and Gretel (BARITONE)

ACT I
The broom-maker's house

Hänsel and Gretel are doing chores. Both are bored and hungry, and to cheer themselves up they start to dance. Their games are interrupted by Gertrud, their mother, who is angry to find them playing instead of working. In her anger she knocks over the milk jug, loosing what was to have been their supper. She sends them into the forest to gather strawberries instead. Wearied by their precarious existence, she sinks into a chair, only to be woken by the return of Peter, her husband. She is irritated to find him tipsy, but calms down when he produces a sack full of food. When he enquires after Hänsel and Gretel, he is alarmed to hear they are in the forest: he warns of the Witch who lives there, and both parents set out to look for the children.

ACT II
The wood

Hänsel and Gretel happily gather and eat strawberries. When night falls they realize they are lost, and are frightened by the mysterious shapes in the mist. But a Sandman appears and settles them. They say their evening prayers, and go to asleep. The mist around them turns to clouds from which angels appear, who guard the children from harm.

ACT III
The gingerbread house

At dawn the Dew Fairy comes to wake Hänsel and Gretel. They are excited to see a gingerbread house not far away, but when they begin to nibble at it, the Witch emerges and captures them, casting a spell. She puts Hänsel in a cage, telling Gretel that her brother needs fattening. She releases Gretel with a spell, in order that the girl may help her with the oven. But Gretel uses the spell to free Hänsel, and as the Witch demonstrates to Gretel how to check the oven, the children push her into it. As the witch dies, the fence of gingerbread people is transformed back into motionless children. Hänsel invokes the formula for breaking the spell, and the children jump up and thank Hänsel and Gretel for saving them. Peter and Gertrud appear, and the family is reunited. All celebrate when they find that the Witch has herself been transformed into gingerbread.

L'HEURE ESPAGNOLE (The Spanish Hour)
Maurice Ravel (1875-1937)

ONE ACT. TEXT BY FRANC-NOHAIN. PREMIERE IN PARIS, 9 MAY 1911.

For his first opera, Ravel set Franc-Nohain's vaudeville *L'Heure espagnol* (1904) virtually as it stood, with only small cuts and changes. The comedy draws a parallel between the spring-driven clocks in the shop where it is set and the sexually-driven characters who visit it, and Ravel amplified this in the opera, by means of the score's delightful assortment of clock noises and the depiction of almost mechanical people. Another element in the score is Spanish colour (the opera is set in Toledo), but in its sophisticated lightness the opera remains thoroughly French.

CHARACTERS

Concepción, Torquemada's wife (SOPRANO); *Torquemada*, clock-maker (TENOR); *Gonçalve*, a poet (TENOR); *Ramiro*, a muleteer (BARITONE); *Don Inigo Gomez*, a banker (BASS)

Torquemada the clock-maker and his wife Concepción are in their shop. It is her custom to receive lovers during her husband's weekly, hour-long round to attend the city's clocks. Just as Torquemada is about to set off, the muleteer Ramiro enters, hoping to have his watch fixed. Torquemada tells him to wait the hour until he returns, much to the mutual embarrassment of Ramiro and Concepción: she because she is expecting her lover, the poet Gonçalve, and he because of his shyness. She decides to put his muscles to use, by asking him to carry a grandfather clock up to her bedroom.

While Ramiro is performing the task, Gonçalve arrives for his assignation. He is hidden in another clock, and Concepción asks Ramiro to switch the two clocks around. But before he has finished, another of Concepción's admirers, the banker Don Inigo, enters. His is concealed in yet another clock. The tireless Ramiro is asked to swop clocks again. Concepción is disappointed with both her lovers. Finally, she abandons Gonçalve and Don Inigo, and instead invites Ramiro up to her room. While they are there Torquemada returns home, to find both Gonçalve and Don Inigo lodged inside clocks. Their excuses are that they are interested customers, and Torquemada is happy to make a sale. When Concepción and Ramiro reappear, all address the audience with a moral from Boccaccio: 'In the pursuit of love, there comes a moment when the muleteer gets his turn'.

LES HUGUENOTS (The Huguenots)
Giacomo Meyerbeer (1791-1864)

FIVE ACTS. LIBRETTO BY EUGENE SCRIBE AND EMILE DESCHAMPS. PREMIERE IN PARIS, 29 FEBRUARY 1836.

Giacomo Meyerbeer's adopted name reflects his cosmopolitan experience. A German-Jewish composer, born Jakob Liebmann Meyer, he spent seven years in Italy, where he came under the influence of Rossini, before settling in Paris in 1826. There he formed a successful partnership with the librettist Scribe, and composed four of the most spectacular grand opéras ever written, of which *Les Huguenots* is perhaps the finest. Though not his longest score (*L'Africaine* lasts over six hours), *Les Huguenots* prompted Berlioz's enigmatic comment that it contains enough material for ten operas. There is much in it—everything that Parisian audiences of the day demanded—but the music and five-act plot (which sets the doomed love of the Protestant Raoul and the Catholic Valentine against the background of the bloody St Bartholomew massacre of 1572) are powerfully integrated. The subject is painfully topical today; perhaps the biggest reason for its neglect in recent times is the shortage of singers suited to the demands which Meyerbeer makes.

CHARACTERS

Valentine, Saint-Bris's daughter, betrothed to Count de Nevers (SOPRANO); *Marguérite de Valois*, betrothed to Henry IV of Navarre (SOPRANO); *Urbain*, Marguérite's page (SOPRANO); *Raoul de Nangis*, Huguenot nobleman (TENOR); *Cossé*, Catholic gentleman (TENOR); *Tavannes*, Catholic gentleman (TENOR); *Bois-Rosé*, Huguenot soldier (TENOR); *Comte de Saint-Bris*, Catholic nobleman, father of Valentine (BARITONE); *Comte de Nevers*, Catholic nobleman (BARITONE); *Méru*, Catholic gentleman (BARITONE); *Thoré*, Catholic gentleman (BARITONE); *De Retz*, Catholic gentleman (BARITONE); *Marcel*, Huguenot soldier, Raoul's servant (BASS); *Maurevert*, Catholic nobleman (BASS)

With Catholic and Huguenot *courtiers*, *soldiers*, and *burghers*, *Nightwatchman*, *monks*, *students*

ACT I
A hall in Nevers's château
The Count of Nevers is hosting a banquet for his fellow Catholics. In the spirit of peace, he has also invited the Huguenot Raoul, who entertains the company with a story of how he fell in love with an unknown beauty whom he saved from a group of molesters. Raoul is interrupted by his servant Marcel, who disapproves of his fraternising with the Catholics. News comes that a lady is waiting to meet Nevers. Raoul watches, and realizes that she is the woman of whom he had been talking. It is revealed that she is Valentine, daughter of the Catholic Count Saint-Bris, who has ordered that she marry Nevers. But she has come—under pressure from Queen Marguérite—to beg that she be freed from her engagement. Raoul is invited to a meeting: the Catholic noblemen identify the writing on the invitation to be that of Queen Marguérite, and their attitude to the Huguenot changes instantly.

ACT II

The château gardens at Chenonceaux

Marguérite and her ladies-in-waiting long for an end to religious disputes. She hopes that a marriage between the Catholic Valentine and Huguenot Raoul will help to bring peace, and has thus summoned Raoul. Although he is enraptured by Marguérite herself, he agrees to her plan. But when Valentine appears, Raoul presumes her to be Nevers's mistress, and refuses to be part of the pact. Old prejudices flare up.

ACT III

The Pré-aux-clercs on the banks of the Seine

Catholics and Huguenots are celebrating the holiday. Nevers and Valentine are about to be married when Marcel arrives with a note from Raoul to Valentine's father, Saint-Bris, challenging him to a duel. Saint-Bris, Nevers, and Maurevert plan to retaliate, but Valentine overhears them and—since she is still in love with Raoul—alerts Marcel. Marguérite intervenes, and reveals to Raoul the purpose of Valentine's earlier visit to Nevers. But it is too late, and Saint-Bris derives satisfaction from telling Raoul that Valentine is already married.

ACT IV

Outside Valentine's bedroom in Nevers's château

Raoul pays a secret visit to Valentine to explain the misunderstanding that led him to reject her. He hides when Saint-Bris and the Catholic leaders appear, and thus overhears them plotting a massacre of Huguenots. Nevers declines to collaborate. Priests bless the weapons before the Catholics set off. When they have left, Valentine confesses her love to Raoul. He lapses into a reverie, only to be awoken by the sound of bells, the signal for the massacre to begin. Raoul runs off to fight.

ACT V

SCENE 1 *A ballroom of the Hôtel de Nesle*

The Huguenots are celebrating the wedding of Queen Marguérite and Henry of Navarre when Raoul rushes in to warn them of the impending massacre.

SCENE 2 *A Huguenot cemetery*

Raoul, Marcel, and Valentine take cover from the fighting in a churchyard. Nevers is dead, and in order to marry the injured Raoul, Valentine disavows her Catholicism. Marcel conducts an impromtu wedding, but Catholic soldiers pursue them to the street.

SCENE 3 *A street*

Saint-Bris finds Valentine and Marcel comforting the dying Raoul. He orders the execution of all three, not recognizing his daughter until she is dead. The fighting continues until Queen Marguérite intervenes.

IDOMENEO, RE DI CRETA
(Idomeneus, King of Crete)
Wolfgang Amadeus Mozart (1756-1791)

THREE ACTS. LIBRETTO BY GIAMBATTISTA VARESCO, AFTER ANTOINE DANCHET'S *IDOMENÉE*. PREMIERE IN MUNICH, 29 JANUARY 1781.

Idomeneo, Mozart's first mature opera, came about as the result of a prestigious commission to compose for the court in Munich. Inspired by the possibilities there—a magnificent theatre and a legendary orchestra—he was able to write on a grand scale, producing what is generally held to be the greatest opera seria. He did so by undermining some of the strict conventions of opera seria, and by blending the genre with elements of French opera, emphasizing the choruses and ballet. The story of Idomeneus—king of Crete during the period of the Trojan War—is given noble, human depth in Mozart's music. The opera was greatly revised for a 1786 Vienna concert performance.

CHARACTERS

Ilia, a Trojan princess (SOPRANO); *Elettra* (Electra), a Greek princess (SOPRANO); *Idamante* (Idamantes), Idomeneo's son (SOPRANO or TENOR); *Idomeneo* (Idomeneus), King of Crete (TENOR); *Arbace* (Arbaces), confidant of Arbace (TENOR); *High Priest of Neptune* (TENOR); *Voice of Neptune* (BASS)

ACT I
Ilia's apartments in the royal palace

The Trojan princess Ilia languishes in Crete, having been carried off as a prisoner. She laments her fate, and is tormented by an inner struggle: she feels loyalty towards her homeland and father, King Priam, but also recognizes her growing love for her captor, Idamantes, whom she is sure loves his compatriot Electra rather than her. Idamantes enters, assures Ilia of his love for her, and proves it by releasing the Trojan prisoners. His move drives Electra into a jealous rage, which is interrupted by Arbace's bringing a report of Idomeneus's death. Electra now sees her chances of marrying Idamantes diminishing, and angrily invokes the Furies.

A sea-shore

The cries of storm-tossed sailors can be heard. Neptune rises up to calm the sea, but spares Idomeneus only on condition that he sacrifices the first person he meets. A victim appears on the shore: it is his son, Idamantes. Idomeneus flees in horror, leaving his son upset at his rejection. The Cretan people praise Neptune's apparent benevolence.

ACT II
The royal apartments

Idomeneus admits to Arbace the vow he has taken, and is advised to send Idamantes out of the country, to accompany Electra back to her home. Ilia comes to Idomeneus, to accept him as a second father, and the King's realization that his vow will ruin two lives increases his despair. Electra, meanwhile, is happy at the prospect of embarking with Idamantes.

The port of Sidon

Idamante and Electra bid Idomeneo farewell, but a storm breaks before they can sail. The people recognize the storm as a symbol of Neptune's anger, and Idomeneus admits his guilt. The crowd scatters, confused.

ACT III

The royal gardens

Ilia bids the breezes carry her message of love to Idamantes. He comes to Ilia, explaining that he is off to fight the sea monster that has been wreaking havoc. The lovers are interrupted by Idomeneus and Electra, and all four express their varied emotions. Arbaces announces that the people, led by the High Priest of Neptune, are threatening revolt and demand to speak to Idomeneus.

A square in front of the palace

On behalf of the suffering people, the High Priest demands that Idomeneus fulfils his vow.

The temple of Neptune

Preparations are made for the sacrifice. Jubilant sounds are heard, indicating that Idamantes has killed the monster, but the victor returns and offers himself as the sacrificial victim. As Idomeneus is about to strike the blow, Ilia intervenes and offers herself in his place. But Neptune is satisfied, and commands Idomeneus to abdicate in favour of the lovers. Electra departs in a rage. Idomeneus accepts willingly the new order, and all celebrate.

L'INCORONAZIONE DI POPPEA
(The Coronation of Poppaea)
Claudio Monteverdi (1567-1643)

PROLOGUE AND THREE ACTS. LIBRETTO BY GIOVANNI FRANCESCO BUSENELLO, BASED PRIMARILY ON TACITUS AND SUETONIUS. PREMIERE IN VENICE, AUTUMN 1643.

L'incoronazione di Poppea has long been held to be Monteverdi's last opera, the crowning glory of his long career. Now, scholars are troubled by its authorship and by establishing an 'authentic' text. Neither of the two surviving manuscripts is in the composer's hand, and no-one can be certain how much of the opera was written by Monteverdi himself, and how much of it was put together by other composers. But these questions need not worry audiences, for *Poppea*'s dramatic power—it is the first known opera based on real historical events, in which the emperor Nero divorces his wife and disposes of his general in order to make his mistress, Poppaea, empress—makes it an undisputed masterpiece.

CHARACTERS

La Fortuna (Fortune), the Goddess of Fortune (SOPRANO); *La Virtù* (Virtue), the Goddess of Virtue (SOPRANO); *Amore* (Cupid), the Goddess of Love (SOPRANO); *Poppea* (Poppaea); Nero's mistress (SOPRANO); *Nerone* (Nero), Roman emperor (SOPRANO); *Ottavia* (Octavia), empress (SOPRANO); *Drusilla* Octavia's lady-in-waiting (SOPRANO); *Ottone* (Otho), Poppaea's former lover (MEZZO-SOPRANO); *Arnalta*, Poppaea's old nurse (CONTRALTO); *Nutrice*, Octavia's nurse (CONTRALTO); *Lucano* (Lucan), friend on Nero (TENOR); *Liberto*, captain of the guard (BARITONE); *Seneca*, philosopher, Nero's former tutor (BASS); *Mercurio* (Mercury), messenger of the gods (BASS)

With *servants, soldiers, friends* of Seneca, *consuls, tribunes, cupids,* etc

PROLOGUE

Fortune, Virtue, and Cupid argue over their respective powers. Cupid claims that events about to be witnessed will prove her supremacy.

ACT I

When Otho returns from service abroad, he finds Nero's guards outside his house. It soon becomes clear that his lover Poppaea has betrayed him, and that she is with the emperor. Nero's guards gossip and grumble about life at the Roman court, but keep quiet when Nero and Poppaea appear in the light of dawn, and bid each other a languid farewell. Poppaea confides to her nurse Arnalta her ambitions for the crown, but the old woman urges caution. In her palace, the empress Octavia laments her fate, and dismisses her nurse's advice that she take a lover. The old philosopher Seneca urges her to be strong (advice which Octavia's page thinks fatuous), and is left alone to contemplate stoically his own death. Nero enters and tells Seneca of his scheme to send Octavia into exile and make Poppaea empress, but the old man's counsel raises Nero to anger. Poppaea intervenes, and suggests that Seneca be killed. When Otho begs Poppaea to change her heart, she dismisses him. He goes to Drusilla, who is in love with him, for comfort.

ACT II

Seneca is warned of his impending death by Mercury, and soon Liberto arrives to convey Nero's death sentence to him. The old man accepts the news happily. He calls upon his household to prepare the bath in which his blood will flow. Back at the court, Octavia's page and lady-in-waiting are enjoying a moment of passion when news of Seneca's death comes through; Nero and his friend Lucan rejoice. Otho, still in love with Poppaea, is joined by Octavia, who commands him to kill Nero's new mistress. Drusilla, so in love with Otho that she will do anything for him, agrees to lend him her clothes so that he will be disguised when he kills Poppaea. In her garden, Poppaea welcomes news of Seneca's death, as she realizes that there are now no more obstacles to her ambition. Arnalta lulls her to sleep. Cupid is keeping watch, and prevents Otho—who has entered disguised as Drusilla—from killing Poppaea.

ACT III

Drusilla is happy to think that her rival is dead, but she is soon arrested for the attempted murder. Brought before Nero, she pleads guilty in order to save Otho, and is condemned to death. But Otho confesses the plot and Octavia's part in it, and all three are sent into exile. Arnalta rejoices in her mistress's imminent coronation, not least because it will improve her own station. Greeted by the consuls and tribunes, Poppaea is crowned by Nero. Cupid descends from heaven with Venus to claim success, and Nero and Poppaea celebrate their love.

IOLANTA
Pyotr Ilich Tchaikovsky (1840-1893)

ONE ACT. LIBRETTO BY MODEST TCHAIKOVSKY AFTER HENRIK HERTZ'S *KING RENÉ'S DAUGHTER*. PREMIERE IN ST PETERSBURG, 18 DECEMBER 1892.

The one-act *Iolanta*, Tchaikovsky's last opera, was conceived as part of a double-bill and premiered on the same night as *The Nutcracker*. As a pair of works, they bear witness to Tchaikovsky's multi-faceted genius, and although the opera is now completely overshadowed by the ballet, it is a minor masterpiece. *Iolanta* is fragile, far removed from *Eugene Onegin* or *The Queen of Spades*, and direct comparisons with these are fruitless. The chamber-like proportions of *Iolanta* place it in a category of its own, and the lack of dramatic conflict is compensated for by intimate music of affecting poignancy. Above all, the young, vulnerable Iolanta is unmistakably another of Tchaikovsky's heroines, and it is clear that he identified strongly with her.

CHARACTERS

Iolanta, blind daughter of the King (SOPRANO); *Brigitte*, Iolanta's friend (SOPRANO); *Laura*, Iolanta's friend (MEZZO-SOPRANO); *Martha*, Iolanta's nurse, Bertrand's wife (CONTRALTO); *Count Vaudémont*, a Burgundian knight (TENOR); *Alméric*, the King's armour-bearer (TENOR); *Robert*, Duke of Burgundy (BARITONE); *Ibn-Hakia*, a Moorish doctor (BARITONE); *René*, King of Provence (BASS); *Bertrand*, gate-keeper of the castle (BASS)
With *servants* and *friends* of Iolanta, *members* of the court and the Duke's regiment

Princess Iolanta and her companions are in the castle garden listening to music. The plants around her are lush, but she cannot see them: blind from birth, she has been kept hidden by her well-meaning father and is unaware of her condition, believing that she has been given eyes only so that she may weep. Brigitte, Laura, and Martha try to soothe her with a lullaby. Bertrand ushers in Alméric, who announces that King René is bringing the famous oriental doctor Ibn-Hakia who he hopes can cure his daughter. Ibn-Hakia makes his diagnosis, and tells the King that Iolanta can only be cured if she is made aware of her blindness. Robert and Vaudémont have made their way to castle: they are hoping that the King will release

Robert from his engagement to Iolanta—they were betrothed in childhood—since he has now fallen in love with another woman. Neither knows of Iolanta's blindness, and although Robert finds the atmosphere strange, Vaudémont is enchanted by the sleeping Princess. He confesses his love to her. Once he realizes that she is blind, he explains the meaning of light to her. The King is horrified to discover a stranger at Iolanta's side, but uses the situation to force her into accepting a cure: he threatens Vaudémont with death unless Iolanta gains her sight, whereupon she willingly submits to Ibn-Hakia's treatment. Vaudémont asks the King for Iolanta's hand in marriage, and is at first refused; but Robert intervenes, and waives his claim to her in favour of Vaudémont. When the cured Iolanta is brought in, the King is happy to grant Vaudémont his wish. All join in praising God.

IPHIGÉNIE EN TAURIDE (Iphigenia in Tauris)
Christoph Willibald Gluck (1714-1787)

FOUR ACTS. LIBRETTO BY NICOLAS-FRANÇOIS GUILLARD, BASED ON GUYMOND DE LA TOUCHE'S *IPHIGÉNIE EN TAURIDE*, ITSELF DRAWN FROM EURIPIDES. PREMIERE IN PARIS, 18 MAY 1779.

Iphigénie en Tauride is widely considered to be Gluck's greatest opera, the fulfillment of his operatic reforms. Gluck's name is most closely associated with his reform of Italian serious opera (of which *Orfeo ed Euridice* is an example) as practised in Vienna in the 1760s. There he had gained inspiration from contemporary French opera, and in Paris from the mid-1770s, he confronted that tradition on its own territory, with long-lasting consequences that changed the course of operatic history. *Iphigénie en Tauride* exemplifies the plain, lyrical simplicity Gluck sought, in which he reconciled the demands of music and libretto: the conventional French dance episodes are harnessed for dramatic ends, and the economical, expressive orchestration is rich in psychological perception.

CHARACTERS

Iphigénie (Iphigenia), Priestess of Diana (SOPRANO); *Diane* (Diana), goddess of hunting (SOPRANO); *Pylade* (Pylades), Orestes's friend (TENOR); *Oreste* (Orestes), Iphigenia's brother (BARITONE); *Thoas*, King of Tauris (BASS)
With *Scythians, priestesses* of Diana, *Greeks*

ACT I
A grove in the temple of Diana

Five years after the end of the Trojan War, Iphigenia is living on the island of Tauris as a priestess of Diana. A violent storm conjures up inner turmoil in Iphigenia herself. As she relates to the priestesses, she has had a vision in which she saw the death of her father Agamemnon at the hands of her mother Clytemnestra (events which have happened since her departure from home, and of which in reality she knows nothing); she has also been reminded of her long-lost brother, Orestes.

The sorrowing priestesses are interrupted by the agitated Thoas: he has been frightened by the storm and, to appease the gods, orders Iphigenia to sacrifice two victims of a shipwreck who have made it to the shore. The two, Orestes and Pylades, are brought in, and Thoas informs them of their fate.

ACT II
The temple of Diana

The captive Orestes and Pylades await their deaths. In despair, Orestes is haunted by memories of how he killed his mother, Clytemnestra, to avenge her murder of his father. Pylades is unable to comfort his friend, and only Iphigenia's entrance calms him. She has come to question him, and he gives her news of the deaths of Agamemnon, Clytemnestra, and—he says—Orestes. He claims that only one member of the noble family, Electra, survives.

ACT III
Iphigenia's room

Iphigenia is stirred by the resemblance of the one of the prisoners to her brother Orestes. She decides to save him by sending him to Greece with a message for her sister Electra. But the two prisoners are unwilling to be separated, since neither will let the other die. Finally, when Orestes threatens to kill himself once set free, Pylades agrees to undertake the errand, and resolves to use his freedom to rescue Orestes.

ACT IV
The temple of Diane

Iphigenia, utterly against her will, is about to sacrifice Orestes when they recognize each other as brother and sister. Their happiness is cut short by the entrance of the angry Thoas, who demands that the sacrifice go ahead. He is about to perform the ritual himself, when Pylades returns with Greek soldiers and kills Thoas. Diana intervenes to stop further bloodshed, reprieves Orestes, and allows the Greeks safe passage home.

L'ITALIANA IN ALGERI
(The Italian Girl in Algiers)
Gioacchino Rossini (1792-1868)

TWO ACTS. LIBRETTO BY ANGELO ANELLI (ORIGINALLY FOR LUIGI MOSCA'S *L'ITALIANA IN ALGERI*). PREMIERE IN VENICE, 22 MAY 1813.

Rossini already had ten operas completed when, at the age of 21, he composed *L'italiana in Algeri* in just 27 days. Although Rossini always wrote with prolific ease, here he was under pressure to fill a gap in the schedule of the Teatro San Benedetto in Venice, and so adapted the libretto of an already existing opera. The result—which quickly overshadowed the earlier (1808) opera—was an instant success, and established Rossini as a composer of comic operas. It remains one of his most popular works, less for the absurd plot than for the brilliant, witty music.

CHARACTERS

Elvira, Mustafà's wife (SOPRANO); *Zulma*, Elvira's confidante (MEZZO-SOPRANO); *Isabella*, Italian lady (CONTRALTO); *Lindoro*, an Italian slave of Mustafà (TENOR); *Mustafà*, Bey of Algiers (BASS); *Haly*, captain of the Algerian corsairs (BASS); *Taddeo*, an old Italian (BARITONE)
With *women* and *eunuchs* of the harem, *corsairs, slaves, sailors*

ACT I

Elvira, wife of the Bey Mustafà, is suffering the rejection of her husband, and no amount of sympathy from her confidante, Zulma, or the court eunuchs, will help. Matters are only made worse when the bad-tempered Mustafà enters, announces that Elvira will have to marry his Italian slave Lindoro, and instructs Haly to find him an Italian wife. Lindoro has only recently been captured, and is lamenting the absence of his Isabella, but when Mustafà suggests that he returns to Italy, taking Elvira with him, he sees his opportunity of returning home. Meanwhile, there has been news of Isabella: searching for Lindoro, she has been shipwrecked on the Algerian coast, and along with her elderly admirer Taddeo (whom she passes off as her uncle) captured by Haly. Isabella is brought in, and immediately resolves to use her feminine wiles to defeat Mustafà. As Elvira and Lindoro prepare to depart for Italy, Lindoro and Isabella recognize each other. Isabella complains to Mustafà about his treatment of Elvira, and demands that Lindoro be allowed to remain behind as her slave.

ACT II

Mustafà is besotted with Isabella, and invites her to drink coffee with him. Once Lindoro has convinced Isabella of the circumstances of his 'marriage'to Elvira, the two plan their escape, to Lindoro's great joy. Mustafà's next attempt to flatter Isabella involves making her 'uncle'the Kaimakan of Algeria: Taddeo would like to refuse, but Mustafà's anger persuades him to accept. When it is time for coffee, Isabella requests enough for three: she plans to include Elvira in the party to teach her how to deal with men. Mustafà, along with Lindoro and Taddeo, watches Isabella prepare herself; when he goes in for coffee he is unable to get rid of the other men, and when the four are joined by Elvira, he realizes angrily that he has been tricked. Haly, alone, muses over the wiles of Italian women. He is soon to be proved right when Isabella puts her plan against Mustafà into action. She offers to admit him to the Italian order of the 'Pappatacci', model husbands who eat, sleep, and leave their wives in peace. Lindoro and Isabella prepare him for the initiation ceremony. A boat arrives offshore, which Mustafà assumes to be part of the ceremony. The jealous Taddeo tries to warn him that the lovers are escaping, but Mustafà discovers the truth too late. He begs Elvira's forgiveness, blesses the departing lovers, and all are reconciled.

THE ITALIAN GIRL IN ALGIERS
see L'italiana in Algeri

IVAN SUSANIN
see **A Life for the Tsar**

JENŮFA
Leoš Janáček (1854-1928)

THREE ACTS. LIBRETTO BY THE COMPOSER AFTER GABRIELA PREISSOVA'S *JEJI PASTORKYNA* (HER STEPDAUGHTER). PREMIERE IN BRNO, 21 JANUARY 1904.

Though Janáček was born in 1854, his late development as a composer and his musical language mean that he is thought of as a twentieth-century figure. Indeed, it was the premiere of *Jenůfa* in 1904—when the composer was 50—that effectively launched his career. The opera is set in an oppressive rural community. Janáček had for several years been studying folk-lore and the sounds of human speech and, although there are no direct quotations of folk music in *Jenůfa*, 'speech-melody' pervades the score and the rural setting is beautifully evoked; even the turning mill-wheel has its motif.

CHARACTERS
Kostelnička Buryjovka, Grandmother Buryja's daughter-in-law (SOPRANO); *Jenůfa*, the Kostelnička's stepdaughter (SOPRANO); *Barena*, servant at the mill (SOPRANO); *Jano*, shepherd boy (SOPRANO); *Mayor's Wife* (MEZZO-SOPRANO); *Karolka*, Mayor's daughter (MEZZO-SOPRANO); *Grandmother Buryjovka*, former owner of the mill (CONTRALTO); *Laca Klemen*, stepbrother of Steva Buryja, grandson of Grandmother Buryjovka (TENOR); *Števa Buryja* stepbrother of Laca Kleen (TENOR); *Foreman at the mill* (BARITONE); *Mayor* (BASS)
With *recruits, musicians, country-people*

ACT I
The Buryovka mill; late afternoon
Both Števa and his half-brother Laca are in love with their cousin Jenůfa. She is anxiously waiting to see whether or not Števa has been conscripted: if he is not to go into the army, they will be able to marry without revealing that she is pregnant with his child. Three people wait with her: Jano, the herd-boy she has taught to read, her Grandmother Buryjovka, and the jealous Laca, who taunts her. Even before the recruits appear, Jenůfa hears from the foreman that Števa has not been conscripted. The lovers are overjoyed, but when the drunken Števa leads Jenůfa in a riotous dance, her stern stepmother, the Kostelnička ('female sacristan'), intervenes: she announces that the couple can marry only after a year, and only if Števa gives up drinking. When all have dispersed, Laca tries to convince the shattered Jenůfa of the shallowness of Števa's emotions: he believes that his half-brother loves her only for her looks, and—as if out to prove it—slashes her cheek.

ACT II
The Kostelnička's living-room; five months later, winter
Jenůfa has given birth in secret, tended by the Kostelnička.

She gives Jenůfa a sleeping potion. Števa has been called in by the Kostelnička, but is unwilling to look at his child and refuses to marry Jenůfa, now that her cheek is scarred; he also admits that he is now engaged to Karolka, the Mayor's daughter. Laca—who, along with the other villagers, believed Jenůfa to be in Vienna—comes to see the Kostelnička, and begs her to let him marry Jenůfa. He is told about the baby's birth, but that the boy is dead. Once he has gone, the Kostelnička resolves to kill the baby to save the family's honour: she takes him from the sleeping Jenůfa, and goes to drown him in the stream. When Jenůfa wakes, she is told the news that she has been unconscious for two days, during which time the baby died. When she learns that Števa is going to marry another, she decides to accept Laca.

ACT III
The Kostelnicka's cottage; two months later
The Kostelnička, though haunted by her guilty secret, is overseeing preparations for Jenůfa's wedding. Villagers—even the Mayor and his wife, Števa and Karolka—come to wish Jenůfa well, and Grandmother Buryjovka gives her blessing. The Kostelnička is about to do the same when an uproar is heard outside: the corpse of a baby has been found under the ice. Jenůfa recognizes it as hers, and fears the crowd, who assume that she is the murderer. The Kostelnička confesses, and Jenůfa tries to understand the motives of her step-mother, who is taken away to court. Karolka breaks off her engagement to Števa. Jenůfa and Laca are left alone: she fears that he may reject her in these circumstances, but he remains devoted. Jenůfa sees that happiness has come out of all her pain.

JULIUS CAESAR
see **Giulio Cesare**

KATERINA ISMAILOVA
see **Lady Macbeth of Mtsensk**

KATYA KABANOVA
Leoš Janáček (1854-1928)

THREE ACTS. LIBRETTO BY THE COMPOSER AFTER ALEXANDER OSTROVSKY'S *THE STORM*. PREMIERE IN BRNO, 23 NOVEMBER 1921.

Katya Kabanova was the first of four operatic masterpieces Janáček wrote in his sixties—it was followed by *The Cunning Little Vixen*, *The Makropoulos Case*, and *From the House of the Dead*—inspired by his friendship with Kamila Stösslová, and after the long-overdue first production of *Jenůfa* in Prague (1916) boosted his confidence. If such a multi-faceted composer can be represented by one work, perhaps *Katya Kabanova* serves best: it reveals his love of Russian literature, his deep humanity and concern for social issues (the opera depicts a stifling village community), and his identification with his tragic heroines. Janáček described Katya as 'a woman so gentle by nature a breeze would carry her away, let alone the storm that breaks over her'.

CHARACTERS

Katya (Katerina Kabanova), Tikhon's wife (SOPRANO); *Varvara*, Kabanicha's foster-daughter (MEZZO-SOPRANO); *Glasha*, a servant (MEZZO-SOPRANO); *Feklusha*, a servant (MEZZO-SOPRANO); *Kabanicha* (Marfa Kabanova), a rich merchant's widow (CONTRALTO); *Tikhon Ivanich Kabanov*, Kabanicha's son (TENOR); *Boris Grigoryevich*, Dikoy's nephew (TENOR); *Vanya Kudrjash*, clerk to Dikoy (TENOR); *Kuligin*, friend of Vanya (BARITONE); *Dikoy*, a wealthy merchant (BASS)

ACT I

SCENE 1 *On the banks of the Volga, in front of the Kabanovs'house*
Vanya and Glasha are admiring the river when the tranquility is shattered by the entrance of Dikoy and his nephew Boris, arguing with each other. When Dikoy goes off to find Kabanicha, Boris confesses to the disapproving Vanya that he has fallen in love with a married woman, Katya Kabanova. When the Kabanov family return from church, the repressive Kabanicha orders her son Tikhon off to the market in Kazan. She is jealous of the attention he has been paying her daughter-in-law, Katya, and feels neglected. Soon Kabanicha turns on Katya herself. Only Varvara is prepared to stand up for Katya, and she urges Tikhon not to be so meek towards his mother.

SCENE 2 *In the Kabanovs' house*
Katya tells Varvara how unhappy she is, and how free she felt before her marriage. She admits to the sympathetic Varvara that she loves another man. Tikhon is ready to leave on his trip, and Katya begs him to take her with him. He refuses, and fails to understand when she asks him to make her swear an oath to remain faithful. Only his domineering mother can make him administer that oath. Kabanicha scolds Katya for embracing her departing husband in public, but then forces her son to bid his mother goodbye.

ACT II

SCENE 1 *In the Kabanovs' house*
Katya, Varvara, and Kabanicha are sewing, and the old woman complains to Katya that she does not seem to be missing her husband. Varvara plans to help Katya meet Boris, and gives her the key to the garden gate, should she wish to come to an assignation that night. Katya is frightened to give in to her emotions, but soon succumbs. The drunken Dikoy visits Kabanicha, hoping for chastisement for all his sins.

SCENE 2 *Beyond the Kabanovs'garden gate, on a summer night*
Varvara has not only arranged for Katya and Boris to meet; she has organized a rendezvous of her own, with Vanya. Vanya and Boris arrive before the women, and Vanya warns his companion about ruining a married woman. When they

meet, the contrast between the two couples is great: Katya and Boris are unable to enjoy their guilty love, but the others are carefree.

ACT III

SCENE 1 *At a ruined building overlooking the Volga*

Vanya and Kuligin take shelter from a heavy storm, and see that the walls protecting them are decorated with murals depicting sinners in hell. Other villagers come to shelter, including Dikoy, who is sure that thunderstorms are a sign of God's punishment. Next to appear is Varvara, who has come to warn Boris of Tikhon's unexpected return. She tries to calm Katya, but to not avail: at the height of the storm, and under pressure from Kabanicha, Katya confesses everything and flees from the villagers.

SCENE 2 *On the banks of the Volga*

A search-party, led by Tikhon, is looking for Katya. Varvara and Vanya decide to escape their oppressive life in the village by running away to Moscow. The tormented Katya appears, and is able only to think of Boris, whose life she fears she has ruined. Before long he finds her, and bids her farewell: as he explains, his uncle is sending him to Siberia. She realizes that she will find peace only in her grave, and drowns herself in the Volga. Her body is pulled from the river, and Tikhon blames his mother for driving Katya to her death. The callous Kabanicha simply thanks the villagers for their help.

KHOVANSHCHINA (The Khovansky Affair)
Modest Mussorgsky (1839-1881)

FIVE ACTS. LIBRETTO BY THE COMPOSER AND VLADIMIR VAILY'EVICH STASOV, FROM HISTORICAL SOURCES. PREMIERE IN ST PETERSBURG, 21 FEBRUARY 1886.

Because Mussorgsky's name is immortally linked with *Boris Godunov*, four other operas the composer left in various states of completeness at his death are often overlooked. These are *Salammbô*, *Marriage*, *Sorochinsky Fair*, and—most importantly—*Khovanshchina*, a second national epic on the lines of *Boris*, which Rimsky-Korsakov completed and orchestrated, thus ensuring its place in the repertory today. (Since then other composers, notably Shostakovich, have also provided editions.) *Khovanshchina*'s contemporary resonance—it depicts a Russia racked by conflict between old and new orders—is inescapable. The opera is set approximately seventy-five years later than *Boris Godunov*, early in the reign of Peter the Great: the title refers to a plot by the Khovansky princes (father Ivan, and son Andrey) against the Tsar. Though a detailed knowledge of the historical background is of little help in understanding the opera—real events are conflated and imaginary characters introduced—it should be noted that this period saw the violent repression of a sect, the Old Believers, which opposed the religious reforms of the Orthodox Church. Rather than face persecution by the state, large numbers resorted to mass suicide, usually by burning.

CHARACTERS

Emma, a young girl from the German quarter (SOPRANO); *Susanna*, a member of the Old Believers (SOPRANO); *Marfa*, a young widow, member of the Old Believers (MEZZO-SOPRANO); *Prince Andrey Khovansky*, Ivan's son (TENOR); *Prince Vasily Golitsin* (TENOR); *A Scrivener* (TENOR); *Streshnev*, a young boyar (TENOR); *The Boyar Shaklovity* (BARITONE); *Kuzka*, a musketeer (BARITONE); *Prince Ivan Khovansky*, leader of the Streltsy musketeers (BASS); *Dosifey*, leader of the Old Believers (BASS); *Varsonofiev*, Golitsin's attendant (BASS); *Pastor* (BASS) With *musketeers* and *wives, refugees, Old Believers, maid-in-waiting* and *Persian slaves* to Prince Ivan Khovansky, Peter the Great's *guard, crowd*

ACT I

Red Square in Moscow

Dawn over the Moscow River (depicted in the orchestral prelude) reveals a group of Streltsy (musketeers, under the command of Ivan Khovansky) on guard outside the Kremlin. One of them, Kuzka, dreams about going into battle, while others brag about their recent rampage. As they march off, a Scrivener sets himself up on the square. Soon the boyar Shaklovity appears, and forces the Scrivener to take dictation of an anonymous letter to the Tsarevna (mother of the future Peter the Great), alerting her to Ivan Khovansky's plot against the crown. Muscovites enter, and get the Scrivener to read to them a poster listing the names of the Streltsy's victims. All are filled with horror, but when Khovansky enters, many are taken in by his pledge to protect the Tsarevna. Meanwhile, Khovansky's son Andrey has been trying to force his attentions on a young Lutheran girl, Emma. She is saved only by the intervention of Marfa, Andrey's former mistress and a member of the schismatic Old Believers. Father and son are pitted against each other when Ivan declares that he desires Emma for himself, but the situation is resolved when Dosifey, leader of the Old Believers, entrusts Emma to Marfa's care. Dosifey leads his followers in a prayer for the preservation of their faith.

ACT II

Golitsin's study

Prince Vasily Golitsin is a shrewd enough politician to wonder if he can trust the love letter he has received from the Tsarevna. His attendant, Varsonofiev, announces a visitor: it is the Lutheran Pastor, who has come to protest at the Khovanskys' harassment of Emma, and to beg for Golitsin's help in establishing a German church. Both requests fall on deaf ears, and another visitor is shown in. Marfa has come disguised as a fortune-teller, and predicts Golitsin's imminent downfall; Golitsin commands Varsonofiev to dispose of her and her prophecies in a nearby swamp. Ivan Khovansky comes to Golitsin to discuss political developments, but their meeting degenerates into a quarrel motivated by the personal ambition of each. The power struggle deepens when Dosifey enters. Marfa has escaped death at the hands of Varsonofiev, and reports to the three men that she was saved by the young Tsar Peter's troops. The news of their proximity is enough to shake Golitsin and Khovansky, but worse is still to come: Shaklovity announces that a denunciation (his own, delivered anonymously) has alerted the Tsar to the 'Khovansky Affair', and that the Tsar is preparing to act.

ACT III
The Streltsy quarter

A procession of Old Believers passes through the Streltsy district of Moscow. Marfa, among them, muses over her continuing love for Andrey Khovansky; she is overheard by Susanna, who denounces her for her passion, but Dosifey comes to Marfa's defence. Shaklovity enters, and laments the troubles facing Russia. Around him, the drunken Streltsy wake up and soon become angry at their reproachful wives. All are diverted by Kuzka's entertaining song. The Scrivener runs in with news that Tsar Peter's troops have attacked the Streltsy, who immediately look to Ivan Khovansky for deliverance. But Khovansky is too shocked to take action.

ACT IV

SCENE 1 *Ivan Khovansky's estate*

The melancholy Khovansky has withdrawn to his estate outside Moscow. He orders peasant women, and later Persian slave girls, to cheer him with dancing. Meanwhile, he has had Varsonofiev flogged for bringing advice from Golitsin. Suddenly, Shaklovity appears and summons Khovansky to a meeting with the Tsarevna. But as Khovansky leaves, the triumphant Shaklovity has him murdered.

SCENE 2 *Red Square*

As Golitsin is sent into exile, Dosifey realizes that the fate of Golitsin and Khovansky bodes ill for the Old Believers; he and Marfa agree that the time has come for the Old Believers to burn themselves to death. When Andrey Khovansky comes in search of Emma, Marfa tells him that she has been sent away to safety, and that his father has been killed. He refuses to believe this, and summons the Streltsy. But they are now demoralized, and arrive carrying blocks for their own execution. Andrey persuades Marfa to lead him away to safety, but when Tsar Peter's troops appear it is revealed that the Tsar has pardoned the Streltsy.

ACT V
The Old Believers' hermitage

Dosifey knows that the Tsar's troops are closing in on the Old Believers, and resolves that the time has finally come for them to take their lives. Andrey, still searching for Emma, is reminded by Marfa of a vow of fidelity they once made, and accepts his fate on the pyre alongside Marfa and the other Old Believers. All pray as they perish in the flames.

KING PRIAM
Michael Tippett (b. 1905)

THREE ACTS. LIBRETTO BY THE COMPOSER AFTER HOMER'S *ILIAD*. PREMIERE IN COVENTRY, 29 MAY 1962.

Tippett composed the second of his five operas, *King Priam*, in a stark musical idiom—completely different in style and tone from that of his luxuriantly beautiful first opera, *The Midsummer Marriage*—as befits a work drawn from the brutal world of Greek myth. Nevertheless, there is respite from the violence of the Trojan War in moments of humanity and love—characteristic of a composer who has always addressed human issues with insight and sympathy. In one respect *Priam* is different from his other operas: it is the only one set in the past and based on a well-known story.

CHARACTERS

Hecuba, Priam's wife (SOPRANO); *Andromache*, Hector's wife (SOPRANO); *Helen*, wife to King Menelaus of Sparta (MEZZO-SOPRANO); *Paris*, Priam's second son (TENOR or BOY SOPRANO); *Achilles*, a Greek hero (TENOR); *Hermes*, messenger of the gods (TENOR); *Patroclus*, Achilles's friend (BARITONE); *Hector*, Priam's eldest son (BARITONE); *Priam*, King of Troy (BASS-BARITONE)
With *Nurse, Old Man, Young Guard, hunters, wedding guests, serving women, warriors*

ACT I

SCENE 1 *The royal palace at Troy*
Queen Hecuba has just given birth to Priam's son, Paris, when she is troubled by a dream: interpreted by an Old Man, it reveals that the baby boy will, in time, bring about his father's death. Hecuba resolves to kill the child; Priam is less certain, but finally realizes that his duty as king is to order Paris's death. In an Interlude, the Nurse, Old Man, and Young Guard address the audience on the moral issues raised.

SCENE 2 *The countryside outside Troy*
Priam and his son Hector are hunting. They meet a young boy whose physical prowess impresses them, and they offer to teach him the arts of war. But it is revealed that his name is Paris: Priam hesitates, remembering Hecuba's dream, and then accepts Paris as his son, regardless of what fate that will bring. A second Interlude brings further commentary, and informs the audience that Hector has married Andromache, and Paris has sailed for Greece, where he will fall in love with Helen, wife of Menelaus.

SCENE 3 *Menelaus's palace at Sparta*
Paris and Helen have consummated their love, and he demands that she chooses between him and Menelaus. She promises to leave with him, but Paris reflects that taking her back to Troy will lead to war. As he ponders these matters, the god Hermes appears and tells him to choose between three goddesses, Athene, Hera, and Aphrodite. The first two remind him of his mother and sister-in-law, so he chooses

Aphrodite, who represents Helen. The two elope, and thus trigger war between Greece and Troy.

ACT II

SCENE 1 *Troy*

Paris's adulterous affair has led to war. In the besieged Troy, Hector ridicules his brother Paris for not having gone to war against the Greeks. Priam intervenes, and eventually Paris follows his brother into battle. In an Interlude, Hermes conducts the Old Man through battle lines to the Greek camp, to see the hero Achilles sulking in his tent.

SCENE 2 *Achilles's tent*

Achilles is unwilling to go into battle because of an argument with his commander, Agamemnon. Patroclus reminds him of the Greeks' military plight, and they resolve that Patroclus should fight the Trojans dressed in Achilles's armour. In another Interlude, the Old Man asks Hermes to warn Priam of the threat posed by Patroclus.

SCENE 3 *Troy*

Hector has killed a figure dressed in Achilles's armour in battle. He is joined by his father and brother in gloating over the dead body, but they are surprised by the battle cry of Achilles himself, now stirred to fight.

ACT III

SCENE 1 *The royal palace at Troy*

Andromache, Hecuba, and Helen wait nervously for news of the war, and blame each other for the turn events have taken. They join in praying to their goddesses. In an Interlude, serving women discuss rumours of the expected fall of Troy, and confirm news of Hector's death.

SCENE 2 *The royal palace at Troy*

Paris breaks the news to his father of Hector's death. Priam reflects that the war has been caused by Paris, whom he should never have spared, but resolves to accept Fate.

SCENE 3 *Achilles's tent*

Priam goes to the Greek camp to plead with Achilles for the body of his son Hector. It is returned in a deal which gives Achilles the body of his friend Patroclus. Both men accept their destiny: Achilles knows that he will be killed by Paris, and Priam that he will dies at the hands of Achilles's son Neoptolemus. In an Interlude, Hermes prepares for the protagonists' deaths by reminding the audience of the healing powers of music.

SCENE 4 *Troy*

Priam is withdrawn. He is unaffected by Paris's announcement that he has killed Achilles, and refuses to speak to Hecuba or Andromache. He finds hope only in Helen, before going to his inevitable death.

THE KNOT GARDEN
Michael Tippett (b.1905)

THREE ACTS. LIBRETTO BY THE COMPOSER. PREMIERE IN
LONDON, 2 DECEMBER 1970.

The 'Garden' in the title of Tippett's third opera is sometimes a
literal outdoor setting, sometimes a metaphorical maze. Tippett
has described his opera as dealing with 'the loves and hates of
seven people in modern England'; certainly, it addresses contemporary issues, including marriage, homosexuality, race relations,
and the torture of political prisoners. Despite a jumble of musical
influences—including blues, a Schubert Lied, and a snatch of
'We Shall Overcome'; the orchestra includes jazz kit and electric
guitar—the structure is taut, and *The Knot Garden* remains one
of the strongest examples of modern musical theatre.

CHARACTERS

Flora, an adolescent girl, ward of Thea and Faber (SOPRANO);
Denise, Thea's sister, a freedom-fighter (SOPRANO); *Thea*, Faber's
wife, a gardener (MEZZO-SOPRANO); *Dov*, Mel's white friend, a
musician (TENOR); *Mangus*, a psychoanalyst (TENOR-BARITONE);
Faber, a civil engineer, aged about 35 (BARITONE); *Mel*, a black
writer in his late 20s (BASS-BARITONE)

ACT I Confrontation

Thea and Faber have invited a psychoanalyst, Mangus, to sort
out the adolescent problems they imagine their ward, Flora, is
experiencing. Mangus soon realizes that it is not Flora who
needs help, but Thea's and Faber's marriage. As therapy he
plans a series of charades from Shakespeare's *The Tempest*: Faber
will play Ferdinand and Flora Miranda, while two friends, the
homosexual couple Dov and Mel, will be Ariel and Caliban. As
Prospero, Mangus intends to solve their problems. Mangus is
delighted with the way the play-acting is proceeding, but tensions soon appear. The relationship of Dov and Mel is fragile,
and it does not take much for Mel to become attracted to Thea.
Dov rages in despair and latches on to Faber. All changes when
Thea's sister, Denise, arrives: as a freedom-fighter who has
endured disfiguring torture, she mocks the triviality of the others'preoccupations. They react with an outpouring of feeling.

ACT II Labyrinth

The characters are whirled around a labyrinthine maze by
Mangus's 'tempest', which releases their suppressed feelings.
Thea and Denise meet, then Denise and Faber, before Faber
attempts to rape Flora. Her screams alert Thea, who takes a
horsewhip to her husband. Faber and Dov—each humiliated
by a woman—comfort each other, but Mel appears and taunts
them. He has found his excuse for ending his affair with Dov,
and becomes attracted to Denise. It is left to the two most
emotionally battered, Flora and Dov, to comfort each other.

ACT III Charade

Mangus's plans culminate in charades he organizes for an

audience consisting of the sisters Thea and Denise. In a complicated series of situations, most of the characters come to
terms with their problems: Flora gains freedom and confidence, and Thea recognizes that Faber has matured. Only
Dov (possibly a self-portrait of the composer) remains isolated.
As a scene is about to end in chaos, Mangus dissolves the proceedings: he realizes that only love can solve human problems,
and the others accept this. Mel and Denise now leave together, and Thea and Faber reaffirm the bond of marriage.

KULLERVO
Aulis Sallinen (b.1935)

TWO ACTS. LIBRETTO BY THE COMPOSER, AFTER ALEKSIS
KIVI'S PLAY OF THE SAME TITLE AND THE *KALEVALA*. PREMIERE
IN LOS ANGELES, 25 FEBRUARY 1992.

With four full-scale operas to his name—a fifth is due to be
premiered in 1995—Aulis Sallinen is not only Finland's leading opera composer, but one of the most significant
practitioners of the genre living today. *Kullervo*, Sallinen's
fourth opera, was written in celebration of the 75th anniversary
of Finnish independence, and in it the composer returned to
the roots of Finnish culture: the basis of the libretto is Kivi's
tragedy *Kullervo*, considered to be the starting point of Finnish
drama, itself derived from the Finnish national epic, the
Kalevala. In spite of these sources, this is no 'fur-hat'opera: the
powerfully-drawn characters all have modern resonance, especially Kullervo himself, an angry youth trapped by society.
With its thick-textured blocks of sound, Sallinen's score suggests the primitivism of Finnish myth; the opera has only one
'number', the jazz-flavoured 'Song of the Sister's Ravishing'
sung by the Blind Singer, on which the whole plot hinges.

CHARACTERS

Kullervo's Mother (SOPRANO); *Kullervo's Sister* (SOPRANO); *Smith's Young
Wife* (MEZZO-SOPRANO); *Unto's Wife* (CONTRALTO); *Kimmo*, Kullervo's
friend (TENOR); *Hunter* (TENOR); *Kullervo* (BARITONE); *Unto*,
Kullervo's uncle (BARITONE); *Blind Ballad Singer* (MIDDLE RANGE
VOICE); *Kalervo*, Kullervo's father (BASS-BARITONE); *Tiera* (BASS)
With chorus of *observers*

ACT I

The Prologue describes the war which Kullervo's uncle Unto
has waged against his brother Kalervo. The feud culminated in
the destruction of Kalervo's home and entire clan. Only a single woman was spared: she was carried away by Unto and later
gave birth to Kullervo, Kalervo's son. In Scene 1, Unto is
haunted by his deeds. But his Wife reproaches him for having
spared Kullervo, who meanwhile realizing who his father's
murderer is, swears vengeance; his rage is directed at Kimmo,
his childhood friend with whom he has been enslaved. Unto's
Wife urges her husband to kill Kullervo before he takes his
revenge, but instead Unto sells the young man to the Smith as

a herdsman. The beginning of Scene 2 finds the Smith's Young Wife awaiting Kullervo's return from minding the cattle. That morning she baked him bread for lunch, but maliciously put a stone in it, which broke Kullervo's knife (the only heirloom from his father). In revenge, he has driven the cattle into the woods to be devoured by beasts, an incident related to the Young Wife by a passing Hunter. When Kullervo returns, she tries to seduce him, but he kills her with the remnants of the knife. Scene 3 is preceded by an Entr'acte in which Kimmo discovers that Kullervo's parents have miraculously survived, and he plans to reunite the family. In the scene that follows, the fugitive Kullervo arrives at his parents' house. When Kalervo discovers that his son is a murderer he disowns him, but his Mother urges him to stay.

ACT II

In Scene 4 (Kullervo's Dream), the Blind Singer's 'Song of the Sister's Ravishing' reminds Kullervo of how he met his long-lost sister: unaware of her identity, he seduced her, and when the truth was revealed, she threw herself into a torrent. In Scene 5 he relates the dream to his parents; now that it is impossible for him to remain at home, he sets off to vent his frustrations by burning down Unto's house. During Scene 6, while Kullervo is on his way to Unto's house, he is intercepted by Kimmo, who brings news of his parents' death. More determined than ever, Kullervo continues and with Tiera, the Hunter, and two strangers whom they meet, finally lays waste to Unto and his people. This accomplished, he sets out to find Kimmo. In the Epilogue, Kullervo finds Kimmo alone at home, deranged. He fails to recognise Kullervo as his friend. Kullervo sees Kimmo's insanity as a merciful respite from the world, and takes his life by self-immolation.

LADY MACBETH OF MTSENSK
Dmitry Shostakovich (1906-1975)

FOUR ACTS. LIBRETTO BY THE COMPOSER AND ALEXANDER PREYS, AFTER THE SHORT STORY BY NIKOLAY LESKOV. PREMIERE IN LENINGRAD, 22 JANUARY 1934 (AND, REVISED AS *KATERINA ISMAILOVA*, IN MOSCOW, 26 DECEMBER 1963).

Shostakovich's second opera came early during his career but remained his single most provocative work. After two years of success in the theatre, *Lady Macbeth* was condemned by Stalin in an anonymous *Pravda* article in 1936 and, with the exception of an operetta and an incomplete opera, Shostakovich thereafter abandoned the genre. *Lady Macbeth* was revised and rehabilitated in the Soviet Union as *Katerina Ismailova* in 1963, but Shostakovich was never able to complete his projected trilogy dedicated to the women of Russia, of which *Lady Macbeth* was intended as the first part. The libretto alters the tone of Leskov's tale of passion and murder in provincial Russia by painting a more sympathetic portrait of the heroine Katerina, and justifies her actions on the grounds that she is a victim of her oppressive environment. Shostakovich's music is vivid—the scoring is extreme and often blaringly loud—and the structure—in four acts, with orchestral interludes and big choruses—masterful.

CHARACTERS

Katerina Lvovna Ismailova, Zinovy's wife (SOPRANO); *Aksinya*, the Ismailovs's cook (SOPRANO); *Sonyetka*, a convict (CONTRALTO); *Zinovy Borisovich Ismailov*, a merchant, Boris's son (TENOR); *Sergey*, employee of the Ismailovs (TENOR); *Shabby Peasant* (TENOR); *Chief of Police* (BARITONE); *Boris Timofyevich Ismailov*, a merchant (HIGH BASS)
With *Millhand, Steward, Coachman, Ghost of Boris, Porter, Priest, Teacher, Drunken Guest, Sergeant, Sentry, workpeople, policemen, guests, convicts*

ACT I

SCENE 1 *Katerina's bedroom*
Katerina, wife of the merchant Zinovy, is bored by her existence and resents her husband. Boris, her father-in-law, complains that she is childless, but she retorts that his son is impotent. When Zinovy leaves home for several days on business, Boris forces Katerina to swear an oath of fidelity to her husband. The cook Aksinya tells Katerina that the new worker, Sergey, is a notorious womanizer, who even seduced his previous employer's wife.

SCENE 2 *The Ismailovs' yard*
The workmen, led by Sergey, molest Aksinya. Katerina intervenes, defending the equality of women. Sergey offers to put this equality to the test by wrestling with Katerina, and forces her to the ground as Boris enters.

SCENE 3 *Katerina's bedroom*
Boris, keeping a watchful eye on his daughter-in-law, prowls around as she is preparing for bed. After he leaves, a knock at the door reveals Sergey, who has come ostensibly to borrow a book. Before long—and after only half-hearted protests from Katerina—he seduces her.

ACT II

SCENE 4 *The Ismailovs' yard*
Unable to sleep, and aroused by memories of his philandering youth, Boris decides to visit his daughter-in-law, 'relieve'her loneliness, and provide the family with an heir. But he finds that Sergey has got there first, and carries out a bloody assault on the younger man, in front of the household and Katerina herself. He orders Katerina to bring him some mushrooms. She laces them with poison, and her father-in-law dies an agonizing death. A Priest is summoned, and conducts Boris's funeral.

SCENE 5 *Katerina's bedroom*
In bed, Katerina and Sergey are disturbed by the Ghost of Boris. When Zinovy returns home, he soon hears rumours of his wife's infidelity. He confronts her, and she summons Sergey's help. They murder Zinovy and hide his body in the cellar.

ACT III

SCENE 6 *The Ismailovs' yard*

While Katerina and Sergey are away at church getting married, the Shabby Peasant goes to the cellar in search of vodka. He stumbles on Zinovy's corpse, and rushes off to alert the police.

SCENE 7 *The police station*

The police are so bored that they discuss their own importance and amuse themselves by interrogating a Teacher. Most of all, they long for an excuse to attend the wedding party. When the Shabby Peasant arrives with news of the corpse, they can hardly believe their good fortune. They head off to the Ismailovs' house.

SCENE 8 *The Ismailovs' garden*

During the wedding celebration, Katerina notices to her horror that the cellar door is open: someone must have found the body. But it is too late for her and Sergey to escape—the policemen are already entering. The bride and groom are arrested.

ACT IV

SCENE 9 *The banks of a river*

Prisoners—including the convicted Katerina and Sergey—are marching to exile in Siberia. They stop for the night on the banks of a river. Sergey has lost interest in Katerina, and turned his attentions on the beautiful young convict Sonyetka. Together they taunt Katerina, who reacts by dragging Sonyetka into the rapids, where they both drown. An Old Convict asks, 'Why is our life so dark, so horrifying? Is this the life one is born to?', as the prisoners march on.

LICHT: DER SIEBEN TAGE DER WOCHE
(Light: The Seven Days of the Week)
Karlheinz Stockhausen (b. 1928)

CYCLE (AS YET INCOMPLETE) OF SEVEN OPERAS. LIBRETTOS BY THE COMPOSER. TO DATE, FOUR OPERAS HAVE BEEN PREMIERED: *DONNERSTAG AUS LICHT* (MILAN, 15 MARCH 1981), *SAMSTAG AUS LICHT* (MILAN, 25 MAY 1984), *MONTAG AUS LICHT* (MILAN, 7 MAY 1988), *DIENSTAG AUS LICHT* (LISBON, 10 MAY 1992).

In 1977 Stockhausen, Germany's leading avant garde composer, embarked on his magnum opus, a seven-opera cycle scheduled to take 25 years: the final work is expected in 2002. Each opera is named after a day of the week, and as the composer's biographer Michael Toop writes, *Licht* is an 'attempt to create a cosmic World Theatre which summarizes and intensifies his lifelong concern: the unity of music and religion'. The three principal characters are drawn from religious tradition, Eva (Eve, SOPRANO), the archangel Michael (TENOR), and Luzifer (Lucifer, BASS). Each character is also acted by a dancer, and represented by an instrument: Eve with a basset horn, Michael with trumpet, Lucifer with trombone.

In addition, each protagonist is represented by a melodic formula (analogous to a leitmotif), one of the many parallels with

Wagner's *Ring*. Like Wagner, Stockhausen aims at an integration of text, music, and action, both within each work and in the cyclical context. Like his predecessor, Stockhausen's work shows his preoccupation of socio-spiritual issues.

In barest outline, the complete cycle will be organized as follows, with different prominence given to the characters in each opera: Eve is the central figure in *Montag*, which deals with her birth; war between Michael and Lucifer dominates *Dinstag*; Eve and Lucifer motivate the collaboration in *Mittwoch*; Michael's awakening and learning is the subject of *Donnerstag*; Eve and Michael have the important roles in *Freitag*, which focuses on Eve's temptation; *Samstag* relates Lucifer's death; and all three characters are united mystically in *Sonntag*.

A LIFE FOR THE TSAR (or Ivan Susanin)
Mikhail Glinka (1804–1857)

FOUR ACTS AND EPILOGUE. LIBRETTO BY BARON GEORGY FYODOROVICH ROSEN, VASILY ZHUKOVSKY AND NESTOR KUKOLNIK. PREMIERE IN ST PETERSBURG, 9 DECEMBER 1836.

A Life for the Tsar was not only Glinka's first opera, but the first full-scale Russian opera. Glinka came to be called 'the father of Russian music', but although there are distinctive Russian traits in this early work of his, it is clear that he was still under Italian and French influences. *A Life for the Tsar* is set in 1613, during political turmoil following the death of Boris Godunov, and its epic subject makes it the forerunner of the great historical operas—such as Mussorgsky's *Boris Godunov* and Borodin's *Prince Igor*—central to the Russian repertory.

CHARACTERS

Antonida, Susanin's daughter (SOPRANO); *Vanya*, orphan boy, adopted by Susanin (CONTRALTO); *Bogdan Sobinin*, Antonida's fiancé (TENOR); *Polish Messenger* (TENOR); *Polish Commander* (BARITONE); *Ivan Susanin*, a peasant (BASS); *Russian Commander* (BASS)

ACT I
The village of Domnino
Peasants celebrate the imminent return of the Russian army from a campaign against the Poles. Antonida is waiting for her fiancé, Sobinin, one of the Tsar's troops, whom she hopes to marry soon. But her father Susanin has heard that Moscow is about to fall to the Poles, and will not agree to the wedding going ahead while Russia is suffering. Even when Sobinin arrives with news that Moscow is secure, Susanin remains resolute. Only the news that their own overlord, Mikhail Romanov, has been elected Tsar changes Susanin's mind. All rejoice.

ACT II
The Polish headquarters
A ball is in progress, and the high spirits reflect the confidence of the Poles that they are about to defeat the Russians. Suddenly a Messenger comes to the Polish Commander with

news of Romanov's election. Soldiers are immediately dispatched to the monastery at Kostroma, where the Tsar-elect is living, to capture him.

ACT III
Susanin's house

Susanin comes to join his adopted son, Vanya, who longs for the day he will grow up and enter the Tsar's army. Peasants arrive to congratulate Antonida and Sobinin, and the family expresses its happiness. After Sobinin has left to collect some wedding guests, the peace is disturbed by the sound of soldiers—Poles, who have come to force Susanin to lead them to the Tsar. At first Susanin refuses, but when the men become more threatening he agrees, having first told Vanya to ride ahead and warn the Tsar, while he will mislead the Poles. Antonida is horrified to see her father going off with the enemy; he, realising that he may not see her again, tells her to go ahead with the wedding in his absence. Sobinin organizes a party of men to rescue Susanin.

ACT IV
SCENE 1 *A forest glade*

Sobinin's men brave the snowy night in the forest, confident of success.

SCENE 2 *Gates of the Kostroma monastery*

Vanya arrives at the monastery on foot—his horse has died of exhaustion—and conveys his warning to the Tsar's servants.

SCENE 3 *A forest*

Susanin has led the Poles astray, deep into an enchanted, impassable forest. When the men rest, his thoughts turn to his daughter's wedding. But a snowstorm wakes the Poles, who angrily force Susanin to confess his plot. They kill him.

EPILOGUE
Red Square, Moscow

As the new Tsar is about to be crowned in Moscow, Antonida, Sobinin, and Vanya join the crowd celebrating liberation from the Poles, and relate Susanin's bravery. All join in praising their new leader and Susanin.

LIFE WITH AN IDIOT
Alfred Schnittke (b.1934)

TWO ACTS. LIBRETTO BY VIKTOR YEROFEYEV, BASED ON HIS OWN NOVELLA. PREMIERE IN AMSTERDAM, 13 APRIL 1992.

The contemporary Russian composer Alfred Schnittke—of German and Jewish descent, and now resident in the West—inherited to a certain extent the mantle of Shostakovich after the senior composer's death. But he rebelled more openly than Shostakovich against the conformism of Soviet musical method, as the confusion of musical styles (labelled 'polystylism' by the composer) present in his opera reveals. Yerofeyev wrote his novel *A Life with an Idiot* in 1980, but kept it hidden from the eyes of the Soviet authorities; Schnittke's initial inspiration to set this Gogol-like black comedy came when he heard the author recite it some years later. The story has been interpreted as an allegory of life under the old Soviet regime: Vova (Lenin's nickname) the 'Idiot'organizes life for those around him in a way that makes 'normality' impossible.

CHARACTERS

Wife (SOPRANO); *Vova* (TENOR); *'I'* (BARITONE); *Marcel Proust* (BARITONE); *Guard* (BASS)

ACT I

'I' is a good-natured man, without pretension. His eccentric Wife, also well-meaning, is keener on reading Proust than on doing household chores. For an unspecified misdemeanour at work, 'I' is threatened with expulsion from the Party, but in the end is punished by having to take in an idiot to share their flat. 'I' goes off to choose an idiot, and selects Vova from around a hundred lunatics. Vova can say nothing except the monosyllabic 'Ekh', but at first everything goes smoothly.

ACT II

One day Vova begins to create havoc, ransacking the couple's fridge, tearing up their books, and running around naked. Soon he seduces the Wife, who falls pregnant. Her decision to have an abortion upsets Vova, who turns his attention to 'I'. His Wife, jealous of the tenderness 'I' and Vova have found, becomes increasingly disturbed (she has visions of Marcel Proust), and tries to starve them out of the room they have adopted as their love-nest. She tries to get Vova back, even promising him a son, but Vova kills her and disappears. 'I' surrenders himself to the Guard of the asylum where he found Vova, and is admitted.

LOHENGRIN
Richard Wagner (1813-1883)

THREE ACTS. LIBRETTO BY THE COMPOSER. PREMIERE IN WEIMAR, 28 AUGUST 1850.

Lohengrin stands at the crossroads of German Romanticism. Like Wagner's three successful operas which preceded it— *Rienzi, Der fliegende Holländer*, and *Tannhäuser—Lohengrin* is firmly rooted in the traditions of 19th-century Romantic opera, yet in its structure and use of leitmotifs it hints of things to come, of the seamless, self-contained music dramas Wagner went on to write. As in all his operas, Wagner was himself the librettist: he drew his text from several medieval German sources, chiefly Wolfram von Eschenbach's *Parzifal* and the epic *Lohengrin*. Because Wagner went into political exile after the attempted revolutions 1848-9, he did not hear the whole opera until almost eleven years after its premiere, which was conducted by his future father-in-law, Franz Liszt.

CHARACTERS

Elsa of Brabant (SOPRANO); *Ortrud*, Friedrich's wife (MEZZO-SOPRANO); *Lohengrin* (TENOR); *Friedrich von Telramund*, Count of Brabant (BARITONE); *Heinrich der Vogler* (Henry the Fowler), King of Germany (BASS); *The King's Herald* (BASS); *Duke Gottfried*, Elsa's brother (SILENT) With *Saxon, Thuringian,* Brabantian *counts* and *nobles, noblewoman, page, attendants, serfs*

ACT I

On the banks of the river Scheldt near Antwerp

Fearing a renewed threat from the Hungarian army, King Henry has come to Antwerp to recruit soldiers from among his Brabantine subjects. But Brabant is torn by discord, and Henry demands an explanation from Friedrich von Telramund. Telramund claims that the late Duke's daughter, Elsa, has murdered her brother Gottfried, at the suggestion of her mysterious lover, in order to claim her father's throne; Telramund tells him that he thus broke off his engagement to Elsa and married Ortrud in her place, and is claiming the throne himself. Elsa is brought in to defend the charge, but refuses to answer, recalling instead the vision she had of a knight who will protect her. The King decrees that the dispute be settled by combat, but nobody dares face Telramund. Twice the King's Herald calls for a champion, and finally a swan-drawn boat appears, carrying her knight in shining armour. It is Lohengrin, who has come to defend Elsa. He offers her his hand in marriage on condition that she never enquires after his name or family. Lohengrin beats Telramund, but spares his life, and the crowd acclaim the couple. Ortrud frets about the strange knight who is frustrating her plans.

ACT II

Outside the castle of Antwerp

Telramund and Ortrud are in disgrace. She has exercised her evil power over him—it was she who plotted Elsa's downfall—and now he accuses her of discrediting him. She suggests that in revenge they induce Elsa to ask the forbidden question. She sees her chance when Elsa appears on a balcony, singing of her happiness. Convincing Elsa of her friendship—but at the same time invoking the help of pagan gods—she begins to sow doubts in Elsa's mind: can she really trust Lohengrin not to disappear as swiftly as he came? At dawn, the Herald proclaims that Telramund has been banished, and that Brabant has been put under Lohengrin's protection; furthermore, Lohengrin will marry Elsa that day, before setting off to lead an army against the Hungarians. First Ortrud, and then Telramund, disrupt the wedding procession with their accusation that Lohengrin defeated Telramund by evil means, and although Elsa pledges her love for Lohengrin, it is clear that the suspicion that Ortrud planted in Elsa has taken root.

ACT III

SCENE 1 *The bridal chamber*

The King blesses the couple, who declare their love. But their happiness gives way to hysteria as Elsa demands to know her knight's background. At the moment she asks him his name, Telramund and four of his nobles burst in. Lohengrin kills Telramund and promises to answer, in front of the Brabantine people, Elsa's questions.

SCENE 2 *On the banks of the Scheldt*
The King and his court assemble. Lohengrin announces that he can no longer lead the Brabantine army, and must now leave: he reveals that he has come from the Temple of the Holy Grail in Monsalvat, that his father is Parsifal (King of the Grail), and that he himself is Lohengrin. He bids Elsa farewell, and prepares to board the boat drawn by the swan, which has returned. Ortrud bursts in and boasts that the swan is Gottfried, Elsa's brother, transformed by her own spell. When the swan sinks and reappears as Gottfried, Lohengrin declares him leader of Brabant. Ortrud is now vanquished, and even though Elsa is overjoyed to see her brother restored, she so heart-broken at Lohengrin's departure—his boat is now drawn by a white dove of the Grail—that she collapses and dies.

THE LOVE FOR THREE ORANGES
Sergey Prokofiev (1891-1953)

PROLOGUE AND FOUR ACTS. LIBRETTO BY THE COMPOSER, AFTER GOZZI'S *FIABA DELL'AMORE DELLE TRE MELARANCIE*. PREMIERE IN CHICAGO, 30 DECEMBER 1919.

The Love for Three Oranges, Prokofiev's second opera, was the only one of his operas to achieve success during his lifetime, and it remains the most popular. Though it was first given in Chicago (early during Prokofiev's period of exile), in French, it remains a very Russian work: its overstated, knockabout humour is typical of the anti-realist Russian theatre of that time. There is little character development, and the score lacks set numbers like arias and choruses; rather, Prokofiev uses dazzling, brittle music to evoke the *commedia dell'arte* atmosphere of Gozzi's play.

CHARACTERS

Ninetta, a princess (hidden at first in an orange) (SOPRANO); *Fata Morgana*, a witch, and protector of Leandro (SOPRANO); *Nicoletta*, a princess (hidden at first in an orange) (MEZZO-SOPRANO); *Smeraldina*, Fata Morgana's servant (MEZZO-SOPRANO); *Princess Clarissa*, the King's niece (CONTRALTO); *Linetta* a princess (hidden at first in an orange) (CONTRALTO); *The Prince*, the King's son (TENOR); *Truffaldino*, a jester (TENOR); *Leandro*, the prime minister (BARITONE); *Pantaloon*, courtier and confidant of the King (BARITONE); *The King of Clubs*, ruler of an imaginary kingdom (BASS); *Chelio*, a magician, and protector of the King (BASS); *Cook* (BASS); *Farfarello*, a devil (BASS)
With *Herald, Master of Ceremonies, Eccentrics, Tragicals, Comicals, Empty Heads, Romantics, Little Demons, Doctors, Courtiers, Servants, Sentries*

PROLOGUE

Supporters of various forms of theatre argue, each group demanding to see their favourite type of entertainment. It is the Eccentrics who win, and they call for *The Love for Three Oranges*, which tells the story of the evidently incurable hypochondria of the King of Clubs's son. Throughout the performance the spectators will interrupt, commenting on events.

ACT I
The Prince lies sick in bed, with too many illnesses for the King's doctors to cure. Their advice is that his melancholia can be cured only by laughter, and the King orders Truffaldino to oversee the entertainments. The prime minister, Leandro, has no wish to see the Prince recover, and so opposes the plans. Chelio (the King's protector) in beaten in a symbolic game of cards by Fata Morgana (Leandro's protector). Leandro and Princess Clarissa plot to prevent the Prince's recovery, in the hope that Princess Clarissa will be able to claim the throne herself. Smeraldina, who has been caught listening to their plans, suggests that her mistress Fata Morgana be brought in to prevent the Prince from laughing at Truffaldino's entertainments.

ACT II
The Prince remains unamused by Truffaldino's lavish entertainments, and it is only when Fata Morgana—who has come to ensure that he remains glum—collides with Truffaldino and slips, that he begins to laugh uncontrollably. In revenge, Fata Morgana curses him to fall in love with three oranges, for which he will have to search to the ends of the earth. the Prince sets off on his mission, accompanied by Truffaldino, swept along by the devil Farfarello's bellows.

ACT III
The Prince and Truffaldino are in the desert. Chelio comes to their aid, and informs them that the oranges they seek are in the kitchen of the witch Creonta's palace, guarded by her fearsome Cook. He supplies Truffaldino with a magic ribbon for protection against the Cook, and Farfarello reappears to blow them on their way. The travellers reach their destination but are soon apprehended by the giant Cook. But the Cook is so taken with the ribbon that the Prince and Truffaldino are able to escape—with the oranges. As the pair make their way across the desert, the oranges become bigger and bigger. Soon they are forced to stop, and though the Prince sleeps, Truffaldino is too thirsty to rest. He cuts open an orange, from which a fairy princess (Linetta) steps. She calls for water, but when none can be found, she dies. The same fate awaits Nicoletta, inside the second orange. The Prince wakes to find two dead princesses, but nevertheless cuts open the third orange, to reveal Ninetta, with whom he falls in love. She is saved by the spectators, who provide water. Before the Prince can take her back to his father's palace, he has to find her a suitable dress. While he is away getting her clothes, Fata Morgana and Smeraldina appear: they turn Ninetta into a rat, leaving Smeraldina to take her place. The Prince is forced, reluctantly, to take Smeraldina back to meet his father. The King commands his son to marry her.

ACT IV

Fata Morgana and Chelio argue about each other's magical powers. The spectators intervene, allowing Chelio to head for the palace and warn the court of his rival's evil plan. The King, Prince, and Smeraldina enter for the wedding, only to find a giant rat sitting on the throne. Confusion breaks out, but Chelio uses his powers to transform the rat back into Ninetta. Truffaldino denounces Smeraldina and her accomplices Leandro and Clarissa, and all three are sentenced to hang. Fata Morgana helps them to escape, but the King and his court are content to celebrate the union of the happy Prince and his Princess.

LUCIA DI LAMMERMOOR
Gaetano Donizetti (1797-1848)

THREE ACTS. LIBRETTO BY SALVATORE CAMMARANO, AFTER SIR WALTER SCOTT'S NOVEL *THE BRIDE OF LAMMERMOOR*. PREMIERE IN NAPLES, 26 SEPTEMBER 1835.

Sir Walter Scott's historical novel *The Bride of Lammermoor* had already served as the basis for at least three other Italian operas before it was adapted for Donizetti. The novel's popularity (it was known throughout Europe) ensured Donizetti a great success, and unlike many of the composer's seventy-or-so operas, it has remained in the repertory ever since. Because it demands a great deal of florid singing from the soprano in the title role, for a long time it was regarded chiefly as a vehicle for prima donnas (to the extent that many 19th-century productions cut the final scene so as to end with Lucia's spectacular Mad Scene), but now the opera is appreciated as much for its musico-dramatic power.

CHARACTERS

Lucia (SOPRANO); *Alisa*, Lucia's companion (MEZZO-SOPRANO); *Lord Arturo Bucklaw*, Lucia's bridegroom (TENOR); *Edgardo*, Master of Ravenswood (TENOR); *Normanno*, huntsman, retainer of Ashton (TENOR); *Lord Enrico Ashton*, Lucia's brother (BARITONE); *Raimondo Bidebent*, chaplain at Ravenswood (BASS)
With *retainers, servants, huntsmen, wedding guests*

ACT I

SCENE 1 *The grounds of the Ravenswood castle*
Enrico Ashton is in despair over the declining fortunes of his family. He rages against his loathed rival, Edgardo, whom he imagines to be gloating at the Lammermoors' impending ruin. He is angry that his sister Lucia refuses to marry Arturo Bucklaw, whose wealth would help to save the Lammermoor family. The chaplain Raimondo tries to explain that Lucia is not interested in marriage because she still mourns her mother, but Normanno reveals that she has been meeting secretly with the enemy Edgardo, with whom she is in love. Enrico swears vengeance.

SCENE 2 *The park at the Lammermoor castle*
Lucia, with her companion Alisa, waits at a fountain for her rendezvous with Edgardo. She is frightened, and relates to

Alisa the story of a young woman once murdered on that spot by a member of the Ravenswood family. When Edgardo comes, he explains that he has to depart for France to fight for the Stuart cause. He wants to make peace with Enrico in order to ask for Lucia's hand, but when she insists on keeping their love a secret, they exchange vows and rings anyway.

ACT II

SCENE 1 *Henry's apartments at the Lammermoors*

Enrico and Normanno are making plans for Lucia's wedding to Arturo, and have forged a letter to persuade her of Edgardo's unfaithfulness. When Lucia rejects her brother's plans for her—she announces that she is engaged to another—Enrico breaks her resolve by showing her the letter. Enrico tells her that by marrying Arturo she will save the family from ruin, a fact of which she is also reminded by the chaplain Raimondo. Longing for death, she agrees to their plan.

SCENE 2 *The great hall of the Lammermoors*

Guests assemble to welcome Arturo to his wedding. Lucia, pale and dishevelled, is brought in and made to sign the marriage contract. At that moment, Edgardo bursts in and has to be restrained. When he sees Lucia's signature on the contract, he angrily returns her ring, and demands his back, stamping on it. He curses Lucia and leaves.

ACT III

SCENE 1 *The ruined hall at Ravenswood*

Edgardo is alone. At the height of a storm, Enrico arrives to challenge him to a fight.

SCENE 2 *The great hall at Lammermoor*

The wedding celebrations are terminated by the tragic news which Raimondo brings: Lucia has slain Arturo with his own sword. She enters, demented and covered in blood, and conducts herself through an imagined wedding ceremony with Edgardo before fainting.

SCENE 3 *The graveyard at Ravenswood castle*

Edgardo, unaware of Lucia's fate, has come to the cemetery to fight the duel with Enrico. Because of Lucia's apparent infidelity, he intends to die. A tolling bell conveys to Edgardo the news of Lucia's death, and he looks forward to reunion with her in heaven. As he stabs himself his last thoughts are of Lucia.

LULU
Alban Berg (1885-1935)

THREE ACTS. LIBRETTO BY THE COMPOSER, COMPILED FROM TWO WEDEKIND PLAYS, *ERDGEIST* AND *DIE BÜSCHE DER PANDORA*. PREMIERE (UNFINISHED, AS LEFT BY THE COMPOSER AT HIS DEATH) IN ZURICH, 2 JUNE 1937; FIRST PERFORMANCE WITH COMPLETED ACT III IN PARIS, 24 FEBRUARY 1979.

Berg left *Lulu*, his second and last opera, incomplete at his death. (He finished Acts I and II, but only a little of Act III.) At first his widow tried to persuade close friends and colleagues of the composer, Arnold Schoenberg and Anton Webern, to tackle the unfinished sketches, though both declined; after the Second World War—which had effectively put a stop to performances of Berg's music in Europe—Frau Berg began to restrict access to the manuscript, for reasons ostensibly artistic but probably also personal. Only after her death in 1976 was it revealed that the Austrian composer Friedrich Cerha had secretly completed the score during the 1960s, and the full three acts were first performed in 1979. *Lulu* has always been accepted as one of the operatic masterpieces of the 20th-century. Its lurid subject matter reflects the troubled inter-war Europe in which it was composed, and its music is largely written in the twelve-note, serial system originally developed by Schoenberg in response to the breakdown of tonality in turn-of-the-century composition.

CHARACTERS

Lulu (HIGH SOPRANO); *Countess Geschwitz* (MEZZO-SOPRANO); *Wardrobe-mistress/Schoolboy/Groom* (CONTRALTO); *Painter/Negro* (LYRIC TENOR); *Alwa*, Dr Schön's son, a composer (HEROIC TENOR); *Prince/Manservant/Marquis* (BUFFO TENOR); *Dr Schön*, a newspaper editor/Jack the Ripper (HEROIC BARITONE); *Schigolch*, an old man (HIGH CHARACTER BASS); *Doctor/Banker/Professor* (HIGH BASS); *Animal Tamer/Athlete* (HEROIC BUFFO BASS)
With *Theatre Manager, Clown, Stagehand, Police Commissioner, Fifteen-year-old Girl, Her Mother, Woman Artists, Journalist, Manservant*

PROLOGUE

The Animal Tamer welcomes his audience, and introduces the animals of his circus: Lulu, who represents the snake, is brought on.

ACT I

SCENE 1 *A Painter's studio*
Dr Schön and his son Alwa look on as Lulu's portrait is painted. Alwa takes his father off to the dress rehearsal of his new ballet, and the Painter proceeds to seduce Lulu. They are interrupted by the entry of Lulu's husband, a Doctor, who is so shocked by what he sees that he suffers a stroke and dies. Lulu is unconcerned, and happy to stay with the Painter.

SCENE 2 *A salon in the Painter's house*
Lulu and the Painter are now married. They receive news of Schön's engagement. A visitor comes to the house: it is Schigolch, an old acquaintance of Lulu (perhaps a former lover, perhaps her father), who is pleased to see how comfortably she is now living. Schön arrives, obviously still in love with Lulu, but wants to be free of her so that he will be able to live honestly with his future wife. Schön sees the Painter, who he tells of Lulu's sordid past. The Painter commits suicide. With Alwa, who has just arrived, Schön discovers the Painter's

body, and summons the police. Unperturbed by her new husband's death, Lulu taunts Schön about his engagement, and tells him that they will still marry after all.

SCENE 3 *A theatre dressing room*
Lulu is in her dressing room, preparing to go on stage as a dancer, and reminisces with Alwa, whom she tells about the Prince who wants to marry her. Soon the Prince arrives at the theatre, full of praise for Lulu. During her act, Lulu sees Schön and his fiancée in the audience, and pretends to faint. She is given time to compose herself, and Schön comes to her side; she pressurizes him into breaking off his engagement.

ACT II

SCENE 1 *A living room in Dr Schön's house*
Lulu has now married Schön, but still attracts admirers. The first to arrive is the lesbian Countess Geschwitz, who provokes Schön's jealousy. Geschwitz hides, and other admirers—the Athlete, Schoolboy, and Schigolch—enter and do the same. Overheard by Schön, Alwa makes his love for Lulu clear to him. Schön snaps, and confronts Lulu, handing her a revolver with which he urges her to commit suicide. She is driven to kill Schön instead, and pleads with Alwa to save her from the police.

In an Interlude, a silent film shows Lulu's arrest, imprisonment, and escape, which she effects by deliberately catching cholera from Geschwitz, and then changing places with her in a hospital.

SCENE 1 *The same living room, a year later*
Alwa, Geschwitz, and the Athlete wait for Schigolch, who plans to take Geschwitz to the hospital and free Lulu. The Schoolboy enters, having devised his own plan for her escape, but is chased away by the Athlete, who tells him that Lulu is dead. When Lulu is brought in, the Athlete is so appalled by her appearance that he rejects her. She and Alwa admit their love.

ACT III

SCENE 1 *A Parisian salon*
Discussion at the casino is of railway shares in which many of those present have invested. The Athlete proposes a toast to Lulu, but she is being blackmailed by the Marquis. The Athlete joins the Marquis in demanding money, and the situation is made more desperate by the Banker's news that the shares have collapsed: all are now bankrupt. Schigolch and Geschwitz distract the Athlete while the Marquis is away at the police, giving Lulu the chance to escape.

SCENE 2 *A garret in the East End of London*
Lulu has fled to London, and is about to begin work as a prostitute. Her earnings will keep Alwa and Schigolch. Her first client is a Professor, whose trouser pockets Alwa and Schigolch take the opportunity to search. Geschwitz arrives from Paris, bringing with her the portrait of Lulu she saved. Lulu's second client is a Negro, who argues about money and kills Alwa when he intervenes. Geschwitz is considering her return to Germany when

she hears the dying Lulu's screams: she goes to investigate, and is herself murdered by Lulu's last client, Jack the Ripper.

DIE LUSTIGE WITWE (The Merry Widow)
Franz Lehár (1870-1948)

THREE ACTS. LIBRETTO BY VICTOR LÉON AND LEO STEIN AFTER HENRI MEILHAC'S *L'ATTACHÉ D'AMBASSADE*. PREMIERE IN VIENNA, 30 DECEMBER 1905.

The enormous success which *Die lustige Witwe* enjoyed in the years after its premiere gave Viennese operetta a new lease of life. Franz Lehár inherited Johann Strauss II's mantle, and took the form into the 20th century: Lehár's blend of nostalgia, worldly wit, and irony was exactly what turn-of-the-century audiences appreciated. Like Strauss's *Fledermaus*—and many celebrated operettas—*Die lustige Witwe* is based on a French source (by one of *Carmen*'s librettists). Its score is packed full of fresh, irresistible melodies, of which the most famous is perhaps the 'Vilja' Song: sung by the widow Hanna Glawari to entertain guests at her party, it tells the story of Vilja, a mountain nymph in her Balkan homeland.

CHARACTERS

Hanna Glawari (SOPRANO); *Valencienne*, Zeta's wife (SOPRANO); *Count Danilo Danilowitsch*, attaché at the Pontevedrian embassy (TENOR); *Camille de Rosillon*, Valencienne's admirer (TENOR); *Baron Mirko Zeta*, Pontevedrian envoy in Paris (BARITONE)
With *Vicomte Cascada, Raoul de St Brioche, Bogdanowitsch, Sylviane, Olga, Krolmow, Pritschitsch, Praslowia, Njegus, Lolo, Dodo, Jou-Jou, Frou-Frou, Clo-Clo, Margot, Pontevedrian* and Parisian *society, musicians, servants*

ACT I
The Pontevedrian embassy in Paris
The Pontevedrian envoy Baron Mirko Zeta and his wife Valencienne are holding a party to celebrate the birthday of the head of their Balkan state. Valencienne is playing the perfect hostess, but Zeta is oblivious to the fact that she is paying special attention to her admirer, the French aristocrat Camille. Zeta is preoccupied with looking after Hanna Glawari, widow of a Pontevedrian banker and one her country's wealthiest citizens: to prevent her millions from leaving the country, he must ensure that she does not marry a foreigner. He instructs his attaché Danilo to woo her. It is revealed that Hanna and Danilo were once lovers, but that he dropped her when she became wealthy, anxious not to be identified with the men who pursued her for her money. Although he now prefers the girls at Maxim's, Danilo agrees to dance with Hanna.

ACT II
The garden of Hanna Glawari's mansion
Hanna's guests, in national costume, listen to her story of the faithless nymph Vilja. Zeta is concerned to hear rumours that Hanna is going to marry the Frenchman Camille. Meanwhile,

Camille has persuaded Valencienne to join him in the pavilion: as Valencienne is about to be caught by her husband, Danilo substitutes Hanna for the envoy's wife. Camille's protestations of love for Hanna convince Zeta of his wife's innocence, but also arouse Danilo's jealousy. He storms off, to Maxim's.

ACT III

Inside Hanna Glawari's mansion

To please Danilo, Hanna has decorated her mansion to resemble Maxim's, and invited girls from the cabaret. During a dance, Hanna assures the relieved Danilo that she never intended to marry Camille, but it is only when she explains that (in terms of her late husband's will) she will lose all her money on marrying again, that Danilo proposes. It transpires that the money will pass to her second husband, and Danilo is happy to accept his fate.

MACBETH
Giuseppe Verdi (1813–1901)

FOUR ACTS. LIBRETTO BY FRANCESCO MARIA PIAVE AND ANDREA MAFFEI. PREMIERE IN FLORENCE, 14 MARCH 1847. (REVISED VERSION PERFORMED IN PARIS, IN FRENCH, 21 APRIL 1865.)

Macbeth was the first of Verdi's Shakespeare operas (decades later he returned to the playwright for *Otello* and *Falstaff*). It never achieved great popularity during the composer's lifetime—even after substantial revisions in 1865 it remained relatively obscure—though Verdi counted it amongst his favourite works. *Macbeth* is now highly regarded, and held to be the best of his pre-*Rigoletto* operas, especially for its bold and imaginative instrumental music.

CHARACTERS

Lady Macbeth, Macbeth's wife (SOPRANO); *Lady-in-waiting to Lady Macbeth* (MEZZO-SOPRANO); *Macduff*, a Scottish nobleman (TENOR); *Malcolm*, Duncan's son (TENOR); *Macbeth*, a general in Duncan's army (BARITONE); *Banco* (Banquo), a general in Duncan's army (BASS); *A Doctor* (BASS); *Duncano* (Duncan), King of Scotland (SILENT); *Fleanzio* (Fleance), Banquo's son (SILENT)

With Macbeth's *Servant*, the *Ghost* of Banquo, a *Herald*, *witches*, *murderers*, *messengers* of the King, Scottish *nobles*, English *soldiers*, *bards*, *apparitions*

ACT I

SCENE 1 *A wood*

Returning from battle, King Duncan's generals Macbeth and Banquo encounter a coven of witches, who prophecy that Macbeth will become king and Banquo the father of future kings. The ambitious Macbeth feels uneasy to hear his secret longings out in the open, and even more disquiet when part of the prophecy is suddenly fulfilled: messengers arrive to say that the title and estate of the executed Thane of Cawdor have been given to Macbeth by the King. He is horrified to realize that complete fulfillment of what the witches fortold will involve him removing Duncan from the throne. The witches dance.

SCENE 2 *A room in Macbeth's castle*
Lady Macbeth learns of her husband's promotion and of the witches' prophecy, and realizes that without her encouragement he is unlikely to commit the murder that will put him on the throne. When he arrives, she urges him to act. Both greet the King when he enters (escorted by Banquo, Malcolm, and Macduff), but that night Macbeth's vision of a bloodstained dagger prompts him to kill the King. He returns from the King's chamber with a dripping dagger, and Lady Macbeth takes it back to the scene of the murder to smear the blood over the sleeping guards and implicate them. Banquo and Macduff come to wake the King and discover him dead. The Macbeths join the company in denouncing the assassin.

ACT II

SCENE 1 *A room in Macbeth's castle*
Macbeth, now king of Scotland, remembers the witches' prophecy—that the throne will fall to Banquo's line—and with Lady Macbeth plots to remove Banquo and his son Fleance.

SCENE 2 *A park*
Banquo and his son are heading for Macbeth's castle when they are set upon by assassins sent by the king. Banquo is killed, but Fleance survives.

SCENE 3 *A grand hall*
The Macbeths are hosting lavish entertainments. One of Banquo's assassins comes in to report Fleance's escape, and Macbeth becomes gloomy. Lady Macbeth attempts to lighten the mood of the party, but her husband is haunted by Banquo's Ghost. The guests become anxious, and Macduff resolves to flee to England.

ACT III

A gloomy cavern
In their lair, the witches are visited by Macbeth, who is desperate to know more about what the future holds. Various assurances are given but Macbeth is warned obliquely of the danger of Birnam Wood and told to be careful of Macduff; a vision of Banquo reminds him of the threat from his line. Macbeth faints, but is revived by the witches. When they have left, he is joined by Lady Macbeth, and they resolve again that those who threaten them must die.

ACT IV

SCENE 1 *A deserted place on the borders of England and Scotland*
Refugees, gathered near Birnam Wood, lament the fate of Scotland under Macbeth's rule. Macduff is devastated by news that his wife and children have been killed, and encouraged by Malcolm—who has arrived with his army—to attack. For camouflage they gather branches from Birnam Wood.

SCENE 2 *A room in Macbeth's castle*
Lady Macbeth sleep-walks, tormented by her crimes.

SCENE 3 *A room in Macbeth's castle*
The brooding Macbeth realizes that his fate is near. He is so
disturbed by reports of Birnam Wood 'on the move', that he
hardly reacts to news of his wife's death. Battle ensues, and
Macbeth acknowledges his defeat.

MADAMA BUTTERFLY
Giacomo Puccini (1858-1924)

TWO ACTS. LIBRETTO BY GIUSEPPE GIACOSA AND LUIGI ILLICA
AFTER DAVID BELASCO'S PLAY *MADAME BUTTERFLY*, ITSELF
BASED ON A SHORT STORY BY JOHN LUTHER LONG. PREMIERE
IN MILAN, 17 FEBRUARY 1904.

Madama Butterfly is the archetypal Puccini opera. Like
Puccini's heroines Manon and Mimì before her, Cio-Cio-San is
a doomed, fragile woman. The composer was immediately
moved by the subject when he saw Belasco's play in London in
1900, and it also provided the possibility of incorporating exotic
colours into his music—something he continued to do throughout his career, whether he was evoking the Wild West in *La
fanciulla* or Peking in *Turandot*. Butterfly's premiere was one of
the great fiascos of operatic history—the composer was accused
of plagiarising his own music and that of others—and Puccini
withdrew it after only one performance. Three months later,
after revision, it was triumphantly acclaimed, but Puccini made
further modifications before a definitive edition was published.

CHARACTERS

Cio-Cio-San (Madam Butterfly) (SOPRANO); *Suzuki*, her servant
(MEZZO-SOPRANO); *Kate Pinkerton*, Pinkerton's American wife (MEZZO-
SOPRANO); *F.B. Pinkerton*, Lieutenant in the US Navy (TENOR); *Goro*,
a marriage broker (TENOR); *Prince Yamadori*, a rich Japanese (TENOR);
Sharpless, US consul at Nagasaki (BARITONE); *The Official Registrar*
(BARITONE); *The Bonze*, Cio-Cio-San's uncle (BASS); *The Imperial
Commissioner* (BASS); *Trouble*, Cio-Cio-San's child (SILENT)
With Cio-Cio-San's *relatives* and *friends, servants*

ACT I

A house on a hill overlooking Nagasaki
Pinkerton, a Lieutenant in the US Navy, is about to marry
Cio-Cio-San, the geisha Madam Butterfly. He is being shown
around the house he has leased by the marriage broker Goro,
when his friend Sharpless, the American consul, enters.
Sharpless is anxious to dissuade Pinkerton from marrying
Butterfly, for he knows that the sailor does not intend to take
the ceremony seriously, in contrast to the bride-to-be, who has
even renounced her religion for it. Butterfly arrives and reveals
a few details of her life—she is fifteen, the daughter of an
impoverished mother and a father who committed hari kiri—
before going through with the ceremony. The celebrations are

interrupted by the angry intervention of the bride's uncle, the Bonze, who rails against her for abandoning her religion. When all the guests have finally gone, the couple express their love.

ACT II

PART 1 *Inside Butterfly's house, three years later*

Pinkerton has sailed back to America on duty, but Butterfly— cared for by her servant Suzuki—is confident that he will return to her and their son, Trouble, who he has never met. Suzuki is sceptical, but Butterfly sure enough to refuse an offer of marriage from the wealthy Prince Yamadori. Sharpless has heard from Pinkerton that he is about to return with an American wife, and tries to prepare Butterfly for the shock. But she is so excited by the first part of the news that Sharpless cannot bring himself to tell her the whole truth; he tries instead to persuade her to accept Yamadori's offer. As the harbour cannon announces the arrival of Pinkerton's ship, Butterfly and Suzuki decorate the house with flowers. As night falls, they begin their wait for him.

PART 2 *Inside Butterfly's house*

Next morning, Butterfly is resting when Pinkerton and his wife Kate arrive together with Sharpless. Suzuki is the first to meet them, and when she sees Kate she guesses the truth. Butterfly realizes what has happened, but not before Pinkerton, unable to face the situation, has rushed out. At first Butterfly seems to accept that her husband will not return, and when Kate offers to adopt her husband's son, Butterfly agrees. But left alone with her son, she takes a last farewell of him before stabbing herself. She dies as Pinkerton enters the house to fetch his son.

THE MAGIC FLUTE
see **Die Zauberflöte**

THE MAKROPOULOS CASE
Leoš Janáček (1854-1928)

THREE ACTS. LIBRETTO BY THE COMPOSER, AFTER KAREL ČAPEK'S PLAY. PREMIERE IN BRNO, 18 DECEMBER 1926.

Janáček's penultimate opera is based on a cruel play—called a comedy by the author, but really a tragedy—by his compatriot Karel Čapek, which tells the supernatural tale of a 300-year-old heroine who finally accepts her mortality. The role of Emilia Marty/Elina Makropoulos is a gift to the singing-actress, as Čapek's description of her makes plain: '...a tall, strangely beautiful woman. What so many lesser actresses try to be, she is: cold but dazzling, unique, impelling, mysterious, and always at ease.' The score—sometimes harsh, as befits the story—contains some of Janáček's most imaginative music.

CHARACTERS

Emilia Marty, a famous singer (SOPRANO); *Kristina*, Vitek's daughter, a singer (MEZZO-SOPRANO); *Albert Gregor*, Dr Kolenatý's client (TENOR);

Vitek, Dr Kolenatý's clerk (TENOR); *Janek*, Prus's son (TENOR); *Count Hauk-Šendorf*, elderly ex-diplomat (TENOR); *Jarolsav Prus*, Hungarian nobleman (BARITONE); *Dr Kolenatý*, a lawyer (BASS-BARITONE)
With *Cleaning Woman, Chambermaid, Stage-hand, Doctor*

ACT I
Dr Kolenatý's chambers

Emilia Marty is a woman with a long past. Born Elina Makropoulos in 1585 and given and elixir of life by her father, she has held a series of identities, each under a different name but always with the same initials, E.M. Consequently, she has an intimate knowledge of past events. She is also a singer, and years of practise have given her an unrivalled technique. For this and many other reasons, she fascinates all those who meet her. By co-incidence, a century-old lawsuit is drawing to a close as she returns to her birthplace, Prague.

In the long-running Gregor-Prus case, valuable property left by Baron Josef Prus in 1827 has been contested by successive generations of the Gregor family. Albert Gregor comes to Kolenatý's clerk Vitek for news of the case. They are interrupted by the arrival of Vitek's daughter Kristina, mesmerized by Emilia Marty's singing, which she has just heard at a theatre rehearsal. Vitek and his daughter leave when Kolenatý and Emilia Marty enter. She is anxious to be updated on news of the case, and soon reveals vital information. She claims that Ferdinand Gregor was in fact an illegitimate son of Baron Prus, and that a will in favour of Gregor survives; she also discloses information about Baron Prus's mistress—a singer Elian MacGregor. When the will is located, Prus protests that further evidence is still needed, and Emilia Marty promises to find it. Both sides in the case are now equally fascinated by her.

ACT II
The empty stage of a theatre

Those cleaning up the stage discuss Emilia Marty's triumphant performance the night before. The singer herself appears, but is rude to all those who around her except the old, senile Hauk-Šendorf; he thinks he recognizes something of his long-dead gypsy girl, Eugenia Montez, in her. When Prus brings up some complications—he claims that Ferdinand's mother was not Elian MacGregor but Elina Makropoulos, and therefore no Gregor can inherit anything from the Prus estate—it becomes clear that Emilia Marty's real interest in the case is self-centered: she not trying to help Gregor win, but hoping to retrieve the document detailing a potion which will give her a new lease of life (for the first time in her life she is beginning to feel her age). She discovers that the vital envelope is in Prus's possession, and persuades him to hand it over in return for a favour.

ACT III
A hotel room

Prus has spent the night with Emilia Marty and handed her the envelope. His disillusion at her coldness turns to horror when he learns of his son's suicide. Hauk-Šendorf and Emilia Marty plan to elope, but are thwarted by the arrival of Kolenatý, who comes to accuse her of forgery. Her trunk is searched, and reveals documents connected to her various personas. Eventually she confesses, telling everyone assembled that she was born Elina Makropoulos in 1585, and that she had passed on the secret of her elixir to her lover Josef Prus and is now desperate to retrieve it. But she collapses, and begins to realize that death would bring relief from her tortured existence. She offers the secret formula to Kristina, who burns it as the old woman dies.

LES MAMELLES DE TIRÉSIAS
(The Breasts of Tiresias)
Francis Poulenc (1899-1963)

PROLOGUE AND TWO ACTS. LIBRETTO BY THE COMPOSER, AFTER GUILLAUME APPOLLINAIRE'S PLAY. PREMIERE IN PARIS, 3 JUNE 1947.

Poulenc's first opera, *Les Mamelles de Tirésias*, was composed during the Second World War and premiered two years after its end. Many people in a country just emerging from that horror thought the frivolity of the work in bad taste, but underneath the highjinks—the story tells of how Thérèse tires of her womanly responsibilities and changes sex with her husband, who is left to have 40,000 children—the message was of the need for a higher birthrate in order to repopulate France. Poulenc drew on the French traditions of operetta and café music, and combined them in a score full of his customary charm and sophisticated wit.

CHARACTERS

Thérèse (SOPRANO); *Newspaper Vendor* (MEZZO-SOPRANO); *An Elegant Lady*, member of the audience (MEZZO-SOPRANO); *A Woman*, member of the audience (MEZZO-SOPRANO); *Thérèse's Husband* (TENOR or BARITONE); *Monsieur Lacouf* (TENOR); *Journalist from Paris* (TENOR); *Theatre Director* (BARITONE); *Monsieur Presto* (BARITONE); *The Policeman* (BARITONE); *The Son* (BARITONE); *A Bearded Gentleman*, member of the audience (BASS)

PROLOGUE

The Theatre Director urges the audience to 'make babies', before the curtain rises on 'Zanzibar' a town in Poulenc's imagination somewhere near Monte-Carlo.

ACT I

Thérèse is tired of being a woman, and longs to be president, a soldier, or a waiter. Her Husband's call for his meat only increases her determination to break free. She grows a beard and opens her blouse to release her breasts—two coloured balloons fly away. Her husband enters to find her completely transformed: at first he fails to recognize her, and thinks she has been killed, but she explains that she is no longer his wife and that her name is Tirésias. They are interrupted by a quarrel between two old friends who kill each other. This alerts a Policeman, who encounters the Husband, by now dressed in

Thérèse's clothes. He tells the Policeman that with women emancipated, the men will have produce the babies themselves.

ACT II

At a dance, the band portrays the noises of the over 40,000 children the proud Husband has produced in a single day. A curious Journalist arrives to interview the Husband, and assumes that he must be very wealthy to support such a large family. The Husband replies that it is the children who provide for him: one, Joseph, has already produced a best-selling novel. This prompts the Journalist to ask for a loan, whereupon he is kicked out. The visitor has given the Husband an idea: he turns one Son into journalist, who unfortunately immediately starts to blackmail his father. To feed his enormous family the Husband goes to get ration-cards from the Cartomancer (fortune-teller), who turns out to be Thérèse in disguise. The Policeman confronts her about her illegal work and ends up being strangled. Thérèse and her Husband are reunited, and the Policeman revives. To restore her womanhood, her Husband buys her balloons, and though she promptly looses them all ends happily.

MANON
Jules Massenet (1842-1912)

FIVE ACTS. LIBRETTO BY HENRI MEILHAC AND PHILIPPE GILLE AFTER PRÉVOST'S NOVEL *L'HISTOIRE DU CHEVALIER DES GRIEUX ET DE MANON LESCAUT*. PREMIERE IN PARIS, 19 JANUARY 1884.

Manon was Massenet's greatest success and also one of the composer's few works to have maintained a firm place in the repertory when other of his operas became unfashionable. Its initial success (so great that he provided a one-act sequel, *Le portrait de Manon*, ten years later) was partly guaranteed by the popularity of the novel on which it is based, the Abbé Prévost's *Manon Lescaut*, published in 1731. Before Massenet set it, *Manon Lescaut* had served as the basis for a ballet by Halévy in 1830, an opera by Auber in 1856; nine years after Massenet's opera appeared, it provided Puccini with his first triumph. Massenet's heady music is tempered with 18th-century pastiche—including minuets and gavottes—to evoke the period setting.

CHARACTERS

Manon Lescaut (SOPRANO); *Chevalier des Grieux* (TENOR); *Guillot de Morfontaine*, a nobleman (TENOR); *Lescaut, of the Royal Guard*, Manon's cousin (BARITONE); *De Brétigny*, a tax farmer (BARITONE); *Comte des Grieux*, father of Chevalier des Grieux (BASS)
With *Poussette, Javotte, Rosette, Innkeeper, Maid, Guardsmen, citizens* of Ameins, *travellers, gamblers*

ACT I
An inn at Amiens

In the courtyard of an inn, Guillot, Brétigny, and the actresses Poussette, Javotte, and Rosette are carousing. The coach from Arras arrives, and Lescaut prepares to meet one of its passengers, his cousin Manon. She is on her way to enter a convent, but is entranced by the brilliance of a life she has never experienced before. Guillot tries of proposition her, and Lescaut intervenes, warning the innocent girl about unsavoury strangers. Left alone when Lescaut goes off to gamble, Manon meets the handsome, young Des Grieux. They fall in love, and elope in the carriage Guillot had planned to abduct her in.

ACT II
The apartment of Manon and Des Grieux in Paris

Des Grieux has written to his father with news that he intends to marry Manon. This news placates Lescaut, who has come with his friend De Brétigny. Brétigny tells Manon that Des Grieux's father plans to abduct her lover, and that she might as well come and live a life of luxury with him. Manon is easily persuaded, and while Des Grieux is out posting the letter, she bids farewell to their cosy life together. Des Grieux returns and tells her of his dream, in which they were no longer together. Des Grieux answers a knock at the door and is abducted by his father's men, leaving Manon full of pity for him.

ACT III
SCENE 1 *The Cours-la-Reine*

Crowds are out enjoying the public holiday: Lescaut is running through his money in his usual carefree way, and Manon is promenading on De Brétigny's arm. She hears Des Grieux's father tell De Brétigny that his son is about to enter the priesthood and is to preach his first sermon at St Sulipice that day. Guillot has organized an entertainment, but Manon is preoccupied with the news of her old lover, and rushes off to find him.

SCENE 2 *The seminary at St Sulpice*

With the sermon over, Des Grieux is congratulated by his father. But he still resents his father's intervention, and longs for Manon. No sooner has Des Grieux returned to the service than Manon enters. She waits for him: they are reunited, and after a short struggle with his conscience, Des Grieux departs with her.

ACT IV
The Hôtel Transylvanie

Lescaut, Guillot and the gamblers are joined by Des Grieux and Manon: Des Grieux has realized that to keep her in style he needs more money. When Guillot loses to him, Des Grieux is accused of cheating; he is arrested, together with Manon, charged with being a prostitute.

ACT V
On the road to Le Havre

The Count des Grieux has intervened on behalf of his son and obtained his release, but Manon faces deportation. Lescaut and Des Grieux bribe a sergeant to let them speak to her. Left alone with Des Grieux she begs his forgiveness for having shamed him. She is too ill to escape with him, and dies leaving Des Grieux in despair.

MANON LESCAUT
Giacomo Puccini (1858-1924)

FOUR ACTS. LIBRETTO BY RUGGERO LEONCAVALLO, MARCO PRAGA, DOMENICO LIVIA, LUIGI ILLICA, GIUSEPPE GIACOSA, GUILIO RICORDI, AND THE COMPOSER, AFTER PRÉVOST'S NOVEL *L'HISTOIRE DU CHEVALIER DES GRIEUX ET DE MANON LESCAUT*. PREMIERE IN TURIN, 1 FEBRUARY 1893.

Manon Lescaut—Puccini's third opera but his first international success, it came after *Le villi* (1884) and *Edgar* (1889), neither of which have remained in the repertory—appeared just nine years after Massenet's popular opera on the subject. Puccini, understandably anxious to make his setting as different as possible to that of his French colleague, avoided some of the episodes Massenet set but ended up with a version that follows the original novel more closely. In the process Puccini used several librettists, and it was Luigi Illica and Giuseppe Giacosa—destined to write *La Bohème*, *Tosca*, and *Madama Butterfly*—who completed the text. It was with *Manon Lescaut* that Puccini found his voice as a composer, and the youthful, fresh music already bears the fingerprints of the composer's mature style.

CHARACTERS

Manon Lescaut (SOPRANO); *Chevalier Des Grieux* (TENOR); *Edmondo*, a student (TENOR); *Lescaut*, Manon's brother, sergeant of the Royal Guards (BARITONE); *Geronte di Ravoir*, Treasurer General (BASS) With *Innkeeper, Musician, Wig-maker, Dancing Master, Lamplighter, Sergeant of the Archers, Naval Captain, singers, townsfolk, old men* and *abbés, students, prostitutes, archers, sailors*

ACT I

A square in Amiens

Des Grieux interrupts some of his fellow-students, gathered on the square to enjoy the summer evening, with a song mocking the way they fall in love. But he himself is soon to be smitten: when the stagecoach from Arras arrives he is immediately captivated by one of its passengers, Manon. On her father's orders, she is on her way to enter a convent, but she nevertheless agrees to meet Des Grieux. It is the turn of the students, led by Edmond, to tease him. Two more of the passengers, Manon's brother Lescaut and the wealthy Geronte, fall into conversation, and Geronte hears of Manon's fate. He plots to abduct her, but his plans are overheard by Edmond, who alerts Des Grieux to the situation. When Manon arrives to keep her meeting with Des Grieux, he tells her of Geronte's plans and persuades her to elope with him in the old man's coach. Geronte is furious, but Lescaut philosophical about the developments: he advises him to patient, since he is sure that Manon will soon tire of living in poverty and will easily be lured by Geronte's riches.

ACT II

Geronte's house

As her brother predicted, Manon has indeed deserted Des Grieux and become Geronte's mistress. But she has begun to regret her move; when Lescaut comes to visit, she asks for news of Des Grieux and is told that he has taken up gambling in order to get the money he needs to win her back. She is bored by life with Geronte, unimpressed by the madrigal he has composed in her honour and the dancing lessons that are laid on. Tipped off by Lescaut, Des Grieux at last manages to find Manon: his reproaches soon give way to a rekindling of love, but the couple are discovered by Geronte. In spite of Manon's reluctance to abandon the jewels that have been lavished on her they prepare to escape, but their plans are thwarted by the arrival of the police. Geronte has denounced Manon to them, and she is arrested.

ACT III

Near the harbour in Le Havre

Manon has been sentenced to exile in America, along with a group of prostitutes. Her unhappy journey to Le Havre is depicted in an orchestral Intermezzo. At dawn, Lescaut and Des Grieux wait to attempt her rescue, but their scheme falls through. As the women prepare to embark, Des Grieux and Manon bid each other an anguished farewell. In desperation, Des Grieux begs the ship's Captain to allow to him join the ship as a cabin boy: the Captain takes pity on him, and Lescaut is left behind as they sail to America.

ACT IV

The desert outside New Orleans

Manon, on the run with Des Grieux from the French colonial authorities, is weakening steadily. She sends Des Grieux off to search for water. He returns, empty-handed, to find her loosing consciousness, and with a last assurance of her love she dies in his arms.

MARIA STUARDA (Mary Stuart)

Gaetano Donizetti (1797-1848)

TWO ACTS (SOMETIMES THREE). LIBRETTO BY GIUSEPPE BARDARI AFTER ANDREA MAFFEI'S TRANSLATION OF SCHILLER'S *MARIA STUART*. PREMIERE IN MILAN, 30 DECEMBER 1835.

English Tudor history was a rich source for Donizetti, whose over 70 operas include *Elisabetta al Castello di Kenilworth* (1829), *Anna Bolena* (1830), *Maria Stuarda* (1835), and *Roberto Devereux* (1837). Donizetti matched the tragic story of Mary Stuart with music of great power; indeed, there is hardly anything in opera of this period to equal the confrontation between the two queens—fictional, invented by Schiller—in the second scene of Act I.

CHARACTERS

Maria Stuarda (Mary Stuart), Queen of Scots (SOPRANO); *Elisabetta* (Elizabeth), Queen of England (SOPRANO); *Anna* (Hanna) (MEZZO-SOPRANO); *Leicester* (TENOR); *Talbot* (BARITONE); *Cecil* (BASS); *A Herald* (BASS)

With *courtiers, huntsmen, soldiers, servants*

ACT I
SCENE 1 *The Palace of Westminster*
Courtiers are excited by the rumours of Elizabeth's marriage to the French king, but her affections are more inclined towards Leicester. Elizabeth's indecisiveness extends to her dealings with Mary Stuart, imprisoned at Fotheringay: Cecil advises her to be wary of her Scottish rival, while Talbot begs her to show mercy. When Leicester arrives, Talbot solicits his help: he shows him a letter from Mary requesting an audience with Elizabeth, thus arousing Leicester's sympathies. When Elizabeth enters she is jealous to see Leicester holding the latter from one who in the past coveted both her throne and the man she favours, but Leicester still succeeds in persuading her to meet Mary.

SCENE 2 *The Park at Fotheringay*
Mary dreams of freedom. Leicester arrives, followed by Elizabeth, who resents the beauty of her younger rival. They insult each other, and when Mary calls Elizabeth a 'vile bastard' who 'sullies the English throne', the older queen calls in her guard and swears vengeance.

ACT II
SCENE 1 *Westminster*
Elizabeth is about to sign Mary's death warrant, but wavers. Cecil encourages her to act, and when Leicester's intervention convinces her of his affection for her rival, she commands him to watch the execution.

SCENE 2 *Fotheringay*
Mary takes the news of her sentence stoically. Talbot hears her confession, and Mary prays with her supporters (who include Hanna). The distraught Leicester watches as Mary walks towards the block.

THE MARRIAGE OF FIGARO
see **Le nozze di Figaro**

A MASKED BALL
see **Un ballo in maschera**

THE MASTERSINGERS OF NUREMBERG
see **Die Meistersinger von Nürnberg**

IL MATRIMONIO SEGRETO
(The Secret Marriage)
Domenico Cimarosa (1749–1801)

TWO ACTS. LIBRETTO BY GIOVANNI BERTATI, AFTER COLMAN'S AND GARRICK'S *THE CLANDESTINE MARRIAGE*. PREMIERE IN VIENNA, 7 FEBRUARY 1792.

Of the hundreds of operas written by Mozart's contemporaries, *Il matrimonio segreto* remains the most frequently performed today. It was popular from the first, as the legend of Emperor Leopold II ordering a repeat performance after dinner on the day of its premiere—two months after Mozart's death—suggests. The prolific Cimarosa (composer of about 80 operas) began and ended his career in his native Italy, but his international reputation took him for extended periods to St Petersburg and Vienna. The brilliantly paced *Matrimonio segreto* exemplifies his work, with its sunny music both echoing Mozart and anticipating Rossini.

CHARACTERS

Carolina, daughter of Geronimo (SOPRANO); *Elisetta*, daughter of Geronimo (MEZZO-SOPRANO); *Fidalma*, Geronimo's sister (CONTRALTO); *Paolino*, clerk to Geronimo (TENOR); *Geronimo*, a wealthy merchant (BASS); *Count Robinson* (BASS)

ACT I

Geronimo, a wealthy citizen of Bologna, hopes to marry off his two daughters, Carolina and Elisetta. But for several months Carolina and her father's clerk, Paolino, have been secretly married, and they are troubled over the best way to break the news to him. They hope that Count Robinson's proposal of marriage to Elisetta will appease Geronimo, and when the old man comes in, Paolino gives him Robinson's letter. Geronimo is overjoyed, but Carolina's lack of enthusiasm is misinterpreted as jealousy of her sister's romantic success. Talk of a wedding leads Geronimo's widowed sister Fidalma—who runs the household—to ponder remarriage, and she reveals that she has her eye on none other than the secretly-married Paolino. The situation gets more embarrassing when Count Robinson arrives and is immediately struck by Carolina's beauty; in fact he prefers even Fidalma to Elisetta whom he is supposed to marry. Even though Carolina tries in vain to put the Count off by listing all her flaws, her sister still accuses her of having seduced him. Geronimo comes to inspect preparations for the celebratory banquet he is to host later, and is left thoroughly confused by the accusations and counter-accusations of his household.

ACT II

SCENE 1

Count Robinson persuades Geronimo to allow him to marry Carolina instead.

SCENE 2

In desperation, Paolino goes to Fidalma to help; but she interprets his sighs as a sign of love, whereupon he faints. Carolina enters to find Fidalma trying to revive him, and imagines that he has been unfaithful to her. Meanwhile, the Count has been depicting himself as an ogre to Elisetta, in a vain attempt to persuade her to break off the engagement. Elisetta and Fidalma, having discovered that they share a rival, seek Geronimo's permission to banish Carolina to a convent. The distressed Carolina is being comforted by the Count, and is about to tell him the truth when they are interrupted by Elisetta, Fidalma, and Geronimo, who assume that they have caught them in a compromising position. Now Carolina must go to the convent, and Paolino is dispatched with a letter to the Mother Superior.

SCENE 3

Paolino and Carolina are planning their elopement. Alarmed by a noise, they retreat into Carolina's room, but their whispering is overheard by Elisetta. She imagines that it is the Count with Carolina, and invites Geronimo and Fidalma to help her trap him. But the Count answers their call from his own room, and it is Paolino who comes out with Carolina. They confess that they are already married. All is forgiven, and the Count decides to marry Elisetta after all.

MAZEPPA
Pyotr Ilich Tchaikovsky (1840-1893)

THREE ACTS. LIBRETTO BY VIKTOR BURENIN AND THE COMPOSER AFTER PUSHKIN'S *POLTAVA*. PREMIERE IN MOSCOW, 15 FEBRUARY 1884.

Mazeppa is Tchaikovsky's seventh complete opera and, like his two most successful operas (*Eugene Onegin* and *The Queen of Spades*), is drawn from Pushkin. Its historical basis—an unsuccessful bid by the Cossack leader Mazeppa in 1709 to gain Ukrainian independence—gives it a political significance not found elsewhere in his output. Tchaikovsky provided imposing music for the execution (Act II, Scene 3) and the Symphonic Picture depicting the Battle of Poltava, but balanced it with some of his most beautiful writing in evoking the tragic sub-plot. Maria, one of Tchaikovsky's most touching heroines, is driven out of her senses, and sings a haunting lullaby as the opera ends.

CHARACTERS

Maria, Kochubey's daughter (SOPRANO); *Lyubov*, Kochubey's wife (MEZZO-SOPRANO); *Andrei*, a young Cossack (TENOR); *Iskra*, governor of Poltava (TENOR); *A Drunken Cossack* (TENOR); *Mazeppa*, the Cossack leader (BARITONE); *Kochubey*, a wealthy Cossack (BASS); *Orlik*, Mazeppa's henchman (BASS)
With *Cossacks, women, guests,* Kochubey's *servants,* Mazeppa's *bodyguards, monks, executioners*

ACT I

SCENE 1 *Kochubey's estate*

Maria, preoccupied with her love for Mazeppa, is unable to join her friends' dances, and rejects the attentions of her admirer, Andrei. Her powerful father, Kochubey, is hosting Mazeppa, who takes the opportunity to ask for Maria's hand in marriage. Kochubey is outraged by the suggestion—the elderly Mazeppa is none other than Maria's godfather—and an argument breaks out involving the whole household. Maria is caught between her lover and her parents, and when Mazeppa forces her to make a choice, she resolves to leave with him.

SCENE 2 *Kochubey's house*

Kochubey plots revenge for what he sees as the abduction of his daughter. His wife Lyubov urges immediate action, but he has hatched a more devious plan. Kochubey remembers that, in happier days, Mazeppa confessed to him his plot to collaborate with the Swedish king in throwing the Tsar out of the Ukraine; he decides to denounce Mazeppa to Tsar Peter. Andrei sets out for Moscow with the message.

ACT II

SCENE 1 *A cell in the Byelotserkovsky Palace*

Kochubey's plan has backfired on him. Far from believing the allegations against Mazeppa, the Tsar has handed over to him both Kochubey and his friend Iskra. They are to be executed, but first Mazeppa's henchman Orlik interrogates Kochubey, determined to find out where he has stashed his wealth.

SCENE 2 *A room in the Palace*

Mazeppa worries how he will break to Maria the news of her father's death. When she enters and chides Mazeppa for paying her so little attention, he reveals to her his plan to secure an independent Ukraine. Unaware of her father's plight, she pledges loyalty to Mazeppa's cause. Lyubov comes to find her daughter, and brings her the news of Kochubey's impending execution. Maria is aghast, and the two rush off to intervene.

SCENE 3 *A field*

A Drunken Cossack entertains the crowd assembled for the execution. Kochubey and Iskra mount the scaffold. Maria and Lyubov rush up, too late to stop the deaths.

SYMPHONIC PICTURE *The Battle of Poltava*

Tsar Peter's troops defeat both Mazeppa's Cossacks and the Swedish army.

ACT III

Kochubey's estate, the night after the battle

Andrei, unable to take revenge on Mazeppa during the battle, has returned to Kochubey's estate, hoping to find Maria. He hears the clattering of hooves: Mazeppa and Orlik are in flight. Andrei tries to kill Mazeppa, but the older man is faster and Andrei is shot. Maria—driven out of her mind by the sight of her father's death— approaches, but Orlik persuades Mazeppa to abandon her. She sees the mortally wounded Andrei, and mistaking him for a child, cradles him as he dies.

DIE MEISTERSINGER VON NÜRNBERG
(The Mastersingers of Nuremberg)

Richard Wagner (1813-1883)

THREE ACTS. LIBRETTO BY THE COMPOSER. PREMIERE IN MUNICH, 21 JUNE 1868.

Though it had long been on his mind, Wagner composed *Die*

Meistersinger only after *Tristan und Isolde* and when he was halfway through the four operas of *The Ring*. It was his only excursion into comedy as a mature composer, but it is not a conventional comedy. *Die Meistersinger* is genial—though some have detected a dark side—rather than light, over four hours long, and deals with questions about the purpose of art. Set in 16th-century Nuremberg, famous for its guilds which included the Mastersingers, the story tells of a singing competition and how its winner is given the hand of a beautiful maiden. Wagner's subplot is more than simply a glorification of German art, and too detailed even to outline here; in making his point, the composer returned to a 'conservative' musical style, with identifiable musical numbers and set-pieces, he had long since abandoned.

CHARACTERS

Eva, Pogner's daughter (SOPRANO); *Magdalene*, Eva's companion (MEZZO-SOPRANO); *Walther von Stolzing*, a young knight from Franconia (TENOR); *David*, Hans Sachs's apprentice (TENOR)

MASTERSINGERS

Kunz Vogelgesang, furrier (TENOR); *Balthasar Zorn*, pewterer (TENOR); *Ulrich Eisslinger*, grocer (TENOR); *Augustin Moser*, tailor (TENOR); *Sixtus Beckmesser*, town clerk (BARITONE); *Hans Sachs*, cobbler (BASS); *Veit Pogner*, goldsmith (BASS); *Konrad Nachtigall*, tinsmith (BASS); *Fritz Kothner*, baker (BASS); *Hermann Ortel*, soapmaker (BASS); *Hans Schwarz*, stocking weaver (BASS); *Hans Foltz*, coppersmith (BASS); A *Nightwatchman* (BASS)

With guild *members* and their *wives, journeymen, apprentices*, young *women*

ACT I

St Catharine's Church

The knight Walther is visiting Nuremberg, where he has fallen in love with Eva, daughter of Pogner. Walther goes to find her in church, hoping to propose to her, only to be told by Magdalene that, as head of the Mastersingers, Pogner has promised Eva's hand in marriage to the winner of the singing competition to be held the following day. Eva returns his feelings, and so Magdalene instructs her lover, David, to give Walther a lesson in the convoluted rules of the Mastersingers. Although David is doubtful of the outsider's chances when the guild convenes, Walther presents himself for membership when the guild convenes. He immediately finds a rival in the Marker, Beckmesser, who is himself in love with Eva and who therefore gives Walther a low score for the song he performs. Walther's song is fresh and adventurous but does not conform to the guild's rules; only Hans Sachs recognizes Walther's talents, and resolves to help him.

ACT II

The street in front of Pogner's and Sachs's houses

Word reaches Eva that Walther has failed in his bid to become a Mastersinger. She goes to seek Sachs's advice, and though he too loves Eva, he agrees to help her and Walther. A Nightwatchman passes as the couple are preparing to elope, and Sachs, determined that they would do better not to run away, thwarts their disappearance. Beckmesser appears, ready to serenade Eva with the song he intends to sing in the following day's contest, but it is Magdalene in disguise who comes to the window. Beckmesser is constantly interrupted by Sachs's hammering—Sachs pretends to be working late on a pair of shoes, and even when the cobbler agrees to 'mark' Beckmesser's song with hammer strokes the noise is continuous—and soon the neighbourhood is roused by the din. David jealously imagines that Beckmesser is courting Magdalene and sets upon him, provoking an ugly riot. The Nightwatchman's horn disperses the crowd, and calm returns.

ACT III

SCENES 1-4 *Sachs's workshop*

It is Midsummer's Day. Sachs sends David on an errand, and, left alone, reflects on the madness of human nature as revealed in the events of the previous night. He is visited by Walther, whom he helps shape a song for the contest. While they are preparing to leave for the competition, Beckmesser arrives and jumps to the conclusion that the freshly composed song, though incomplete, is Sachs's and he has yet another rival. To prove him wrong, Sachs offers the text to Beckmesser, who leaves overjoyed. Eva's appearance inspires Walther to complete his song, and the sight of the happy couple convinces Sachs that he must forget his feelings for Eva. They are joined by David and Magdalene in 'baptising' the song, before setting off for the contest.

SCENE 5 *A meadow on the banks of the Pegnitz*

Townsfolk and the various guilds assemble in anticipation of the competition. The Mastersingers enter, and Sachs opens the proceedings. Beckmesser is the first to take the stand, and performs a muddled version of Walther's song. Humiliated, he tries to blame Sachs, whom he accuses of being the composer. Sachs defends himself by calling on Walther, whose performance of the same song is so accomplished that he is immediately acclaimed by all present. Eva crowns Walther; at first he stubbornly refuses to accept the Mastersingers' chain which Pogner offers, but Sachs persuades him, and Walther becomes a Mastersinger and claims Eva as his bride.

THE MERRY WIDOW
see **Die lustige Witwe**

THE MIDSUMMER MARRIAGE
Michael Tippett (b.1905)

THREE ACTS. LIBRETTO BY THE COMPOSER. PREMIERE IN LONDON, 27 JANUARY 1955.

Tippett, who has composed five full-scale operas, came to the genre relatively late. Possibly inspired by the success of his friend Benjamin Britten with *Peter Grimes* (1945), Tippett began composing *The Midsummer Marriage* in 1946, but it did not reach the stage until the year of his 50th birthday. *The*

Midsummer Marriage has been described as a 'quest' opera, and likened to Mozart's *Magic Flute* (*Die Zauberflöte*); each has two pairs of lovers who search for enlightenment, but unlike Mozart's fairy-tale setting, Tippett's opera is set in everyday life, in the ordinary English countryside, with ordinary English characters. Separated from the opera as a concert suite, the Ritual Dances (from Acts II and III) are Tippett's most frequently performed music. Tippett's outpouring of lyrical invention is perhaps unequalled anywhere in post-war opera.

CHARACTERS

Jenifer, a young woman betrothed to Mark (SOPRANO); *Bella*, King Fisher's secretary (SOPRANO); *She-Ancient*, priestess of the temple (MEZZO-SOPRANO); *Sosostris*, a clairvoyant (CONTRALTO); *Mark*, a young man of unknown parentage (TENOR); *Jack*, Bella's boyfriend, a mechanic (TENOR); *King Fisher*, Jenifer's father, a businessman (BARITONE); *He-Ancient*, priest of the temple (BASS); *Strephon* (DANCER) With *Friend's* of Mark and Jenifer, *dancers* attendant on the Ancients

ACT I
Morning

Jenifer and Mark have run away to get married. Friends are gathering in an outdoor clearing for their midsummer marriage. Music is heard from a strange temple nearby, and the crowd hides as Strephon and the other dancers lead the He-Ancient and She-Ancient out. Mark approaches them and stops the dancing: he, confident and full of passion, wants a new dance for his wedding, but soon the dancers go back to their old routines. The He-Ancient trips Strephon, Mark's alter-ego—a sign that change can be traumatic. The dancers and Ancients return to the temple, and Mark waits for Jenifer's arrival. When she enters, it is to cancel the wedding: she is frigid, and afraid of Mark's ardour. The couple quarrel and part: she disappears up a staircase into light, he down into a cave. King Fisher, Jenifer's father, arrives with his secretary, Bella, in pursuit of his runaway daughter. He bribes some onlookers to search for Mark, and gets Bella's boyfriend, Jack, to try to open the gates of the temple. As they attempt to break in, the voice of Sosostris is heard warning them off. Suddenly, Jenifer reappears, followed by Mark, and the Ancients order them to recount their respective adventures: Jenifer claims to have been freed by the purity of her experience, while Mark has felt only increasing physical urges. Mark is persuaded to join her in the light, and they depart on a spiritual journey, leaving King Fisher and the onlookers amazed.

ACT II
Afternoon

In the temple, Strephon hears voices and takes cover. Jack and Bella enter, and talk of marriage. Three Ritual Dances follow, depicting animals hunting (and representing sexual pursuit). The final one frightens Bella, but Jack comforts her. Before they run off light-heartedly, she tells him that King Fisher has another task for them.

ACT III

Evening and Night

Festivities in the clearing near the temple are interrupted by the entrance of King Fisher and Bella. He confronts the Ancients, who warn him not to interfere in the destiny of Jenifer and Mark. Unperturbed, he summons the clairvoyant Sosostris, whom he hopes will outsmart the Ancients and reveal Jenifer's whereabouts; an imposter appears instead, who turns out to be Jack disguised under veils. When the real Sosostris enters, her crystal bowl reveals a vision of Mark and Jenifer making love, which outrages King Fisher. He orders Jack to derobe Sosostris, but Jack refuses and leaves with Bella. Ignoring the Ancients' warnings, King Fisher himself tears the veils from Sosostris to uncover a huge flower, whose petals contain Mark and Jenifer locked in embrace. King Fisher points his gun at Mark, but the couple's defiant stare induces his death. His body is taken into the temple, where the fourth Ritual Dance is performed. In a sacrifice, Strephon is drawn into the giant petals with Mark and Jenifer. The flower closes and burst into flame, and darkness descends as the glow dies out. At dawn the couple emerge reborn, fulfilled, and ready to celebrate their wedding.

A MIDSUMMER NIGHT'S DREAM
Benjamin Britten (1913-1976)

THREE ACTS. LIBRETTO BY THE COMPOSER AND PETER PEARS AFTER SHAKESPEARE. PREMIERE IN ALDEBURGH, 11 JUNE 1960.

The special appeal for Britten—a composer always attracted to the themes of night and sleep—of Shakespeare's *A Midsummer Night's Dream* is clear in this score, one of the most beautiful he wrote. He characterizes each of the three strata—the fairies, the lovers, and the mechanicals—with its own sound-world: harps, harpsichord, celesta, and percussion represent the fairies, strings and woodwind the lovers, and bassoon and low brass the mechanicals. Britten is one in a line of composers to have based operas on *A Midsummer Night's Dream*—the first was Purcell, in *The Fairy Queen*—but his work stands out; Britten's adaptation of Shakespeare has been likened to Verdi's handling of *Othello* and *Falstaff* in his final masterpieces.

CHARACTERS

Tytania, Queen of the Fairies (COLORATURA SOPRANO); *Helena*, in love with Demetrius (SOPRANO); *Hermia*, in love with Lysander (MEZZO-SOPRANO); *Hippolyta*, Queen of the Amazons, betrothed to Theseus (CONTRALTO); *Oberon*, King of the Fairies (COUNTER-TENOR or CONTRALTO); *Lysander* (TENOR); *Flute*, a bellows-mender (TENOR); *Snout*, a tinker (TENOR); *Demetrius* (BARITONE); *Starveling*, a tailor (BARITONE); *Bottom*, a weaver (BASS-BARITONE); *Theseus*, Duke of Athens (BASS); *Quince*, a carpenter (BASS); *Snug*, a joiner (BASS); *Puck* (ACROBAT, SPEAKING ROLE)

With *fairies*, including *Cobweb*, *Peaseblossom*, *Mustardseed*, and *Moth*

ACT I
The wood; twilight

Oberon and Tytania have argued over possession of an Indian page-boy whom she refuses to give up. Oberon begins to plot his revenge, and sends Puck to collect a magic herb, whose liquid, when squeezed in drops onto Tytania's eyelids, will cause her to fall in love with the first creature she sees. Four Athenian lovers enter, Hermia and Lysander, and Helena and Demetrius (though Demetrius prefers Hermia and rejects Helena's advances). Oberon resolves to help Helena by ordering Puck to put drops of the liquid on Demetrius's eyelids. Before Puck can carry out his task, the mechanicals (Athenian craftsmen) arrive to prepare for a play in celebration of the marriage of their duke, Theseus and Hippolyta. When Puck can at last carry out his task, he mistakes Lysander for Demetrius: Lysander is woken by Helena and goes off with her, leaving Hermia to search for him. Tytania and her attendants return, and as soon as she falls asleep, Oberon sprinkles the magic drops onto her eyelids.

ACT II
The wood; night

Puck watches the mechanicals rehearsing their play, and mischievously gives Bottom the head of an ass to wear. Bottom's singing wakes Tytania, who is infatuated in an instant. The Athenian lovers return, and Oberon seeks to correct Puck's mistake by anointing Demetrius's eyes. But it is Helena who wakes him, and the situation has been reversed: both men now love Helena. The four quarrel, and Oberon resolves to straighten things out; he tells Puck to put the drops in Lysander's eyes.

ACT III
SCENE 1 *The wood; early the next morning*

Oberon is satisfied that he has won the Indian boy from Tytania. Out of pity for her humiliation—she remains bewitched by the ass's head—he removes the spell. Bottom is freed and returns to the mechanicals, and the four lovers are reconciled.

SCENE 2 *Theseus's palace*

Theseus and Hippolyta arrive in the wood. After hearing the tale of the four lovers, Theseus invites them to marry alongside him and his bride, and a triple wedding is celebrated. The rustics perform their play. The lovers retire, and Puck, Tytania, Oberon, and the fairies enter. Peace has returned, and Puck delivers the Epilogue to the audience.

MOSES UND ARON (Moses and Aaron)
Arnold Schoenberg (1874-1951)

THREE ACTS (ACT III NOT COMPOSED). LIBRETTO BY THE COMPOSER. PREMIERE IN ZURICH, 6 JUNE 1957 (A CONCERT PERFORMANCE WAS GIVEN IN HAMBURG, 12 MARCH 1954).

Schoenberg's masterpiece reflects his identification with his Jewish religion. Acts I and II were composed between 1930 and 1932, shortly before he was forced to flee Nazi Germany for exile in the United States, and though he wrote the libretto for the short, final act, he was never able to complete the opera. (The first two acts are performable as they stand.) Schoenberg calls for a large cast, but the drama centres on the conflict between the spiritual Moses and his fallible brother Aaron. The score is complex, though, like all Schoenberg's serial works, derived from a single twelve-note row.

CHARACTERS

A *Young Girl* (SOPRANO); A *Sick Woman* (CONTRALTO); *Aron* (Aaron), Moses's brother (TENOR); A *Young Man* (TENOR); A *Naked Youth* (TENOR); *Another Man* (BARITONE); *Ephraimite* (BARITONE); A *Priest* (BASS); *Moses* (SPOKEN ROLE, DEEP VOICE)
With four *Naked Virgins, Naked Men, Voice from the Burning Bush*, Old Men, twelve *Tribal Chieftains*, Beggars, seventy *Elders*, Israelite *People*

ACT I

Moses hears God's call from the Burning Bush, and though he doubts his eloquence and ability to inspire the Israelites he is to lead into the Promised Land, he receives assurance that Aaron will act as his mouthpiece. In the wilderness, Moses and Aaron discuss their task: Moses cannot see how their mysterious God can be realistically represented, but Aaron believes that only images and idols will impress the people. The Israelite people wait for the return of Moses and Aaron, fearing the message they may bring. When the brothers arrive, the people are scornful of Moses's view of an invisible God, and Aaron is forced to convince them of God's power by performing miracles. Persuaded, the people vow to serve this God and prepare to flee Egypt for the Promised Land.

ACT II

Moses is away on Mount Sinai receiving God's commandments, and the people fear that he will not return. They rebel, and Aaron is forced to provide them with a tangible symbol of one of their old gods. He fashions the Golden Calf, and sacrifices give way to an orgy of drunken and sexual excess. As it reaches its height with the killing of four Naked Virgins, a voice warns of Moses's descent from the mountain. He arrives carrying the tablets of the law, and destroys the Golden Calf as the people flee. Aaron defends himself against his brother's anger, claiming that even Moses needs symbols with which to impress the people, and that his are the tablets he has brought down. This provokes Moses to smash them, and Aaron goes off to join the Israelites who have moved on, following a pillar of fire. Moses is left in despair at his lack of eloquence.

ACT III

In the uncomposed final act, the imprisoned Aaron was to have been brought before Moses, reproached for favouring actions over words, before dying upon his release.

NABUCCO (Nebuchadnezzar)
Giuseppe Verdi (1813-1901)

FOUR PARTS. LIBRETTO BY TEMISTOCLE SOLERA, AFTER THE PLAY *NABUCODONOSOR* BY ACICET-BOURGEOIS AND FRANCIS CORNUE, AND THE BALLET *NABUCODONOSOR* BY ANTONIO CORTESI. PREMIERE IN MILAN, 9 MARCH 1842.

'With *Nabucco*,' wrote Verdi of his third opera, 'my career began'. Indeed, the great success of *Nabucco* cancelled memories of his second opera's failure, and established him as one of Italy's leading composers. It appealed so much to nationalist feeling that the chorus in which the Hebrew slaves dream of their homeland, 'Va pensiero', became widely known as a patriotic hymn. None of the principal roles is characterized in depth; the drama centres on the fate of the Hebrew people, and it is the big choral moments that give the score its flavour.

CHARACTERS

Abigaille, a slave, presumed to be the daughter of Nabucco (SOPRANO); *Fenena*, daughter of Nabucco (SOPRANO); *Anna*, Zaccaria's sister (SOPRANO); *Ismaele*, nephew of the King of Jerusalem (TENOR); *Abdallo*, elderly officer in Nabucco's service (TENOR); *Nabucco*, King of Babylon (BARITONE); *Zaccaria*, High Priest of Jerusalem (BASS); *High Priest of Baal* (BASS)
With Babylonian and Hebrew *soldiers*, *Levites*, Hebrew *virgins*, Babylonian *women*, *magi*, Babylonian *lords*, *people*

PART I Jerusalem
Inside Solomon's Temple

The Hebrews take refuge in the Temple, fearing the besieging Babylonian army. The high priest Zaccaria tries to raise his people's spirits, assuring them of God's protection, and announcing that he has taken Fenena, Nabucco's daughter, hostage. She is left alone with Ismaele, and it transpires that they have been lovers since he was imprisoned in Babylon years earlier. They are interrupted by Abigaille, who has crept into the Temple with a group of disguised Babylonian soldiers; Abigaille taunts them, offering to save Ismaele from the fate of the other Hebrews in return for his love. Zaccaria rushes in to warn of Nabucco's approach, and soon the Babylonian king enters on horseback. Ismaele prevents Zaccaria from killing Fenena, and Nabucco is now free to call for the sacking of the Temple.

PART II The Wicked Man
SCENE 1 *The palace in Babylon*

The Hebrews have been taken into captivity in Babylon, where, in Nabucco's absence, Fenena rules. Abigaille is jealous of Fenena, who holds a position she might have, had rumours not circulated suggesting that she was the child of slaves, rather than Nabucco's daughter. She enlists the help of the High Priest of Baal, who brings news that Fenena is releasing the Hebrews and urges Abigaille to seize power.

SCENE 2 *A room in the palace*

Zaccaria, having led the Hebrews in prayer, announces that Fenena has converted to their faith. Rumours of Nabucco's death inspire Abigaille to challenge Fenena's position, but when she arrives to do so, it is Nabucco himself who intervenes. When Nabucco orders both Babylonians and Hebrews to worship him as a god, he is hit by a thunderbolt for blasphemy; he survives, but is left mad and incoherent. Abigaille grabs his crown, proclaiming that Babylon will still triumph.

PART III The Prophecy

SCENE 1 *The Hanging Gardens of Babylon*

Abigaille holds the reins of power with the approval of the Babylonians, who insist that the Hebrews be killed. She tricks Nabucco into signing Fenena's death sentence. Nabucco realizes what has happened, and a confrontation develops: he reminds Abigaille that she is not his daughter but of lowly birth, whereupon she destroys the documentary evidence. He begs her to show mercy on Fenena, but she remains unmoved.

SCENE 2 *The banks of the Euphrates*

The Hebrews long for their lost homeland, and are roused by Zaccaria's prophecy of the fall of Babylon.

PART IV The Broken Idol

SCENE 1 *The palace in Babylon*

Nabucco wakes from his tormented dreams to hear the procession leading Fenena to her execution. In desperation he prays to the Hebrew God; his sanity is restored and he sets off with a band of men to save Fenena.

SCENE 2 *The Hanging Gardens*

Fenena and the Hebrews pray in preparation for their deaths. Nabucco enters, is hailed as king, and the idol of Baal shatters in pieces. All—including Abigaille, who, having taken poison, asks for Fenena's forgiveness before she dies—join in praising the Hebrew God.

NORMA

Vincenzo Bellini (1801-1835)

TWO ACTS. LIBRETTO BY FELICE ROMANI, AFTER ALEXANDRE SOUMET'S TRAGEDY *NORMA*. PREMIERE IN MILAN, 26 DECEMBER 1831.

Norma, the eighth of Bellini's ten operas, is his most noble and eloquent work. The story is of the clash between Druids and Romans in first century B.C. Gaul, but Bellini places emphasis on the human element—the secret love of a Druid priestess for a Roman general. Though the great title role makes vocal and emotional demands few sopranos have ever been able to meet, the work's enduring qualities have kept it in the repertory; the score includes the famous aria 'Casta diva' ('Chaste goddess'), Norma's invocation to the moon for peace on earth.

CHARACTERS

Norma, Druidess, Oroveso's daughter (SOPRANO); *Adalgisa*, a priestess in the temple (SOPRANO); *Clotilde*, Norma's confidante (MEZZO-SOPRA-NO); *Pollione*, Roman proconsul in Gaul (TENOR); *Flavio*, Pollione's friend (TENOR); *Oroveso*, high priest of the Druids (BASS)
With *Children* of Norma and Pollione, *Druids*, *priestesses*, Gallic *soldiers*

ACT I

SCENE 1 *The sacred grove of the Druids*

Druids and Gallic soldiers assemble, and are led by their high priest Oroveso in begging the gods to rouse people to war against the hated Roman occupiers. They disperse, to wait for the new moon, when Norma will come to the altar to prophesy. Pollione, the Roman proconsul, enters with his friend Flavio, and reveals that he has grown tired of his mistress, Norma, and fallen in love with a young priestess, Adalgisa; he fears Norma's revenge. The Druids gather, impatient for war, but Norma—still in love with the Roman—prays for peace. All leave, except for Adalgisa, who is soon joined by Pollione. Like Norma, she has broken her vows of chastity, and though she at first resists Pollione's advances, she agrees to run away with him to Rome.

SCENE 2 *Norma's secret dwelling in the forest*

Norma confides to Clotilde her worry that Pollione may return to Rome without her. She instructs Clotilde to hide the two children she has borne Pollione. Adalgisa enters, and Norma listens sympathetically when she relates how she has fallen in love with a Roman and broken her vows. When Pollione enters, Norma immediately realizes that Adalgisa is her rival. Norma berates Pollione furiously, and Adalgisa, not wanting to come between them, renounces her love for the Roman. Norma remains bent on vengeance.

ACT II

SCENE 1 *Inside Norma's dwelling*

The desperate Norma plans to kill her children, but cannot bring herself to act. Instead, she summons Adalgisa and asks her to take the children to Rome with their father. Adalgisa replies that she will visit Pollione only to urge him to return to Norma and their children. The women renew their bond of friendship.

SCENE 2 *A clearing near the Druids' grove*

Oroveso reports to the Druids and Gallic soldiers that Pollione is to be succeeded by an even more tyrannical proconsul; he suggests that they lie low until a better opportunity for rebellion presents itself.

SCENE 3 *The Druids' temple*

Clotilde tells Norma that Pollione has ignored Adalgisa's pleas. Angered, Norma calls the Druids to assemble, and urges war against the Romans. A ritual sacrifice is required, and as Oroveso asks Norma to name the victim, Pollione is brought in, having been apprehended while attempting to abduct Adalgisa. She is about to raise her knife to Pollione when she hesitates, asking to be left alone to question him. Norma hopes he will save himself by renouncing Adalgisa, but he refuses, even when she threatens to sacrifice both Adalgisa and their children. She summons the Druids and soldiers to prepare a funeral pyre for a priestess who has broken her vows, whom they believe to be Adalgisa. But Norma confesses her own guilty secret and, having begged Oroveso to care for her children, prepares to die. Pollione is moved to remorse, and joins Norma on the burning pyre.

THE NOSE
Dmitry Shostakovich (1906-1975)

THREE ACTS. LIBRETTO BY THE COMPOSER, AFTER GOGOL'S SHORT STORY. PREMIERE IN LENINGRAD, 12 JANUARY 1930.

Shostakovich's first opera reflects the experimental mood of the Soviet arts during the years that followed the Russian Revolution. The harmonies are dissonant, the rhythms jerky and abrasive, the vocal lines uncompromising, and the few moments of lyricism are ironic, or there for comic effect. The orchestration is eccentric, an extreme example being the entr'acte between Scenes 2 and 3 of Act I, scored for untuned percussion only. *The Nose* has been labelled an 'anti-opera'; with nearly 80 sung roles it is certainly an exercise in excess. It is based on Gogol's tale, set in St Petersburg, of a petty official who wakes one morning to find his nose missing, and of the ridiculous episodes that follow. It cocks a snook in every direction, at the civil service, the police, the church, the medical profession, even the press.

CHARACTERS
Praskovya Ossipovna, Ivan Yakovlevich's wife (SOPRANO); *Madame Podtochina's Daughter* (SOPRANO); *Madame Podtochina* (MEZZO-SOPRANO); *Police Inspector* (VERY HIGH TENOR); *Ivan*, Kovalyov's servant (TENOR); *The Nose* (TENOR); *Platon Kuzmich Kovalyov* (BARI-TONE); *Ivan Yakovlevich*, a barber (BASS-BARITONE); *Clerk in a newspaper office* (BASS-BARITONE); *A Doctor* (BASS)
With *servants, policemen, students, passers-by, worshippers, travellers, townsfolk, eunuchs, onlookers*, etc.

ACT I
During the introduction the protagonist, Kovalyov, a petty bureaucrat, is shaved by the barber, Ivan Yakovlevich. Kovalyov remarks that, as usual, the barber's hands stink.

SCENE 1 *Yakovlevich's barber shop*
The barber's wife, Praskovya Ossipovna, bakes bread for breakfast. When Yakovlevich finds it contains a nose, they quarrel, and his wife drives him out to dispose of the appendage.

SCENE 2 *The embankment*
Obeying his wife, Yakovlevich rushes to the embankment, but his attempts to get rid of the nose are thwarted by the appearance of acquaintances. Finally, he throws it into the river, only to be confronted by the Police Inspector, who detains him.

SCENE 3 *Kovalyov's bedroom*
Kovalyov wakes; checking in a mirror for a pimple which appeared on his nose the night before, he finds to his horror that his nose has disappeared. His servant Ivan confirms this, and Kovalyov rushes off to report the incident to the Chief of Police.

SCENE 4 *Kazan Cathedral*
En route to the police Kovalyov enters the cathedral, where a service is being held, to find the Nose (dressed in the uniform of a state councillor) at its devotions. Kovalyov, confused about addressing higher rank, nevertheless confronts the Nose, who replies condescendingly. Kovalyov is distracted by a pretty girl, and the Nose escapes.

ACT II
SCENE 1 *Residence of the Chief of Police*
Kovalyov arrives, only to be told that the Chief has left. He heads for the newspaper office in desperation.

SCENE 2 *Newspaper office*
Kovalyov plans to place an advertisement for his missing nose, but finds the office full of servants on errands. He meets no sympathy, and the Clerk refuses to let him place his notice lest it damage the newspaper's reputation. The Clerk offers Kovalyov snuff, whereupon he loses his temper.

SCENE 3 *Kovalyov's house*
Kovalyov arrives home in a temper, and chases his drunken servant out. He despairs of his bleak future without a nose.

ACT III
SCENE 1 *Outskirts of St Petersburg*
The police suspect that the Nose may attempt to leave the city, and scrutinize passengers for the stagecoach. Amid the bustle, the Nose appears, trying to stop the stagecoach. It is apprehended and beaten mercilessly down to normal size and shape. The police wrap it in paper and take it off to Kovalyov's house.

SCENE 2 *Kovalyov's house and Madame Podtochina's house (the stage is divided)*
Kovalyov is overjoyed to be reunited with his nose, and is happy to reward the Chief of Police. His mood changes when he is unable to stick it on again; even the Doctor lacks a remedy, and suggests that he pickle it for posterity. Kovalyov blames his trouble on a spell he imagines Madame Podtochina has cast, in revenge for his unwillingness to marry her Daughter. He writes to her, demanding that she revoke the spell; she replies denying responsibility. Meanwhile, the townspeople, unaware of the nose's return, gossip on its whereabouts.

SCENE 3 *Kovalyov's house*
Kovalyov wakes to find his nose back in its customary place. The barber arrives to shave him, and Kovalyov registers his usual complaint, that Yakovlevich's fingers smell.

SCENE 4 *Nevsky Prospekt*
In high spirits Kovalyov parades along the street, greeting acquaintances. He flirts with a vendor, inviting her to visit, to prove to himself that he is indeed fully restored to health.

LE NOZZE DI FIGARO (The Marriage of Figaro)
Wolfgang Amadeus Mozart (1756-1791)

FOUR ACTS. LIBRETTO BY LORENZO DA PONTE, AFTER PIERRE AUGUSTIN BEAUMARCHAIS'S *LA FOLLE JOURNÉE OU LE MARIAGE DE FIGARO*. PREMIERE IN VIENNA, 1 MAY 1786.

Le nozze di Figaro has been described as the most perfect opera ever written; it is admired for its elaborate ensembles, but it is the tuneful arias (such as Cherubino's 'Voi che sapete') that have made it one of the most popular works in the repertory. *Figaro* marked the beginning of the celebrated collaboration between Mozart and his librettist Lorenzo Da Ponte, and was followed by *Don Giovanni* and *Così fan tutte*. All three are comedies, but they are more than simply funny. In *Figaro*, the least dark of the three and the one with the warmest characterization, Mozart brought a new depth of feeling to comic opera: the music paints a vivid picture of the social and sexual tensions that motivate the plot. Da Ponte's libretto is based on the second of Beaumarchais's three plays about the barber Figaro, which picks up the story where *The Barber of Seville* left off.

CHARACTERS

Countess Almaviva (SOPRANO); *Susanna*, the Countess's maid, betrothed to Figaro (SOPRANO); *Cherubino*, the Count's page (SOPRANO); *Barbarina*, Antonio's daughter (SOPRANO); *Marcellina*, Bartolo's housekeeper (SOPRANO); *Don Basilio*, a music teacher (TENOR); *Don Curzio*, a magistrate (TENOR); *Count Almaviva* (BARITONE); *Figaro*, the Count's valet (BARITONE); *Doctor Bartolo* (BASS); *Antonio*, a gardener (BASS)
With *villagers* and *servants*

ACT I

An unfurnished room in the Almavivas' mansion
It is the wedding day of Figaro and Susanna, and the couple are making last-minute preparations. Figaro is measuring the room their master has provided them, but Susanna warns that it is too close to the bedroom of the Count, who regrets his earlier revoking of the *droit de seigneur*. Figaro, who has served the Count loyally, is shattered by Susanna's disclosure, and resolves to thwart his master's moves. Both Marcellina and Bartolo have scores to settle with Figaro: Bartolo is keen to avenge the humiliation he has suffered at Figaro's hands (in *The Barber of Seville*) and is thus happy to assist Marcellina, who had once lent Figaro money on condition that he marry her should he fail to repay it. With Figaro's marriage to Susanna now imminent, Marcellina is determined to act, and begins by confronting her 'rival'. The page Cherubino comes to Susanna for help: he is to be dismissed by the Count after having been caught *in flagrante* with

Barbarina, and begs Susanna to intercede on his behalf. Cherubino can hardly understand the passion he feels for nearly every woman he sees, but admits to Susanna that he feels something even for the Countess. When the Count approaches, Cherubino hides; he overhears the Count making advances to Susanna. The Count himself hides when Basilio comes to gossip with Susanna about Cherubino's infatuation with the Countess, but bursts out in anger at what he has heard, only to discover Cherubino there too. The arrival of Figaro and his fellow servants, who have come to ask the Count to start the wedding ceremony, halts the confrontation. Realizing that Cherubino overheard his own indiscretion, the Count is forced to forgive him, but sends him away to join his regiment.

ACT II
The Countess's room

The Countess, who has just been told (before curtain up) of the Count's designs on Susanna, laments the loss of her husband's love. She approves of Figaro's two-pronged attack on the Count's self-esteem. Figaro sends an anonymous letter warning of a rendezvous the Countess is planning to keep, while also arranging for Cherubino, disguised as Susanna, to meet with the Count. Cherubino is trying on his disguise when the Count is heard at the door, coming to confront his wife about her supposed infidelity, and in a panic hides in the Countess's dressing-room. The Count demands to know who is in it, and while he is off (with the Countess in tow) fetching tools to force the lock, Susanna comes to the rescue by taking Cherubino's place and allowing the page to escape out the window. When the lock is opened, the Count and Countess are both equally astonished to see Susanna step out. Husband and wife are reconciled when the women reveal that the letter was Figaro's joke, but when Figaro enters he persists in denying knowledge of it. Further embarrassment is caused by the gardener Antonio's complaints that a man jumped from the window and damaged his flowers. Calm is almost restored, but when Marcellina, Bartolo and Basilio arrive to plead Marcellina's case against Figaro, confusion reigns.

ACT III
A large hall in the Almavivas' mansion

Susanna is persuaded by the Countess to rendezvous with the Count, in exchange for money to pay off Marcellina. The Countess intends to go disguised as Susanna, but the Count suspects he is being tricked when he overhears Susanna telling Figaro that they have won their case. The lawyer Don Curzio has found in Marcellina's favour, and Figaro is ordered to repay her or marry her. But Figaro is saved when it transpires that he is in fact the long-lost son of Marcellina and Bartolo, who decide to marry. The Countess, still determined to ensnare her husband, dictates a letter from Susanna to the Count, and seals it with a pin that must be returned by the Count when he has read it. A group of girls arrives to present flowers to the Countess: Cherubino is spotted among them, having been dressed up by Barbarina in order that might stay. The Count is angry, but forced again to forgive Cherubino when he is reminded by Barbarina that he promised her whatever she wanted in exchange for her embraces. The wedding celebrations begin, during which Susanna passes her letter to the Count. Figaro notices him pricking his finger on the pin.

ACT IV
The garden of the Almavivas' mansion
Barbarina, having been given the pin by the Count to return to Susanna, has lost it. Unaware of its significance, she tells her story to Figaro, who jumps to the conclusion that Susanna has made a real assignation with the Count. He is outraged, and hides when the Countess and Susanna appear in the garden. Figaro is unable to see in the dark that they have exchanged clothes, and can distinguish them only by their voices. Cherubino comes into the garden, and seeing the opportunity for a little flirtation, makes advances to the Countess (thinking her to be Susanna). The same disguise tricks the Count into pouring out his love to his own wife. Figaro is relieved to realize what is happening, but indulges in a little teasing of his own by flirting with the real Countess. This upsets Susanna, but they are soon reconciled. The Count returns to find Figaro and the 'Countess' together, and is so outraged that he summons his entire household. But when the real Countess reveals herself, he is moved to ask for her forgiveness. All are reconciled, and the wedding celebrations can continue joyfully.

OEDIPUS REX (King Oedipus)
Igor Stravinsky (1882-1971)

TWO ACTS. LIBRETTO BY JEAN COCTEAU (FRENCH SECTIONS TRANSLATED BY JEAN DANIÉLOU), AFTER SOPHOCLES'S *OEDIPUS TYRANNUS*. PREMIERE IN PARIS, 30 MAY 1927 (CONCERT); IN VIENNA 23 FEBRUARY 1928 (STAGED).

Oedipus Rex, described by its composer as an 'opera-oratorio', is one of Stravinsky's greatest neo-classical works. Its musical influences are wide-ranging, though Handel is one of the strongest; the use of a chorus (the people of Thebes) to comment on the action suggests both the Bach oratorios and Greek theatre. On the surface the music is cold and stark, but Stravinsky's setting of Sophocles's tragedy—Oedipus is the Theban king who unwittingly killed his father (Laius) and married his mother (Jocasta)—is humane. The 'monumental' side of the work is emphasized by its Latin text, though Stravinsky and his librettist, Cocteau, kept the spoken narration in the language of the original audience.

CHARACTERS
Jocaste (Jocasta), Oedipus's wife (MEZZO-SOPRANO); *Oedipe* (Oedipus), King of Thebes (TENOR); *Shepherd* (TENOR); *Créon* (Creon), Jocasta's brother (BASS-BARITONE); *Messenger* (BASS-BARITONE); *Tirésias* (Tiresias), a soothsayer (BASS); *Narrator* (SPOKEN)

ACT I

The Narrator announces that the action will recount the closing of the trap laid for Oedipus at his birth. Oedipus is introduced: he is being implored by the Theban people to save them from the plague, and promises to intervene. Creon, Oedipus's brother-in-law, arrives from Delphi, where the gods disclosed to him that Laius's murderer is still at large in Thebes, and that only his capture will bring relief from the plague. Oedipus promises to find the culprit. He consults the blind soothsayer Tiresias, who reluctantly reveals that Laius's murderer is a king himself. Oedipus responds by angrily accusing Creon and Tiresias of plotting to remove him from the throne, but the argument is interrupted by the arrival of Oedipus's wife, Jocasta.

ACT II

Jocasta chides the men for arguing. She acknowledges that an oracle prophesied that her former husband, Laius, would be murdered by his son, but reminds them that he was in fact killed by thieves at a crossroads. Oedipus, horrified, admits to Jocasta that once he killed a stranger at a crossroads. A Messenger arrives with news of the death of Polybus, king of Corinth, and reveals that Oedipus was Polybus's adopted, rather than natural, son. The Shepherd admits to having found the baby Oedipus abandoned on a mountain slope. Jocasta understands the significance of the news and flees before Oedipus realizes that he was born to Laius and Jocasta but abandoned, and that he has murdered his father and wed his mother. The Theban people are told that Jocasta has hanged herself and Oedipus blinded himself with her brooch, and although they are filled with sympathy for his plight, they drive their former king out.

L'ORFEO (Orpheus)
Claudio Monteverdi (1567-1643)

PROLOGUE AND FIVE ACTS. LIBRETTO BY ALESSANDRO STRIGGIO. PREMIERE IN MANTUA, 24 FEBRUARY 1607.

The legend of Orpheus and Eurydice served as subject for three early operas: Jacopo Peri's *Euridice* (1600), Giulio Caccini's *Euridice* (1600), and Monteverdi's *L'Orfeo*. It took Monteverdi's genius to fuse together the elements of the new medium—dancing, poetry and singing, recitative and aria, solos and ensembles, varied orchestral effects—into a disciplined dramatic structure. *L'Orfeo* drew on the traditions of the Florentine 'Camerata' (a group who sought to recreate the style of Greek drama), but also anticipated the Baroque and set the history of opera on course.

CHARACTERS

La Musica (Music), the Prologue (SOPRANO); *Euridice* (Eurydice) (SOPRANO); *Silvia* (Sylvia), the Messenger (SOPRANO); *Speranza* (Hope) (SOPRANO); *Proserpina*, queen of the underworld (SOPRANO); *Orfeo* (Orpheus) (TENOR); *Apollo*, *Caronte* (Charon) (BASS); *Plutone* (Pluto), king of the underworld (BASS)
With *nymphs*, *shepherds*, *spirits*

PROLOGUE

The fields of Thrace

The personification of Music reveals her power to 'calm every troubled heart, and inflame even the chilliest mind, now to anger, now to love'.

ACT I

The fields of Thrace

Orpheus and Eurydice are joined by nymphs and shepherds in celebrating their wedding.

ACT II

The fields of Thrace

Eurydice has gone off, leaving Orpheus and the shepherds to rejoice in his new-found love. They are interrupted by the Messenger bearing news of Eurydice's death from a snakebite. Orpheus is distraught, and resolves to rescue his bride from the underworld. The shepherds take up his lament.

ACT III

The underworld

Orpheus is led by Hope as far as the River Styx, where she leaves him to cross into the underworld. The boatman Charon is unmoved by Orpheus's music and refuses to take him across the river; at last Orpheus's lyre lulls Charon to sleep, and Orpheus rows across himself.

ACT IV

The underworld

Pluto and Proserpina have listened to Orpheus's music. Moved by it, the queen begs her husband to release Eurydice and he agrees, on condition that Orpheus does not look back until they reach earth. Orpheus sets out triumphantly, but when he looks to see if Eurydice is following, she vanishes from his sight. The spirits regret his lack of discipline.

ACT V

The fields of Thrace

Orpheus, left to wander alone, mourns his loss. He is rescued by his father, Apollo, who takes Orpheus back with him into the heavens. Apollo promises Orpheus that he will be able to see his Eurydice among the stars.

ORFEO ED EURIDICE (Orpheus and Eurydice)
Christoph Willibald Gluck (1714-1787)

THREE ACTS. ITALIAN VERSION: LIBRETTO BY RANIERI DE'CALZABIGI. PREMIERE IN VIENNA, 5 OCTOBER 1762. FRENCH VERSION (*ORPHÉE ET EURIDICE*): LIBRETTO BY PIERRE-LOUIS MOLINE, AFTER CALZABIGI. PREMIERE IN PARIS, 2 AUGUST 1774.

Gluck's most famous opera—the score includes Orpheus's 'Che farò senza Euridice'—is a milestone in the history of opera, the first of the composer's 'reform-operas'. It marked the beginning of a collaboration between Gluck and the librettist Calzabigi, and revealed them moving away from the decorative formality of operatic convention towards a simpler, restrained style more in keeping with dramatic truth. *Orfeo ed Euridice* was a great success at its premiere, but in 1774 Gluck rewrote it completely for Paris, according to French convention (*Orphée et Euridice* is longer, with a greatly extended ballet). Thus—ignoring other modifications Gluck made along the way—there are two different versions performed today, though increasingly the trend has been to revert to the leaner 1762 original.

CHARACTERS

Euridice (Eurydice) (SOPRANO); *Amore* (Cupid), god of love (SOPRANO); *Orfeo* (Orpheus), Eurydice's husband (CONTRALTO or COUNTER-TENOR)
With *shepherds* and *shepherdesses*, *furies* and *demons*, *heroes* and *heroines* from Elysium

ACT I

SCENES 1 and 2 *The grove at Eurydice's tomb*
Orpheus has lost his wife Eurydice—she died from a snake bite—and weeps at her tomb. Shepherds join in his lament, and only Cupid, the god of love, brings encouragement: Orpheus will be allowed to descend into the underworld to rescue Eurydice, but only on condition that while leading her out he does not look back. Orpheus is concerned how Eurydice will feel if he refuses to look at her, but realizes that he must attempt the task.

ACT II

SCENE 1 *A terrifying rocky area at the entrance to the underworld*
The fierce Furies try to block Orpheus's passage into the underworld, but his music soothes them and he is allowed through.

SCENE 2 *A beautiful landscape*
Orpheus reaches the Elysian fields, resting place of the blessed dead. He admires its beauty, but remains unhappy until he is reunited there with Eurydice. A group of heroes and heroines urge her to return to Orpheus.

ACT III

SCENES 1 and 2 *A dark cave*
Orpheus is leading Eurydice out of the underworld. When Orpheus does not look at her she frets that she has lost his love; she cries out, and on impulse Orpheus turns round, only to see Eurydice dying. Orpheus realizes that he has nothing left to live for, and resolves to join Eurydice in death. But Cupid intervenes, prevents Orpheus from killing himself, and restores Eurydice to life. The couple return to earth.

SCENE 3 *The temple of Cupid*
Orpheus, Eurydice and the shepherds join in praising Cupid.

ORPHÉE AUX ENFERS
(Orpheus in the Underworld)
Jacques Offenbach (1819-1880)

FOUR ACTS. LIBRETTO BY HECTOR CRÉMIEUX AND LUDOVIC HALÉVY. PREMIERE IN PARIS, 21 OCTOBER 1858.

The third well-known work based on the story of Orpheus turns the legend on its head: Offenbach's operetta parodies Greek myth and pokes fun at Gluck's masterpiece (see *Orfeo ed Euridice*), as well as being a political satire. *Orpheus in the Underworld* was a *succès de scandale* at its premiere, and has remained popular ever since—not least for the can-can in Act 4, danced by the merry inhabitants of the underworld.

CHARACTERS

Eurydice, Orpheus's wife (SOPRANO); *Diane* (Diana), goddess of chastity (SOPRANO); *Vénus* (Venus), goddess of beauty (SOPRANO); *Junon* (Juno), wife of Jupiter (SOPRANO); *Minerve* (Minerva), goddess of wisdom (SOPRANO); *L'Opinion Publique* (Public Opinion) (MEZZO-SOPRANO); *Cupidon* (Cupid), god of love (MEZZO-SOPRANO); *Orphée* (Orpheus), a musician (TENOR); *Pluton* (Pluto), god of the underworld (TENOR); *John Styx*, Pluto's servant, formerly king of Boeotia (TENOR); *Mercure* (Mercury), Jupiter's messenger (TENOR); *Jupiter*, king of the gods (BARITONE); *Morphée* (Morpheus), god of sleep (BARITONE); *Mars*, god of war (BASS); *Bacchus*, god of wine (SPOKEN); *Cerbère* (Cerberus), watchdog of the underworld (BARKED)
With *gods, goddesses, shepherds, shepherdesses, spirits*

ACT I
Near Orpheus's house in the Theban countryside
Public Opinion introduces the story. Orpheus and Eurydice are tired of their marriage, and a particular bone of contention is Orpheus's violin-playing, which Eurydice cannot bear. Orpheus taunts his wife with his music, and also reveals that he has laid a trap in the fields (a poisonous snake) for her lover, Pluto, who is in his earthly disguise as the shepherd Aristaeus. It is Eurydice who gets bitten, but she dies in ecstasy at the prospect of being carried off by Pluto to his underworld kingdom. Orpheus is also delighted at the outcome, but is pressed by Public Opinion to retrieve her—for appearance's sake.

ACT II
Mount Olympus
The gods, asleep, are joined by others of their number—Cupid, Venus, and Mars—returning from their nocturnal activities. Diana's hunting-horn signals the morning, and they wake to complain about Jupiter's autocratic treatment of them. Mercury informs them of the woman Pluto has kidnapped and taken to the underworld, and Pluto is summoned to explain his behaviour. Before he can defend himself the gods rise up in protest against their regime, and Jupiter can only calm them by inviting them to accompany him to the underworld. Public Opinion has bullied Orpheus into asking for the return of Eurydice, and Jupiter descends to the underworld to ensure that this happens.

ACT III
Pluto's palace in the underworld
Eurydice is being watched over by John Styx, who reminisces about his days as king of Boeotia. She is locked away when the gods arrive. Jupiter, who has fallen in love with Eurydice, is advised by Cupid to transform himself into a fly in order to get through the keyhole into Eurydice's room. Eurydice admires the fly, catches it and kisses it, whereupon Jupiter resumes his usual form. He promises to take her back to Olympus.

ACT IV
The banks of the Styx
Pluto has thrown a party for his fellow gods, including Jupiter and Eurydice (disguised as a Bacchante). Jupiter and Eurydice are about to set out for Olympus when the jealous Pluto points out triumphantly that Orpheus and Public Opinion are about to arrive. Orpheus, who reluctantly agrees to be reunited with his wife, is told that he can lead her back to earth on condition that he does not glance around. They set off, but Jupiter conjures up a thunderbolt, which shocks Orpheus into looking behind him. Eurydice is forced to remain in the underworld, as one of Bacchus's priestesses. Everyone—except Public Opinion—is happy with the outcome.

ORPHEUS IN THE UNDERWORLD
see **Orphée aux Enfers**

OTELLO (Othello)
Giuseppe Verdi (1813-1901)

FOUR ACTS. LIBRETTO BY ARRIGO BOITO, AFTER SHAKESPEARE'S *OTHELLO*. PREMIERE IN MILAN, 5 FEBRUARY 1887.

Verdi's penultimate opera was long in the making. *Otello* appeared 16 years after his previous opera, *Aida*, and marked the beginning of a new, final phase in the composer's life. It brought him the collaboration of Arrigo Boito (composer of *Mefistofele*), who provided librettos for *Otello* and *Falstaff*—widely considered to be the twin peaks of the whole Italian repertory. Verdi had a lifelong fascination with Shakespeare (he had set *Macbeth* half a century earlier), and now his mature musical powers and Boito's taut libretto (3,000 lines of play reduced to 800 in the opera) enabled him to indulge it. The music is more integrated than in Verdi's earlier operas, and each of the acts plays without a break.

CHARACTERS
Desdemona, Otello's wife (SOPRANO); *Emilia*, Iago's wife, Desdemona's companion (MEZZO-SOPRANO); *Otello*, a Moor, general in the Venetian army (TENOR); *Cassio*, Otello's lieutenant (TENOR); *Roderigo*, a Venetian gentleman (TENOR); *Iago*, Otello's ensign (BARITONE); *A Herald* (BARITONE); *Lodovico*, ambassador of the Venetian Republic (BASS); *Montano*, Otello's predecessor as governor of Cyprus (BASS)

With *soldiers* and *sailors* of the Venetian Republic, Venetian *ladies* and *gentlemen*, Cypriot *men* and *women*, *Greeks*, *Dalmatians*, *Albanians*, *innkeeper*, inn *servants*, common *sailors*, *children*

ACT I
Outside the castle

Otello, fresh from playing a part in the Venetian defeat of the Turks, arrives in Cyprus to take up his post as governor, bringing with him his beautiful wife, Desdemona. He appoints Cassio as his second-in-command. Iago is jealous at having been passed over, and to get his revenge on both Otello and Cassio he plots with Roderigo, who desires the love of Desdemona. Iago and Roderigo take the first opportunity to make Cassio drunk, and provoke him into fighting a duel with the former governor, Montano. Roderigo raises the alarm, bringing Otello out to investigate. Finding Montano wounded, and believing Iago's explanation of the events, Otello strips Cassio of his office and orders Iago to restore calm. The crowd disperses, leaving Otello and Desdemona alone to reflect on their love; Otello fears that he will never be as happy again.

ACT II
A room in the castle

Iago, satisfied that the first part of his plan has worked, now considers how best to turn Otello against Desdemona and bring about his downfall. After advising Cassio to ask Desdemona to intercede with her husband on Cassio's behalf, Iago reveals his evil philosophy of life. Iago goes to Otello and plants in his mind seeds of jealousy, warning him to watch Desdemona's behaviour. Otello is untroubled at first, but is reminded of Iago's words when Desdemona comes to intervene on Cassio's behalf. In anger, Otello throws aside Desdemona's handkerchief, but Emilia (her companion and Iago's wife) picks it up. Later, Iago snatches the handkerchief from her, planning to use it as evidence against Desdemona. He goes to Otello, tells him how he heard Cassio speaking in his sleep of his affair with Desdemona, and offers the handkerchief—which he claims to have seen in Cassio's hand. Together Otello and Iago swear an oath of vengeance.

ACT III
The great hall of the castle

Otello questions Desdemona, who has come to him to appeal again on Cassio's behalf, about her feelings for Cassio. She insists on her innocence, but her inability to produce the handkerchief he demands heightens his suspicions. Iago persuades Cassio to talk about his mistress, Bianca, but allows the eavesdropping Otello to conclude they are discussing Desdemona. When Cassio innocently produces the handkerchief (hidden in his lodgings by Iago), Otello flies into a jealous rage. Ambassadors from Venice, led by Lodovico, arrive to recall Otello and announce that Cassio (whom they notice is absent) is to be installed in his place. Otello insults Desdemona in public, and then plots behind the scenes with Iago: Otello will kill

Desdemona, and Iago murder Cassio (though, behind Otello's back, Iago relegates the task to Roderigo). Insane with jealousy, Otello curses the innocent Desdemona and drives everyone out—except for Iago, who gloats triumphantly.

ACT IV
Desdemona's bedroom

As she prepares for bed, Desdemona laments Otello's change of attitude towards her. She is asleep when Otello creeps in and kisses her. She wakes and realizes that he has come to kill her, and her pleas of innocence are in vain: Otello smothers her. Emilia is horrified to find Desdemona dying when she comes to announce that Cassio has killed Roderigo. Cassio, Iago, Lodovico and Montano are raised by Emilia's alarm, but Iago flees when Otello learns of his duplicity and Desdemona's innocence. Otello bids a broken-hearted farewell to his dead wife before stabbing himself.

PAGLIACCI (The Players)
Ruggero Leoncavallo (1857-1919)

Two acts. Libretto by the composer. Premiere in Milan, 21 May 1892.

Leoncavallo's operatic output was substantial, but apart from his *La Bohème* (overshadowed by Puccini's opera, with which it was written in competition), which is occasionally revived today, his fame rests entirely on *Pagliacci*. Like Mascagni's *Cavalleria rusticana*, with which it was soon paired, *Pagliacci* is a *verismo* opera, depicting a 'slice of life'. Leoncavallo wrote his own libretto, drawing on memories of an incident that occurred during his childhood in which a jealous actor murdered his wife after a performance; the magistrate who presided over the case was Leoncavallo's father. The opera's most famous number is 'Vesti la giubba', Canio's sad aria at the end of Act I.

CHARACTERS
Nedda (in the play 'Columbine'), Canio's wife (SOPRANO); *Canio* (in the play 'Pagliccio'), leader of the troupe (TENOR); *Beppe* (in the play 'Harlequin') (TENOR); *Tonio* (in the play 'Taddeo'), a clown (BARITONE); *Silvio*, a villager (BARITONE)
With *villagers*

PROLOGUE
Tonio announces a real-life drama.

ACT I
Canio's troupe of players is welcomed by the villagers. His jealous nature is apparent from the start: he reacts violently when someone in the crowd suggests that the hunchback Tonio desires his wife, Nedda. She remains behind when the villagers disperse, unhappy at her stifling life with Canio. Soon Tonio appears, but his advances are rejected. Tonio's opportunity for revenge presents itself when he sees Nedda with her

lover, the villager Silvio. He overhears them planning to elope
after the performance that evening, and rushes off to alert
Canio. Silvio slips away just in time to avoid Canio, who enters
armed with a dagger. He demands to know the name of
Nedda's lover, but she refuses to tell him. Beppe disarms
Canio: it is almost time for the performance, and with difficul-
ty the heartbroken Canio prepares to go on as a clown.

ACT II

The play begins. Harlequin (Beppe) serenades Colombine
(Nedda). Taddeo (Tonio) makes advances to Colombine, but—
as in real life—is rebuffed. Harlequin and Colombine are
interrupted by Pagliaccio (Canio), who, hearing her use the same
words of farewell as she spoke to her lover Silvio, gets confused
between the play and reality. Struggling to stay in character as
the clown, he breaks down in a jealous rage and demands to
know the name of her lover. As before, she continues to defy
him and he stabs her. Nedda dies, crying out for Silvio, who
rushes up: Canio recognizes him as the lover, and kills him.
Tonio tells the horrified audience that 'The comedy is ended'.
For many years it was Canio who appropriated this punch-line.

PARSIFAL
Richard Wagner (1813-1883)

THREE ACTS. LIBRETTO BY THE COMPOSER. PREMIERE AT
BAYREUTH, 26 JULY 1882.

Like many of his operas, Wagner's final work—the composer
died a few months after its premiere—had occupied his mind
for several decades. In some ways *Parsifal* represents a creative
summing-up. Wagner thought of it as a theatrical representa-
tion of a religious rite rather than as an opera, and described it
as a 'Stage Dedication Festival Play'. *Parsifal* relates the tale of
the Holy Grail, and its allegorical, pseudo-Christian message is
conveyed in slow-moving drama (Act 1 alone lasts over two
hours) and solemn, sensuous music.

CHARACTERS

Kundry (SOPRANO); *Parsifal* (TENOR); *Amfortas*, ruler of the Kingdom
of the Grail (BARITONE); *Gurnemanz*, veteran Knight of the Grail
(BASS); *Klingsor*, a magician (BASS); *Titurel*, Amfortas's father (BASS)
With *knights, squires*, Klingsor's *flowermaidens, youths*

ACT I

Parsifal is set in Spain, on a mountain range inhabited by two
opposing orders. The castle of Monsalvat was built by the Grail
community as a shrine to house the chalice used at the Last
Supper and the holy spear that pierced Christ's side at the
Crucifixion. Not far away is Klingsor's magic castle: Klingsor
once attempted to join the Grail community, but, unable to overcome his lust, he castrated himself and was driven away by the
order. Intent on acquiring the holy relics himself, he has taken
up wizardry and, with the help of seductive flowermaidens, traps

Grail knights in his magic kingdom. The ambiguous Kundry assists both orders. She has a double nature: for her sins, she serves at Monsalvat as a slave; under Klingsor's spell she is also a temptress. The leader of the Grail knights is Amfortas, who suffers from a wound that will not heal. Once, he set off with the holy spear to conquer Klingsor, but was seduced by Kundry and robbed of the spear by Klingsor, who used it to inflict the wound.

SCENES 1 and 2 *A forest glade near the castle of the Grail*

At dawn trumpets rouse Gurnemanz and his knights to prayer. They prepare to bathe the wounds of their ruler, Amfortas. Suddenly Kundry rushes in, dishevelled after the long journey from Arabia, where she obtained a balm to soothe Amfortas's wounds. Amfortas, carried on a litter, enters on his way to bathe, and thanks Kundry for the medicine—unaware of her earlier role in his downfall. Gurnemanz tells the knights the story of Amfortas and Klingsor, and that only the touch of the lost spear will heal their ruler's wounds. He relates Amfortas's dream: only an 'innocent fool' made 'wise through pity' will be able to overthrow Klingsor and gain the spear. At that moment one of the sacred white swans is shot down, and the huntsman enters. Gurnemanz reprimands the youth, who is unable to answer questions about his origin, or even his name; only Kundry recognizes him. Gurnemanz hopes that he may have found Amfortas's redeemer, and the youth is led into the castle of the Grail.

SCENE 3 *The castle of the Grail*

The youth witnesses the ceremonial unveiling of the Grail by the suffering Amfortas, supervised by his father Titurel. The ritual has caused Amfortas to bleed again, and he is carried off. Though impressed by the ceremony, the youth has understood nothing of it, and Gurnemanz dismisses him.

ACT II

Klingsor's magic castle

Klingsor orders Kundry to ensnare the youth seen approaching his castle. Flowermaidens tease him first, but he does not succumb until Kundry calls him by his name—Parsifal—and conjures up for him memories of his mother and youth. Kundry's kiss reveals to him the nature of Amfortas's suffering, and he realizes his sacred mission: Parsifal has been made 'wise through pity'. He rejects Kundry's further advances, even when she pleads that her own redemption can only come through being loved. In revenge, both she and Klingsor try to bar Parsifal's way back to Amfortas. Klingsor hurls the holy spear at Parsifal, but he grabs it, using it to make the sign of the cross. Klingsor's kingdom and magic powers are shattered.

ACT III

SCENE 1 *A forest glade near the castle of the Grail*

Some years have passed and Gurnemanz is now an old man. Amfortas's desperate condition has lowered morale among the knights, and Gurnemanz is now living as a hermit. He discovers and revives the half-dead Kundry, who becomes his serving-maid. Parsifal returns to Monsalvat, and is recognized by Kundry—though not, at first, by Gurnemanz. The old knight rebukes him for being armed on Good Friday, but when Parsifal kneels in prayer Gurnemanz recognizes him by the holy spear. Gurnemanz realizes that the Grail community's redeemer has come: he anoints Parsifal as their new ruler while Kundry bathes his feet. Parsifal's first task is to baptize Kundry, granting her absolution from her sins. Gurnemanz interprets the events as the magic of Good Friday. The three set off for the castle of the Holy Grail.

SCENE 2 *The castle of the Grail*
The knights have assembled for Titurel's funeral. It is Amfortas's responsibility to unveil the Grail, but he is unable to perform the task. He uncovers his incurable wound, and begs the knights to kill him. Parsifal, now filled with understanding, steps forward and touches the wound with the holy spear, healing it. All are restored by the miracle, except Kundry, who collapses lifeless. Parsifal unveils the Grail, and the knights pay homage to their new ruler.

THE PEARLFISHERS
see **Les Pêcheurs de Perles**

LES PÊCHEURS DE PERLES (The Pearl Fishers)
Georges Bizet (1838-1875)

THREE ACTS. LIBRETTO BY EUGENE CORMON AND MICHEL CARRÉ. PREMIERE IN PARIS, 30 SEPTEMBER 1863.

Les Pêcheurs de perles is thought of as Bizet's 'other' opera. His operatic output was large, but only *Carmen* and, to a lesser extent, *Les Pêcheurs de perles*, have gained a place in the repertory. *Les Pêcheurs de perles* was Bizet's first success, and though it shows little of the dramatic cogency of *Carmen*, it is cherished for its lyrical beauty. Indeed, the opera's fame rests chiefly on the tenor-baritone duet, 'Au fond du temple saint', and Nadir's 'Je crois entendre encore', both in Act I.

CHARACTERS
Leïla, priestess of Brahma (SOPRANO); *Nadir*, a fisherman (TENOR); *Zurga*, leader of the fishermen (BARITONE); *Nourabad*, high priest of Brahma (BASS)
With *fishermen, Indians, Brahmins*

ACT I
A wild beach in Ceylon
Fishermen are going about their business when Zurga enters and announces that it is time to choose a leader. Their unanimous choice is Zurga himself. Nadir arrives and is recognized by Zurga as his old companion. When the fishermen disperse, Zurga and Nadir recollect how once at a temple they both fell in love with the same beautiful woman, and that they both

vowed to renounce her in order to save their friendship. A boat brings Leïla, the priestess who will protect the pearl fishers during the seasonal expedition. The crowd welcomes her. Nadir recognizes her as the woman he and Zurga were recalling; although she too remembers him, she reaffirms her vows of chastity and is installed in her temple. Nadir listens to Leïla's incantation and is so overcome with emotion that he interrupts her. They declare their love.

ACT II
The ruins of a temple

Leïla recalls for the high priest Nourabad how she risked her life to save a stranger, who in gratitude gave her the necklace she continues to wear. When Nourabad departs she reflects with joy that Nadir is nearby; soon he enters, and the lovers are reunited. Aware of the risk, Nadir slips away but is spotted by Nourabad, who denounces them to the angry people. Zurga intervenes and spares their lives, but when Leïla is unveiled he recognizes her and realizes that Nadir has broken their vow. No longer inclined to mercy, he orders their deaths.

ACT III
SCENE 1 *Zurga's tent*

Zurga is filled with remorse when he remembers Nadir's friendship and Leïla's beauty. At first he is sympathetic when Leïla comes to ask for clemency, but his jealousy is rekindled when she admits her continuing love for Nadir. He orders Nourabad to take her to the sacrificial pyre. As she goes, he asks a fisherman to take her necklace to her mother. Zurga recognizes it as the one he gave to the young girl who had once saved his life, and snatches it from the fisherman.

SCENE 2 *A desolate spot*

The pearl fishers gather in anticipation of the execution. At the last moment Zurga intervenes, distracting the people with news of a fire in the camp that he has deliberately lit. All run off, leaving Zurga to free Nadir and Leïla. Before revealing a secret escape route, Zurga shows them the necklace and the three reflect on their strange circumstances. As Nadir and Leïla flee, Zurga watches the frightened community scatter from the flames.

PELLÉAS ET MÉLISANDE
(Pelléas and Mélisande)
Claude Debussy (1862-1918)

FIVE ACTS. LIBRETTO BY THE COMPOSER, AFTER MAURICE MAETERLINCK'S PLAY. PREMIERE IN PARIS, 30 APRIL 1902.

Debussy contemplated numerous operatic projects but completed only *Pelléas et Mélisande*, a setting (with few incisions) of an enigmatic play by the symbolist writer, Maeterlinck. It occupies a special place both in his output and in French music, for it has no obvious antecedents but opened up new directions for French composers in the 20th century. Debussy rejected set-piece numbers in favour of a seamless symphonic structure, which he filled with atmospheric orchestration and—the opera's most celebrated feature—fluid speech rhythms in the vocal writing.

CHARACTERS

Mélisande (SOPRANO); *Yniold*, Golaud's son from an earlier marriage (SOPRANO); *Geneviève*, mother of Pelléas and Golaud (CONTRALTO); *Pelléas*, grandson of Arkel (TENOR or HIGH BARITONE); *Golaud*, grandson of Arkel (BARITONE); *Doctor* (BARITONE); *Shepherd* (BARITONE); *Arkel*, King of Allemonde (BASS)

With *sailors, servants, paupers*

ACT I

SCENE 1 *A forest*
Golaud, lost in the forest, discovers a mysterious girl sobbing near a well. She will answer none of his questions except to give her name: Mélisande. Eventually she agrees to go home with Golaud.

SCENE 2 *A room in the castle*
Golaud has written to his half-brother, Pelléas, telling him of his marriage to Mélisande. He has delayed breaking the news to his family, fearing the reaction of his grandfather, King Arkel, who had hoped for a politically advantageous marriage following the death of Golaud's first wife. When Golaud's mother, Geneviève, reads the letter to Arkel, the old man accepts the news resignedly. Pelléas enters, announcing his intention to visit a dying friend, but Arkel opposes his wish, reminding him that his own father lies ill.

SCENE 3 *Outside the castle*
Mélisande has arrived at the castle, and Geneviève takes her into the gardens, where they are joined by Pelléas. Left alone by Geneviève—who has gone off to attend to Yniold, Golaud's son by his first marriage—Pelléas tells Mélisande that he has to go away the following morning. She is upset by this news, an indication of the tenderness between them.

ACT II

SCENE 1 *At a well in the park*
Pelléas has postponed his departure, and accompanies Mélisande to the well in the park. While Mélisande is looking at her reflection in the water, her wedding rings slips off and falls into the depths. She is distraught, but Pelléas reassures her that Golaud will not be angry so long as she tells him the truth.

SCENE 2 *A room in the castle*
Mélisande is nursing Golaud. At the moment that her ring slipped off, her husband was thrown from his horse. Golaud observes that the ring is missing from her hand, but Mélisande is too afraid to tell him the truth; instead she claims to have lost it in a seaside cave while looking for seashells for Yniold. Angrily, he orders her to search for it, even though it is dark, and Pelléas accompanies her.

Scene 3 *Outside a cave*
Pelléas and Mélisande have stumbled through the dark to the cave, both aware that the ring is not there. They encounter three dishevelled beggars, a sight that frightens Mélisande into heading back.

ACT III

Scene 1 *In a tower of the castle*
At the tower window, Mélisande is combing her hair. Pelléas has now decided to depart the following day and comes to say farewell, persuading her to lower her hair so that he can kiss her goodbye. Golaud appears and reproaches them.

Scenes 2 and 3 *The castle vaults*
Golaud shows Pelléas the dank castle vaults. The unhealthy air leaves them feeling faint and they emerge. Outside the entrance to the vault, Golaud warns Pelléas against getting too close to Mélisande.

Scene 4 *Outside the castle*
Golaud's jealousy is increased by Yniold's ambiguous reply to his questions about the relationship of Pelléas and Mélisande. Seeing a light in Mélisande's room, Golaud holds Yniold up to look through the window: the boy sees Pelléas and Mélisande sitting motionless. Golaud's increasing violence of emotion terrifies the child.

ACT IV

Scene 1 and 2 *A room in the castle*
Pelléas's father, now recovered, has advised his son to travel. Pelléas comes to Mélisande to arrange their final meeting: she will find him at the well in the park that evening. Arkel is telling Mélisande how happy he is at the recovery of Pelléas's father when Golaud bursts in. In a jealous rage, he drags her across the room by her hair. Arkel intervenes.

Scenes 3 and 4 *At a well in the park*
Yniold is playing in the park. He encounters a Shepherd, whose mysterious answer to the boy's question disturbs him. Yniold runs off home, and Pelléas and Mélisande appear. They confess their love for each other, and embrace passionately. But Golaud is watching from behind a tree, and he emerges to kill his brother with his sword. He pursues Mélisande into the darkness.

ACT V

Mélisande's bedroom
Mélisande has given birth to a girl and now lies dying. Golaud is wracked by guilt, but the Doctor reassures him that the small wound he inflicted on her is not the cause of her worsening condition. He is still jealous, however, and questions her about her relationship with Pelléas, doubting the innocence she protests to the end. Arkel tries to console the grieving man, suggesting that Mélisande's daughter will fill her place.

PETER GRIMES
Benjamin Britten (1913–1976)

LIBRETTO BY MONTAGU SLATER, AFTER GEORGE CRABBE'S POEM *THE BOROUGH*. PREMIERE IN LONDON, 7 JUNE 1945.

Peter Grimes was Britten's first full-scale opera (it was preceded by the operetta *Paul Bunyan*) and remains the most successful of all 20th-century British operas. Set in Aldeburgh—near to where Britten was born, and where he was to settle shortly after writing the opera—it charts the conflict between a narrow-minded fishing community and the strange fisherman, Grimes, the first of the composer's misfit anti-heroes. The powerful score is constructed on traditional lines, with self-contained choruses and arias. The orchestral Interludes—the best-known music in *Grimes*, four of which are often heard in concert—are effective evocations of the sea as well as reflections of Grimes's mental state.

CHARACTERS

Ellen Orford, a widowed schoolmistress (SOPRANO); *First Niece* and *Second Niece*, main attractions of 'The Boar' (SOPRANOS); *Mrs Sedley*, a widow (MEZZO-SOPRANO); *Auntie*, landlady of 'The Boar' (CONTRALTO); *Peter Grimes*, a fisherman (TENOR); *Bob Boles*, fisherman and Methodist (TENOR); *Rev. Horace Adams*, the rector (TENOR); *Captain Balstrode*, retired merchant skipper (BARITONE); *Ned Keene*, apothecary and quack (BARITONE); *Swallow*, a lawyer (BASS); *Hobson*, carrier (BASS); *John*, Grimes's apprentice (SILENT); *Dr Crabbe* (SILENT) With *townspeople* and *fisherfolk*

PROLOGUE
The Moot Hall
An inquest is taking place into the death in suspicious circumstances of Peter Grimes's apprentice. After hearing Grimes's testimony, Mr Swallow returns a verdict of accidental death. Grimes protests when he is cautioned not to get another apprentice. The townsfolk are suspicious of Grimes, and only the widowed schoolmistress Ellen Orford stands by him.

ACT I
Interlude I Dawn
SCENE 1 *A street by the sea*
People are going about their business when Grimes calls for help with his boat. Only Balstrode and Ned Keene defy the mood of antagonism by helping him land his catch. Keene tells Grimes that he has found him a new apprentice, but Hobson can only be persuaded to fetch him from the workhouse when Ellen offers to accompany him. A storm blows up, during which Balstrode tries to convince Grimes not to take on another boy, but to start a new life elsewhere. Grimes is defiant, saying he intends to remain in the community, get wealthy, and marry Ellen.

Interlude II Storm
SCENE 2 *'The Boar'*
Townsfolk are gathered in the pub and are joined by others in search of shelter. The landlady, known as Auntie because of

the two 'Nieces' she keeps there, is annoyed with her customers, particularly the disruptive Baltsrode and Bob Boles. Ned Keene announces that the storm has caused a landslide near Grimes's hut, and soon Grimes himself enters. When Ellen and Hobson arrive with the new apprentice, John, Grimes wastes no time in ordering the boy to work.

ACT II
Interlude III Sunday Morning
SCENE 1 *A street by the sea*

While most of the town is in church, Ellen sits at the beach with John playing around her. When she notices a tear in his clothing and then a bruise, she confronts Grimes and accuses him of mistreating the boy. Angry and defiant, Grimes drags the boy off to his boat, but not before the community—emerging from church—have witnessed the quarrel. They resolve to take action against Grimes, and men set off for his hut.

Interlude IV Passacaglia
SCENE 2 *Grimes's hut*

Grimes is haunted by the death of his previous apprentice and the accusations against him. Nevertheless, he roughly orders the boy to get ready for fishing. At the sound of the men approaching he panics, and hurries the boy out onto the cliff top in order to go down to the sea by another route. But the boy slips and falls to his death, and Grimes is climbing down after him when the men reach his empty hut.

ACT III
Interlude V Moonlight
SCENES 1 and 2 *A street by the sea*

The village dance is in full swing. People come and go, and Ellen takes Balstrode aside to show him John's jersey, which has been washed up. Mrs Sedley, having seen the evidence and noticed that Grimes's boat is back, calls for a mob to track down Grimes. They set off, crying 'Peter Grimes'.

Before the man-hunt reaches Grimes, Ellen and Balstrode find him alone and deranged. He fails to recognize them, but accepts Balstrode's advice, to sail his ship out to sea and scuttle it. When day comes, the community resumes its business. News of a boat sinking far out to sea is met with indifference.

PORGY AND BESS
George Gershwin (1898-1937)

THREE ACTS. LIBRETTO BY DUBOSE HEYWARD AFTER HIS NOVEL *PORGY*; LYRICS BY HEYWARD AND IRA GERSHWIN. PREMIERE IN NEW YORK, 10 OCTOBER 1935.

Porgy and Bess, which was described by its composer as a 'folk opera' and started life on Broadway, is now recognized as one of the great 20th-century operas and a classic of American theatre history. Its acceptance was slow: although it was one of the first 'white' works to portray its 'negro' subject seriously, some found it condescending and dismissed it as a product of its time. However, it has not dated, since the South Carolina society depicted is universal in its emotions. *Porgy* turned out to be the climax of Gershwin's career—he died at only 38—and reveals his considerable experience of the musical theatre. The powerful score is sophisticated, but its jazzy numbers have entered the popular repertory: highlights include 'Summertime', 'I got plenty o' nuttin'', 'Bess, you is my woman now', and 'It ain't necessarily so'.

CHARACTERS

Bess (SOPRANO); *Serena*, Robbins's wife (SOPRANO); *Clara*, Jake's wife (SOPRANO); *Annie* (MEZZO-SOPRANO); *Lily*, Peter's wife (MEZZO-SOPRANO); *Strawberry Woman* (MEZZO-SOPRANO); *Maria*, keeper of the cook-shop (CONTRALTO); *Sportin' Life*, a dope pedlar (TENOR); *Mingo* (TENOR); *Robbins* (TENOR); *Peter*, the Honey Man (TENOR); *Nelson* (TENOR); *Crab Man* (TENOR); *Crown*, a stevedore (BARITONE); *Jake*, a fisherman (BARITONE); *Frazier*, a lawyer (BARITONE); *Jim*, a cotton-picker (BARITONE); *Undertaker* (BARITONE); *Porgy*, a cripple (BASS-BARITONE); *Jasbo Brown* (PIANIST)
With *Mr Archdale*, *Detective*, *Policeman*, *Coroner*, *Scipio* (all SPOKEN); *residents* of Catfish Row

ACT I

SCENE 1 *Catfish Row*
On a quiet evening, the sounds of Jasbo Brown playing the piano and Clara singing her baby a lullaby are soon interrupted. The men have started a game of crap, which attracts both Porgy and the belligerent Crown, the latter high on Sportin' Life's 'happy dust'. When Crown loses, he picks a fight with Robbins and kills him. Serena mourns her dead husband, while Crown's woman, Bess, is given refuge from the angry tenement dwellers by Porgy.

SCENE 2 *Serena's room*
Porgy and Bess join the mourners at Serena's house, though Bess is treated with suspicion. A detective arrives and accuses Peter of the murder; the old man panics and reveals that Crown is the guilty one. Nevertheless, Peter is held as a witness. The Undertaker is persuaded to bury Robbins, even though Serena lacks the money to pay him.

ACT II

SCENE 1 *Catfish Row*
Normality has returned to Catfish Row. Jake is preparing his fishing nets, though his wife Clara warns about threatening storms. Porgy sings contentedly, and Maria comments how much happier Bess has made him. The lawyer Mr Frazier enters and sells Porgy a 'divorce' between Bess and Crown—even though they were never married. Porgy warns that the buzzard flying overhead is a bad omen, but everyone makes ready for a picnic on Kittiwah Island. Bess pledges to be Porgy's woman—she has spurned Sportin' Life's offer of 'happy dust'—before setting out with the others for the island. Porgy is left alone.

SCENE 2 *Kittiwah Island*
Sportin' Life entertains the picnickers with his un-Biblical 'sermon'. Serena scolds them before they embark to return home. Bess is waylaid by Crown—who has been hiding on the island since the murder—and, ignoring her protestations of love for Porgy, he overcomes her and she remains behind as the others sail.

SCENE 3 *Catfish Row*
In spite of a storm warning, Jake bids Clara farewell and sets off fishing. Bess, who had been missing for two days and returned feverish, gains consciousness and confesses to Porgy that she was with Crown, but assures Porgy that she would rather stay with him. Clara and Maria wait anxiously for Jake. The hurricane bell is heard.

SCENE 4 *Serena's room*
Prayers are offered for deliverance from the storm. At the height of the noise, Crown breaks his way in. He has come to claim Bess, but she refuses to leave with him. The wreck of Jake's boat is spotted, and Crown goes to help Clara—but threatens Porgy that he will return.

ACT III
SCENES 1–3 *Catfish Row*
With the storm over, the community mourns the dead, Jake, Clara, and—they believe—Crown. Sportin' Life, however, is sure that Crown is alive, and warns that he will be returning to confront Porgy. Bess comforts Clara's baby, and as she leaves, Crown enters the courtyard where Porgy lies in wait.

Crown has been killed by Porgy, and the police take Porgy off to identify the corpse. Playing on Bess's fears, Sportin' Life persuades her to start a new life with him in New York.

Porgy, having been released, returns to Catfish Row. When he is unable to find Bess, Serena and Maria break the news to him that she has run away. Inconsolable, and despite his crippling disability, he sets off in search of her.

PRINCE IGOR
Alexander Borodin (1834–1887)

PROLOGUE AND FOUR ACTS. LIBRETTO BY THE COMPOSER, AFTER A SCENARIO BY VLADIMIR VASILEVICH STASSOV, ITSELF DRAWN FROM A 12TH-CENTURY EPIC POEM *THE SONG OF IGOR'S CAMPAIGN*. PREMIERE IN ST PETERSBURG, 4 NOVEMBER 1890.

Borodin—an amateur composer whose profession was chemistry—worked at his opera for 18 years but died leaving it unfinished, unaware that it would become a success and a milestone in Russian nationalist music, ranking with Mussorgsky's *Boris Godunov*. The two operas have much in common: like *Boris*, *Prince Igor* deals with an historical subject, and just as Rimsky-Korsakov edited a performing edition of Mussorgsky's opera, so he (together with Glazunov) completed *Prince Igor*, thus ensuring its place in the repertory. *Prince Igor* tells the story of the conflict between the Russians and the Polovtsians, and the opposing sides are distinguished musically: folk idioms were used as inspiration (rather than directly) in depicting the Russians, and the Polovtsians are characterized in exotic and sometimes—as in the famous Polovtsian Dances—wild music.

CHARACTERS

Yaroslavna, Igor's wife (SOPRANO); *Yaroslavna's Nurse* (SOPRANO); *A Polovtsian Maiden* (SOPRANO); *Konchakovna*, Konchak's daughter (MEZZO-SOPRANO); *Vladimir Igorevich*, Igor's son by his first marriage (TENOR); *Ovlur*, a Christian Polovtsian (TENOR); *Yeroshka* , a gudok player (TENOR); *Igor Sviatoslavich*, Prince of Seversk (BARITONE); *Prince Galitsky* (Vladimir Yaroslavich), Yaroslavna's brother (BASS); *Khan Konchak*, a Polovtsian leader (BASS); *Skula*, a gudok player (BASS); *Khan Gzak*, a Polovtsian leader (SPOKEN)

With Russian *princes* and *princesses*, *boyars* and their *wives*, *elders*, *warriors*, *maidens*, *people*, Polovtsian *Khans*, Konchakovna's *companions*, Konchak's *slave girls*, *guards*, Russian *prisoners of war*

PROLOGUE

The town square in Putivl

Prince Igor and his son Vladimir make preparations for war against the barbaric Polovtsians. Igor is not superstitious, and takes no notice when an eclipse of the sun instils fear into his subjects and wife, Yaroslavna; but two of his soldiers, Skula and Yeroshka, interpret the eclipse as a bad omen, and desert to become followers of the hedonistic Galitsky, Yaroslavna's brother, who is not going to war. Prince Igor appoints Galitsky to govern Putivl in his absence and protect Yaroslavna.

ACT I

SCENE 1 *Prince Galitsky's house*

Galitsky's followers have kidnapped a girl for him. He encourages them by promising them wine and women for all should he succeed Prince Igor as ruler of Putivl, and takes no notice when the captive girl's friends come to beg for her release. The drunken Skula and Yeroshka are so taken with their new lifestyle that they stir up the crowd in calling for Prince Igor to be deposed.

SCENE 2 *Yaroslavna's quarters*

Yaroslavna, alone except for the company of her Nurse, receives a deputation of friends of the captive girl, asking her to intervene. She confronts Galitsky, and obtains the girl's release. Boyars inform Yaroslavna of the defeat and capture of Igor and Vladimir. Soon the Polovtsians encircle Putivl.

ACT II

The Polovtsian camp

Vladimir has fallen in love with Konchakovna, the enemy commander's daughter; she is sure that her father will accept their marriage, but Vladimir knows that his father will oppose it vehemently. They move off as Prince Igor enters, downcast at his military mistakes and full of longing for Yaroslavna.

Ovlur, a convert to Christianity who feels no loyalty to Khan Konchak, offers to secure Igor's escape, but the Prince declines on honourable grounds. Konchak himself comes to offer freedom to Igor—he suggests a truce, in order that they can unite against the rest of the world—but the Prince remains unmoved. In order to impress his captive, Khan Konchak orders his slaves to perform the Polovtsian Dances for Igor.

ACT III
The Polovtsian camp
News of the sacking of Putivl and the Polovtsians' atrocities delights the bloodthirsty Konchak and convinces Igor and Vladimir of the need to defend their people. They seek out Ovlur, who is able to provide horses, but Konchakovna plays on Vladimir's emotions. When he makes up his mind to defend his country and abandon his lover, she raises the alarm: Vladimir is captured, and the Polovtsians attempt to torture him. But Khan Konchak intervenes and, admitting his admiration for Igor, unites his daughter and Vladimir in marriage.

ACT IV
Putivl
Yaroslavna and her people lament their fate. She fears the worst when two horsemen are spotted in the distance, but is soon overcome with joy when she recognizes one of them as Igor. They are reunited and the people—including even the deserters Skula and Yeroshka, who join in for fear of being exposed as followers of the now discredited Galitsky—rejoice.

PUNCH AND JUDY
Harrison Birtwistle (b.1934)

PROLOGUE AND ONE ACT. LIBRETTO BY STEPHEN PRUSLIN. PREMIERE IN ALDEBURGH, 8 JUNE 1968.

Birtwistle is one of the most original voices in contemporary music, and among British composers of his generation one of the most prolific in writing for the musical theatre. He has composed full-scale works for London's opera houses (*The Mask of Orpheus* for English National Opera, *Gawain* for Covent Garden), but his first opera remains perhaps the most important. *Punch and Judy* is a work of the 1960s, juxtaposing extremes of sex and violence with moments of great lyrical beauty. Its brutality and decibel level scandalized some, but it is now accepted as a masterpiece of post-war British music.

CHARACTERS
Pretty Polly (later Witch) (HIGH SOPRANO); *Judy* (later Fortune Teller) (MEZZO-SOPRANO); *Lawyer* (HIGH TENOR); *Punch* (HIGH BARITONE); *Choregos* (later Jack Ketch) (BARITONE); *Doctor* (DEEP BASS)

In the Prologue, Choregos opens his Punch-and-Judy show. The first of four 'Melodramas' follows, in which Punch is cradling a baby, which he soon throws into the fire. Judy challenges him about the murder, and she too ends up being killed. In the first 'Quest for Pretty Polly' (there are three, interspersed between the 'Melodramas'), Punch sets out on a hobby-horse to woo Pretty Polly. He finds her, but she is unmoved by his serenade and spurns his offer of a huge sunflower. Punch's confrontation with the Lawyer and the Doctor (the second 'Melodrama') leads to the death of the two men. The second 'Quest for Pretty Polly' recalls the first, but brings Punch no nearer to winning her over; this time she rejects the giant gemstone he offers. With the third 'Melodrama', Punch's creator Choregos enters the action, but his battle of wits with Punch ends in his own death inside a bass-viol case. In Punch's 'Nightmare', he is haunted by his victims (Judy has been transformed into a Fortune Teller) and confronted by a Witch (none other than Pretty Polly), but escapes on his hobby-horse. He is unable to find Pretty Polly on his third 'Quest', and is comforted by Choregos (who has miraculously reappeared). Punch languishes in prison for his crimes (the fourth 'Melodrama') and soon he is visited by the hangman Jack Ketch (Choregos in disguise). He dupes Jack Ketch into putting his own head in the noose, and the hangman dies. By performing a good deed at last—the murder of the hangman—he is rewarded with the love of Pretty Polly. The tale ends with Choregos's Epilogue, in which he announces that tragedy has turned into comedy.

I PURITANI (The Puritans)
Vincenzo Bellini (1801-1835)

THREE PARTS. LIBRETTO BY CARLO PEPOLI, AFTER THE PLAY *TETES RONDES ET CAVALIERS* BY J.-A.P.F. ANCELOT AND J.X. BONIFACE. PREMIERE IN PARIS, 25 JANUARY 1835.

Although Bellini's death at the age of 34 was untimely, *I Puritani*, never intended to be his final opera, seems to summarize his achievements. It is his most sophisticated work, though it lacks none of the lyricism of his earlier operas. Like most operas of the period, it is dominated by its soprano role but also makes great demands on its ensemble of four principal singers. Indeed, the singers at the premiere were so perfectly suited to their parts and remained so closely identified with the opera's great success that they are to this day known as the '*Puritani* Quartet'.

CHARACTERS
Elvira, Lord Walton's daughter (SOPRANO); *Enrichetta di Francia*, widow of Charles I (MEZZO-SOPRANO); *Lord Arturo Talbo*, Cavalier, Stuart supporter (TENOR); *Sir Bruno Robertson*, Puritan (TENOR); *Sir Riccardo Forth*, Puritan (BARITONE); *Lord Walton*, Puritan governor-general (BASS); *Sir Giorgio*, Lord Walton's brother (BASS)
With Puritan *soldiers*, Arturo's *followers*, *ladies*, *pages*

PART I
SCENE 1 *The courtyard of a fortress near Plymouth*
The Puritans are anticipating both a victory over the Stuarts and the marriage of their governor's daughter, Elvira. Lord Walton had earlier promised her hand to Riccardo, a fellow

supporter of Cromwell, but relented when he discovered that she was in love with a Cavalier, Lord Arturo Talbo.

SCENE 2 *Elvira's chambers*
Giorgio, Elvira's uncle, comforts his niece: she still fears that she will be forced to marry Riccardo, but Giorgio reveals how he brought about her father's change of heart. She can scarcely believe his news that Arturo is arriving at the fortress.

SCENE 3 *The armoury*
The bridal couple are welcomed. Walton gives them his blessing, but announces that he is unable to attend their wedding as he has been ordered to escort a woman, believed to be a Stuart spy, to London. Arturo discovers that the prisoner is none other than Queen Enrichetta, widow of Charles I, and resolves to save her. Elvira enters briefly, and leaves her bridal veil behind. Arturo uses it to disguise the Queen, and they succeed in passing the guards. They are confronted only by the jealous Riccardo, but, when he realizes that the veiled woman is not Elvira, are allowed to escape. Elvira believes that Arturo has deserted her, and loses her reason. The wedding guests denounce Arturo for his treachery, and a warrant for the fugitives' arrest is given.

PART II
A hall in the fortress
All are concerned for the delirious Elvira, who dreams of Arturo. Riccardo's announcement that Cromwell has placed a death sentence on Arturo's head worries Giorgio: he knows that Arturo's execution would drive Elvira to her death. He convinces Riccardo to save the Cavalier, but both agree that he can have only one reprieve: if they encounter Arturo fighting against them in battle, he must die.

PART III
A grove near the fortress, three months later
Arturo is attempting to seek out his lover. During a storm he creeps up to the fortress, and is reunited with Elvira, explaining his actions. Her joy temporarily restores her senses, but the noise of soldiers closing in upsets her again, and she imagines that she is about to be deserted a second time. Riccardo discovers them and pronounces the death sentence on Arturo, which jolts Elvira back to sanity. The sight of the lovers moves Giorgio and even Riccardo to pity, but the soldiers demand punishment, even when Elvira is determined to stand by Arturo in the face of death. Suddenly news arrives of victory over the Stuarts and a general amnesty. Elvira and Arturo are free to marry.

THE QUEEN OF SPADES
Pyotr Ilich Tchaikovsky (1840-1893)

THREE ACTS. LIBRETTO BY MODEST TCHAIKOVSKY AND THE COMPOSER AFTER PUSHKIN'S NOVELLA. PREMIERE IN ST PETERSBURG, 19 DECEMBER 1890.

'Unless I am making a dreadful and unforgivable mistake *The Queen of Spades* really will be my masterpiece,' wrote Tchaikovsky to his brother Modest, the opera's librettist. Though audiences today favour the composer's *Eugene Onegin*, *The Queen of Spades* is his second most popular opera, cherished both for its powerful music and Modest Tchaikovsky's melodramatic adaptation of Pushkin's cynical tale. *The Queen of Spades* is a late work—Tchaikovsky's penultimate opera—and inhabits the same haunted emotional world as the composer's Fifth and Sixth Symphonies. It is further distinguished by its combination of backwards-looking charm (in its affectionate evocation of Rococo and Baroque style), Grand Opera panoply and High Romantic turbulence.

CHARACTERS

Lisa, granddaughter of the Countess (SOPRANO); *Chlöe*, player in the Interlude (SOPRANO); *Masha*, Lisa's maid (SOPRANO); *The Countess* (MEZZO-SOPRANO); *Governess* (MEZZO-SOPRANO); *Pauline*, Lisa's companion (CONTRALTO); *Daphnis*, played by Pauline in the Interlude (CONTRALTO); *Herman* (TENOR); *Chekalinsky* (TENOR); *Chaplitsky* (TENOR); *Master of Ceremonies* (TENOR); *Count Tomsky* (BARITONE); *Plutus*, played by Tomsky in the Interlude (BARITONE); *Prince Yeletsky* (BARITONE); *Surin* (BASS); *Narumov* (BASS) With *nurses*, *governesses*, *promenaders*, *children*, *gamblers*

ACT I

SCENE 1 *The Summer Garden, St Petersburg*

Children play in the park, watched by their nurses. A troop of boy soldiers marches in, and soon the officer Surin and gambler Chekalinsky appear. They discuss the strange, brooding Herman—a poor man, not quite of the 'officer class'—who had spent the whole of the previous evening watching the gambling but refused to join in. Herman enters with Count Tomsky, and admits that he has fallen in love with a young woman he does not know. He is driven to jealous torment when Prince Yeletsky is complimented on his engagement by Surin and Chekalinsky and points out his fiancée: she is Lisa, and Herman recognizes her as the woman he loves. In turn, Lisa and her Countess grandmother are alarmed to see Herman: he is the stranger who has been following them. When they have gone, Tomsky tells how the Countess became known as the 'Queen of Spades'.

During her youth in Paris, where she was renowned for her beauty, the Countess sought to regain her husband's wealth she had lost at gambling by exchanging the secret of three winning cards for a night of passion with a French Count. She won her fortune back and disclosed the secret to two men, but was warned by a ghost that she would die if she divulged it again.

A storm scatters the crowd, leaving Herman alone. He is gripped by the idea of using the cards to win Lisa from Yeletsky.

SCENE 2 *Lisa's room*

Lisa—though distracted—joins Pauline and friends in dancing and singing. The noise rouses Lisa's Governess, who reprimands them. When Lisa is finally left alone she admits to herself that she loves Herman rather than the gentlemanly Yeletsky. Suddenly, Herman appears on her balcony, declaring his love. He hides when the Countess is heard ordering Lisa to bed, but when they are alone again Lisa gives in to his feelings.

ACT II
SCENE 2 *The ballroom of a mansion*
At a masked ball, Chekalinsky and Surin mock Herman for his preoccupation with the Countess's 'three cards'. Lisa, too, is clearly distracted, and Yeletsky begs her to explain the reason for her coldness. Herman receives a letter from Lisa, arranging an assignation for that evening. An allegorical interlude, 'The Faithful Shepherdess', is performed for the company, in which Chlöe chooses the love of the poor but sincere shepherd Daphnis in preference to the wealthy Plutus. The performance over, Lisa gives Herman the key to the Countess's house in order that he may come to her room. Their conversation is interrupted by the Master of Ceremonies announcing the arrival of the Empress, and guests wait to welcome her.

SCENE 2 *The Countess's bedroom*
At midnight Herman steals into the Countess's house. He reaches her bedroom and hides when she is brought in by her servants, who she soon dismisses. She muses to herself, recalling her youth in Paris, and takes fright when Herman emerges. He begs for her secret, then threatens her with a pistol; she is overcome by fear and dies. Lisa appears and accuses him of murder. When he reveals that he was after the Countess's secret she is certain that his declarations of love were false.

ACT III
SCENE 1 *Herman's barracks*
Herman is reading a letter from Lisa, begging him to meet her on the embankment. The sounds of a church service bring memories of the Countess's funeral back to Herman, and suddenly the old woman's ghost appears with the secret—'three, seven, ace'.

SCENE 2 *An embankment*
Lisa has almost given up hope seeing Herman when he appears. But her joy is shattered again by the realization that his obsession is now entirely with the cards. As he rushes off to the gambling house to test his secret, Lisa throws herself into the canal.

SCENE 3 *A gambling house*
Yeletsky, shattered by his broken engagement, has come to gamble for the first time. Tomsky entertains the men with a song, and play has resumed when the ashen-faced Herman enters. Staking a huge sum on 'three', Herman plays and wins; placing his winnings on the table, he is lucky again with the 'seven'. Yeletsky, seeking revenge, steps forward: Herman plays on 'ace', but the card is the Queen of Spades. The Countess's ghost reappears. Herman kills himself, and prayers for the peace of his soul are offered.

THE RAKE'S PROGRESS
Igor Stravinsky (1882-1971)

THREE ACTS AND EPILOGUE. LIBRETTO BY W.H. AUDEN AND
CHESTER KALLMAN, AFTER WILLIAM HOGARTH'S SERIES OF
ENGRAVINGS *A RAKE'S PROGRESS*. PREMIERE IN VENICE, 11
SEPTEMBER 1951.

Stravinsky's music divides into three categories: the works written in his native Russia before the First World War, the
neo-classical compositions that he began writing soon after he
went into exile in Western Europe, and his serial works, written
in the 1950s and '60s in the United States (where he had settled
in 1939). *The Rake's Progress*—inspired by seeing Hogarth's
series of engravings at the Chicago Art Institute in 1947—was
his last major neo-classical work. It alludes to late 18th-century
opera (the three Mozart-Da Ponte works especially), to the
extent of including harpsichord-accompanied recitatives. Like
Mozart's *Don Giovanni*, Stravinsky's opera ends with the princi-
pals pointing out the story's moral to the audience.

CHARACTERS
Anne, Trulove's daughter (SOPRANO); *Mother Goose*, a brothel keeper
(MEZZO-SOPRANO); *Baba the Turk*, bearded lady displayed in a cir-
cus (MEZZO-SOPRANO); *Tom Rakewell*, in love with Anne (TENOR);
Sellem, auctioneer (TENOR); *Nick Shadow* (BARITONE); *Trulove* (BASS)
Keeper of the Madhouse (BASS)

ACT I
SCENE 1 *The garden of Trulove's house in the country*
Tom and Anne are in love, but Anne's father is worried about
the match: Trulove suspects that Tom is lazy, and his fears are
confirmed when Tom declines his offer of a respectable job in
the city. The young man is busy explaining that he has put his
trust in fortune when a stranger who introduces himself as
Nick Shadow brings the message that Tom has been left a
large inheritance. Tom adopts Shadow as his servant—at a
price to be settled at the end of a year and a day—and sets off
for London to claim his wealth.

SCENE 2 *Mother Gooses's brothel, London*
Tom is introduced to the physical pleasures that money can
buy. Shadow and Mother Goose make Tom recite the creed of
his new-found lifestyle, but he hesitates at the mention of
'love', when memories of Anne flood back. The whores com-
miserate with Tom, but do not get a chance to comfort him:
Mother Goose takes him off for initiation.

SCENE 3 *Trulove's garden*
Anne, upset at having heard nothing of Tom, resolves to go to
London to rescue him.

ACT II
SCENE 1 *The morning room of Tom's house in London*
Tom is already tired of his new life. He longs for excitement,

and in response Shadow suggests that he marry the bearded woman, Baba the Turk, who has been causing such a stir. They set off to woo her.

SCENE 2 *The street outside Tom's house*
Anne is waiting outside Tom's house when he returns and steps out of a sedan chair. He advises Anne that London is no place for her and urges her to forget him. She leaves when Tom admits that the bearded woman he has helped from the chair is Baba the Turk, his new wife.

SCENE 3 *Tom's morning room*
Tom's house is strewn with the strange objects Baba the Turk has collected from her many admirers. He is irritated by her constant babble, and they argue until Tom silences her by covering her face with his wig. He seeks solace in sleep, but is interrupted by Shadow, who introduces his machine for turning stones into bread. Tom is convinced that by abolishing the world's hunger he will be worthy of Anne's love, but Shadow knows that his scheme will complete his master's downfall.

ACT III
SCENE 1 *Tom's morning room*
Shadow's scheme has left Tom bankrupt, and a crowd is gathering for the auction of his possessions. Anne joins the people, but can see no sign of Tom. Sellem, the auctioneer, directs the sale until a mysterious object is offered: it is Baba, still on the spot where Tom silenced her, who is suddenly revived. Anne returns when she hears the voice of Tom, who is singing with Shadow outside, and Baba reassures her that Tom still cares for her. Baba leaves, to resume her career on the stage.

SCENE 2 *A graveyard*
A year and a day since their first encounter, Shadow is claiming his wage: Tom's soul. His grave is dug, and Shadow orders him to commit suicide. But at the last minute Shadow proposes instead a game of cards to settle his fate. When Tom wins—inspired by thoughts of Anne—Shadow gets his revenge by condemning him to insanity.

Scene 3 *Bedlam*
Surrounded by madmen, Tom imagines himself to be Adonis and is convinced that Anne, who comes to visit him, is Venus. She calms him with a lullaby before leaving with her father. Tom wakes to find her gone and dies of a broken heart.

EPILOGUE
The principal characters address the audience with a moral: 'For idle hearts and hands and minds the Devil finds a work to do.'

THE RETURN OF ULYSSES TO HIS HOMELAND
see **Il ritorno d'Ulisse in patria**

DAS RHEINGOLD
see **Der Ring des Nibelungen**

RIGOLETTO
Giuseppe Verdi (1813-1901)

THREE ACTS. LIBRETTO BY FRANCESCO MARIA PIAVE AFTER
VICTOR HUGO'S PLAY *LE ROI S'AMUSE*. PREMIERE IN VENICE, 11
MARCH 1851.

Rigoletto was Verdi's first outright masterpiece. It is one of his
most tuneful works, but was also innovative in breaking firmly
established conventions of operatic form and structure. From
Rigoletto onwards, each of Verdi's operas has its own distinctive
colour: *Rigoletto* is dark (there are no female voices in the chorus),
in keeping with the mood of Hugo's *Le Roi s'amuse*, on which it is
based. Verdi admired Hugo's play as 'perhaps the greatest drama
of modern times'. He responded by making Rigoletto (Hugo's
Triboulet) one of the great operatic roles, full of contradictions—a
malevolent jester softened by tenderness for his daughter. Verdi
provided no other baritone role with such range of emotion.

CHARACTERS
Gilda, Rigoletto's daughter (SOPRANO); *Giovanna*, Gilda's nurse
(SOPRANO); *Countess Ceprano* (MEZZO-SOPRANO); *Maddalena*,
Sparafucile's sister (CONTRALTO); *The Duke of Mantua* (TENOR);
Matteo Borsa, a courtier (TENOR); *Rigoletto*, the Duke's jester (BARI-
TONE); *Marullo*, a nobleman (BARITONE); *Sparafucile*, a hired
assassin (BASS); *Count Monterone* (BASS); *Count Ceprano* (BASS)
With *courtiers, pages, servants*

ACT I
SCENE 1 *A hall in the palace of the Duke of Mantua*
The Duke, a compulsive philanderer, tells the courtier Borsa
how he plans to seduce a young woman he has seen in church.
When he turns his attentions on Countess Ceprano, the jester
Rigoletto taunts her jealous husband. Marullo counters by
revealing to the company that Rigoletto keeps a woman locked
up at home. Their amusement is interrupted by the entrance of
Monterone, who denounces the Duke for having ravished his
daughter. Rigoletto seizes the opportunity to mock him too,
but in doing so provokes Monterone's curse on him.

SCENE 2 *A blind alley leading to Rigoletto's house*
On his way home, Rigoletto is still reeling from the curse when
he is waylaid by a professional assassin, Sparafucile, who offers
his services. He is welcomed home by Gilda—the daughter he
is over-protective of, not his mistress (as the courtiers
believe)—and reminds her nurse, Giovanna, never to let any-
one in. But before long the Duke steals in undetected. Gilda is
telling Giovanna about the young man she has seen at church
when the Duke steps forward—she recognizes him as the man
she loves, and is smitten when he convinces her that he is only
a poor student. Not long after the Duke has departed, Ceprano

leads some of his fellow courtiers up to the house to avenge Rigoletto's taunts: they plan to abduct his 'mistress'. Rigoletto encounters them in the street, is tricked into thinking they are about to kidnap the Countess Ceprano, and is blindfolded. He holds the ladder as they carry Gilda off. Rigoletto is haunted by the curse when he discovers the crime.

ACT II
A hall in the Duke's palace

The Duke, crestfallen when he discovers that Gilda has gone, is cheered by the news that the courtiers have brought her to him. He rushes off to seduce her. Rigoletto enters in search of her and soon realizes where she is, but his way is barred by the courtiers. Gilda emerges and throws herself into her father's arms. The courtiers are shamed into leaving, and Rigoletto comforts her as she relates her story. Provoked by the sight of both Monterone being conducted to prison and the Duke's portrait, Rigoletto swears vengeance.

ACT III
A run-down inn on the bank of the river

Gilda is still infatuated with the Duke, and Rigoletto has brought her to see her lover's true character: they hide and watch as the Duke flirts with Maddalena, Sparafucile's sister. Rigoletto sends Gilda home (with orders to disguise herself as a man and leave the city) before making arrangements with Sparafucile, whom he has hired to kill the Duke. When Rigoletto has left and the Duke retired to bed, the disguised Gilda returns to the inn and overhears Maddalena—who herself has fallen in love with the Duke—persuade her brother not to murder him, but to substitute another body in Rigoletto's sack. Gilda decides to sacrifice herself, enters the inn at the height of a storm, and is stabbed. Rigoletto comes to collect the victim, who he intends to dump in the river. But as he triumphantly drags the sack away, he hears the voice of the Duke. He rips open the sack to find his dying daughter, and realizes in horror that Monterone's curse has been fulfilled.

DER RING DES NIBELUNGEN
(The Ring of the Nibelungs)
Richard Wagner (1813-1883)

CONSISTING OF FOUR OPERAS—*DAS RHEINGOLD, DIE WALKÜRE, SIEGFRIED,* AND *GÖTTERDÄMMERUNG*—*THE RING* IS DESCRIBED AS 'A STAGE FESTIVAL PLAY FOR THREE DAYS AND A PRELIMINARY EVENING'. LIBRETTOS BY THE COMPOSER, BASED ON THE NIBELUNG SAGA. PREMIERES: *DAS RHEINGOLD,* MUNICH, 22 SEPTEMBER 1869; *DIE WALKÜRE,* MUNICH, 26 JUNE 1870; *SIEGFRIED,* BAYREUTH, 16 AUGUST, 1876; *GÖTTERDÄMMERUNG,* 17 AUGUST 1876. FIRST PERFORMANCE OF THE COMPLETE CYCLE AT BAYREUTH, 13-17 AUGUST 1876.

Der Ring des Nibelungen, the greatest achievement of a composer who probably influenced the course of music more than any other, occupies a unique place in musical history. Indeed, some would claim *The Ring* to be the greatest single achievement in the history of Western art. Though Wagner set the course for modern music by stretching the tonal system to its limit and opening the way for the breakdown of harmony in the 20th century, his theories about opera (or 'music-drama' as he called his works), as exemplified in *The Ring*, were almost as influential. Wagner believed in the concept of a *Gesamtkunstwerk*, literally a 'total artwork', in which music, poetry, drama, and visual design were all combined and equally important. Central to this is the *leitmotif*, a recurring theme or musical idea associated with characters or concepts both large and small. There are over 100 *leitmotifs* in *The Ring*, unifying it at many different levels over its 14 hours of music.

Wagner believed in the power of myth, and *The Ring* is timeless—about more than the giants, gods, dwarfs and humans it portrays—and has been interpreted in many different ways. While on one hand it seems to be a warning against the abuse and retention of power in which love ultimately triumphs, on the other it has been taken as a manifesto for German nationalism and unsavoury racial views. *The Ring* has also been viewed as comment on the industrialization of Wagner's time, as a socialist allegory, even in terms of Jungian psychology—all of which testifies to the fascination it holds for people.

Wagner took over 28 years to complete *The Ring*, and it was first performed as a complete cycle at the opening of his Festspielhaus ('Festival Theatre') in Bayreuth in 1876. It still forms the centrepiece of the Wagner Festival there.

DAS RHEINGOLD (The Rhinegold)
'Preliminary evening'. Four scenes.

CHARACTERS
RHINEMAIDENS
Woglinde (SOPRANO); *Wellgunde* (SOPRANO); *Flosshilde* (MEZZO-SOPRANO)

GODS
Freia, goddess of youth (SOPRANO); *Fricka*, Wotan's wife (MEZZO-SOPRANO); *Erda*, earth goddess (CONTRALTO); *Froh*, god of spring, brother of Freia (TENOR); *Loge*, god of fire (TENOR); *Wotan*, king of the gods (BASS-BARITONE); *Donner*, god of thunder, brother of Freia (BASS-BARITONE)

GIANTS
Fasolt (BASS-BARITONE); *Fafner* (BASS)

NIBELUNGS (DWARFS)
Mime, Alberich's brother (TENOR); *Alberich*, lord of Nibelheim, the underworld (BASS-BARITONE)

SCENE 1 *At the bottom of the Rhine*
The Rhinemaidens, guarding the sacred Rhinegold, taunt the dwarf Alberich when he appears on the banks of the river. He

glimpses the gold gleaming on the riverbed, and they tell him that whoever forges it into a ring will become ruler of the world, but that it can only be gained by renouncing love. Alberich duly curses love and steals the treasure.

SCENE 2 *High in the mountains*

Wotan, the one-eyed ruler of the gods, is woken by his wife Fricka and admires his new castle, Valhalla. It has been built by the giants Fasolt and Fafner, who demand as their payment Freia, the goddess of youth. She rushes in, begging for protection, followed by Fasolt and Fafner. They remind Wotan of their contract, and Freia's brothers, Donner and Froh, come to her defence. A confrontation follows, broken up only by the arrival of Loge, the god of fire. Loge reveals that Alberich has stolen the Rhinegold, and the giants offer to accept the treasure in Freia's place, but demand Freia as a hostage until the gold is delivered to them. Fearing that without Freia the gods will grow old and die, Wotan and Loge resolve to rob Alberich of the gold.

SCENE 3 *The subterranean cavern of Nibelheim*

Alberich, having fashioned the ring, is lording it over the dwarfs in Nibelheim. He torments even his brother Mime, who has made for him from the gold the magic *Tarnhelm*, a helmet that has the power to make its wearer assume any shape. Wotan and Loge arrive in the underworld and observe Alberich's cruelty before he notices them. Alberich puts on a display of his power, and shows Wotan and Loge the *Tarnhelm*. The gods trick Alberich into transforming himself into a toad, making it easy for them to capture him.

SCENE 4 *An open space high in the mountains*

On their way to Valhalla, the gods release Alberich and snatch the treasure, including the ring and *Tarnhelm*. Before disappearing, Alberich puts a curse on the ring and its future owners. Preparing to hand the gold over to the giants, Wotan at first tries to keep the ring, but Fricka and then Erda—who understands the consequences of keeping it—convince him to give it over. The curse begins to work at once: Fasolt and Fafner fight over division of the treasure, and Fasolt is killed. The hostage Freia is released back to the gods, who, with the help of Donner's thunderstorm and Froh's rainbow bridge, are able to enter their new castle. Loge watches cynically, knowing that the gods are now dishonourable and that their triumph will be short-lived.

DIE WALKÜRE (The Valkyrie)
'First day'. Three acts.

CHARACTERS

Brünnhilde, a Valkyrie, Wotan's daughter (SOPRANO); *Sieglinde*, a Volsung, Wotan's daughter (SOPRANO); *Fricka*, Wotan's wife (SOPRANO); *Siegmund*, a Volsung, Wotan's son (TENOR); *Wotan*, king of the gods (BASS-BARITONE); *Hunding*, Sieglinde's husband (BASS);

Gerhilde, Helmwige, Ortlinde, Waltraute, Rossweisse, Siegrune, Grimwerde, and *Schwertleite*, Valkyries, the daughters of Wotan and Erda (SOPRANOS and CONTRALTOS)

ACT I
Inside Hunding's hut

Siegmund (one of the human children—or Volsungs—whom Wotan has fathered to rid the gods of Alberich's curse, and the son he hopes will one day slay Fafner and return the ring to the Rhinemaidens) is driven by a violent storm to seek shelter in Hunding's hut. There he encounters Sieglinde, Hunding's wife, who nurses him back to health. Siegmund recalls his youth for Sieglinde, who seems to understand what he is saying. Hunding arrives home and is disturbed by the mysterious attraction his wife and Siegmund clearly feel for each other—and by their physical resemblance—and when he recognizes Siegmund as one of a group of men he has recently been fighting in the forest, he challenges him to a duel.

Left alone when Hunding and Sieglinde retire for the evening, Siegmund remembers that he is without a weapon. He has noticed something metallic in the trunk of an ash tree when Sieglinde returns from drugging her husband's drink to tell Siegmund that, on her wedding-day, a stranger (Wotan) thrust a sword into the tree, declaring that only a hero would be able to draw it out. At Sieglinde's suggestion that he become her lover if he can get the sword (called 'Nothung'), Siegmund pulls it out. The bright moonlight of a spring night shines on them as they recognize each other as brother and sister—and acknowledge their love.

ACT II
A wild mountainside

Wotan orders his favourite daughter, Brünnhilde, to rush to the defence of Siegmund, who is being hunted by Hunding. Brünnhilde is happy to oblige, but warns Wotan that his angry wife is on the way. Fricka, as the goddess of matrimony, cannot allow the incest and adultery of Siegmund and Sieglinde, and forces Wotan to countermand Brünnhilde's orders. Wotan, though distressed by his dilemma, warns Brünnhilde not to help Siegmund, and when she encounters the fleeing couple, Brünnhilde tells Siegmund of his impending death. But she is filled with pity at their exhausted state and by Siegmund's devotion to Sieglinde, and ignores her father's command by promising to protect Siegmund against Hunding. Brünnhilde is shielding Siegmund in the battle when Wotan arrives and allows Hunding to kill Siegmund. Having collected the pieces of Siegmund's shattered sword, Brünnhilde flees with Sieglinde to the rock of the Valkyries. With a commanding gesture, Wotan strikes Hunding dead and sets off in pursuit of the defiant Brünnhilde.

ACT III
The summit of a rocky mountain

The Valkyries (warrior daughters of Wotan and Erda) ride back to their mountain home, followed by their sister Brünnhilde, who arrives carrying Sieglinde on the saddle of her horse. Sieglinde longs for death, but is revived by Brünnhilde's prophecy that she will bear Siegmund's son, Siegfried, destined to be a great hero. Brünnhilde gives her the remains of the sword Nothung—from which a new one will one day be forged—and advises her to hide in the forest near Fafner's cave, where Wotan never ventures.

Wotan enters and confronts Brünnhilde, and the Valkyries are horrified when their sister is sentenced to be cast out of Valhalla in a magic sleep until the first man who passes wakes her. Brünnhilde explains her actions to her father, and he is moved to grant her request that she be protected by a circle of magic fire that only a fearless hero will be able to penetrate. Wotan bids Brünnhilde farewell, and summons Loge to conjure up the magic flames.

SIEGFRIED
'Second day'. Three acts.

CHARACTERS

Brünnhilde, Wotan's daughter (SOPRANO); *Woodbird* (SOPRANO); *Erda*, earth goddess (CONTRALTO); *Siegfried*, son of Sieglinde and Siegmund (TENOR); *Mime*, Alberich's brother (TENOR); *The Wanderer*, Wotan in disguise (BASS-BARITONE); *Alberich*, lord of Nibelheim, the underworld (BASS-BARITONE); *Fafner*, transformed into a dragon (BASS)

ACT I

A cave in the forest

The dwarf Mime is struggling to forge a sword strong enough for his ward Siegfried. As a baby Siegfried had been entrusted to Mime by the dying Sieglinde, together with the fragments of Siegmund's sword (Nothung). The crafty Mime has tried in vain to restore Nothung, reasoning that Siegfried could use it to kill Fafner (now transformed into a dragon) and win the treasure for him, making him ruler of the world. Siegfried returns from the forest with a bear to taunt Mime. Siegfried has come to realize that Mime, for whom he has little respect, is not his father, and forces him to reveal the circumstances of his birth. Having told Siegfried about his mother and father, Mime admits that the broken Nothung once belonged to Siegmund, and Siegfried demands that Mime repair it.

They are interrupted by the arrival of a Wanderer (Wotan in disguise), who challenges Mime to a game of riddles in which both parties are allowed three questions. One question—the identity of the man destined to restore Nothung—stumps Mime, and the Wanderer tells him that it will be someone completely fearless. When Siegfried remains undaunted by Mime's horrifying descriptions of the dragon Fafner, and then begins to forge Nothung anew, Mime realizes that his foster-son is destined to become the fearless hero. He brews a poisoned soup so as to be able to kill Siegfried once he has slain Fafner and obtained the treasure. Siegfried announces triumphantly that Nothung is now complete.

ACT II

Deep in the forest

Alberich, Mime's brother, is lurking near Fafner's cave in the hope of one day being able to regain the ring. He is disturbed by the Wanderer's appearance, and told of Mime's plan to use Siegfried against Fafner. The Wanderer rouses the sleeping dragon, suggesting that he could escape danger by handing the treasure over. Fafner is unmoved and goes back to sleep; the Wanderer leaves and Mime hides when his brother and Siegfried approach.

Mime keeps a safe distance from the dragon's cave, hoping for an easy outcome in which Fafner and Siegfried will kill each other. Siegfried listens to the peaceful sounds of the forest, and muses about his own birth. He tries unsuccessfully to imitate the birdcalls on his reed pipe and, when he resorts to calling on his horn, wakes Fafner instead. A confrontation between the apparently unequal combatants ensues, and Siegfried succeeds in thrusting his sword into the dragon's heart. Recognizing that Siegfried must have been carrying out another's plans, the dying Fafner warns him of Mime's treachery. As Siegfried withdraws his sword from the dragon, he accidentally tastes Fafner's blood, which gives him an understanding of the Woodbird's message. She advises him to take the ring and *Tarnhelm* from the cave.

Alberich and Mime scuttle onto the scene, and are arguing over the treasure when Siegfried emerges carrying it. Alberich hides while Mime tries to persuade the youth to taste the poisonous drink he has brewed, but Siegfried remember's Fafner's warning and kills Mime with his sword. The Woodbird tells Siegfried about Brünnhilde, the woman who lies asleep surrounded by fire waiting for a fearless hero to liberate her. The Woodbird leads him off towards Brünnhilde's rock.

ACT III

SCENES 1 and 2 *The foot of a rocky mountain*

Wotan the Wanderer summons the earth goddess Erda to foretell the future, but she—having passed on the rope of destiny to the Norns—is clueless, and when Wotan informs her that he is resigned to the downfall of the gods she retires into eternal sleep. Wotan accepts that his power will pass to a new order under Siegfried and Brünnhilde, but must first put Siegfried to the test. He goes to bar the youth's way to Brünnhilde's rock: Siegfried ridicules Wotan without recognizing him as his grandfather, and with Nothung shatters Wotan's previously invincible spear. Wotan withdraws to await his own death.

SCENE 3 *Brünnhilde's rock*

Siegfried breaks through the flames and is astonished to find Brünnhilde sleeping in warrior's armour. He has never seen a woman before and hopes he has found his mother. But Brünnhilde wakes to tell Siegfried that his mother will never return. Siegfried, however, is mesmerized by Brünnhilde's beauty, and his ardour gradually awakens her passion. Transformed by their ecstatic love, they reject the gods of Valhalla and vow to go fearlessly into the world.

GÖTTERDÄMMERUNG (Twilight of the Gods)
'Third day'. Prologue and three acts.

CHARACTERS

Brünnhilde, Wotan's daughter (SOPRANO); *Gutrune*, Gunther's sister (SOPRANO); *Woglinde*, a Rhinemaiden (SOPRANO); *Wellgunde*, a Rhinemaiden (SOPRANO); *Third Norn* (SOPRANO); *Waltraute*, a Valkyrie (MEZZO-SOPRANO); *Flosshilde*, a Rhinemaiden (MEZZO-SOPRANO); *Second Norn* (MEZZO-SOPRANO); *First Norn* (CONTRALTO); *Siegfried*, son of Sieglinde and Siegmund (TENOR); *Gunther*, chief of the Gibichungs (BASS-BARITONE); *Alberich*, lord of Nibelheim, the underworld (BASS-BARITONE); *Hagen*, Alberich's son, half-brother of Gunther (BASS)
With *vassals* and *women*

PROLOGUE

The Valkyries' rock
The three Norns, reading their rope of destiny, prophecy the end of the gods and the destruction of Valhalla. Under Alberich's curse the rope breaks, and unable to divine anything further, the silent Norns return into the earth. Siegfried is now ready to perform great deeds in the world, and sets off on Brünnhilde's steed, having entrusted the ring to her keeping.

ACT I

SCENES 1 and 2 *The hall of the Gibichungs*
Hagen, son of Alberich, plots to obtain the ring and with it its powers. His plan involves getting his half-brother, Gunther, the weak-willed chief of the Gibichungs, and half-sister, Gutrune, to destroy the marriage of Siegfried and Brünnhilde. They are inspired by his scheme—Gunther will win the 'world's fairest woman', Gutrune the 'world's strongest hero'—and Gutrune agrees to give Siegfried a potion that will erase his memories of Brünnhilde.

Siegfried arrives at the hall of the Gibichungs and is shown hospitality. Having drunk the potion, he falls in love with Gutrune, and agrees to help Gunther win Brünnhilde. As the only one capable of penetrating the flames around Brünnhilde, Siegfried will use the transforming *Tarnhelm* to impersonate Gunther and woo her. Left to watch over the Gibich hall Hagen, who knows that the ring is on Brünnhilde's hand, rejoices that power will soon be his.

SCENE 3 *The Valkyries' rock*
Brünnhilde is visited by her sister Waltraute, who tells her how Wotan and the gods are suffering from Alberich's curse. Only by restoring the ring to the Rhinemaidens will the curse be lifted, and Waltraute begs Brünnhilde to release the ring. Brünnhilde stubbornly refuses to hand over Siegfried's token of love. Suddenly Siegfried returns, but Brünnhilde does not recognize him; with the help of the *Tarnhelm*, he has taken on Gunther's form. 'Gunther' swears that she shall become Gunther's wife, and during a struggle pulls the ring from her finger.

ACT II

In front of the hall of the Gibichungs

In Hagen's dream, Alberich appears to his son and reminds him of his duty to obtain the ring for him. Siegfried, restored to his proper form, returns to the Gibichung castle and announces that Gunther and Brünnhilde are about to arrive. The Gibichung vassals prepare to welcome them. Brünnhilde enters downcast, but is roused to recrimination when she sees Siegfried in Gutrune's arms. The sight of the ring on his hand provokes charges of treachery, but Siegfried—who truly retains no memory of his love for Brünnhilde—confusedly denies her accusations. Hagen, Gunther, and Brünnhilde plot to kill Siegfried, and the vengeful Brünnhilde confides that only Siegfried's back is vulnerable to a spear.

ACT III

SCENES 1 and 2 *A wild forest on the banks of the Rhine*

Siegfried is resting on the banks of the river, when the Rhinemaidens beg him to return the ring. They warn him of Alberich's curse on the ring, and laugh at his stupidity when he obstinately holds on to it. He is joined by Hagen's and Gunther's hunting party, and entreated to entertain them with tales of his adventures. Hagen gives Siegfried an antidote to Gutrune's draught, enabling him to recall Brünnhilde. As Siegfried happily tells of how he fell in love with her, Hagen drives his spear into his back. He dies swearing eternal love for Brünnhilde and is borne on his shield back to the Gibichung castle.

SCENE 3 *The hall of the Gibichungs*

Gutrune is filled with foreboding. The curse of the ring continues to work when, in an argument over it, Hagen kills Gunther. Brünnhilde intervenes: she ignites Siegfried's funeral pyre and rides into the flames herself, confident that her self-sacrificing love will break the curse on the ring and restore peace. As the Rhine overflows its banks, the Rhinemaidens swim up to retrieve the ring. In a desperate, unsuccessful attempt to reach it, Hagen is swept away by the flood. The hall of the Gibichungs collapses and Valhalla, with its gods, is engulfed in flames. The survivors watch apprehensively as a new era of love dawns.

IL RITORNO D'ULISSE IN PATRIA
(The Return of Ulysees to his Homeland)
Claudio Monteverdi (1567-1643)

PROLOGUE AND THREE ACTS. LIBRETTO BY GAICOMO BADOARDO AFTER HOMER'S *ODYSSEY*. PREMIERE IN VENICE, FEBRUARY 1640.

Though Monteverdi's early operas had been given—like all operas of the time—as court entertainments, from 1637 opera houses had opened to the public in Venice (other cities soon followed suit) and Monteverdi became one of the leading composers for them. *Il ritorno d'Ulisse in patria*, the first of three operas he wrote for Venice, shows how far his style evolved over the decades that separate *Ulisse* and his earliest opera, *Orfeo*: the sensuous music was truly modern for its time, and the characters—though drawn from mythology—were given a new depth of emotion.

CHARACTERS

L'Humana Fragilità (Human Frailty) (SOPRANO); *La Fortuna* (Fortune) (SOPRANO); *Amore* (Cupid) (SOPRANO); *Minerva* (SOPRANO); *Giunone* (Juno) (SOPRANO); *Melantho*, Penelope's maid (MEZZO-SOPRANO); *Ericlea* (Eurycleia), Penelope's old nurse (MEZZO-SOPRANO); *Penelope*, Ulysses's wife (CONTRALTO); *Anfinomo* (Anphi-nomus), one of Penelope's suitors (COUNTER-TENOR); *Ulisse* (Ulysses) (TENOR); *Telemaco* (Telemachus), son of Penelope and Ulysses (TENOR); *Giove* (Jupiter) (TENOR); *Pisandro* (Peisander), one of Penelope's suitors (TENOR); *Eurimaco* (Eurymachus), Melantho's lover (TENOR); *Eumete* (Eumaeus), a swineherd (TENOR); *Iro* (Irus), a jester (TENOR); *Nettuno* (Neptune) (BASS); *Antinoo* (Aninous), one of Penelope's suitors (BASS); *Il Tempo* (Time) (BASS)
With *Phaeacians, celestial spirits, sea spirits*

PROLOGUE

Human Frailty admits that it is ruled by Time, Fortune, and Cupid.

ACT I

Penelope laments the long absence of her husband, Ulysses, at war. Her loneliness is only heightened by the sight of the lovers Melanto and Eurymachus, and her nurse Eurycleia is unable to comfort her. The Phaeacians have rescued Ulysses and laid him on the beach of his homeland Ithaca, but in doing so have disobeyed Neptune. In his wrath, Neptune (who is supported by Jupiter) turns the Phaeacians and their ship into a rock. Ulysses wakes in despair, believing himself to be on a foreign shore, but he learns from Minerva that he is in Ithaca. She also tells him that, during his absence, three suitors—Antinous, Peisander, and Anphinomus—have laid siege to Penelope in her palace, but that she has remained faithful, and advises him to return home disguised as an old beggar. Ulysses sets off to find his former servant Eumaeus, and Minerva goes to Sparta to summon the help of Ulysses's son, Telemachus. Back at the palace, Melantho tries in vain to interest Penelope in one of her suitors. At last Ulysses finds Eumaeus, who has been living as a swineherd after being driven out of the court by Penelope's suitors and has had to endure the taunts of the suitors' jester, Irus. Ulysses, disguised as a beggar, brings Eumaeus news that his master is still alive. Eumaeus is overjoyed and the two set off.

ACT II

Telemachus has been brought back to his native country, where he is welcomed by Eumaeus. Telemachus sends Eumaeus to the palace to announce to Penelope her son's return and the rumours of her husband's homecoming. Ulysses reveals his identity to his son, and the two are joyfully reunited. At the palace, Penelope, in spite of Melantho's urgings and the renewed attempts of the suitors, remains steadfast in her devotion to the absent Ulysses. The suitors overhear Eumaeus telling Penelope of the expected homecomings, and resolve to murder Telemachus when he arrives. But the appearance of an eagle, which they take to be a bad omen, convinces them instead to intensify their efforts to win Penelope's hand. Meanwhile, Ulysses has been given Minerva's assurance that he will be able to defeat the suitors, and he sets off with Eumaeus for the palace. There, Telemachus and Penelope have been reunited when Ulysses (still disguised as a beggar) and his servant draw near. They are confronted by Antinous and Irus, but finally reach the palace and are made welcome by Penelope. The beggar observes the suitors' renewed efforts to woo his wife, and is allowed to enter the competition she has announced: Penelope agrees to marry the one who succeeds in stringing Ulysses's bow. The three suitors fail, but the beggar—having renounced the prize—wins. In a furious rage he turns on the suitors and kills them.

ACT III
Irus mourns the suitors and, driven to despair, commits suicide. Eumaeus and Telemachus try in vain to convince Penelope that the beggar who strung Ulysses's bow was indeed her husband. Prompted by Minerva and Juno, Jupiter restores Ulysses to his proper form, but even Ulysses cannot convince his wife of his identity. Eurycleia steps forward to tell Penelope that Ulysses is recognizable by a scar on his shoulder, but she is fully convinced only when Ulysses is able to describe the cover on her bed. Ulysses and Penelope are joyfully reunited.

ROBERTO DEVEREUX
Gaetano Donizetti (1797-1848)

THREE ACTS. LIBRETTO BY SALVATORE CAMMARANO AFTER FRANÇOIS ANCELOT'S *ELISABETH D'ANGLETERRE*. PREMIERE IN NAPLES, 29 OCTOBER 1837.

Roberto Devereux, Donizetti's 57th opera, is the third of his so-called 'Tudor trilogy', and includes the composer's most rounded portrayal of Queen Elizabeth I. The opera is only loosely based on historical fact, and among the anachronistic touches is the inclusion of 'God save the Queen' (an 18th-century tune) in the overture Donizetti provided when he revised the opera for Paris a year after its premiere.

CHARACTERS
Elisabetta (Elizabeth), Queen of England (SOPRANO); *Sara* (Sarah), Duchess of Nottingham (MEZZO-SOPRANO); *Roberto Devereux*, Earl of Essex (TENOR); *Cecil* (TENOR); *Nottingham* (BARITONE); *Raleigh* (BASS) With *Page*, Nottingham's *Servant*, *courtiers*, *guards*, *attendants*

ACT I
Devereux has returned from his disastrous military campaign in Ireland and faces charges of treason. Sarah, the new Duchess of Nottingham, longs for him, although during his lengthy absence she was forced into marrying Nottingham.

The Queen, who pines for Devereux almost as much, is ill at ease and suspects that his affections lie elsewhere, though she is unaware of his love for Sarah. Nevertheless, the Queen gives Devereux a ring with the guarantee that it will always obtain a pardon in an emergency. The Duke of Nottingham is upset by his wife's coolness, and confesses his worries to the embarrassed Devereux. Sarah is rebuked by Devereux for allowing herself to enter into her loveless marriage. They pledge their love again, he giving her the Queen's ring, she him the scarf she has been embroidering.

ACT II

Ruling against Nottingham's arguments, the Queen's council has found Devereux guilty of treason. Raleigh returns from arresting Devereux, bringing with him Sarah's scarf, found when his house was searched. Both Nottingham and the Queen are roused to jealous fury. She gives Devereux the choice of either naming the woman or dying on the block, and he chooses the latter. He is sent to the Tower of London.

ACT III

Sarah resolves to take the ring to the Queen in order to save Devereux, but is prevented from doing so by her husband. In his cell, Devereux waits for the ring to effect his release; the Queen is also waiting anxiously for it, in order that she may commute his sentence. Sarah finally arrives, having broken out of captivity, but too late: the Queen is giving orders to halt the execution at the very moment that a cannon shot from the Tower announces that it is over. Nottingham enters, admitting that he deliberately delayed Sarah in order to avenge her betrayal. He is arrested together with his wife, and the despairing Queen abdicates.

ROMÉO ET JULIETTE (Romeo and Juliet)
Charles Gounod (1818-1893)

Five acts. Libretto by Jules Barbier and Michel Carré after Shakespeare's *Romeo and Juliet*. Premiere in Paris, 27 April 1867.

Shakespeare's tragedy *Romeo and Juliet* has inspired countless musical settings—among them Berlioz's 'dramatic symphony', Tchaikovsky's overture, Prokofiev's ballet, and Bernstein's *West Side Story*. (Bellini's opera *I Capuleti e i Montecchi* is based on a substantially different Italian source of the story.) Gounod's version follows the Shakespeare original closely, though some scenes are cut and a few incidents added for operatic effect. Bernard Shaw praised 'the spell of the heavenly melody . . . the exquisite orchestral web of sound colours . . . the unfailing dignity and delicacy of the accent and rhythm'; there are no less than four love duets.

CHARACTERS

Juliette (Juliet), Capulet's daughter (SOPRANO); *Stéphano*, Romeo's page (SOPRANO); *Gertrude*, Juliet's nurse (MEZZO-SOPRANO); *Roméo* (Romeo),

Montague's son (TENOR); *Tybalt*, Lady Capulet's nephew (TENOR); *Benvolio*, Montague's nephew (TENOR); *Mercutio*, Romeo's friend (BARITONE); *Count Paris* (BARITONE); *Grégorio* (Gregory), Capulet's servant (BARITONE); *Count Capulet* (BASS); *The Duke of Verona* (BASS); *Frère Laurent* (Friar Laurence) (BASS); *Frère Jean* (Friar John) (BASS)
With *servants*, *kinsfolk* of both Houses, *maskers*

ACT I

A hall in the Capulet house

At a masked ball, Paris and Tybalt are discussing Juliet when she is escorted in by her father, Capulet. Montague intruders, including Romeo and his friends Mercutio and Benvolio, enter disguised; Romeo's nerves are calmed by Mercutio. Juliet, left alone by her nurse Gertrude, meets Romeo and the two fall instantly and deeply in love. When Tybalt realizes that Juliet is with a Montague he tries to attack him and his followers; Capulet intervenes, and Romeo and his friends escape.

ACT II

The Capulet garden

At night Romeo steals into Juliet's garden, where he overhears her admitting her longing for him. He emerges from the shadows, but soon the lovers are interrupted by Capulet servants in pursuit of a Montague intruder (Stephano). Once quiet has returned they exchange vows of love, before Juliet is called in by her nurse.

ACT III

SCENE 1 *Friar Laurence's cell*

Romeo and Juliet persuade Friar Laurence of their devotion to each other, and he marries them in secret.

SCENE 2 *A street near the Capulet house*

Romeo's page Stephano provokes the Capulets to a bloody confrontation in which Tybalt attacks Mercutio; determined to avenge that injury, Romeo kills Tybalt (now a relative by marriage). He is ordered into exile by the Duke.

ACT IV

SCENE 1 *Juliet's room*

Romeo has spent the night with Juliet and at dawn they part. Juliet is told by her father that she is to be married immediately to the young nobleman Paris. She appeals for help to Friar Laurence, who advises her to take a sleeping potion so strong that she will be taken for dead, and that in her tomb she will wake to be reunited with Romeo. Nervously, she drinks the potion.

SCENE 2 *A hall in the Capulet house*

Guests assemble and Juliet is brought in for her wedding. To their horror, she collapses and is pronounced dead.

ACT V

The Capulet tomb

Friar John reveals to Friar Laurence that Romeo has not been informed of the scheme. Indeed, when Romeo arrives to bid the apparently dead Juliet farewell, he is overcome with grief and poisons himself. She wakes to discover what he has done and after a final embrace stabs herself.

DER ROSENKAVALIER (The Knight of the Rose)
Richard Strauss (1864-1949)

THREE ACTS. LIBRETTO BY HUGO VON HOFMANNSTHAL. PREMIERE IN DRESDEN, 26 JANUARY 1911.

Der Rosenkavalier, Strauss's fifth opera, is undoubtedly the composer's most popular. Its sophisticated, bittersweet love story and waltz-infused score—which ends with the famous trio, some of the most incandescent music in all opera—captivates audiences. Strauss called *Der Rosenkavalier* a 'comedy for music' and intended it as a homage to Mozart: it is set in 18th-century Vienna (Octavian, a travesti role, is inspired by Mozart's Cherubino), and marks an radical change of direction from the brutal, expressionistic worlds of his preceding operas, *Elektra* and *Salome*.

CHARACTERS
The Feldmarschallin, Princess Werdenberg (Marschallin) (SOPRANO); *Sophie von Faninal* (SOPRANO); *Octavian*, Count Rofrano, the Marschallin's young lover (SOPRANO or MEZZO-SOPRANO); *Marianne*, Sophie's duenna (SOPRANO); *Annina*, an intriguer, Valzacchi's niece (CONTRALTO); *Valzacchi*, an Italian intriguer (TENOR); *Major-domo*, to the Marschallin (TENOR); *Major-domo*, to Faninal (TENOR); *Innkeeper* (TENOR); *A Singer* (TENOR); *Herr von Faninal*, Sophie's nouveau riche father (BARITONE); *Baron Ochs auf Lerchenau*, the Marschallin's cousin (BASS); *A Police Commissioner* (BASS); *A Notary* (BASS)
With *Mohammed, Flautist, Hairdresser, Scholar, Noble Widow*, three *Noble Orphans, Dressmaker, Animal-seller, servants, waiters, children*

ACT I
The Marschallin's bedroom
Princess von Werdenberg, the Marschallin (Field Marshal's wife), has passed the night with her passionate young lover, Count Octavian. They are breakfasting, when noises at the door alarm the Marschallin: imagining that her husband has returned earlier than expected, she orders Octavian to hide. But it is her boorish cousin, Baron Ochs, who has come to announce his coming marriage to Sophie von Faninal. His engagement does not stop him flirting with the Marschallin's 'chambermaid' when Octavian emerges disguised: he even suggests that 'Mariandel', as the Marschallin calls the 'maid', join his household after his marriage. For the moment, Ochs requires the services of a nobleman who can perform the custom of presenting a silver rose to his betrothed, and he asks the Marschallin to recommend someone. She suggests Octavian as the 'Rosenkavalier'. When the time arrives for the Marschallin's daily levee, she receives a room full of people anxious to secure her patronage. An Italian tenor serenades her while Ochs consults the Marschallin's lawyer about his marriage contract. The Marschallin is unhappy at how old her hairdresser has made her look. The intriguers Annina

and Valzacchi offer to find out more about 'Mariandal' for Ochs. The Marschallin, feeling melancholy, dismisses the company. She reflects on her advancing age (though she is only in her early thirties) and the fact that before long, Octavian will probably leave her for a younger lover. Octavian reappears, and unable to understand her feelings leaves the room again. The Marschallin realizes that, for the first time, he left without kissing her. She instructs her page Mohammed to take the silver rose to him.

ACT II
Faninal's house
The Faninal household is abuzz with preparations for the marriage. Herr von Faninal has gone to collect the bridegroom Ochs when the Rosenkavalier enters to present the rose to Sophie. The couple fall in love at first sight. Sophie is strongly repelled by the behaviour of Baron Ochs, and pleads with Octavian to help her escape her marriage. Their declarations of love are interrupted by the intriguers Annina and Valzacchi, who immediately summon Ochs. Octavian and Ochs enter into a duel, and though only superficially wounded, Ochs makes a huge fuss. Faninal is horrified to see his plan for marrying his daughter into the aristocracy falter, and orders Sophie either to go ahead with the wedding or enter a convent. But the situation is diffused when the delighted Ochs receives a note from 'Mariandal', the Marschallin's 'chambermaid'—Octavian has now enlisted the help of the intriguers himself—inviting him to an assignation.

ACT III
A private room at an inn
With the help of Annina and Valzacchi, Octavian prepares to humiliate Ochs. When 'Mariandal' and Ochs sit down to supper, the Baron is struck by the resemblance between 'her' and the impudent Octavian he encountered at Faninal's. The dinner degenerates into chaos as Annina, claiming to be Ochs's abandoned wife, enters with several screaming children in tow. The noise alerts the Police Commissioner—who refuses to believe Ochs's story that 'Mariandal' is his fiancée, Sophie—followed by Faninal, then Sophie, and finally the Marschallin herself. Ochs sees that he has been duped when Octavian reveals his true identity, and is relieved when the Marschallin advises him to flee as quickly as possible. Left alone with Sophie and Octavian, the Marschallin realizes that they are deeply in love, and gives up her claim on Octavian with good grace. She blesses the couple.

RUSALKA
Antonín Dvořák (1841–1904)

THREE ACTS. LIBRETTO BY JAROSLAV KVAPIL, AFTER FRIEDRICH DE LA MOTTE FOUQUE'S *UNDINE*. PREMIERE IN PRAGUE, 31 MARCH 1901.

The Czech composer Dvořák is best known today for his nine symphonies, but his large and varied output also includes ten operas. Though several are still given in his homeland, only

Rusalka—the undoubted masterpiece among them—is performed in the West. The story, drawn from folklore, is evoked in music of sensuous lyricism, nowhere better exemplified than in Rusalka's famous 'Song to the Moon'.

CHARACTERS

Rusalka, a water nymph (SOPRANO); *Foreign Princess* (SOPRANO); *First and Second Wood Nymphs* (SOPRANOS); *Ježibaba*, a witch (MEZZO-SOPRANO); *Kitchen-boy* (MEZZO-SOPRANO); *Third Wood Nymph* (CONTRALTO); *Prince* (TENOR); *Forester* (TENOR); *Hunter* (BARITONE); *Vodnìk*, a water spirit, Rusalka's grandfather (BASS) With *wood nymphs, courtiers, wedding guests*

ACT I

A clearing on the lakeshore

The playful games of the Wood Nymphs rouse Vodnìk from the depths of the moonlit lake. On the shore he encounters the water nymph Rusalka, who confesses to him that she has fallen in love with a human Prince, and in order to become visible to him wants to take on human form herself. Vodnìk warns her of the dangers she faces, but before sinking back into the gloomy depths advises her to consult the witch Ježibaba . Rusalka invokes the help of the moon and calls on Ježibaba. The witch agrees to assist, but warns that though she may become human Rusalka will remain dumb, and that both she and Prince will be damned if he proves unfaithful to her. The spell is cast and the Prince appears. Captivated by Rusalka's beauty, he leads her off.

ACT II

The grounds of the Prince's castle

Guests have assembled to witness the wedding of the Prince and his mysterious Rusalka. Both the Kitchen-boy and Forester are disturbed by the dumb bride, and fear that their master has come under a dangerous spell. When a Foreign Princess arrives, the Prince realizes that he is already bored by the silent Rusalka's shyness. He transfers his attentions to the Foreign Princess, and despite Rusalka desperate pleas, he rejects her. Vodnìk is heard reiterating the witch's curse, and the Prince discovers that he has been damned. He appeals to the Foreign Princess, but she coldly refuses to help.

ACT III

The lakeshore

Rusalka wanders mournfully at the lakeside. Ježibaba appears and suggests that she break the curse by killing the Prince. Unable to contemplate such an action, Rusalka sinks into the water, only to be rejected there by her sisters. Soon the Kitchen-boy and Forester come to seek out Ježibaba, hoping to save their master, but are promptly chased off. Finally, the Prince himself arrives in search of Rusalka, begging for forgiveness. Rusalka warns him that her kiss will prove fatal, but the Prince, longing for peace of mind, accepts his fate. They embrace and he dies in her arms. Rusalka, still haunted by his initial rejection, vanishes into the depths.

RUSLAN AND LUDMILA
Mikhail Glinka (1804-1857)

FIVE ACTS. LIBRETTO BY VALERIAN SHIRKOV, NESTOR KUKOLNIK, NIKOLAY MARKEVICH, AND MIKHAIL GEDEONOV, AFTER ALEXANDER PUSHKIN'S POEM. PREMIERE IN ST PETERSBURG, 9 DECEMBER 1842.

'The Tsar of operas', Tchaikovsky called it; Alexander Serov, Russian critic and composer, countered with 'not a drama, not a play, hence not an opera, but a randomly assembled gallery of musical scenes'. *Ruslan and Ludmila*, Glinka's second opera, continues to divide critical opinion, but its seminal importance in the history of Russian music is indisputable; it became a veritable source-book for Russian operatic composers even into the 20th century. *Ruslan* earned Glinka the title 'father of Russian music', a label fitting for a composer who mixed Italian convention with bold new forms, 'fantastic' harmonies, vivid oriental colours, and magical subjects. *Ruslan* was also the first of countless Russian operas to be derived from Pushkin's works.

CHARACTERS

Ludmila, Svetozar's daughter (SOPRANO); *Gorislava*, Ratmir's slave, in love with him (SOPRANO); *Naina*, an evil witch (MEZZO-SOPRANO); *Ratmir*, an oriental prince (CONTRALTO); *Finn*, a benevolent magician (TENOR); *Bayan*, a bard (TENOR); *Ruslan*, a Kiev knight, betrothed to Ludmila (BARITONE); *Svetozar*, Prince of Kiev (BASS); *Farlaf*, a warrior (BASS); *Chernomor*, an evil dwarf (SILENT)
With Svetozar's *courtiers*, Naina's *maidens*, Chernomor's *slaves*

ACT I
Svetozar's court
Svetozar is hosting the feast that will precede the wedding of his daughter, Ludmila, and Ruslan. The bard Bayan is called on to entertain the guests, but he warns that dark events will intervene before the couple's eventual happiness. Ludmila bids a sad farewell to the home where she grew up and pays her respects to her unsuccessful suitors, the prince Ratmir and warrior Farlaf, before proceeding with the marriage ceremony. The couple have received Svetozar's blessing when a sudden clap of thunder plunges everyone into darkness. Ludmila is nowhere to be found when light returns, and Svetozar promises her hand in marriage and half of his kingdom to the one who will bring her back. Ruslan, Ratmir, and Farlaf all set off in search.

ACT II
SCENE 1 *Finn's cave*
Ruslan consults the sage Finn, who reveals that Ludmila has been abducted by the evil dwarf Chernomor and taken to his northern kingdom; Finn also warns Ruslan to beware of the evil witch Naina, who will turn against Ruslan if she discovers he has taken advice from Finn.

SCENE 2 *A lonely spot*
Farlaf encounters Naina, who promises to help him win Ludmila.

SCENE 3 *A deserted battlefield*

On a battlefield strewn with the relics of war, Ruslan finds a giant head and underneath it a sword. Initially hostile, the head tells Ruslan that he once belonged to Chernomor's brother's body, but that Chernomor decapitated him with the sword now in Ruslan's hands. He advises him that by cutting off Chernomor's magic beard—only with the sword—Ruslan can defeat him.

ACT III

Naina's magic castle

Naina instructs her maidens to seduce and distract the men searching for Ludmila. Much to the dismay of Gorislava—though Ratmir's slave, she loves him—they turn their attentions on Ratmir and succeed in ensnaring him. Naina rejoices when Ruslan arrives and becomes entranced by Gorislava, forgetting Ludmila. But Finn enters and breaks the spells: Ratmir and Gorislava acknowledge their love for each other, and together with Finn join Ruslan on his quest for Ludmila.

ACT IV

Chernomor's magic garden

Having failed to drown herself in the river, Ludmila languishes miserably in Chernomor's magic garden and spurns his flattery. When Ruslan's arrival is announced, Chernomor puts Ludmila into an enchanted sleep and goes off to fight his rival. Ruslan defeats the dwarf by cutting off his beard, and prepares to take Ludmila home. But he is downcast to discover that he is unable to rouse her from her sleep. With the help of his companions and Chernomor's now liberated slaves, he sets off with the sleeping Ludmila for Kiev.

ACT V

SCENE 1 *The steppes*

Guarding their overnight camp, Ratmir is so distracted by his love for Gorislava that he fails to notice when Naina and Farlaf abduct the sleeping Ludmila. Ruslan has set off in pursuit when Finn arrives with a magic ring that will break the spell over Ludmila; he entrusts it to Ratmir.

SCENE 2 *Svetozar's court*

Farlaf arrives triumphantly at Svetozar's court, but is unable to wake Ludmila. When Ruslan, Ratmir, and Gorislava enter, Ruslan breaks the spell with the help of the magic ring. All rejoice, and the wedding feast is resumed.

SADKO
Nikolay Rimsky-Korsakov (1844-1908)

SEVEN SCENES (THREE OR FIVE ACTS). LIBRETTO BY THE COMPOSER AND VLADIMIR BELSKY, BASED ON OLD RUSSIAN BALLADS. PREMIERE IN MOSCOW, 7 JANUARY 1898.

Rimsky-Korsakov, who drew many of his 15 operas from Russian folklore, was especially proud of *Sadko*, a vibrant series of seven tableaux depicting the adventures of the eponymous minstrel. The opera juxtaposes scenes set in the historic world of ancient Novgorod with those in the fantasy world of an underwater sea kingdom (the latter calling for an elaborate ballet). The colourful, exotic score includes the famous 'Song of India', sung by the Hindu Merchant in Scene 4.

CHARACTERS

Volkhova, the Sea King's beautiful daughter (SOPRANO); *Lyubava*, Sadko's wife (MEZZO-SOPRANO); *Nezhata*, a psaltery player from Kiev (MEZZO-SOPRANO); *Sadko*, a singer from Novgorod (TENOR); *Hindu Merchant* (TENOR); *Venetian Merchant* (BARITONE); *Apparition* (BARITONE); *Sea King* (BASS); *Viking Merchant* (BASS)

With *entertainers, wizards, town dignitaries, townsfolk, foreign traders, pilgrims, mermaids, swans, sea creatures*

SCENE 1 *Novgorod*

The merchants of Novgorod are feasting, entertained by jesters and Nezhata, a psaltery player from Kiev. Sadko, a local psaltery player who longs to be wealthy, takes his turn at entertaining the company, but his song insults the town elders and they banish him. The revelry resumes.

SCENE 2 *The shore of Lake Ilmen*

Roaming along the lakeshore, the mournful Sadko is startled by the appearance of swans who transform themselves into beautiful maidens. One lingers behind with Sadko, and tells him she is Volkhova, the Sea King's youngest daughter, and that the others are her sisters. She reveals that she is destined to marry a human being. They fall in love—Sadko instantly forgetting his wife Lyubava—and when Volkhova has to return to the lake at dawn, she tells him to cast his net into Lake Ilmen, where he will find fish with golden scales to make him rich.

SCENE 3 *Sadko's house*

Lyubava's fears that she has lost Sadko's love are confirmed when he arrives home distracted. Before long he sets off again, his mind on the golden fish Volkhova promised him.

SCENE 4 *The shore of Lake Ilmen*

The crowd at the keyside mock Sadko when he appears and boasts of the riches he is planning to land. The merchants enter into bets with him, which they lose when he catches—with the help of Volkhova, whose voice is heard—three fish with golden scales. The mood changes, and the people of Novgorod now acclaim Sadko as the hero of their city. Nezhata leads the singing in praise of him. He gathers a crew and before leaving for distant lands, seeks the advice of foreign merchants. Having heard the tales of the Viking, Hindu, and Venetian guests, Sadko sets sail.

SCENE 5 *Sadko's ship*

After twelve years at sea, Sadko is returning home a wealthy man. Suddenly his ship is becalmed: the Sea King is demanding his dues, and no amount of casting treasure overboard

brings up the wind. Lots are cast, and Sadko himself is selected to be set adrift. Immediately the ship sails off, and Sadko
sinks into the Sea Kingdom.

SCENE 6 *The Sea Kingdom*
Sadko's singing placates the angry Sea King, who gives him
his daughter Volkhova's hand in marriage. The dancing at the
underwater wedding celebrations churns up the sea so much
that ships begin to sink. An Apparition of an old warrior intervenes, proclaiming the end of the Sea King's reign. Sadko and
Volkhova depart, seated in a giant shell.

SCENE 7 *The shore of Lake Ilmen*
The sleeping Sadko is lulled by Volkhova's singing, but at
dawn she bids him farewell and turns into a rapidly flowing
river. Sadko wakes alone, but soon hears the cries of his wife
Lyubava. They are happily reunited, and welcomed home by
the people of Novgorod.

SAINT FRANÇOIS D'ASSISE
(St Francis of Assisi)
Olivier Messiaen (1908–1992)

THREE ACTS. LIBRETTO BY THE COMPOSER, AFTER 14TH CEN-
TURY WRITINGS. PREMIERE IN PARIS, 28 NOVEMBER 1983.

Although the static, ritual drama of *Saint François d'Assise* has
none of the human conflict usually associated with opera and
is more like an oratorio in its conception, Messiaen's slow-
moving work (which lasts approximately four hours) has a
powerful effect in the theatre. Messiaen, one of this century's
leading composers, found in the subject of St Francis the possibility of combining two life-long interests, both important
influences on his music: it embodies his deep religious faith
and—in the scene of St Francis preaching to the birds—also
reflects his musical exploration of bird song.

CHARACTERS

L'Ange (The Angel) (SOPRANO); *Le Lépreux* (The Leper) (TENOR);
Frère Massée (Brother Masseo) (TENOR); *Frère Elie* (Brother Elias)
(TENOR); *Saint François* (St Francis) (BARITONE); *Frère Léon*
(Brother Leo) BARITONE); *Frère Sylvestre* (Brother Sylvester) (BASS);
Frère Rufin (Brother Rufin) (BASS); *Frère Bernard* (Brother
Bernardo) (BASS)

ACT I

St Francis teaches one of his monks, Brother Leo, that spiritual perfection can be achieved only by overcoming suffering. At
the end of a service, Francis prays that God will help him rise
above the instinctive aversion he feels towards lepers. When
he finally encounters a sufferer from the disease, the Leper
senses his revulsion and rejects his preaching. But an Angel
intervenes and moves Francis to embrace the sick man.
Immediately, the Leper is cured and dances for joy.

ACT II

The Angel appears at the monastery and is mistaken for a traveller: Brother Elias refuses to answer his questions about predestination, but Brother Bernardo listens patiently. The Angel departs, but reappears to the praying Francis and entrances him with music evoking celestial bliss. Inspired, Francis preaches to the birds.

ACT III

Francis prays that before his death he will experience the pain of Christ's crucifixion. In response he receives the stigmata. The dying Francis bids his fellow monks farewell and is soothed by the Angel and the Leper he cured. He prays for the light of divine truth, and dies.

SALOME

Richard Strauss (1864-1949)

ONE ACT. LIBRETTO BY THE COMPOSER, AFTER A GERMAN TRANSLATION OF OSCAR WILDE'S PLAY. PREMIERE IN DRESDEN, 9 DECEMBER 1905.

Salome, though preceded by *Guntrum* and *Feuersnot*, was Strauss's first great operatic success. It established him as an important composer of operas and revealed his musico-dramatic powers. Though the brutal plot—which encompasses several perversions, including necrophilia—scandalized many, it provided Strauss with considerable operatic potential. Using his skills as an orchestrator, he was able to evoke the oppressive heat of the mid-Eastern night and the decadence of Herod's court. The principal roles, with the exception of the spiritual Jokanaan, are studies in neurotic depravity, Salome being one of the great parts for singing-actresses.

CHARACTERS

Salome, Herodias's daughter, Herod's stepdaughter (SOPRANO); *Herodias*, Herod's wife (MEZZO-SOPRANO); *Herodias's Page* (CONTRALTO); *Herod*, Tetrarch of Judea (TENOR); *Narraboth*, captain of the guard (TENOR); *Jokanaan* (John the Baptist) (BARITONE)
With *Jews*, *Nazarenes*, a *Cappadocian*, a *Slave*, *guests*, *soldiers*, *servants*

The terrace of Herod's palace

Watching over Herod's feast, the captain Narraboth stares obsessively at Salome. Herodias's Page warns him that misfortune may befall them if his infatuation persists. The voice of Jokanaan is heard deep inside the cistern where he is incarcerated, announcing the coming of the Messiah. Salome, who has left the banqueting table to avoid the lascivious looks of her stepfather, Herod, is fascinated by the prophet and demands to see him. Narraboth, eager to please Salome, disobeys his orders and fetches the prisoner up. The gaunt, wild-looking Jokanaan rails against Herod and Herodias, and denounces Salome when he discovers she is their daughter. But Salome's interest in him has turned to lust, and her passion drives the jealous Narraboth to suicide. Jokanaan, remaining steadfast, curses her and returns to the cistern.

Herod, Herodias, and their guests leave the table and appear on the terrace. Herodias is disturbed by the voice of Jokanaan, and urges Herod to punish him. Herod is reluctant, saying that Jokanaan is a holy man; this rouses the Jews and Nazarenes to an argument. Salome finally gives in to Herod's advances when he promises to grant her any wish if she will dance for him. At the end of the 'Dance of the Seven Veils' she throws herself at the feet of Herod, whose ecstasy turns to horror when she demands the head of Jokanaan on a plate. Herodias gloats, but her husband tries to persuade Salome to accept lavish gifts instead. Undeterred, she demands her reward again, and Herod finally orders Jokanaan's beheading. Salome waits eagerly: at last she is able to kiss the lips the living Jokanaan denied her. Herod, disgusted by her crazed behaviour, orders his soldiers to kill her.

SAMSON ET DALILA (Samson and Delilah)
Camille Saint-Saëns (1835-1921)

THREE ACTS. LIBRETTO BY FERDINAND LEMAIRE. PREMIERE IN WEIMAR, 2 DECEMBER 1877.

Most of Saint-Saëns's 12 operas are forgotten today, but *Samson et Dalila* has attained status as one of the great masterpieces of French operatic literature. It seems astonishing that it was first received with indifference in its own country—indeed, its premiere was not in France but in Weimar (and sung in German), and it took a further 15 years to reach the Paris Opéra. The spectacular score includes the exotic Bacchanale and Dalila's sensuous aria 'Mon coeur s'ouvre à ta voix'.

CHARACTERS

Dalila (Delilah) (MEZZO-SOPRANO); *Samson* (TENOR); *A Philistine Messenger* (TENOR); *High Priest of Dagon* (BARITONE); *Abimélech* (Abimelech), satrap of Gaza (BASS); *An Old Hebrew* (BASS)
With *Hebrews, Philistines*

ACT I
A square in Gaza, in front of the Temple of Dagon
The Hebrews, enslaved to the Philistines, are led by Samson in prayers for deliverance. They are interrupted by the entrance of Abimelech, the satrap of Gaza, who mocks the Hebrews' God. When Abimelech draws his sword Samson snatches it and kills him; in response, the High Priest of Dagon curses the Hebrews. Samson is hailed by his people as a hero, and Philistine girls, led by Delilah, come to dance for him. Delilah flatters Samson and invites him to visit her. Despite the Old Hebrew's warning that he should be wary of her wiles, Samson is seduced by her provocative dancing.

ACT II
The valley of Sorek
Delilah, outside her remote house, is contemplating her

responsibilities as the Philistines' agent of vengeance. She is visited by the High Priest of Dagon, who urges her to discover the secret of Samson's phenomenal strength. Finally, Samson appears, torn between duty to his people and love for Delilah; he has resolved that this must be their last meeting, but she soon succeeds in overcoming his doubts. As he follows her into the house, Philistine soldiers emerge from hiding and, at a signal from Delilah, capture the Hebrew hero.

ACT III
SCENE 1 *A prison in Gaza*
Samson, blinded and shorn of his hair—the secret of his strength—is chained to a mill-wheel. He prays, begging forgiveness for having betrayed his people, whose reproachful voices he hears from another part of the prison. Guards enter to drag him away to the Philistines' victory celebrations.

SCENE 2 *The Temple of Dagon*
Revelry in the Philistines' temple culminates in a frenzied bacchanale. Samson is led in, and Delilah mocks him for his weakness. Taunted by everyone, Samson is ordered by the High Priest to join the sacrificial ritual in the middle of temple in full view of all. Positioning himself between two central pillars, Samson prays for the return of his old strength in order that he may avenge the Hebrews' humiliation. He gives a mighty push, and the whole temple collapses on all those inside.

THE SECRET MARRIAGE
see **Il Matrimonio Segreto**

SEMIRAMIDE
Gioachino Rossini (1792-1868)

TWO ACTS. LIBRETTO BY GAETANO ROSSI, AFTER VOLTAIRE'S *SÉMIRAMIS*. PREMIERE IN VENICE, 3 FEBRUARY 1823.

Rossini's last opera for Italy—after *Semiramide*, he turned his attentions on Paris—is one of his grandest. This story of intrigue in ancient Babylon has attracted some 40 operatic settings (almost all earlier than Rossini's, though Respighi had the courage to compose one in 1908-10), all of which Rossini surpasses in music of dazzling brilliance, though the florid writing is always used to dramatic ends. The title role provides one of the great challenges of the coloratura soprano repertory.

CHARACTERS
Semiramide, Queen of Babylon (SOPRANO); *Azema*, a princess (SOPRANO); *Arsace*, commander of the Babylonian army (CONTRALTO); *Idreno*, an Indian prince (TENOR); *Mitrane*, captain of the guard (TENOR); *Assur*, a prince (BASS); *Oroe*, high priest of the Magi (BASS); *Ghost of King Nino* (BASS)
With *Magi, Babylonians, Indians, Scythians, Egyptians, satraps, princesses, bards, foreign women, guards, priests, slaves*

ACT I

SCENE 1 *The temple of Baal*

The high priest Oroe stands in the temple where a crowd has assembled to hear Semiramide name her successor to the throne she has occupied for 15 years. Prince Assur, who helped Semiramide murder her husband, King Nino, and gain the throne, expects to be nominated, but the Indian prince Idreno is also a contender; both hope to win the hand of the princess Azema. But Semiramide is smitten with the handsome young commander Arsace, and unaware that he is the son she attempted to murder when she did away with her husband, hopes to make him king. Arsace arrives back in Babylon, carrying possessions of his dead father. His love for Azema arouses the jealousy of the other princes.

SCENE 2 *The Hanging Gardens of Babylon*

Semiramide summons Arsace. She is so infatuated with the youth that she imagines that his vows of love for Azema are addressed to her.

SCENE 3 *The palace*

From her throne, Semiramide announces that she will make Arsace not only king, but her consort too. This sparks off a crisis, with protests from both Arsace and Assur. Idreno is to win Azema's hand, but as the High Priest is about to marry them, the Ghost of King Nino intervenes. He confirms that Arsace will be his successor, and commands him to descend into his tomb to learn the circumstances of his assassination. Rumblings from the tomb terrify Semiramide and the crowd.

ACT II

SCENE 1 *The palace*

Assur tries to blackmail Semiramide into giving him the throne, by threatening to expose her crime; she counters by offering to reveal his.

SCENE 2 *The palace sanctuary*

Oroe, preparing to lead Arsace to the tomb, tells him that Nino was indeed his father and names the assassins. Arsace is reluctant to harm his mother but swears vengeance on Assur.

SCENE 3 *The queen's rooms*

Arsace reveals to Semiramide that he is her son. She is overcome with remorse and offers herself as a sacrifice at Nino's tomb. But Arsace spares her, and the two are reconciled.

SCENE 4 *Near King Nino's tomb in the palace*

Assur, now held guilty by the people, resolves to kill Arsace.

SCENE 5 *Inside King Nino's tomb*

Assur enters the tomb in order to confront Arsace. Semiramide appears too, desperate to warn her son of Assur's plans. As Arsace moves to kill Assur, Semiramide throws herself between the two men and receives a fatal blow. Nino's death is avenged, and Arsace—though aghast at having killed his mother—is persuaded to take the Babylonian throne.

SERSE (Xerxes)
George Frideric Handel (1685-1759)

THREE ACTS. LIBRETTO (ANONYMOUS) AFTER SILVIO STAMPIGLIA'S *XERSE*, ITSELF BASED ON NICOLO MINATO'S *IL XERSE*. PREMIERE IN LONDON, 15 APRIL 1738.

Handel wrote prolifically for the London stage (some 40 operas in the 30 years from 1711-1741) and *Serse* was one of the last operas he composed before changing direction and turning to oratorio. It is perhaps his finest comic work. In keeping with the plot—a lighthearted amorous intrigue—the arias are shorter than in most Handel operas, though the change in style may also have been in part a reaction to the popular ballad operas of the day that were challenging Handel's supremacy. Like Handel's other operas, *Serse* suffered two centuries of neglect, but its name was kept alive through one number, 'Ombra mai fu'—known since Victorian times as 'Handel's Largo', but not in its context as Xerxes's serenade to a plane tree.

CHARACTERS

Romilda, Ariodate's daughter, in love with Arsamene (SOPRANO); *Serse* (Xerxes), King of Persia (MEZZO-SOPRANO); *Arsamene*, his brother (MEZZO-SOPRANO); *Amastre*, a foreign princess, betrothed to Xerxes (MEZZO-SOPRANO); *Ariodate*, commander of the army (BASS); *Elviro*, Arsamene's servant (BASS)

ACT I

Xerxes, after praising the beauty of a plane tree, turns his mind towards Romilda, whose singing he hears in the distance. He is enraptured, and orders his brother, Arsamene, to convey his proposal of marriage to her. But Arsamene makes excuses—he and Romilda are already in love. Romilda's sister, Atalanta, overhears Arsamene warning his beloved, and she resolves to back Xerxes's cause: she herself is secretly in love with Arsamene and sees an opportunity to win him. When Xerxes has no success in wooing Romilda, he banishes Arsamene from the court. Xerxes is already betrothed to the foreign princess Amastre, and soon she arrives—disguised as a soldier—to witness Xerxes's plotting. She sees him congratulating Ariodate on a successful campaign, and promising to arrange a 'royal marriage' for his daughter, Romilda. She swears vengeance. Elviro is dispatched with a letter from his master, Arsamene, to Romilda, begging her not to forget him during their separation. Atalanta tries to convince Romilda of Arsamene's infidelity.

ACT II

Elviro, disguised as a flower seller, arrives on his errand and encounters Amastre, who he tells about Xerxes and Romilda. Instead of delivering the letter to Romilda herself, he entrusts it to Atalanta, who despite her promise to pass it on shows it to

Xerxes, convincing him that it was addressed to her and not Romilda. In turn, Xerxes shows it to Romilda as evidence that Arsamene now loves Atalanta, but she continues to spurn his advances. Elviro prevents the unhappy Amastre from committing suicide, before conveying to Arsamene the news the scheming Atalanta had told him: that Romilda had given in to Xerxes's demands.

Xerxes and Ariodate inspect a great new bridge that will enable them to invade Europe. He encounters the downcast Arsamene, who steadfastly reaffirms his love for Romilda. Atalanta ignores Xerxes's advice to forget about Arsamene. Elviro watches as a violent storm breaks up the new bridge. Amastre reappears, only to see Xerxes's latest attempt to win Romilda. Her intervention provokes Xerxes to order her arrest, but Romilda counters by demanding her release. Once again, Romilda declares her steadfast love for Arsamene.

ACT III

Romilda and Arsamene uncover Atalanta's plot. When Xerxes tries again to persuade Romilda to marry him, she tells him he will require her father's permission. Xerxes finds Ariodate and gets his consent for a 'royal marriage', Ariodate imagining his future son-in-law to be Xerxes's brother, Arsamene. Attempting to deter Xerxes, Romilda tries to cast doubt on her virtue, but this results only in an order for Arsamene's execution. Arsamene accuses Romilda of plotting to dispose of him.

In the temple, Ariodate awaits his daughter and her bridegroom. When Romilda and Arsamene enter he marries them—with, he believes, Xerxes's blessing. Xerxes is furious to discover that he is too late to marry Romilda, and orders Arsamene to kill his bride. But Amastre intervenes and reveals her identity as the one to which Xerxes was originally betrothed. She forgives him, and all are reconciled.

THE SICILIAN VESPERS
see I Vespri siciliani

SIEGFRIED
see Der Ring des Nibelungen

SIMON BOCCANEGRA
Giuseppe Verdi (1813-1901)

PROLOGUE AND THREE ACTS. LIBRETTO BY FRANCESCA MARIA PIAVE AND ARRIGO BOITO, AFTER ANTONIO GARCIA GUTIÉRREZ'S PLAY *SIMON BOCCANEGRA*. PREMIERE IN VENICE, 12 MARCH 1857 (REVISED FOR MILAN, 24 MARCH 1881).

Simon Boccanegra, one of several Verdi operas that exist in two versions, was revised because of the work's failure at its premiere. The dark, convoluted plot and the music Verdi wrote to match it—in search of dramatic truth, he abandoned the more obvious tunefulness of his earlier operas—baffled audiences of 1857. Though the libretto of the 1881 revision, the version almost always heard today, is more coherent, the music remains sombre. The score is now admired as one of Verdi's greatest, but it lacks the popular tunes to make it a universal favourite.

CHARACTERS

Amelia, thought to be Amelia Grimaldi but in fact Maria, Boccanegra's daughter (SOPRANO); *Amelia's Maidservant* (MEZZO-SOPRANO); *Gabriele Adorno*, a Genoese nobleman (TENOR); *A Captain* (TENOR); *Simon Boccanegra*, a corsair in the service of the Genoese Republic, later Doge of Venice (BARITONE); *Paolo Albiani*, a Genoese plebeian, later the Doge's favourite courtier (BARITONE); *Jacopo Fiesco*, a Genoese nobleman, later under the name of Andrea (BASS); *Pietro*, a Genoese plebeian, later a courtier of the Doge (BASS) With *soldiers, sailors, artisans, councillors, courtiers* of the Doge, *servants*, African *prisoners*

PROLOGUE

A square in Genoa
On the eve of elections for a new Doge, Paolo urges his fellow plebeian politician Pietro to support the nomination of the corsair Simon Boccanegra, who they hope will become Genoa's first Doge not to be elected from the nobility. Boccanegra accepts, reasoning that the position might enable him to marry Maria—daughter of the outgoing Doge, Fiesco—whose child he has fathered. Though Fiesco disapproves of Boccanegra and has kept the lovers apart, Boccanegra goes to plead with him for reconciliation. Fiesco is in no mood for appeasement: his daughter has just died, though he does not tell Boccanegra the news. His condition for peace, that his grand-daughter (also named Maria) be surrendered to him, cannot be met, because Boccanegra admits that the child has gone missing. The men part in anger, Boccanegra entering the Fiesco palace to find Maria's corpse. He hears the crowd declaring him Doge.

ACT I

Twenty-five years later
SCENE 1 *The garden of the Grimaldi palace near Genoa*
The lost daughter of Maria and Boccanegra has been brought up as Amelia Grimaldi and is now in the care of a certain Andrea—none other than her grandfather, Fiesco, though neither of them know their relationship. She is in love with the nobleman Gabriele Adorno, and despairs that he may be endangering their lives by plotting against Boccanegra. When Boccanegra's arrival is signalled, she fears that the purpose of his visit may be to force her to marry the Doge's courtier, Paolo. She begs Andrea's permission to marry Gabriele without delay, and it is granted; Gabriele is undeterred by the revelation that his betrothed is not of noble birth after all, but an orphan. Boccanegra enters, and after questioning Amelia and comparing lockets, realizes that she is his long-lost daughter. They are reunited. Boccanegra refuses to allow Paolo to marry his daughter, and out of revenge against the man he helped gain the throne, Paolo plots to abduct her.

SCENE 2 *The council chamber in the Doge's palace*

The Doge urges the opposing plebeian and noble factions on his council to put aside their differences. Their meeting is disrupted by a group of rowdy plebeians who haul Gabriele and Fiesco in. Gabriele announces that Amelia has been abducted, admits that he killed one of the culprits, and accuses Boccanegra of being behind the plot. He attacks the Doge, but Amelia enters and comes to her father's defence. She hints that Paolo was responsible for the plot. When Boccanegra has calmed down the rowdy factions, he torments Paolo by making him curse the criminal.

ACT II

The Doge's room in the Ducal palace in Genoa

Paolo, still bent on revenge, tries to recruit the help of Gabriele and Fiesco, both in prison. He poisons Boccanegra's drinking water. The freedom he offers Fiesco in exchange for assistance in murdering Boccanegra is declined, but he fires Gabriele's anger by telling him that Amelia is Boccanegra's mistress. Indeed, when Gabriele finds her in the Doge's room he accuses her of infidelity. Unable to bear the pressure any longer, Amelia confesses to her father that she loves one of his opponents, and persuades the Doge to pardon Gabriele. Boccanegra drinks from the water containing slow-acting poison and falls asleep. Gabriele steals up to the sleeping Boccanegra, intending to stab him, but Amelia intervenes and their confrontation rouses Boccanegra, who reveals to Gabriele that he is Amelia's father. Gabriele begs forgiveness and offers his services to the Doge. Boccanegra puts him to the test by sending him out to quell the fighting heard outside, promising Amelia's hand if he can bring peace to the city.

ACT III

The Doge's palace

With the rebellion crushed, Paolo—who at the last moment tells Fiesco he has poisoned Boccanegra—is led away to execution. Boccanegra appears in a daze, suffering from the effects of the poison. When Fiesco comes to confront him, Boccanegra startles him by meeting the conditions of peace he demanded 25 years earlier: Amelia, he says, is his grand-daughter. All are reconciled, and as he dies, Boccanegra blesses the couple's marriage and names Gabriele as his successor.

STREET SCENE
Kurt Weill (1900-1950)

TWO ACTS. LIBRETTO BY ELMER RICE, AFTER HIS OWN PLAY, WITH LYRICS BY LANGSTON HUGHES. PREMIERE IN NEW YORK, 9 JANUARY 1947.

Street Scene is the masterpiece of Weill's American years. Although many of the works he composed before fleeing Nazi Germany were harder-hitting social satires than those he wrote for Broadway, his humanism never left him. *Street Scene*, set in a poor New York tenement, had a social message when it appeared in the late 1940s and its conscience is no less strong today. Weill called it an 'American opera', though only one role, Ann Maurrant, requires a truly operatic voice. The music ranges from the Pucciniesque 'Somehow I never could believe' to the jitterbug 'Moonfaced, starry eyed'.

CHARACTERS

Ann Maurrant (SOPRANO); *Rose Maurrant*, daughter of Ann and Frank (SOPRANO); *Sam Kaplan*, in love with Rose (TENOR); *Frank Maurrant*, Ann's husband (BASS-BARITONE)

With *Abraham Kaplan, Mr Fiorentino, Mrs Fiorentino, Mr Olsen, Mrs Olsen, Mr Jones, Mrs Jones, Henry Davis, Mr Buchanan, Mrs Buchanan, Jennie Hildebrand, Harry Easter, Mae Jones, Willie Maurrant, Mr Sankey, graduates, nursemaids, neighbours, policemen*

ACT I

On a stifling summer's evening, the women of the tenement gather to grumble and gossip. The janitor, Henry Davis, goes about his work. The busy-body Mrs Jones brings up the subject of Mrs Maurrant's affair with the milkman, Mr Sankey, but conversation changes when Mrs Maurrant herself joins the group; they tease Mr Buchanan, whose wife is about to have a baby, and greet Sam Kaplan, the studious youth who is in love with the Maurrants' daughter, Rose. The appearance of the unfeeling, inarticulate Mr Maurrant explains his wife's unhappiness. When the neighbours see Mrs Maurrant heading off in the direction of the milkman—pretending to search for her son Willie—they reflect that Mr Maurrant is the only one unaware of the affair. The mood lightens when Mr Fiorentino arrives with ice-creams for all, but their highjinks are interrupted by the reappearance of Mr Maurrant who has begun to suspect something. He picks a political argument with the left-wing Mr Kaplan, Sam's father. Children return from their graduation, and although Mrs Hildebrand is proud of her daughter Jenny, she can only celebrate half-heartedly: her family is to be evicted from their apartment the following day. When most residents retire for the night, Mr Maurrant goes drinking. It is late when Rose is seen home by Harry Easter, a fellow office worker whose advances she spurns, even when he tries to lure her to live with him on Broadway. By the small hours, only the tipsy couple Mae Jones and Dick have the energy left to dance. Sam finds Rose, and they dream romantically of a better life together before bidding each other good-night.

ACT II

Next morning, people set about their chores and children play. Mr Maurrant, preparing to go away for two days on business, quarrels violently with his wife before leaving. When Mrs Maurrant has sent her son Willie off to school and Rose goes to attend a funeral, she invites Sankey to visit her. Suddenly, Sam sees Mr Maurrant returning home unexpectedly: his attempts to bar Maurrant's way are unsuccessful, and gunshots are heard. Sankey is killed, and Rose returns only in time to see her dying mother being carried out.

Later that day, two nursemaids come to stare at the scene of the murder. Shots signal that Maurrant has been apprehended. Before being taken away, he tells Rose of his regrets and asks her to care for her brother. Sam tries to comfort her, but Rose insists on going away alone. Sam is broken-hearted, but for the rest of the tenement dwellers life goes on as usual.

SUOR ANGELICA (Sister Angelica)

Giacomo Puccini (1858-1924)

ONE ACT. LIBRETTO BY GIOVACCHINO FORZANO. PREMIERE IN NEW YORK, 14 DECEMBER 1918.

Suor Angelica is the middle work in Puccini's *Il trittico* (see also *Il tabarro* and *Gianni Schicchi*). The sentimental story and mystical atmosphere provides a contrast with its more direct companions in the triptych. Angelica's aria, 'Senza mamma', is one of Puccini's most touching creations.

CHARACTERS

Suor Angelica (Sister Angelica) (SOPRANO); *Suor Genovieffa* (Sister Genovieffa) (SOPRANO); *Suor Osmina* (Sister Osmina) (SOPRANO); *Suor Dolcina* (Sister Dolcina) (SOPRANO); *La Badessa* (Abbess) (MEZZO-SOPRANO); *La Suora Zelatrice* (Alms Collector) (MEZZO-SOPRANO); *La Maestra delle novizie* (Mistress of the Novices) (MEZZO-SOPRANO); *La Suora Infermiera* (Nursing Sister) (MEZZO-SOPRANO); *La Zia Principessa* (Princess); Suor Angelica's aunt (CONTRALTO)
With Alms Collectors, Novices, Sisters

A cloister garden
The sisters of the convent finish their service before resuming their chores and chatting happily. Only Angelica is downcast: though she will not admit why, her sisters know that she has been in the convent for seven years without hearing from her (aristocratic Florentine) family. The Nursing Sister rushes in to seek Angelica's advice: one of their number has been stung by wasps. She is followed by two Alms Collectors, who bring news that a luxurious carriage has arrived at the convent gates. The Abbess summons Angelica, to tell her that her aunt, a Princess, has come to see her. Cold and aloof, the Princess's conversation is business-like (she has brought legal documents for Angelica to sign) until Angelica asks for news of her baby— whose illegitimate birth led to Angelica being sent to the convent as punishment: the Princess admits that he has been dead for two years, and Angelica is overcome with emotion. When the Princess has gone, Angelica breaks down, distraught that her baby died without knowing his mother's love. Angelica resolves to kill herself and after bidding her sisters farewell drinks poison. But with fear she realizes that her mortal sin will prevent her from ever being reunited with her child. Her fervent prayers to the Virgin Mary are answered with a miracle: radiant light pours from the convent chapel and angels' voices are heard as Angelica sees the Virgin leading her child towards her. She dies ecstatically.

IL TABARRO (The Cloak)
Giacomo Puccini (1858-1924)

ONE ACT. LIBRETTO BY GIUSEPPE ADAMI, AFTER DIDIER GOLD'S PLAY *LA HOUPPELANDE*. PREMIERE IN NEW YORK, 14 DECEMBER 1918.

Il tabarro is the first work in Puccini's triptych of one-act operas, *Il trittico*, which also includes *Suor Angelica* and *Gianni Schicchi*. Intended to be performed as a group (though two are often coupled as a double bill), each work contrasts strongly with the others: *Tabarro* provides the melodrama, and is a dark story of adultery and murder set among barge dwellers on the Seine. The opera reveals Puccini's craftsmanship at its best and his orchestration—especially in the impressionistic picture of dusk on the river, complete with tugs' horns—at its most evocative.

CHARACTERS
Giorgetta, Michele's wife (SOPRANO); *Frugola*, Talpa's wife (MEZZO-SOPRANO); *Luigi*, a stevedore (TENOR); *Tinca*, a stevedore (TENOR); *Michele*, owner of a barge (BARITONE); *Talpa*, a stevedore (BASS)

A barge moored on the Seine, Paris
Michele, a middle-aged barge owner (50 years old, Puccini specifies), relaxes at dusk while his young wife Giorgetta (aged 25) finishes her tasks for the day. Soon his stevedores, led by Luigi (aged 20), come on board and gratefully accept the drink offered by Giorgetta. Tinca dances with Giorgetta, but Luigi has taken his place when Michele enters. His suspicions aroused, Michele stops their dancing and the stevedores go below deck. Giorgetta and Michele quarrel, but are interrupted first by a ballad-seller and then by Frugola, who has come in search of her unreliable husband, Talpa, another of the stevedores. When the coast is clear, Luigi returns to find Giorgetta. She is infatuated with her young lover, and the two arrange to meet again that night; he will appear at her signal, the lighting of a match. Unable to bear the thought of sharing her love with another, Luigi resolves to leave the boat and asks Michele to put him ashore at Rouen the following day, but Michele urges him to stay on.

Michele is troubled by his wife's coldness and tries to show affection by recalling happier times, when their baby was still alive. Giorgetta dismisses the cooling of their passion as a natural consequence of their getting older and goes off to bed. Left alone to ponder the affair he is by now convinced of, Michele lights his pipe. Immediately, Luigi—taking this to be Giorgetta's signal—rushes aboard, and is confronted by Michele. He is forced to confess his illicit love before being strangled to death and wrapped in Michele's cloak. Giorgetta appears on the deck, hoping for a reconciliation with her husband, but he triumphantly reveals the corpse and pushes her face into that of her dead lover.

THE TALES OF HOFFMANN
see **Les Contes d'Hoffmann**

TANNHÄUSER
Richard Wagner (1813-1883)

THREE ACTS. LIBRETTO BY THE COMPOSER. PREMIERE IN DRESDEN, 19 OCTOBER 1845.

Tannhäuser is a transitory work in Wagner's output, breaking away from the operatic conventions of *Der fliegende Holländer* but not achieving the synthesis of music and drama of his mature works. In order to obtain the contrast of carnal and spiritual love on which the plot hinges, Wagner drew on two distinct medieval legends, the first being the seduction of a wandering minstrel by Venus, the goddess of love, the second describing the Wartburg minstrel contest. The score contains many highlights—including the famous Overture, the Pilgrims' Chorus and the Venusberg ballet music—that helped to make *Tannhäuser* once Wagner's most popular opera.

CHARACTERS

Elisabeth, the Landgrave's niece (SOPRANO); *Venus* (SOPRANO); *A Young Shepherd* (SOPRANO); *Tannhäuser, Walther von der Vogelweide* and *Heinrich der Schreiber*, minstrel kights (TENORS); *Wolfram von Eschenbach*, a minstrel knight (BARITONE); *Biterolf* and *Reinmar von Zweter*, minstrel knights (BASSES); *Hermann*, Landgrave of Thuringia (BASS)
With *knights, nobles, ladies, pages, pilgrims, sirens, naiads, nymphs, bacchantes*

ACT I
SCENES 1 and 2 *Inside the Venusberg*
The minstrel-knight Tannhäuser is enjoying the profane delights of the Venusberg. When the wild dancing finishes and he is left alone with Venus, he begins to feel torn between desire for her and a longing to return to the simplicity of the real world. Venus curses Tannhäuser when he begs for release, but his invocation to the Virgin Mary breaks her spell.

SCENES 3 and 4 *The Wartburg valley*
Tannhäuser finds himself in a valley near the Wartburg castle, where he hears a Shepherd singing. The prayers of passing pilgrims move him to confess his sins. Hunting horns signal the approach of the Landgrave and minstrels, and they recognize Tannhäuser as a long-lost comrade. One of their number, Wolfram, reminds Tannhäuser of his love for the Landgrave's niece, Elisabeth, who has been pining for him since his departure for the Venusberg. Tannhäuser resolves to return with them to the Wartburg to see her.

ACT II
The Singers' Hall of the Wartburg
Elisabeth receives Tannhäuser joyfully and the two are reunited, though he does not reveal where he has been during his absence. The Landgrave announces a contest of song on the theme of love, promising Elisabeth's hand as the prize. The first contender is Wolfram, who defines love as pure and tender; Walther and Biterolf express similar feelings. Tannhäuser takes the stand, and to the horror of the company extols

Venus's erotic allure. The angry knights attempt to kill him, but Elisabeth restrains them. Tannhäuser is filled with remorse, and bows to the Landgrave's command: to save his soul he must join the pilgrims heading for Rome.

ACT III
The Wartburg valley

Months have passed and Tannhäuser has not returned. At a shrine near the castle Elisabeth anxiously scans the pilgrim procession, hoping to catch sight of her knight. She prays to the Virgin Mary for his salvation, offering herself as a sacrifice if need be. In turn, Wolfram calls on the evening star to protect Elisabeth. When Tannhäuser finally appears, his garments torn, he encounters Wolfram and tells him that his pilgrimage has been fruitless: the Pope refused to absolve him, saying that his chance of salvation was as great as the papal staff bursting into leaf. Tannhäuser resolves to seek solace in the Venusberg, but Wolfram's mention of Elisabeth helps him to overcome temptation. At that moment a funeral procession passes. Elisabeth has died of a broken heart, and Tannhäuser collapses over her body. More pilgrims enter to reveal a miracle: the papal staff has sprouted leaves, a sign of Tannhäuser's redemption.

THAÏS
Jules Massenet (1842–1912)

THREE ACTS. LIBRETTO BY LOUIS GALLET, AFTER ANATOLE FRANCE'S NOVEL *THAIS*. PREMIERE IN PARIS, 16 MARCH 1894.

Massenet's detractors mock his music for its 'discreet and semi-religious eroticism' (the words of Massenet's contemporary composer Vincent D'Indy), but nowhere are these qualities more apposite than in *Thaïs*, the story of a courtesan's conversion by a monk himself drawn into carnality, set in 4th-century Egypt. The sensuous score has gained notoriety for the beautiful but hackneyed Méditation, which in its dramatic context serves as an effective intermezzo in Act II.

CHARACTERS
Thaïs, a courtesan (SOPRANO); *Crobyle*, a slave (SOPRANO); *Myrtale*, a slave (MEZZO-SOPRANO); *Albine*, an abbess (MEZZO-SOPRANO); *Nicias*, a young philosopher (TENOR); *Athanaël*, a young Cenobite monk (BARITONE); *Servant of Nicias* (BARITONE); *Palémon*, an old Cenobite monk (BASS); *La Charmeuse* (DANCER)
With *actors, philosophers, monks, nuns*, Alexandrian *people*

ACT I
SCENE 1 *The Cenobite refuge*

Monks at their supper are joined by their brother, Athanaël, who has returned from Alexandria. He is shocked to have encountered the courtesan Thaïs there, for in his youth he knew her as an innocent girl. Haunted by images of her plying her trade he is unable to sleep. Ignoring the warnings of the old monk Palémon, Athanaël sets out across the desert, determined to convert her.

SCENE 2 *Nicias's house in Alexandria*
In the city of his childhood, Athanaël meets his old acquaintance Nicias, now a womanizer who has acquired the services of Thaïs for a week. He persuades Nicias to allow him to attend a banquet that evening, and—having changed out of his severe monastic garb—finds himself in Thaïs's presence. She sees the monk as an exciting new challenge, and her blatant advances frighten Athanaël away.

ACT II

SCENE 1 *Thaïs's house*
For the first time, Thaïs is vexed by her conscience. She listens with interest when Athanaël arrives to pursue his mission, warning against the sins of the flesh and promising redemption, but drives him away when voices remind her of her profession.

SCENE 2 *Outside Thaïs's house*
Athanaël's message has had its effect, and later that night the converted Thaïs comes to find him, waiting patiently on the steps of her house. Now dressed plainly, she begs Athanaël to take her to a convent. He agrees, but orders her to break with her past by burning her house and its contents. Some men, resenting Athanaël's power over her, intimidate them, but Nicias intervenes.

ACT III

SCENE 1 *An oasis near Mother Albine's convent*
Athanaël delivers the exhausted Thaïs to her convent.

SCENE 2 *The Cenobite refuge*
Athanaël is troubled by erotic visions of Thaïs and realizes that he is in love with her. He is also haunted by dreams of her death, and at the height of a violent storm—and in spite of further warnings from Palémon—heads for the convent.

SCENE 3 *The convent garden*
Athanaël arrives to find the nuns comforting Thaïs on her deathbed. Left alone with her, Athanaël confesses his unchaste passion for her as she dies, purified by thoughts of heaven.

THE THIEVING MAGPIE
see **La gazza ladra**

TOSCA
Giacomo Puccini (1858-1924)

THREE ACTS. LIBRETTO BY GIUSEPPE GIACOSA AND LUIGI ILLICA, AFTER VICTORIEN SARDOU'S PLAY *LA TOSCA*. PREMIERE IN ROME, 14 JANUARY 1900.

Though *Tosca*—which comes between *La Bohème* and *Madama Butterfly* in Puccini's output—is the composer's most popular opera, it has also drawn more criticism than any of his other works. Its melodramatic emotions and their effects—passion, lust, jealousy, torture, murder, intrigue, suicide—have led one musicologist to denounce it as a 'shabby little shocker', but Puccini manipulates them so compellingly that *Tosca* never fails to grip its audiences. The opera is set in Rome in 1800, against the background of oppressive Austrian rule (upheld in the drama by the police chief Scarpia) and invasion by Napoleon, greeted by Italian patriots (represented by Cavaradossi) as liberation from foreign tyranny.

CHARACTERS

Floria Tosca, a celebrated singer (SOPRANO); *A Shepherd Boy* (ALTO); *Mario Cavaradossi*, a painter (TENOR); *Spoletta*, a police agent (TENOR); *Baron Scarpia*, Chief of Police (BARITONE); *A Sacristan* (BARITONE); *Cesare Angelotti*, a political prisoner (BASS); *Sciarrone*, a gendarme (BASS); *A Gaoler* (BASS)

With *executioner, cardinal, judge, scribe, officer, sergeant, soldiers, police agents, noblemen* and *women, citizens, artisans*

ACT I

The church of Sant'Andrea della Valle

Cesare Angelotti—a former consul of the defunct Roman republic, now an escaped political prisoner on the run—comes to hide in the Attavanti chapel. His sister, the Marchesa Attavanti, has concealed the key in the church. The old Sacristan shuffles past, going about his chores. Cavaradossi enters to resume work on his painting in the church (a portrait of Mary Magdalene, inspired both by his lover, the singer Floria Tosca, and Angelotti's sister) when Angelotti emerges and asks for help. Cavaradossi promises to assist him, but they are disturbed by Tosca calling outside: she has overheard Cavaradossi talking to someone and is jealous. Cavaradossi calms her and sends her away before fleeing with Angelotti to his villa outside Rome. Meanwhile, Angelotti's escape has been discovered, and the Sacristan comes in with news (false, it turns out) of Napoleon's defeat. Plans are made for a victory service and Tosca is ordered to perform that evening for the queen, but the preparations are interrupted by the arrival of Baron Scarpia and his agents, in search of Angelotti. Tosca, looking for Cavaradossi, is confronted by Scarpia: he has discovered the Marchesa Attavanti's fan and uses it to work on Tosca's jealousy, hoping to arrest Cavaradossi and conquer the woman himself.

ACT II

Scarpia's room in the Palazzo Farnese

Scarpia contemplates his double victory. Cavaradossi is brought in for interrogation, but denies knowing of Angelotti's hideout and is taken off for torture as Tosca (who has been singing in the royal gala downstairs) enters. Unable to bear the cries of pain she hears from the torture chamber, she discloses Angelotti's whereabouts. Cavaradossi is brought in, denounces her for her weakness, and then acclaims the news of Napoleon's counter-victory. He is dragged off for execution. Alone with Tosca, Scarpia tries to blackmail her by offering Cavaradossi's freedom in return for her embraces. Resisting at first, she is broken down by news of Angelotti's suicide. Scarpia promises to arrange a mock execution before writing a safe-conduct for Tosca and Cavaradossi. To escape his amorous advances, Tosca stabs Scarpia and leaves with the safe-conduct.

ACT III
The Castel Sant'Angelo
The voice of a Shepherd Boy and church bells greeting the dawn are heard as Cavaradossi is led out to prepare for his execution. He is writing a farewell note to Tosca when she enters with news of her bold success and tells him to go along with the mock execution. They rejoice at the prospect of their freedom, before Cavaradossi is taken to face the firing squad. Shots ring out and when the soldiers have gone, Tosca urges her lover to move. She discovers Scarpia's treachery: the bullets were real. Shouts announce that Scarpia's murder has been discovered, and to escape arrest Tosca—vowing to meet Scarpia before God—leaps over the battlements to her death.

LA TRAVIATA (The Fallen Woman)
Giuseppe Verdi (1813-1901)

THREE ACTS. LIBRETTO BY FRANCESCO MARIA PIAVE, AFTER ALEXANDRE DUMAS'S PLAY *LA DAME AUX CAMÉLIAS*. PREMIERE IN VENICE, 6 MARCH 1853.

Verdi's most popular operas are three consecutive works of his middle period: *Rigoletto*, *Il trovatore*, and *La traviata*. All are distinguished by their melodic richness, but each is different. *Traviata* is an intimate work, dealing with the conflict between the 'real' world of human emotion and the 'false' world of society life. Its lyrical and intoxicating tunes—including the Brindisi, 'Sempre libera' and 'Parigi, o cara'—are often heard out of context, but in place they help to make *Traviata* a great music drama.

CHARACTERS
Violetta Valéry, a courtesan (SOPRANO); *Annina*, Violetta's maid (SOPRANO); *Flora Bervoix*, her friend (MEZZO-SOPRANO); *Alfredo Germont* (TENOR); *Gastone de Letorières*, friend of Alfredo (TENOR); *Giorgio Germont*, Alfredo's father (BARITONE); *Baron Douphol*, Violetta's protector (BARITONE); *Marchese D'Obigny*, friend of Flora (BASS); *Doctor Grenvil* (BASS)
With *ladies, gentlemen, servants, maskers, dancers, guests*

ACT I
Violetta's house
Violetta is hosting one of her glittering parties. Her guests include Flora Bervoix, D'Obigny, Douphol and Gastone, who brings with him Alfredo Germont, for long a secret admirer of Violetta. Alfredo proposes a toast to her, and as the dancers leave for the ballroom, Violetta collapses in a fainting fit (an early sign that she is consumptive). Alfredo lingers behind to help her, and confesses his love. Violetta tries to discourage him, telling Alfredo

that courtesans like herself are incapable of real love, but nevertheless agreeing to meet him again. Left alone, she realizes how moved she is by her declaration but shrugs off her sentimentality and resolves to continue with her life of dizzy pleasure.

ACT II

SCENE 1 *A villa near Paris*

Alfredo and Violetta have been living together for several months when the maid Annina reveals to Alfredo that her mistress has had to sell jewellery to finance their country lifestyle. Alfredo departs for Paris to raise money, and during his absence his father, Giorgio Germont, pays an unexpected visit. Concerned at what his son's relationship is doing to the family's name, he begs Violetta to break their liaison off. Heartbroken—and frightened by the prospect of fighting her illness alone—she agrees, but unable to reveal to Alfredo the truth she writes a note telling him that she is returning to her old life. She is about to leave for Paris when Alfredo returns, and, reassuring him of her love, she departs flustered. Germont's attempts to comfort his son are unsuccessful: Alfredo sets off to find Violetta.

SCENE 2 *Flora's town house*

Violetta arrives at Flora's party—where maskers dress as gypsies and matadors—on the arm of Baron Douphol, whom she pretends to love. Alfredo gambles with Douphol and wins. He confronts Violetta, who keeps her promise to Germont by insisting that she left of her own free will. Driven to fury, Alfredo throws his winnings at her feet in 'payment' for all the pleasure they have shared. The suffering Violetta is unable to bear his insult. He is rebuked for his behaviour by Germont, who has arrived in search of his son. Douphol threatens vengeance.

ACT III

Violetta's bedroom

Violetta lies dying of consumption, comforted by Annina and Dr Grenvil. Realizing that she has only a few hours left to live, Violetta takes out a letter from Germont revealing that he has now told Alfredo about her sacrifice and that his son is on his way to see her. Fearing that he will arrive too late she bids past happiness farewell, but his sudden appearance raises her spirits. The lovers are reconciled, and dream of a future together. She weakens again, and is visited by the doctor and Germont, who begs forgiveness for the pain he has caused. Violetta feels a sudden rush of strength before dying in Alfredo's arms.

TRISTAN UND ISOLDE (Tristan and Isolde)
Richard Wagner (1813-1883)

THREE ACTS. LIBRETTO BY THE COMPOSER. PREMIERE IN MUNICH, 10 JUNE 1865.

Tristan und Isolde is a seminal work in the history of music; in it Wagner pushed the tonal system, on which Western music had been based for centuries, to its limit. Its extreme chromaticism reflects the no less extreme level of Wagner's emotional expression. The opera is autobiographical: in his supremely egotistical way, Wagner took the famous medieval romantic legend and used it to celebrate a love triangle (an affair with Matilde von Wesendonk, whose, husband, Otto, was Wagner's benefactor) he was involved in during its composition; indeed, the passionate turn of events led him to interrupt work on *The Ring* in order that he could write *Tristan*. The opera is full of psychological symbolism beyond the scope of a brief synopsis.

CHARACTERS

Isolde (SOPRANO); *Brangäne*, Isolde's maid (SOPRANO); *Tristan*, nephew of King Mark (TENOR); *Melot*, a courtier (TENOR); *A Shepherd* (TENOR); *A Sailor* (TENOR); *Kurwenal*, Tristan's servant (BARITONE); *A Steersman* (BARITONE); *King Mark*, of Cornwall (BASS) With *sailors, knights, esquires*

ACT I

On board Tristan's ship, at sea
Tristan is returning from Ireland, escorting Isolde to his uncle, King Mark, who has chosen to marry her and make her Queen of Cornwall. Tristan, who is kept company by Kurwenal, avoids Isolde: he is anxious not to rekindle his earlier love for her. She, on the other hand, resents the fact that she is being taken by a former lover—who, years earlier in Ireland (as she recounts for Brangäne) she spared from death when he had killed her betrothed—into a loveless marriage, and demands to speak to him. Tristan appears, and old arguments are ignited: Isolde resolves to avenge Tristan's slaying of her betrothed and end their feud once and for all. She orders Brangäne to prepare a death potion for both of them to share. They drink it expecting to die, but find themselves filled with passionate longing for each other. Brangäne admits to having substituted a love potion. Tristan and Isolde embrace ecstatically as the ship docks in Cornwall, oblivious of the fact that King Mark is waiting to meet his bride.

ACT II

King Mark's castle in Cornwall
With King Mark and his party away hunting at night, Isolde has arranged a rendezvous with Tristan. Brangäne cautions her mistress, suspecting that one of the courtiers, Melot, is spying on the lovers. But Isolde is impatient for Tristan's embraces and extinguishes the torch as a signal to him. He rushes in and they pass a rapturous night together, but at dawn ignore the warnings of Brangäne, who has been keeping watch. Led by Melot, King Mark surprises the lovers together. Mark is too stunned by his nephew's betrayal to act, but Melot strikes Tristan, who allows himself to be wounded.

ACT III

Tristan's castle in Brittany
Kurwenal has taken the injured Tristan to his castle in Brittany. He has sent for Isolde who, he hopes, will once more

save Tristan from death. Kurwenal instructs the Shepherd piper to play a happy tune when Isolde's ship is sighted, and finally her arrival is announced. Tristan breaks out of his delirium and is reunited with Isolde, but dies in her arms. A second ship appears carrying King Mark and Melot. Imagining that they are about to attack, Kurwenal slays Melot and is himself killed before Brangäne can explain that King Mark had come to forgive his wife and Tristan. Realizing that she can only fulfil her love for Tristan in death, Isolde sinks lifeless on his body.

THE TROJANS
see **Les Troyens**

IL TROVATORE (The Troubadour)
Giuseppe Verdi (1813-1901)

FOUR PARTS. LIBRETTO BY SALVATORE CAMMARANO AND LEONE EMMANUELE BARDARE, AFTER ANTONIO GARCIA GUTIÉRREZ'S PLAY *EL TROVADOR*. PREMIERE IN ROME, 19 JANUARY 1853.

Il trovatore's convoluted plot has not prevented it from becoming one of the most popular operas in the repertory. There is little physical action on stage—much of the story occurs before the curtain goes up or between the scenes. Its strengths lie in the music, less sophisticated and innovative than much in middle-period Verdi (the orchestra has been likened to a huge guitar), but earthy and passionate. The score includes the famous 'Anvil Chorus' and Manrico's 'Di quella pira'.

CHARACTERS
Leonora, a lady-in-waiting to the Princess of Aragon (SOPRANO); *Inez*, Leonora's attendant (SOPRANO); *Azucena*, a gypsy woman from Biscay (MEZZO-SOPRANO); *Manrico*, an officer in the Prince of Biscay's army, the supposed son of Azucena (TENOR); *Ruiz*, a soldier in Manrico's service (TENOR); *Count Di Luna*, a young nobleman from Aragon (BARITONE); *An Old Gypsy* (BARITONE); *Ferrando*, a captain in Di Luna's guard (BASS)
With Leonora's *attendants*, the Count's *household*, *nuns*, *soldiers*, *gypsies*

PART I The Duel
SCENE 1 *The palace of Aliaferia*
Ferrando tries to keep his fellow guardsmen awake by recalling for them the story of the Count Di Luna's younger brother, missing for many years. Long ago, the Count's father had accused an old gypsy of casting a spell over his younger, baby son, and burnt her as a witch. Her daughter kidnapped the child in revenge, and when a baby's burnt corpse was discovered not long after, it was assumed that she had murdered him. But the Count hopes that his brother is still alive, and Ferrando is sure he would recognize the gypsy's daughter again.

SCENE 2 *The palace gardens*
Leonora confides to her attendant Inez her love for a mysterious

troubadour who has been serenading her. But Leonora is also being pursued by Count Di Luna, and when he comes to woo her hears the troubadour's music. His jealousy is aroused when, in the dark, Leonora lovingly mistakes him for the troubadour. He confronts the stranger who reveals himself as Manrico, an enemy in the civil war, and challenges him to a duel.

PART II The Gispy
SCENE 1 *A ruined hut in Biscay*
In the gypsy encampment several months later, Azucena is brooding. Gypsies working at anvils try to lighten her mood without success, and she tells Manrico—who believes she is his mother—what is on her mind. She recalls her mother's death at the stake, and how in an act of mad vengeance she accidentally burned her own son and not that of the old Count. Manrico begins to realize the truth, and tells Azucena how, in his duel with the Count, a mysterious feeling prevented him from killing him. Azucena orders him never to show mercy again. A messenger arrives with news that Leonora, believing Manrico dead, has resolved to enter a convent; Manrico rushes off to stop her.

SCENE 2 *A convent near Castellor*
The Count—who also believes that Manrico is dead—plans to abduct Leonora before she takes her vows, and hides with several of his men in the cloister. But as he is about to claim her, Manrico arrives with his followers, who rout the Count's men. In the confusion, Manrico and Leonora escape to the castle at Castellor.

PART III The Gypsy's Son
SCENE 1 *A military camp*
Count Di Luna and his men are besieging the castle at Castellor where Manrico and Leonora are holed up. Gypsies appear on the scene and Azucena is arrested under suspicion of being a spy. Ferrando recognizes her as the supposed murderer of the Count's younger brother, and she denies it by claiming to be Manrico's mother. The Count responds by sentencing the mother of his sworn enemy to death.

SCENE 2 *A room adjoining the chapel at Castellor*
Manrico and Leonora are about to marry, but when Ruiz brings news of Azucena's impending execution, Manrico resolves to rescue her. He leaves Leonora behind.

PART IV The Execution
SCENE 1 *The Aliferia palace*
Manrico's rescue attempt has failed, and he and Azucena have been arrested. Monks are already singing the Miserere that signals an execution when Leonora, desperate to save her lover, comes to bargain with the Count: she offers her love in return for Manrico's freedom, and the Count eagerly accepts. He grants her one condition, that she be allowed to convey the news to Manrico. Determined not to keep her promise to the Count, Leonora takes slow-acting poison.

SCENE 2 *A dark prison*
Manrico is comforting Azucena when Leonora enters with her news. She begs him to flee without asking any questions, but he guesses the price of his freedom and curses her for infidelity. When the poison begins to take effect, Manrico realizes the extent of her selfless love and begs forgiveness. The Count discovers that he has been tricked and orders Manrico's immediate execution. Azucena, forced to witness it, reveals triumphantly to the Count that he has just killed his younger brother and that her gypsy mother has at last been avenged.

LES TROYENS (The Trojans)
Hector Berlioz (1803-1869)

FIVE ACTS. LIBRETTO BY THE COMPOSER, AFTER VIRGIL'S *AENEID*. PREMIERES (ACTS III-V) IN PARIS, 4 NOVEMBER 1863; (COMPLETE) IN KARLSRUHE, 6 DECEMBER 1890.

Berlioz's epic masterpiece unites the influences of two of the composer's idols: Virgil, for whose *Aeneid* Belioz held a life-long passion, and Gluck, whose Classical refinement was a potent inspiration. Aiming for a performance of *Les Troyens* in Paris, Berlioz also adopted some features of Parisian grand opera. He divided the opera into two unequal parts—calling Acts I and II *La Prise de Troie* ('The Fall of Troy'), Acts III-V *Les Troyens á Carthage* ('The Trojans at Carthage')—which contrast with each other in colour and atmosphere: the Trojan acts are harsh and violent, those in Carthage warmer and sensuous. Berlioz was never rewarded with a full performance (the first two acts were not performed until 21 years after his death), and indeed it was not until 1957 at Covent Garden that *Les Troyens* was given in its complete and authentic form.

CHARACTERS

Ascagne (Ascanius) Aeneas's son (SOPRANO); *Polyxène* (Polyxena) Cassandra's sister (SOPRANO); *Hécube* (Hecuba) Queen of Troy (SOPRANO); *Cassandre* (Cassandra) Trojan prophetess, Priam's daughter (MEZZO-SOPRANO); *Didon* (Dido) Queen of Carthage (MEZZO-SOPRANO); *Anna*, Dido's sister (CONTRALTO); *Énee* (Aeneas) Trojan hero (TENOR); *Iopas*, poet at Dido's court (TENOR); *Hylas*, a young Phrygian sailor (TENOR); *Helenus*, Trojan priest, Priam's son (TENOR); *Chorèbe* (Choroebus) Cassandra's fiancé (BARITONE); *Panthée* (Pantheus) Trojan priest (BASS); *Priam*, King of Troy (BASS); *Narbal*, Dido's minister (BASS); *A Greek Captain* (BASS); *Ghost of Hector* (BASS); *Two Trojan Sentries* (BASSES); *Mercure* (Mercury) (BASS); *Priest of Pluto* (BASS); *Andromaque* (Andromache) Hector's widow (SILENT); *Astyanax*, Andromache's son (SILENT)

With *Trojans, Greeks, Tyrians, Carthaginians, nymphs, satyrs, fauns, sylvans, spirits*

ACT I
The abandoned Greek camp at Troy
Trojans exult in the lifting of the long Greek siege, unperturbed by the giant wooden horse the Greeks have abandoned

on the battlefield. Only Cassandra feels a sense of foreboding, and her visions of doom for Troy are dismissed by all, including her lover, Choroebus, who tries to calm her. Victory celebrations have begun when Aeneas rushes in with the news of Laocoon's ghastly death; he reports that Laocoon, while encouraging a crowd to burn the horse, was devoured by two sea monsters. Sensing that the goddess Athena was punishing Laocoon for sacrilege, to appease her King Priam orders the horse to be dragged to Athena's temple in the city. Despite more desperate warnings from Cassandra and the sound of weapons from inside the horse, the Trojan people march happily with it through the city gates.

ACT II

SCENE 1 *A room in Aeneas's palace*

Frightened by the sound of battle, Aeneas's son Ascanius contemplates waking his father, but the noise subsides and he leaves the room. Soon the Ghost of Hector appears to Aeneas with news of the Greek assault, and instructs him to flee Troy and found a new city in Italy. Pantheus enters with the Trojan idols Aeneas is to preserve. Aeneas and his men rush off to defend the citadel.

SCENE 2 *A hall in Priam's palace*

Cassandra tells the Trojan women of their city's fall, of Aeneas's escape towards Italy, and of Choroebus's death. She stirs them by announcing that she would rather kill herself than become a Greek slave, and urges them to do the same. Taking up their lyres, they hymn their vow to die. When the Greek soldiers break in—looking for the treasure which Aeneas has saved—the women commit suicide.

ACT III

A hall in Dido's palace at Carthage

The people of Carthage acclaim their queen, Dido. Left alone with Dido, Anna encourages her sister to think of marrying again and providing Carthage with a king; but although Dido longs for love she has resolved to remain faithful to the memory of her dead husband, Sychaeus. The court poet Iopas enters with news of the arrival of strange ships. The fleet turns out to be Aeneas's (though he is at first disguised), blown off course by a violent storm, and the men come to pay homage to Dido. Suddenly, Dido's minister Narbal warns that Carthage is being attacked by the Numidian warriors under Iarbas; Aeneas reveals his identity to the captivated Dido, who accepts his offer of military help. Leaving his son Ascanius in Dido's care, Aeneas sets off at the head of a joint Trojan and Carthaginian army for battle.

ACT IV

SCENE 1 *A forest near Carthage*

Aeneas (having defeated the enemy) and Dido are attending a hunt. During a storm they take refuge in a cave, where they consummate their love.

SCENE 2 *Dido's garden*

Narbal worries that Aeneas and the Trojans remain in Carthage, but Anna delights in the love her sister may have found. Dido finds no relief from her unease in the dances that are performed, or in Iopas's song, only in Aeneas's story of Pyrrhus and Andromache, which suggests to her a precedent for remarriage. Dido's resolve not to marry again weakens, and she and Aeneas rejoice in their love. As they retire, the god Mercury urges Aeneas not to forget his duties in Italy.

ACT V

SCENE 1 *The Trojan camp at the harbour of Carthage*

The young sailor Hylas longs for his homeland. Pantheus and the Trojan chiefs agree that their mission to Italy cannot be delayed any longer; the only dissenting voices are those of two sentries who are content with their life in Carthage. Aeneas is torn between love for Dido and duty to his country, but resolves to leave when the ghosts of Trojan heroes command him to sail. Despite Dido's pleas, Aeneas gathers his men together.

SCENE 2 *A room in Dido's palace*

Aeneas's ships have put to sea. In anger, Dido gives orders for the building of a pyre on which she will incinerate all reminders of Aeneas; deciding to kill herself too, she bids Carthage and her friends farewell.

SCENE 3 *The palace gardens*

Assisted by Narbal and Anna, Dido mounts the pyre. She sees visions of both the Carthaginian Hannibal (who will avenge her desertion) and also the eventual glory of Rome, before stabbing herself with Aeneas's sword.

TURANDOT
Giacomo Puccini (1858-1924)

THREE ACTS. LIBRETTO BY GIUSEPPE ADAMI AND RENATO SIMONI, AFTER CARLO GOZZI'S FABLE. PREMIERE IN MILAN, 25 APRIL 1926.

As Puccini's final work, *Turandot* is also the climax of the Romantic operatic tradition in Italy, which began with Rossini and ran through Donizetti, Bellini, and Verdi to Puccini (who had no important successors). Puccini left *Turandot* unfinished at his death (a shortened version of the ending provided by the composer Franco Alfano is usually heard today), probably unable to see his way to the end of what is his most sophisticated work. It combines exotic orchestration—the setting is legendary Peking—and some of the composer's most dissonant music with elements of his earlier lyrical style (represented by Turandot's 'In questa reggia' and Calaf's 'Nessun dorma', for instance).

CHARACTERS

Princess Turandot (SOPRANO); *Liù*, a slave girl (SOPRANO); *Calaf*, Timur's son (TENOR); *Emperor Altoum*, Turandot's father (TENOR);

Pang, General Purveyor (TENOR); *Pong*, Chief Cook (TENOR); *Ping*, Grand Chancellor (BARITONE); *A Mandarin* (BARITONE); *Timur*, exiled king of Tartary (BASS)

With the *Prince of Persia*, the *Executioner*, *guards*, the Executioner's *men*, *priests*, Turandot's *ladies*, *phantoms*, *wise men*, *heralds*, *musicians*, *soldiers*, *people* of Peking

ACT I

A square in Peking near the imperial palace

A Mandarin announces that the Emperor's daughter, Turandot, will marry the first suitor capable of answering her three riddles, but that the price of failure is death. One contender, the Prince of Persia, has already failed, and the crowd waits eagerly for his execution. Among the people are old Timur, the exiled king of Tartary, who is accompanied by his faithful slave girl, Liù. During war he became separated from his son, Calaf, and by chance they are now reunited (much to the joy of Liù who harbours a secret love for the prince). As they watch the preparations for the execution, Calaf denounces Turandot for her cruelty, but is immediately smitten by her beauty when she appears on the moonlit balcony to confirm the death sentence. Ignoring the feelings of his father and Liù and the advice of the ministers Ping, Pang, and Pong, Calaf resolves to tackle the riddles. He strikes the gong signalling his intention.

ACT II

SCENE 1 *A pavilion*

Ping, Pang, and Pong lament the misery that China is enduring under the cold-blooded Turandot. They long for her to be softened by love.

SCENE 2 *The palace courtyard*

All assemble for Calaf's trial. Even Turandot's father, Emperor Altoum, tries to dissuade Calaf from his apparently suicidal course, but the prince remains steadfast. Turandot explains that she has taken her terrible vow to avenge the rape and murder of one of her ancestors by a barbarian invader. Calaf astounds the crowd by answering Turandot's riddles, but she protests that she is unable love any man and begs to be released. Calaf compromises, saying that if she can discover his name by dawn he will die like all her other suitors.

ACT III

SCENE 1 *The palace gardens*

Turandot decrees that no-one in Peking shall sleep until the prince's name is revealed. However, Calaf remains confident and looks forward to winning his bride. Ping, Pang, and Pong appear and try one last time to dissuade him from his course. Calaf is shaken only by the sight of Timur and Liù being dragged in for interrogation. Liù is tortured, and answers Turandot's questions by telling her that the secret of her courage is 'love', before stabbing herself and falling at Calaf's feet. Calaf confronts Turandot, who finally succumbs to his kisses. Putting himself in her power, he reveals his name.

Scene 2 *The palace courtyard*
Turandot announces to her father and the crowd that she has discovered the prince's name: 'Love'. The astonished people begin to celebrate.

THE TURN OF THE SCREW
Benjamin Britten (1913-1976)

Prologue and two acts. Libretto by Myfanwy Piper, after Henry James's story. Premiere in Venice, 14 September 1954.

The Turn of the Screw has been called 'Britten's operatic masterpiece'. This may be unfair on some of his other works, but it is hard to name another of his operas that combines such ingenious musical structure (a lucidly worked-out set of variations) with such emotional impact. It is based faithfully on Henry James's great ghost story, whose theme—innocence corrupted—is one that runs throughout Britten's work. *The Turn of the Screw*'s dramatic potency gains from its chamber-opera proportions—an orchestra of 13 players and a cast of just seven (the tenor frequently doubling as the Prologue and Peter Quint).

CHARACTERS
The Governess (SOPRANO); *Mrs Grose*, the housekeeper (SOPRANO); *Miss Jessel*, a former governess (SOPRANO); *Flora*, child in the Governess's charge (SOPRANO); *Miles*, child in the Governess's charge (TREBLE); *The Prologue* (TENOR); *Peter Quint*, a former manservant (TENOR)

PROLOGUE
The 'curious story' of how the Governess came to her post at Bly, an English country-house, is introduced.

ACT I
Scene 1 *The Journey*
The Governess travels by coach to Bly, apprehensive about what is in store for her.

Scene 2 *The Welcome*
The Governess's mind is put at rest by the welcome of the housekeeper, Mrs Grose, and the children who will become her charges, Flora and Miles.

Scene 3 *The Letter*
A letter arrives announcing Miles's expulsion from school. Mrs Grose and the Governess believe he is innocent.

Scene 4 *The Tower*
The Governess is strolling in the grounds when she is startled by a strange figure who appears on the tower of the house.

Scene 5 *The Window*
The Governess is watching the children at play when at the window she glimpses the stranger again. Gripped by fear, she tells Mrs Grose of her experiences, and the housekeeper

replies confidently that it must be Peter Quint. But, she says, Quint—who had evil power over the children and the previous governess, the late Miss Jessel—is dead. The Governess resolves to shield the children from harm.

SCENE 6 *Lessons*
The Governess, supervising the children's lessons, is struck by Miles's melancholia.

SCENE 7 *The Lake*
Accompanying Flora to the lake, the Governess asks her to name the seas of the world. Flora's mood changes and she calls the lake at Bly the Dead Sea: when the Governess sees the ghost of Miss Jessel across the lake, she knows that Flora has been haunted too.

SCENE 8 *At Night*
The voices of Quint and Miss Jessel are heard calling to Miles and Flora. Mrs Grose and the Governess intervene and the ghosts vanish. Miles's answer to the Governess's question suggests that he blames himself for the turn of events.

ACT II

SCENE 1 *Colloquy and soliloquy*
Quint and Miss Jessel discuss their motives. The Governess agonizes over how to protect the children.

SCENE 2 *The Bells*
The children sing and play in the churchyard. Mrs Grose marvels at their innocence, but the Governess fears they are communicating with 'the others'.

SCENE 3 *Miss Jessel*
Intending to flee Bly, the Governess returns to the schoolroom she encounters Miss Jessel, cursing her own fate and contemplating revenge. Once the apparition has gone, the Governess writes to the children's guardian appealing for help.

SCENE 4 *The Bedroom*
The Governess enters to put Miles to bed, but Quint is heard calling and the boy is clearly in his power.

SCENE 5 *Quint*
Prompted by Quint, Miles steals the letter the Governess had written to his guardian.

SCENE 6 *The Piano*
Miles's piano playing distracts Mrs Grose and the Governess, who fail at first to notice when Flora slips out of the room.

SCENE 7 *Flora*
Mrs Grose and the Governess search for Flora and find her at lake. The Governess senses Miss Jessel's presence, but Flora denies it and rails against the Governess, whom she accuses of interference.

SCENE 8 *Miles*
Mrs Grose, realizing that Flora is possessed, takes her away from Bly, leaving the Governess to care for Miles. The Governess questions him, and when pressed, Miles—who can hear Quint urging him to keep his mouth shut—finally names Quint as the one who made him steal the letter. Quint vanishes, leaving the Governess to cradle the body of the dead Miles.

LES VÊPRES SICILIENNES (The Sicilian Vespers)
Giuseppe Verdi (1813-1901)

FIVE ACTS. LIBRETTO BY EUGENE SCRIBE AND CHARLES DUVEYRIER, ADAPTED FROM THEIR OWN LIBRETTO *LE DUC D'ALBE*. PREMIERE IN PARIS, 13 JUNE 1855.

Les Vêpres siciliennes was the first work Verdi composed specifically for the Paris Opéra (he had adapted his *I Lombardi* as *Jérusalem* for Paris in 1847), and as such he wrote it with the French taste for lavish spectacle in mind; it is set in Palermo in 1282, and relates the Sicilian uprising against French rule. Verdi based his opera on a revision of an already existing libretto, which Donizetti had attempted to set in his *Le duc d'Albe* (completed as an Italian opera after his death). It is a sprawling work without the melodic freshness of the three that preceded it (*Rigoletto, Il trovatore, La traviata*), but not as diffuse as the Italian version (*I vespri siciliani*) which is usually heard today suggests.

CHARACTERS
Hélène, sister of Duke Frederick of Austria (SOPRANO); *Ninetta*, Hélène's maid (CONTRALTO); *Henri*, a young Sicilian (Arrigo in the Italian version) (TENOR); *Daniéli*, a Sicilian (TENOR); *Robert*, a French soldier (TENOR); *Mainfroid*, a Sicilian (TENOR); *Guy de Montfort*, Governor of Sicily (BARITONE); *Thibault*, a French soldier (BARITONE); *Jean Procida*, a Sicilian doctor (BASS); *De Béthune*, French officer (BASS); *Count de Vaudemont*, French officer (BASS)
With *Sicilians*, French *soldiers, monks*

ACT I
The main square in Palermo
Carousing French soldiers call on Hélène—who is mourning her brother, Duke Fredrick of Austria, executed by the French—to entertain them. She obliges, but in her song incites the loitering Sicilians to rise up against the French occupiers. Bloodshed is avoided by the appearance of the much-feared governor, Guy de Montfort, and the crowd disperses. Henri comes to find Hélène and tells her of his release from prison, but his seditious comments are overheard by the governor, who dismisses the others before interrogating Henri. Montfort tries to press him into serving the French cause, but Henri refuses and also defiantly ignores Montfort's warning to keep away from Hélène .

ACT II
A valley near Palermo
Procida, a Sicilian revolutionary, has returned from exile to

encourage his followers. He meets with Hélène and Henri, telling them that he has persuaded Spain to back the Sicilians in the event of an uprising. Henri and Hélène declare their love for each other, and he promises to avenge her brother's execution. Henri receives an invitation (conveyed by the French officer De Béthune) from Montfort to attend a ball, and when he refuses it he is arrested. Procida plots to ignite anti-French feeling: he encourages drunken French soldiers to abduct Sicilian women from local festivities, thus angering the Sicilian men.

ACT III

SCENE 1 *Montfort's study in his palace*

Montfort has discovered that Henri is his illegitimate son, brought up by his mother to hate her seducer. He summons Henri, who rejects his overtures of fatherly love.

SCENE 2 *A ballroom*

However, Montfort's revelations do move Henri to intervene when he discovers that Hélène and Procida are to lead an assassination attempt at the ball. He saves Montfort, and the conspirators are arrested. They brand Henri a traitor.

ACT IV

The courtyard of a fortress

Henri visits Hélène in prison, and she forgives him when he reveals his reason for saving Montfort. She and Procida are led out for execution, and Montfort refuses to listen to Henri's requests for pardon until his son acknowledges him. At the last moment, Henri gives in to his father. The prisoners are released, and as part of the amnesty Montfort announces the wedding of his son and Hélène .

ACT V

The gardens of Montfort's palace

Guests have arrived to celebrate the wedding. But Procida has continued to plot rebellion, and discloses to Hélène that the wedding bells will be recognised by the Sicilians as the signal for slaughter. Hélène is horrified, and tries to halt the proceedings. Montfort, however, will hear of no delay, and calls for the bells to ring. The Sicilians, daggers drawn, rush in and attack the French.

DIE WALKÜRE
see **Der Ring des Nibelungen**

LA WALLY
Alfredo Catalani (1854-1893)

FOUR ACTS. LIBRETTO BY LUIGI ILLICA, AFTER WILHELMINE VON HILLERN'S NOVEL *DIE GEYER-WALLY*. PREMIERE IN MILAN, 20 JANUARY 1892.

Alfredo Catalani, a contemporary of Puccini whose career was cut short by his death at the age of 39, composed five operas of which

La Wally was the most successful. It is a finely-crafted work with some attractive music (including the famous 'Ebben? Ne andro lontan'), illustrative of the individual path Catalani pursued.

CHARACTERS

Wally (SOPRANO); *Walter*, a minstrel (SOPRANO); *Afra*, a tavern owner (MEZZO-SOPRANO); *Giuseppe Hagenbach*, from the village of Sölden (TENOR); *Messenger* (TENOR); *Vincenzo Gellner*, Stromminger's bailiff (BARITONE); *Stromminger*, Wally's father (BASS)
With *Tyroleans, shepherds, hunters, children*

ACT I

The village of Hochstoff in the Tyrolean Alps
At his 70th birthday party, the landowner Stromminger discusses with his bailiff Vincenzo Gellner his enemy from the neighbouring village, Giuseppe Hagenbach. The celebration continues—the minstrel Walter sings a song—until Hagenbach himself enters, bragging of the bear he killed while hunting. This provokes a fight, which Stromminger's daughter, Wally, breaks up. Her attempts to protect Hagenbach make it plain that she is in love with him, and when all have left Stromminger and Gellner discuss the situation. Stromminger realizes that Gellner is in love with his daughter, and orders Wally to marry him. She defies her father, is banished, and heads into the mountains, taking Walter with her.

ACT II

A tavern in Sölden
A year has passed, during which Stromminger has died and left Wally a fortune. Wally enters Afra's inn, where Hagenbach and his friends are loitering. Gellner tries to woo her again, and in revenge for being spurned once more tells her that Hagenbach is about to marry Afra. Wally insults Afra, which in turn provokes Hagenbach into humiliating Wally: when dancing begins, he plays the 'kissing game' with her, and only the mocking laughter of the others makes her realize his vows of love are false. Promising to marry Gellner after all, she asks him to kill Hagenbach.

ACT III

Hochstoff
Wally regrets having asked Gellner to kill Hagenbach, and resolves to warn Hagenbach the following day. But it is too late: Gellner arrives to tell her that under cover of darkness he pushed Hagenbach—who was on his way to apologize to Wally for having humiliated her—into a ravine. Horrified, Wally rushes out and rescues the injured man, bringing him to Afra, whom she believes he loves.

ACT IV

High in the mountains
Once again Wally has sought refuge in the mountains. Walter visits her, urging her to come down, but she is determined to stay put. The recovered Hagenbach ascends the mountain and finds Wally, convincing her of his love. Reconciled, the couple

set off down the mountain. Suddenly Hagenbach is swept away by an avalanche, and Wally, hearing no reply to her calls, throws herself into the abyss.

WAR AND PEACE
Sergey Prokofiev (1891–1953)

THIRTEEN SCENES AND EPIGRAPH. LIBRETTO BY THE COMPOSER AND MIRA MENDELSON, AFTER LEO TOLSTOY'S NOVEL. PREMIERED IN VARIOUS VERSIONS BETWEEN 16 OCTOBER 1944 (MOSCOW; CONCERT PERFORMANCE OF EIGHT SCENES ONLY, WITH PIANO ACCOMPANIMENT) AND 15 DECEMBER 1959 (MOSCOW; FIRST UNCUT PERFORMANCE OF ALL 13 SCENES INCLUDING EPIGRAPH).

Cast in the mould of earlier Russian historical operas—*Pince Igor* and *Boris Godunov*, for instance—*War and Peace* is epic in every way: it was composed during wartime (the German siege of Russia), reflects faithfully the scenes drawn from Tolstoy's mammoth novel, and calls for 70-or-so roles. The work's 13 scenes and Epigraph form a sprawling canvas easier to follow if the listener is familiar with Tolstoy's original, but a knowledge of the novel is not essential; Prokofiev, writing for an audience brought up on Tolstoy, assumed nothing more than Tchaikovsky did in his setting of scenes from Pushkin's *Eugene Onegin*. The music of *War and Peace* is instantly accessible, something rare amongst post-1945 operas.

CHARACTERS
Natasha Rostova, Count Ilya Rostov's daughter (SOPRANO); *Madame Peronskaya* (SOPRANO); *Hélène Bezukhova*, Pierre's wife (MEZZO-SOPRANO); *Sonya*, Natasha's cousin (MEZZO-SOPRANO); *Princess Maria Bolkonskaya*, Prince Andrey's sister (MEZZO-SOPRANO); *Maria Dmitrieva Akhrosimova*, Muscovite lady (MEZZO-SOPRANO); *Pierre Bezukhov* (TENOR); *Prince Anatol Kuragin*, Hélène's brother (TENOR); *Prince Andrey Bolkonsky*, Princess Maria's brother (BARITONE); *Napoleon Bonaparte* (BARITONE); *Colonel Vasska Denisov* (BASS-BARITONE); *Dolokhov*, friend of Prince Anatol (BASS); *Prince Nikolay Bolkonsky*, Andrey's father (BASS); *Count Ilya Rostov*, Natasha's father (BASS); *Field Marshal Prince Mikhail Kutuzov* (BASS) With Russian *officers* and *soldiers*, French *officers* and *soldiers*, *Muscovites*, *guests* at the ball, *servants*, *Abbé*, *Doctor*, etc

PART I Peace
Epigraph
A defiant statement of Russia's unyielding might.

SCENE 1 *Count Rostov's estate*
One night while staying at Count Rostov's house, the brooding Prince Andrey Bolkonsky overhears Natasha and her cousin Sonya extoling the beauties of nature. Their singing raises his spirits.

SCENE 2 *A ballroom in a wealthy St Petersburg house*
Natasha is overwhelmed by attending her first ball, and Pierre

Bezukhov eases her discomfort by arranging for Andrey to dance with her. The couple fall in love, but the rake Anatol Kuragin (brother of Hélène, the society beauty married to Pierre) is also attracted to her.

SCENE 3 *The old Prince Bolkonsky's house*
Andrey and Natasha have become engaged, and she arrives with her father at Andrey's father's house to pay their respects. But the old Prince Bolkonsky humiliates Natasha—who he considers to be below his station—and leaves it up to his daughter Maria to receive the guests. In an attempt to break the relationship, he has sent his son away for a year.

SCENE 4 *The Bezuhkov house*
Hélène, as fickle as her brother, has arranged for Anatol to meet Natasha. In spite of her feelings for Andrey and the warnings of Sonya, Natasha falls for Anatol's advances.

SCENE 5 *Dolokhov's house*
Dolokhov—who helped Anatol with his seduction by writing a love letter for him—now advises him not to elope with Natasha. He has many reservations, and reminds Anatol that he is, in any case, already married. But nothing will stop Anatol, who enlists the help of a coachman and bids his gypsy mistress goodbye.

SCENE 6 *Maria Akhrosimova's house*
Natasha is waiting to elope with Anatol, but his plan is foiled (by Sonya) and he escapes. The hostess, Maria Akhrosimova, lectures Natasha about associating with people like Anatol and Hélène; when Pierre enters, he reveals to Natasha that Anatol is a married man. Natasha is thrown into even more emotional turmoil by Pierre's sudden declaration of love.

SCENE 7 *Pierre Bezukhov's study*
Pierre interrupts Hélène and her guests to confront Anatol, ordering him to leave Moscow. A messenger brings news that Napoleon has invaded Russia.

PART II War
(The Epigraph is sometimes placed here.)

SCENE 8 *The battlefield at Borodino*
Andrey is on the front, where encounters with Denisov (once himself in love with Natasha) and Pierre remind him of his love. He longs to die, and turns down the Field Marshal's offer of a safe post at headquaters to fight with his men.

SCENE 9 *Behind French lines*
Napoleon, dreaming of his arrival in Moscow, is distracted by bad news from the front.

SCENE 10 *A peasant hut*
Field Marshal Kutuzov has summoned a council of war. He announces—to the astonishment of his generals—that the

defence of Moscow must be abandoned in order to save the army that in turn has save the whole of Russia.

SCENE 11 *Moscow under French occupation*
Moscow is being ransacked by the French and burnt by the retreating Russians. Pierre's resistance to the French leads to his arrest, but not before he has learned from the Rostovs' old housekeeper that Natasha and her family have left the city, taking injured soldiers into their care. Napoleon enters Moscow to scenes of devastation, and not the reception he had dreamt of.

SCENE 12 *A dark peasant hut*
One of the wounded soldiers the Rostovs are tending turns out to be Andrey. He gains consciousness and is reconciled with Natasha before he dies.

SCENE 13 *The road to Smolensk*
The French army, demoralised by the harsh winter, is retreating. Russian partisans attack the column, releasing among others Pierre. He learns that his wife Hélène has died, that Anatol was injured, and that Andrey died in Natasha's arms. His dreams that he might still find happiness with her one day are interrupted by the arrival of the Field Marshal, who comes to praise the Russians for their momentous victory.

WERTHER
Jules Massenet (1842-1912)

FOUR ACTS. LIBRETTO BY ÉDOUARD BLAU, PAUL MILLIET, AND GEORGES HARTMANN, AFTER GOETHE'S *DIE LEIDEN DES JUNGEN WERTHERS*. PREMIERE IN VIENNA, 16 FEBRUARY 1892.

Werther was Massenet's ninth opera and represented something of a departure for him, since the majority of his operatic sources were French. Indeed, when the composer suggested *Werther*, based on Goethe, to the Opéra-Comique in Paris, it was rejected on the grounds of being too gloomy; but in answer to a later commission from Vienna he was able to provide the already-complete opera, and its basis on *The Sorrows of Young Werther*—once one of the most popular German novels—ensured its popularity there. It is now widely regarded as Massenet's masterpiece.

CHARACTERS

Sophie, Charlotte's sister (SOPRANO); *Charlotte*, the Magistrate's daughter (MEZZO-SOPRANO); *Werther*, a young poet (TENOR); *Schmidt*, friend of the Magistrate (TENOR); *Albert*, a young man (BARITONE); *Le Bailli* (Magistrate) (BARITONE); *Johann*, friend of the Magistrate (BARITONE) With *townsfolk, guests, servants, children*

ACT I

The garden of the Magistrate's house
The Magistrate is teaching his children a carol when his friends Johann and Schmidt arrive. Conversation turns the ball

that evening and the fact that Werther is to escort the Magistrate's daughter, Charlotte, there; the Magistrate also mentions that her fiancé, Albert, is due to arrive. Soon after the friends have left Werther appears. He is impressed by the way in Charlotte cares for her siblings (the Magistrate has recently been widowed). Along with other guests, Charlotte, Werther and the Magistrate depart for the ball, leaving the children in Sophie's care. Albert enters unannounced to find Charlotte out, but promises to return. Charlotte and Werther come back from the ball, and their declarations of love are interrupted by news of Albert's arrival. Charlotte confesses to Werther that she promised her dying mother she would marry Albert, and Werther —though shattered—encourages her not to break her vow.

ACT II
The square in Wetzlar

Charlotte and Albert have married. Werther is in despair, and Albert tries to console him, suggesting that he marry Sophie instead. Charlotte, trying to hide her feelings, urges him to leave and return only at Christmas. Werther contemplates suicide, and implies as much when he tells Sophie he is leaving forever. Charlotte's unhappiness makes it clear to Albert that Werther is still in love with his wife.

ACT III
Albert's house

On Christmas Eve, the melancholy Charlotte is reading Werther's letters again. Sophie tries to cheer her up, but at the mention of Werther's name Charlotte breaks down. Werther arrives. Charlotte's resolve not to give in to his love fails for a moment and the two embrace, but she tears herself away, crying that they must never meet again. Albert confronts his wife, and obliges willingly when a message comes from Werther asking to borrow his pistols. Though Werther requested them for protection on 'a long journey', Charlotte guesses the truth and rushes off to find him.

ACT IV
Werther's study

Charlotte arrives too late, to find Werther suffering from pistol wounds. She assures him that she has loved him from when they first met. Children sing a Christmas carol outside as Werther dies.

WILLIAM TELL
see **Guillaume Tell**

WOZZECK
Alban Berg (1885-1935)

THREE ACTS. LIBRETTO BY THE COMPOSER, AFTER GEORG BÜCHNER'S PLAY. PREMIERE IN BERLIN, 14 DECEMBER 1925.

Berg's work on *Wozzeck* was interrupted by the First World War, but his unhappy experience as a conscript in the Austrian army during that time led him to empathize all the more with the tormented soldier of Georg Büchner's tragedy. The story is evoked in a highly expressionist score, with violence being tempered by great lyricism. *Wozzeck* has a reputation as a 'difficult' opera, but the only difficulties in a first-rate performance are those faced by the singers and orchestra: though they have to battle with the work's complexities, audiences are usually gripped by its extraordinary theatrical power.

CHARACTERS

Marie, Wozzeck's common-law wife (SOPRANO); *Margret*, Marie's neighbour (CONTRALTO); *Marie's Son* (TREBLE); *Drum Major* (TENOR); *Andres*, a soldier (TENOR); *Captain* (TENOR); *Simpleton* (TENOR); *Wozzeck*, a soldier (BARITONE); *Doctor* (BASS)
With *apprentices, soldiers, servants, children*

ACT I

SCENE 1 *The Captain's room*
Wozzeck shaves the Captain.

SCENE 2 *A field*
Wozzeck and his fellow soldier Andres are out cutting sticks. Andres makes light of the visions Wozzeck claims to have had.

SCENE 3 *Marie's room*
Marie has watched a military procession, and is taunted by her neighbour Margret for her interest in the Drum Major. She returns to looking after her Child. Wozzeck arrives home still preoccupied with his visions, and ignores the Child.

SCENE 4 *The Doctor's surgery*
Wozzeck visits the Doctor, who is employing him as a guinea-pig; his oppressive mood convinces the Doctor that his experiments are working.

SCENE 5 *Outside Marie's house*
Encouraged by Marie's obvious interest, the Drum Major visits her.

ACT II

SCENE 1 *Marie's room*
Marie tries on the earrings the Drum Major gave her. When Wozzeck arrives, he is unconvinced by her story of having found the jewellery. Nevertheless, he gives her his wages, leaving her feeling guilty about her infidelity to him.

SCENE 2 *A street*
The Captain and the Doctor meet, and when Wozzeck passes by they taunt him with suggestions of Marie's infidelity.

SCENE 3 *Outside Marie's house*
Wozzeck challenges Marie with his suspicions, but she defies him.

SCENE 4 *A beer garden*
Wozzeck is watching the high-spirited dancing when Marie and Drum Major enter and join in. He contemplates revenge, and the Simpleton tells him he senses blood.

SCENE 5 *A guardroom in the barracks*
Wozzeck is unable to sleep, tormented by memories of the beer garden and his earlier visions. When the Drum Major returns and brags of his conquest, the two fight.

ACT III

SCENE 1 *Marie's room*
Marie reads in her Bible the story of the adulterous woman.

SCENE 2 *A forest path, near a pool*
Wozzeck and Marie are walking together. He tries to reassure her of his love before cutting her throat.

SCENE 3 *A beer garden*
Wozzeck drinks to block out memories of the murder. He dances with Margret, but when she sees blood on his hands, Wozzeck runs away.

SCENE 4 *The forest path near the pool*
Wozzeck has returned to the scene of the crim to dispose of the knife in the pool. He wades in to wash himself of the blood. The Captain and Doctor pass by and think they hear someone drowning.

SCENE 5 *Outside Marie's house*
Marie's Child plays with others. All run off when the discovery of Marie's body is announced.

XERXES
see **Serse**

DIE ZAUBERFLÖTE (The Magic Flute)
Wolfgang Amadeus Mozart (1756-1791)

TWO ACTS. LIBRETTO BY EMANUEL SCHIKANEDER. PREMIERE IN VIÉNNA, 30 SEPTEMBER 1791.

Die Zauberflöte was the last opera Mozart completed; he died just over two months after its premiere, leaving numerous legends surrounding its genesis—more than in the case of any other of his 20 stage works. Part of *Die Zauberflöte*'s fascination is the way in which its surface triviality veils profound significance: it is a *Singspiel* (musical comedy with spoken dialogue in the vernacular) with a fairy-tale story, written for the ordinary Viennese public instead of as a court entertainment, but it is also heavy with Masonic symbolism. It was Mozart's greatest operatic success, but brought little relief from the financial worries of his final months.

CHARACTERS

The Queen of Night (COLORATURA SOPRANO); *Pamina*, her daughter (SOPRANO); *Papagena* (SOPRANO); *Three Ladies*, attendants on the Queen of Night (SOPRANO and MEZZO-SOPRANOS); *Three Boys* (TREBLES); *Tamino*, an eastern prince (TENOR); *Monostatos*, a Moor in the service of Sarastro (TENOR); *Papageno*, a bird-catcher (BARITONE); *Sarastro*, high priest of the sun (BASS); *The Speaker* (BASS)
With *Two Priests, Two Men in Armour, priests, slaves, people*

ACT I

Tamino faints while fleeing for his life from a serpent. He is saved only by the intervention of three Ladies who appear and kill the beast. All are immediately struck by his handsome looks, and they argue about who should stay to watch over him; unable to agree, they reluctantly leave together to inform their mistress, the Queen of Night, about him. Tamino regains consciousness to see Papageno, who claims to have killed the serpent single-handedly. The Ladies reappear, expose Papageno's lie and punish him by padlocking his mouth, before handing Tamino a portrait of the Queen's daughter, Pamina. He is immediately smitten. The Queen herself enters and tells Tamino that her daughter has been abducted by Sarastro, promising Pamina's hand in marriage to him should he recover her. Led by three Boys, Tamino and Papageno set off—equipped with a magic flute and magic bells—to Sarastro's domain to save her.

Sarastro has charged Monostatos to guard the imprisoned princess, and Monostatos is about to take advantage of her when Papageno enters, frightening him off. Papageno comforts Pamina and tells her about Tamino, with whom she falls in love. In turn, Pamina reassures Papageno that before long he will find someone to love too.

Meanwhile, the Boys have led Tamino to Sarastro's temple. At the entrance he is confronted by the Speaker. Once inside, his flute is heard by Papageno and Pamina who are on the run from Monostatos, and the three are united—Tamino seeing Pamina for the first time. Sarastro is impressed by the couple's love for each other. He orders Monostatos to be punished for his treatment of the princess, and invites Tamino and Pamina to prove themselves in a series of trials, promising them initiation into his brotherhood. The people hail him for his wisdom.

ACT II

Tamino and Papageno are taken by the priests into the temple for their trials. They remain steadfast when the Ladies appear and try to lure them back to the Queen's cause. Monostatos finds Pamina asleep and once again tries to steal a kiss, but the Queen of Night enters and chases him off. But he overhears when the Queen gives Pamina orders to kill Sarastro and destroy his power, and as soon as he is left alone with Pamina again, he threatens to reveal the plot to Sarastro if she does not give in to his desires. Sarastro enters and banishes Monostatos, reassuring Pamina that he has no plans for revenge against her mother.

Tamino's and Papageno's next ordeal is a trial of silence: neither is allowed to speak to any woman. Papageno promptly breaks his vow and chats with an old hag who claims to be his sweetheart. She disappears and the Boys enter to remind the men of their duty. Pamina is heartbroken when Tamino remains steadfastly silent. The two initiates are summoned to their next trial. Papageno is dreaming of his companion when the old hag reappears and is suddenly transformed into the beautiful young Papagena. But since he has not completed his trials, she is whisked away.

Pamina, contemplating suicide, is saved by the boys and led to where Tamino is to undergo his final, terrible ordeal of fire and water. Protected by the magic flute, they endure the trial together and are welcomed into the temple. Papageno, pining for his Papagena, is prevented from killing himself by the intervention of the Boys; the couple are at last united. The Queen of Night, her Ladies, and Monostatos make a final assault on Sarastro's temple but are defeated. Bright light shines as Tamino and Pamina are joined in love and to the brotherhood.